Information Literacy Skills Grades 7-12 3rd Edition

Catherine M. Andronik, Compiler

PROFESSIONAL GROWTH SERIES®

A Publication of THE BOOK REPORT & LIBRARY TALK
Professional Growth Series

Linworth Publishing, Inc.
Worthington, Ohio

Library of Congress Cataloging-in-Publication Data

Published by Linworth Publishing, Inc.
480 East Wilson Bridge Road, Suite L
Worthington, Ohio 43085

Copyright © 1999 by Linworth Publishing, Inc.

Series Information:
    From The Professional Growth Series

All rights reserved. Reproduction of this book in whole or in part is prohibited without permission of the publisher.

ISBN 0-938865-82-6

5 4 3 2 1

Table of Contents

INTRODUCTION 1

CHAPTER ONE: **What is Information Literacy?** 3
                         "From School Librarian to Information TeAchnician: A Challenge for the Information Age" 5
                         "Take the Internet Challenge: Using Technology in Context" 9
                         "Information Literacy: More than Pushbutton Printouts" 12
                         "Media Literacy: From Viewing to Doing" 14
                         "Keeping the Ahhh! Alive: The Excitement of Doing Library 'Science'" 16
                         "Information Literacy: Facing the Challenge" 20

CHAPTER TWO: **Orientation and Using Traditional Resources** 23
                         "Surviving the 'New' Library Skills Curriculum" 25
                         "A Model for Library Instruction 28
                         "Wired for Learning New Library Skills" 30
                         "What Do Your Students Know and When Do They Know It? 31
                         "Biography Research" 33
                         "The Relevance of Vertical Files in the Modern Library Media Center" 34
                         "The Influence of 'Infoquest'" 37
                         "Look It Up!" 40
                         Tips 41

CHAPTER THREE: **Research Methods and Models** 43
                         "Survival Skills for the Future" 45
                         "Getting Off to a Solid Start" 47
                         "The Big Six & Electronic Resources: A Natural Fit" 51
                         "Flip It! For Information Skills Strategies" 53
                         "Flip It! as a Planning Strategy" 55
                         "Flip It! Worksheet Formats" 57
                         "Introducing a Problem-Solving Method and Library Resources in a Science Class Research Assignment" 60
                         "Effective Searching Buys Time to Reflect, Ponder & Analyze" 62
                         "Get Student Researchers on Target" 64
                         "6 Steps to Simplifying Student Searches" 66
                         "Technology Helps Students Do More Research Better and Faster" 68
                         "Library Technology Adds Immediacy to Research Assignments" 70
                         "Perfect Partners: Technology and Integrated Instruction" 73
                         "Teaching the Research Process? Check out *The Mind's Treasure Chest!*" 75

Table of Contents continued

CHAPTER FOUR: **Computer Skills** 77
- "How Are We Using Computers in the Classroom?" 79
- "Putting Computer Skills in Their Place" 81
- "Can Information Skills Be Taught with One Computer?" 82
- "In Defense of Dabbling: The Case for Drop-In Session" 83
- "No, You Don't Have to Write Your Name Anymore" 87
- "A Workbook for Accessing University Catalogs from Remote Terminals" 89
- "The Paperless Classroom" 90
- "Synthesizing that Social Studies Unit: Do It with a Database!" 91
- "Generic Instructions for Electronic Resources" 93
- "How to Use Two New Multimedia Encyclopedias" 95
- "Observing Student Searches in an Electronic Encyclopedia" 96
- "Bugs and Frogs and Trees and Doggy Friends: Searching in the Elementary Reference World" 98
- "Boning Up on Boolean Searching" 103
- "A Manual for CD-ROMs" 104
- "Lesson Plans Shared in New PGS Book" 105
- Tips 106

CHAPTER FIVE: **Using the Internet for Research** 109
- "Internet Skill Rubrics for Teachers" 113
- "Internet Staff Development: A Continuum" 117
- "Harnessing Internet Resources for the Student Researcher" 121
- "Guidelines for Using the Internet" 123
- "How to Teach the 'Net" 124
- "Partnering with Teachers for Internet Incorporation" 126
- "The World Wide Web in Three Lessons" 129
- "SCORE One for Students and Teachers" 133
- "Search Engines Become Another Unit in Library Skills" 135
- "Create Your Own Home Page: A Step-by-Step Guide" 137
- "Create a Home Page with Netscape" 140

- "Library Home Pages: A New Knowledge Environment" 142
- "Integrating E-Mail into the Curriculum" 145
- "Telementoring...Providing Authentic Learning Opportunities for Students" 148
- "Adventures in E-Mail Land" 151
- "Making the Most of E-Mail" 152
- "Can the Internet Be Used with K-5 Students? The Answer Is Elementary!" 154

Table of Contents continued

"Seduced and Abandoned on the Web" 156
"It Must Be True. I Found It on the Internet!" 160
"Producing Information Consumers: Critical Evaluation and
       Critical Thinking" 162
"Evaluating Web Resources" 164
"Webliographies: Much More than Just a Bibliography" 167
Tips 169

CHAPTER SIX: **Multimedia Presentation Programs** 171
"Why Students Should Use Multimedia" 173
"Integrating Multimedia into the Curriculum" 175
"Guidelines for Effective Multimedia Design" 177
"The SLAPPS Model: Guiding Students through the SLAPPS
       Process of Multimedia Presentations" 179
"Tokyo Students Create Hypertext Books" 181
"The Romance and the Reality of Developing Hypermedia
       Modules" 183
"PowerPointing the Way" 185
"The Writing-Technology Connection" 187
"Meet the Authors" 189
"Authors! Authors!" 191
"Of Letters, Diaries, and Laserdiscs: The Primary Source" 193
"The Changing Face of Student Research" 195
"Primary Sources: Second to None on the Web" 197
"Laser Discs, Barcodes, and Books...A Great Combination" 201

CHAPTER SEVEN: **Collaboration** 205
"Technology Adds Immediacy, Excitement, and Controversy to
       Research Projects" 207
"Teachers and Librarians; Ideas to Bring the Relationship to Life" 209
"A Research Project Filled with Real World Technology" 211
"Curriculum Integration in Practice" 214
"A Second Grade Unit on Africa" 214
"World Travelers in a School Library" 214
"The Evolution of a Unit: From Dusty Books to Paperless
       Projects" 217
"Teacher-Librarian Collaboration in Practice...Global Warming" 219
"Thumbs Up on Technology Used in Multicultural Research" 223
"Making It Mine: Helping Students Use Information to Create an
       Original Report" 225
"Teaching High School Students How to Use College Libraries
       Online" 227

Table of Contents continued

"The Senior Project: A Chance for the Library to Shine"..............229
"The Computer Lab/Library Connection"...........................231

CHAPTER EIGHT: **Reading and Literature Appreciation**...................233
"Reading Aloud in the Junior High Classroom"....................235
"Student Booktalks Can Motivate Readers".........................237
"Hands on Handout: Raving Reviews".............................240
"Children's Literature Resources on the Web"....................241
Tips...244

CHAPTER NINE: **Training Students and Teachers**..........................245
"A Model for Teacher-Directed Technology Training"..............247
"From Entry Level to Proficient & Exemplary: A Design for Staff
    Technology Development".....................................250
"Singing the Praises of On-site Training"......................252
"Hands on Technology In-Service that Works"....................254
"Tried and True Tips for Technology Training"..................256
"Byte-Sized Technology Sessions Teachers Training Teachers"....258
"Stage a Well-Designed Saturday Session and They Will Come!"...261
"Boolean Burritos: How the Faculty Ate Up Keyword Searching"...263
"Don't Forget the Teachers: Teaching Teachers to Search
    Electronically"...265
"Fantasy and Fact in Computer Training"........................267
"Learned Helplessness"...268
"Computers 101-Back by Popular Demand".........................270
"Developing Library Courses for Credit in High Schools"........272
"Training for Techies: A Schoolwise Commitment"................274
"Training Students as Technology Assistants"...................277
"A Quiz for Student Aides".....................................279
Tips...280

CHAPTER TEN: **Assessing Information Literacy Skills**....................281
"Yes, They Put on Quite a Show, but What Did They Learn?".....283
"Getting What You Ask For"....................................286
"Authentic Assessment of Information Literacy through Electronic
    Products"...288
"Technology Assessment and Curriculum: Teaching What Is
    Tested"...291
"What Does It Look Like? Part 1: The Code 77 Rubrics"..........294
"Rubrics for Restructuring (Continuation of The Code 77 Rubrics)
    Part II"..297

Table of Contents continued

CHAPTER ELEVEN: **Ethical Issues** 301
"How to Help Students Deal with 'Too Much Information'" 303
"Easy to Find But Not Necessarily True" 305
"Using Technology to Cultivate Thinking Dispositions" 306
"Teaching Ethical Technology Behaviors" 309
"Copy, Paste, Plagiarize" 310
"Technology to the Rescue of Senioritis Victims" 311
Tips 312

BIBLIOGRAPHY 313

Introduction

The past 10 years have seen a revolution in information technologies, a revolution that has forever changed the way librarians and library media specialists view, and teach, "library skills." For the vast majority of us, the card catalog has been replaced by an array of OPACs. The red or green bindings of countless volumes of *Readers' Guide to Periodical Literature* have morphed into the equally colorful search screens of CD-ROM and online periodical indexes. Pick-'em-up-and-flip-'em transparencies no longer hold any fascination for the young person who has experienced PowerPoint or HyperStudio. And as we point and click at a terminal hooked up to the global resources of the Internet, do we really miss explaining the obscure codes of Dialog to glassy-eyed patrons? The revolution has been so all-encompassing that the American Library Association has revised *Information Power*, its volume of standards and expectations, to include new media, processes, and applications.

The frightening thing is that 10-perhaps five-years from now, many of today's most exciting and promising innovations will be completely obsolete, and we have no way of knowing which ones, or what will replace them.

For decades, we were safe in teaching students certain concrete skills: how to locate books using the Dewey Decimal or Library of Congress system; how to decipher a catalog card; how to go from the *Readers' Guide* to the neatly labeled boxes in the stacks to find a magazine article; how to use the index of a reference book. As we enter the millennium, change is so rapid that the Net search engine we demonstrate in detail today may be replaced by something more efficient and elegant by the end of the year. In six months, there may be a new version of the presentation program we teach the commands for. The keyboarding instruction we stress may be rendered useless sooner than we think by a generation of computers that understands human language.

What we have learned from all this change, and what we can teach our students, is a spirit of flexibility, an openness to the inescapable reality of change, and an ability to locate common denominators. We can still teach short-term library media skills, but we do so in the larger, more general context of information literacy. We show students how to use what they have available to them today, recognizing that those resources may change tomorrow. If our students understand the broader concepts of research, they should be prepared for those changes, whatever they may be.

In *Information Literacy Skills, Grades 7-12*, I have included very little from the 1990 edition, Library Research Skills, Grades 7-12. This is not to say that there are not fine and useful articles and ideas in the earlier edition; indeed, library media centers that still use card catalogs and print indexes will find excellent skills resources in its pages. What I have tried to do is reflect the technological changes of the past 10 years in my selection of articles, concentrating on broad and current concepts and trends, and the occasional specific popular program.

I begin this volume with a general discussion of the definition of "information literacy." From a few pages on "traditional" library skills (since, when teaching, I tend to progress from a "comfortable" place to newer ideas), I move on to a chapter describing a variety of research models. With the wealth of information available to them, today more than ever, students need to be able to formulate questions and choose the most appropriate resources. Information on computer instruction, including utility programs, is followed by an extensive survey of the Internet and its components: the World Wide Web, search engines, Web pages, and e-mail. Since the product of research is increasingly moving away from the traditional paper report, ideas for student use of a variety of multimedia presentation programs are then offered for consideration, including hypertext, KidPix, and PowerPoint applications. Next, because information skills should always be taught at point of need rather than in an unrelated context, comes a compendium of tried-and-true ideas, most involving collaboration with classroom teachers, that put skills into practice across the curriculum.

Amidst the onslaught of technology, reading and the appreciation of literature are often overlooked, especially in the upper grades. Yet the fostering of a love of the written word is still, thankfully, in the domain of the library media specialist. Several articles in this area are included. *Information Power* advocates that the library media specialist take the lead in faculty inservice training. Since the skills we teach our fellow teachers, and the methods we utilize, are not necessarily the same as those we use with students, developing effective inservice programs merits its own chapter.

Also included here are a few pages on training student library helpers, who need to know a little more about the library media center than their classmates to help them navigate and use it. Because accessing new information sources and synthesizing more information than has ever before been available to young people require a revised concept of product and process assessment, several models are offered. Finally, new technologies carry with them ethical considerations involving copyright, plagiarism (so easy now, with complete term papers available on the Internet, free for the printing), critical reading and selection, and distinguishing between fact and opinion.

Throughout this volume, while I emphasize the positive aspects of teaching information literacy, I have included a few "devil's advocate" pieces, to keep change-for-change's-sake and blind acceptance of all that is new in proper critical perspective. Also, while the focus is on teaching skills to students in grades 7 through 12, some articles involve teaching younger students. Many of us work in schools that encompass a variety of grades (some middle schools, for instance, are now grades 4 through 7 or 8). Also, the methods described may be ability-adjusted, or the lesson might be appropriate for students with limited skills or little previous exposure to the product in question.

Many of the articles in this volume mention related Web sites and home pages. Nothing better illustrates the constantly changing nature of the Internet than the migration of URLs; in a matter of months, the address of a site may disappear or alter. I have checked all the URLs cited in this volume as of late June or early July 1999, and have made revisions as necessary, fully aware that, by the time this book is published, some of my revisions will be obsolete. Most of the pages should still be accessible through the name of the school or the project, however. I have not attempted to update the many e-mail addresses cited.

We live in an exciting time. Unlike many of our younger students, we remember what research was like in the days before CD-ROMs and the Internet, and we can appreciate how much time and work technology can save us. Having witnessed the information technology revolution, we also enjoy a hindsight that allows us to consider not the *how*, but the *why*, involved in the various steps in the research process, whatever method we choose, and to guide our students in the path of lifelong learning through information literacy.

Catherine M. Andronik

Editor's Note: Because many articles are reprints, some URLs mentioned may have changed. URL udates as of the date of publication are located at the end of each chapter introduction.

What Is Information Literacy?

Not so long ago, much in education was pigeon-holed. We were librarians; we selected and recommended good books and showed quiet classes (sometimes quiet with attention, sometimes just quietly bored) how to find and use them. We lived behind the desk in the library, never far from the trusty Gaylord stamper, the card catalog, the accession book, and the circ tray. And it was a *library*. Oh, maybe we purchased the odd filmstrip set, and a bin of 33 1/3 recordings sat discreetly in a corner, but *media* was a newfangled concept, usually the domain of the tech ed person. And while we lived in the library, the teachers inhabited their classrooms-places we entered only to look for missing books at the end of the year. School librarians taught library skills. Teachers taught subject matter.

Today we all teach kids. Sometimes we even teach each other. The dividing line between "library" skills and subject matter is disappearing. Computer programs, CDs and CD-ROMs, videos, and audiotapes have joined books on the media center shelves. The school library media specialist has come out from behind the circulation desk for collaborative projects with teachers from all disciplines. We increasingly invade each other's territory. Meanwhile, the instructional model of the "guide on the side" is replacing the traditional "sage on the stage." The silence of the library is giving way to the excited hum of groups of young people engaged in hands-on activity. And "library skills" are now "information skills."

"Library skills" implies skills useful only in a library setting. There was some application across venues; for instance, with my high school classes I often compared what they were familiar with in our school with what they might find at the local public library or university. But we were still talking about libraries.

"Information skills," on the other hand, have broader and more practical, real-life implications. Students still need to locate information in the school library media center, the public library, and perhaps a local college. They need to be familiar with the print materials-books, periodicals, indices-as well with as the CD-ROMs and electronic resources in these locations. But many of today's information sources are not confined to a library. Educational television shows and cable networks, as well as videotapes, are right in students' living rooms. The Internet has made resources once found only in major research facilities available 24 hours a day-with a laptop, they're available in a person's backyard! That's the positive side. On the negative side, the Internet is also full of misinformation presented on attractive, convincing Web sites. Developing a critical, evaluative eye is one of today's information literacy skills.

Information literacy skills cannot be discrete. Since the realm of information-related technology is changing almost by the minute, we cannot teach a specific resource or program.

We must teach a process broad enough that it can be applied in a variety of contexts and to a variety of materials, including some not even invented yet. We need to help students learn to formulate important questions about their topics. In this age of potential information overload, we need to show them that gathering *every* shred of data on a topic may no longer be feasible; we need to teach them to be selective as they research. We need to offer them many formats from which to gather their information-both because of learning styles and differences, and because of the differences inherent in those formats.

In addition to many information formats, there are an increasing number of presentation formats for students' finished products, which are becoming simpler to create. And there are certainly programs barely in the planning stages today that will be great favorites in 2010. We need to give young people the skills to create presentations in today's print and electronic formats, as well as the background to apply those skills to whatever new programs may come along.

Information literacy skills enable a person to articulate what he or she needs to know, to have a reasonable idea of where to look for that information, to navigate the chosen tools, to locate the needed information, to evaluate its usefulness, and to process and utilize the information found. These are no longer library skills. They are life skills. And we are the primary instructors of those skills.

URL UPDATES

Take the Internet Challenge: Using Technology in Context
http://eric.syr.edu.

Keeping the Ahhh! Alive: The Excitement of Doing Library "Science"
www.ncrel.org/sdrs/areas/issues/content/cntareas/science/sc3nces.htm

http://nueva.pvt.k12.ca.us/~debbie/library.cur/science/bubblesballoons.html

Information Literacy: Facing The Challenge Information Literacy for Lifelong Learning
www.ed.gov.databases/eric_digests/ed358870.html

The National Educational Technology Standards
http://cnets.iste.org/

From School Librarian to "Information TeAchnician"

A Challenge for the Information Age

By Janet Murray

School librarians have a unique opportunity to adapt their professional skills to meet the challenges of the "Information Age." As electronic access to information proliferates in junior and senior high schools, librarians can model the adventure of lifelong learning by teaching faculty and students how to search the Internet for pertinent information, evaluate the reliability of information retrieved, analyze and synthesize the information to construct personal meaning, and apply it to informed decision-making. Library/media centers can be transformed from static repositories of print and audiovisual materials into dynamic and evolving information technology centers.

Skeptics have noted that previous technological revolutions have failed to reform education, pointing to the intransigence of institutions or the resistance of teachers. In my experience, discussions of information technology too frequently focus on hardware, infrastructure, and data, as if these tools and resources alone will "automagically" reform educational practice to produce competent lifelong learners. Experienced educators know that we must add an "A" to "tech"; technology in isolation ignores the "a" in "teAch." School librarians have the professional training and expertise to guide information-processing learning activities, so let's call ourselves "information teAchnicians."

School Librarians and the Electronic World of Information

Librarians at all levels have been exceptionally quick to recognize the potential of an electronic "library without walls." They also have been particularly proactive in identifying and analyzing issues pertaining to Internet use. The American Library Association and the American Association of School Librarians have made significant efforts to guide policy making and standards development.

In January 1996, The American Library Association adopted Access to Electronic Information, Services and Networks, an interpretation of the Library Bill of Rights. It draws upon previous interpretations to guide libraries in the development of policy, notably:

"Providing connections to global information, services, and networks is not the same as selecting and purchasing material for a library collection. Determining the accuracy or authenticity of electronic information may present special problems. Some information accessed electronically may not meet a library's selection or collection development policy. It is, therefore, left to each user to determine what is appropriate. Parents and legal guardians who are concerned about their children's use of electronic resources should provide guidance to their own children."

The new edition of *Information Power*, released in July 1998, incorporates Information Literacy Standards for Student Learning which have been included in "Indicators of Schools of Quality" by the National Study of School Evaluation. This powerful collection of nine standards and 29 indicators of proficiency in information literacy, independent learning, and socially responsible use of electronic information can provide the foundation for recognizing the school librarian's central role in a technology-enriched educational environment. The preface explicitly describes this connection:

"The learning process and the information search process mirror each other: Students actively seek to construct meaning from the sources they encounter and to create products that shape and communicate that meaning effectively. Developing expertise in accessing, evaluating, and using information is in fact the authentic learning that modern education seeks to promote."

ICONnect, a project sponsored by AASL, offers online courses in Internet applications. The Librarians Information Online Network (LION), maintained by the Philadelphia School District, is an exceptional resource for K-12 librarians. Peter Milbury's *School Librarian Web Pages* demonstrates the extent of school librarians' leadership in emerging electronic publication.

Introducing the Internet to Teachers

Successfully enticing teachers to use the Internet with their students may depend more on your teaching skills than your Internet skills. Create a comfortable, nonthreatening learning environment. Avoid overusing technical language. I use analogies to everyday experiences to emphasize that the Internet is not an impenetrable mystery, but merely a new research tool.

Experienced educators know that we must add an "A" to "tech"; technology in isolation ignores the "A" in "teAch."

Demonstrate patience and offer positive reinforcement. Model the adventure of lifelong learning by sharing your enthusiasm for this powerful information resource.

Use a well-designed tutorial to introduce teachers to online research. *Exploring the World Wide Web*, a workshop tutorial on Internet applications, combines text and exercises. Some teachers may prefer *The Internet Island*, a Web tutorial for teachers, because of its graphic replication of the Netscape screen. To learn about the Internet, explore *Hobbes' Internet Timeline*, by Robert H. Zakon, hosted by the Internet Society.

Locating Information

New and novice users frequently complain that finding pertinent and relevant information is like searching for Waldo in the popular children's books! In order for teachers and students to locate appropriate information pertinent to their research inquiries, they must first develop skills in searching electronic databases. Framing a question in terms which lend themselves to successful information retrieval is an important first step. Internet sites with hierarchically organized subjects are useful to students who have not yet pinpointed their research topic. Students may also use concept mapping to refine their inquiry statements so they are neither too broad nor too narrow. They may learn to use synonyms or truncated forms of words to improve the accuracy of their searches. They need to understand the basic principles of Boolean logic in order to use Internet search engines efficiently. It is also important to recognize that different search engines yield different results because they use different methods to build their indexes. Students can benefit from an understanding of the different features of a variety of search engines.

Searching the 'Net is a series of interlinked, short Web pages with some introductory exercises to help students focus on electronic searching skills. Kathy Schrock's presentation at the 1998 National Educational Computing Conference ("Successful Web Search Strategies") provides a valuable overview of searching on the Internet.

Evaluating Information

Rapidly expanding access to the Internet compels school librarians to emphasize the importance of evaluating information retrieved. In an electronic publishing environment which allows anyone to create Web pages, it is imperative that students and teachers examine information sources with a critical eye. The standards which librarians have traditionally applied to print and audiovisual materials are also valid in an electronic setting. Students should consider the authority of the site, identifying the author and his or her qualifications, as well as the organization that sponsors the site. Assess the accuracy and objectivity of the information provided by distinguishing among facts, point of view, and opinion. Consider the currency of information by checking revision dates. Evaluate the relevance of the information; it is easy to lose track of one's original research question when confronted with an overwhelming profusion of resources.

Thinking Critically about World Wide Web Resources can help you apply traditional evaluation criteria to the Internet. *Checklist for an Informational Web Page* can help you structure your instruction in evaluation techniques. *CyberGuides* are useful checklists of Web elements which are important for schools.

Analyzing and Synthesizing Information

Once students have located information from a variety of sources, they need to selectively identify the pieces that are useful, and synthesize them to construct an original product that reflects their engagement in the process of critical thinking. Even in traditional research, prior to the Information Age, students often merely regurgitated facts without considering their significance. The current challenge is to provide students with authentic research tasks by posing fundamental interdisciplinary questions that do not have prescribed answers.

Research and Critical Thinking is a massively detailed site with sections on research skills and tools, search tools, and critical thinking on the Web. *Web Quests* and NASA's *Classroom of the Future* modules both provide models of

> *Librarians who find themselves propelled onto the information superhighway without adequate skills and preparation can use their Internet connectivity to guide their own professional growth. The map is in the glove compartment!*

Sites Cited

American Library Association (<http://www.ala.org>)

American Association of School Librarians (<http://www.ala.org/aasl>)

Access to Electronic Information, Services and Networks, an interpretation of the Library Bill of Rights (www.ala-org/alaorg/oif/electacc.html)

Information Power (www.ala.org/aasl/ip_implementation.html)

Information Literacy Standards (<http://www.ala.org/aasl/ip_nine.html>)

National Study of School Evaluation (<http://www.nsse.org/>)

ICONnect (<http://www.ala.org/ICONN/>)

Librarians Information Online Network (<http://www.libertynet.org/lion/lion.html>)

School Librarian Web Pages (<http://wombat.cusd.chico.k12.ca.us/~pmilbury/lib.html>)

Exploring the World Wide Web (<http://www.gactr.uga.edu/exploring/index.html>)

The Internet Island (<http://www.miamisci.org/ii/ii0.html>)

Hobbes' Internet Timeline (<http://info.isoc.org/guest/zakon/Internet/History/HIT.html>)

Searching the 'Net (<http://www.teleport.com/~janetm/oii/search.html>)

Successful Web Search Strategies (<http://discoveryschool.com/schrockguide/neccsrch/searchingnecc2/ sldool.html >)

Thinking Critically about World Wide Web Resources (<http://www.library.ucla.edu/libraries/college/instruct/web/critical.htm>)

Checklist for an Informational Web Page (www2.widener.edu.wolfgram-memorial-library/inform.htm)

Cyber Guides (<http://www.cyberbee.com/guides.html>)

Research and Critical Thinking (<http://www.execpc.com/~dboals/think.html>)

Web Quests (<http://edweb.sdsu.edu/webquest/overview.htm>)

NASA's Classroom of the Future (<http://www.cotf.edu/ete/modules/modules.html>)

The Big6 Skills (<http://www.big6.com>)

EdWeb (<http://edweb.gsn.org/>)

Child Safety on the Information Highway (<http://www.4j.lane.edu/safety/>)

Acceptable Use Policies (<http://www.netc.org/tech_plans/aup.html>)

Internet-based instruction. Michael Eisenberg and Robert Berkowitz's list of six information-processing skills (*Big6 Skills*) provides a useful framework for organizing instruction.

Applying Information Skills

The Information Literacy Standards developed by the AASL/AECT National Guidelines Vision Committee "describe the content and processes related to information that students must master to be considered well educated." The standards also define the information-literate high school graduate: one who has the ability to use information to acquire both core and advanced knowledge and to become an independent, lifelong learner who contributes responsibly and productively to the learning community.

Internet Implementation Issues

For librarians to successfully redefine themselves as "information teAchnicians," they must also keep informed about the larger issues pertaining to the use of Internet in schools. Andy Carvin's *EdWeb* is an excellent hypertext online "book" that explores technology and school reform. *Child Safety on the Information Highway* is another hypertext guide that is suitable for concerned parents. Defining appropriate acceptable use policies requires thoughtful consideration and experienced leadership.

Resources to guide the successful implementation of technology in schools abound on the Internet, although, ironically one must already have Internet access in order to benefit from them. Librarians who find themselves propelled onto the information superhighway without adequate skills and preparation can use their Internet connectivity to guide their own professional growth. The map is in the glove compartment! ∎

Janet Murray is the Information Specialist at Kinnick High School in Yokosuka, Japan. She has been avidly adopting and promoting electronic access to information since she auto-

mated the first library in Portland (Oregon) Public Schools in 1985. Her new title, Information Specialist, reflects the Department of Defense Dependents Schools' commitment to redefining school librarians as instructional technology leaders. She can be reached via e-mail at janetm@surfline.ne.jp.

The content of this article grew from a workshop presentation to library media specialists at the Texas Computer Education Association annual conference in February 1997. A shorter version was previous published by the Well-Connected Educator <http://www.teleport.com/~janetm/ingotech_wkshp.html>

Notes

Take the Internet Challenge: Using Technology in Context

By Michael B. Eisenberg

Picture this: A slick salesman-type person, broad smile on his face, open arms, extolling, "Technology is the answer, of course. Now what was the question?"

Technology for technology's sake. This is a common lament in education circles. And we aren't alone in this. Businesses and government agencies also suffer from the same concern: technology being touted as an end in itself, the answer to our prayers.

Technology out of context. What a mess, and what a waste. If that wasn't enough, now we have the same situation in relation to the Internet: "The Internet is the answer, of course. Now what was the question?"

Clearly, we must turn this around. The focus should be on the question—what do we want to accomplish in schools? Then, we must ask ourselves how can we use the Internet and other technologies in effective and efficient ways to reach our goals?

The Internet Challenge

For school library media programs the challenge is to use technology in general and the Internet specifically as a means to an end and not as an end in itself. Let's call this the "Internet Challenge." We want to focus on what we are trying to accomplish and how can the Internet help us to do so.

This Internet Challenge provides two tremendous opportunities for library media specialists. First, they are in an excellent position to meet this challenge within the library media program itself. Library media specialists can focus on their central functions of information services and information skills instruction and the use of the Internet meaningfully to meet those goals. Second, and even more importantly, library media specialists can play a key role in helping the entire school meet the Internet Challenge. Their experience with curriculum-focused information services and integrated information skills instruction places library media specialists in a direct and unique position to help classroom teachers integrate the Internet into everyday learning and teaching.

Meeting the Internet Challenge means continually focusing on the fundamentals of vision and purpose. The mission statement from *Information Power* (AASL/AECT, 1988) offers an energetic and essential vision for library media programs: "...the mission of the library media program is to ensure that students...are effective users of ideas and information."

In an information society, there is no mission more important. Library media specialists can accomplish this vital mission by providing essential information services (including access to collections, help and referral, and reading guidance) and teaching essential information literacy skills (as a full process, not just location and access to resources).

In terms of technology and the Internet, it's not "the library" and "technology," it's *the Library* including all information systems and resources used for learning and teaching. Students and teachers shouldn't be thinking about the search for information in terms of using "the library" and then "the Internet." We want them to think about using the Library, which includes the Internet. Today and in the future, the concept of Library should encompass the full range of information resources—electronic and print.

While this concept of a unified library is certainly not a new one, there is a tendency to lose sight of it among the complexities of new and emerging information systems and the ever-changing technological environment. In addition, our own library media systems sometimes work against the unified vision. For example, rather than a common access point and interface to *all* electronic resources, in too many situations we still have an online catalog separate from the full-text resources and separate again from access to the Internet. This doesn't necessarily require a common search system across all resources (although that might be nice), it simply requires that the system includes easy intellectual and physical access to all resources and networks that we would include under the concept of Library.

Commercial library systems should foster and encourage the concept by providing mechanisms for combining local and global systems along with site licensing agreements that allow us to offer Library on every workstation in the school and community.

But library media specialists aren't the only ones focusing on information resources and technology. Many teachers and administrators are getting involved with bringing the Internet and CD-ROM resources into their schools. We may say, "the unified Library should encompass all information systems and resources—including the Internet," but just saying it won't make it so.

This brings us back to our answer to the Internet Challenge. When library media specialists meet the Internet Challenge, they move to fulfill the concept of Library. Using the Internet in context addresses the needs of the library media program and the entire school. The Library is more than just the resources and the technology. The Library means library media specialists using the Internet within the program of information services and as part of information literacy skills instruction to ensure that students are effective users of information.

Here are some examples of how library media specialists can meet the Internet Challenge within each of these two functions—information services and information literacy skills instruction.

ers to link Internet resources to curriculum needs, providing workstations and connections to the Internet, and sharing resources and building cooperative collections across regions.

Reading guidance service centers on promoting literacy and guiding in reading and materials selection. Meeting the Internet Challenge for reading guidance includes identifying and arranging for teachers and students to become involved in special collaborative Internet projects, such as *Live from Antarctica* and *MayaQuest*, and to interact with others globally through e-mail and discussion groups.

Direct information service involves providing assistance in locating and retrieving information. Meeting the Internet Challenge for direct information service includes providing students, teachers, and others direct help, referral, and question-answering service to put them in touch with the information they need.

Curriculum consultation service relates to providing advice on the use of information, resources, and technology in curriculum. Meeting the Internet Challenge for curriculum consultation includes using e-mail and electronic discussion groups to communicate with teachers and help teachers communicate with each other (locally and globally) on curriculum-related matters, professional issues, and decisions.

Curriculum development service refers to collaborating on the design, development, and evaluation of curriculum, particularly those units and lessons integrating information skills instruction.

Meeting the Internet Challenge for curriculum development includes joint efforts to link curriculum and assignments and the plethora of resources, projects, and services available through the Internet, and also to identify and develop relevant Internet-based curriculum projects.

Information Literacy Skills Instruction

Information literacy skills instruction offers another powerful opportunity to meet the Internet Challenge. Over the past 20 years, library media professionals have worked hard to move from teaching isolated library skills to teaching integrated information skills. The key word is "context," and effective integration of information skills requires two contexts:

(1) the skills must directly relate to the content area curriculum and to classroom assignments, and
(2) the skills themselves need to be tied together in a logical and systematic information process model.

Meeting the Internet Challenge also requires library media specialists to focus on both of these contexts. The first context is real need: curricular, life, or work. While it is certainly possible to learn skills in isolation, practice and research confirm that people learn best when the use and purpose are clear.

Students can learn to communicate via e-mail or to access a World Wide Web site, but they will eagerly internalize these skills if they see how the skills directly relate to their school assign-

Information Services

Information services refers to the full range of services and activities available to students, teachers, administrators, and the community. Information services include

- resources provision
- reading guidance
- direct information
- curriculum consultation
- curriculum development.

Resources provision service refers to providing space, materials, and equipment to meet curricular and personal needs. Meeting the Internet Challenge for resources provision includes providing tools that help students and teach-

Internet Applications in a Big Six Context

Big Six Skills	Internet Applications
Task Definition	e-mail, listservs, Internet Relay Chat, MOO, CU-SeeMe
Information Seeking Strategies	network navigation (World Wide Web, Netscape, Lynx, gophers), e-mail, listservs
Location & Access	Web navigation (Netscape) and search tools (Lycos, Webcrawler, Yahoo, Archie, Veronica)
Use of Information	download, upload, ftp
Synthesis	HTML and Web page creation
Evaluation	e-mail, listservs, Internet Relay Chat, MOO, CU-SeeMe

> ...the central question—how can we use the Internet in meaningful ways to help achieve educational goals— is often unanswered. Library media specialists are in a unique position to meet this Internet challenge.

ments or personal interests. Electronic mail, for example, takes on meaning if students realize that it enables them to work with students from another state or country to complete a project for social studies. Accessing a Web site is more than a novelty when it relates directly to answering homework questions.

The second, and often overlooked, context is the information problem-solving process itself. Computer and telecommunications technologies are supposed to extend our abilities to solve problems. That sounds fine in the abstract, but what does it really mean? Again, practice and research tell us that when people understand how specific skills fit into an overall model or process, the power and usefulness of the specific skills are expanded. Yes, students recognize the value of using e-mail for communication, but this takes on new meaning when they realize that e-mail can help them to better define the task of an assignment by being able to interact with teachers and group members. Task definition is step one of Eisenberg and Berkowitz' Big Six information problem-solving model. (Eisenberg & Berkowitz, 1990)

How Internet capabilities can be placed in the Big Six information problem-solving context is shown in the chart on the left. The chart is easily modified as new Internet functions and resources are made available or as teachers and students find new ways to apply existing capabilities. The power of the Big Six model is in this ability to provide an adaptable context for learning and teaching Internet skills; in fact, for learning and teaching any electronic networking or information technology skills. (For a more detailed treatment of computer skills for information problem-solving see Eisenberg and Johnson, 1996).

Conclusion

In the mad rush to technology in general and the Internet in particular, the focus has centered primarily on the hardware and software and the commands and capabilities. Schools and businesses are already investing considerable amounts of money, time, and effort on getting connected to the Internet, but the central question—how can we use the Internet in meaningful ways to help achieve educational goals—is often unanswered. Library media specialists are in a unique position to meet this Internet Challenge. And if they do so, they not only establish a broad and encompassing concept of Library, they also go a long way to fulfilling their mission of ensuring that students are effective users of ideas and information.

Michael B. Eisenberg is the co-owner of LM_NET, Director of the ERIC Clearinghouse on Information & Technology, and a Professor in the School of Information Studies at Syracuse University, Syracuse, New York.

References

AASL/AECT (American Association of School Librarians and Association for Educational Communications and Technology) (1988). *Information Power: Guidelines for School Library Media Programs*. American Library Association.

Eisenberg, Michael B. and Johnson, Doug (1996). "Computer Skills for Information Problem-Solving: Learning and Teaching Technology in Context," ERIC Digest, EDO-IR-96-04, ERIC Clearinghouse on Information & Technology. Available on the Internet:gopher://ericir.syr.edu:70/00/Clearinghouses/16houses/CIT/IT_Digests/Computer Skills.

Eisenberg, Michael B. and Berkowitz, Robert E. (1988). *Curriculum Initiative: An Agenda and Strategy for School Library Media Programs*, Ablex Publishing.

Eisenberg, Michael B. and Berkowitz, Robert E. (1990). *Information Problem-Solving: The Big Six Skills Approach to Library & Information Skills Instruction*, Ablex Publishing.

Notes

Information Literacy: More Than Pushbutton Printouts

By Lesley S.J. Farmer

The author of two books about teacher-librarian partnerships describes a research process that employs this pairing in technology-rich or -poor libraries.

How often do you see this scene in the library: Students stand in line for 20 minutes to use a two-year-old CD-ROM encyclopedia when a brand-new multivolume set is in sight? When asked why they wait, students tell you: "The CD-ROM is easier to use." "I can make printouts." "We don't have to think." Really!

Interestingly, when computers first came into the schools, some educators feared that students wouldn't bother to learn how to spell. The real concern, it turns out, is that students sometimes think "god" is spelled with seven letters: c-o-m-p-u-t-e-r. They confuse data with knowledge. Some librarians call this "information by pill"; students swallow the contents whole without "chewing on the ideas."

When they weren't busy just trying to increase the number of books in a collection, librarians used to worry that students would accept any opinion or "fact" they found in books as truth. Now computer-accessed resources seem to have replaced print as an infallible source. Internet increases the likelihood for unquestioning acceptance of "facts" as it brings vast quantities of data into every library, even the smallest.

Does this mean we should pull the plug on computers? No, the issue would still be there, though not as obvious. Along with teaching location skills, we need to teach the overriding literacy skill: the ability to reflect on information, to select what is useful, and evaluate its value.

Paper Power

One of the reasons that students swallow information whole is their feeling that they don't have enough time to reflect on their research. The value schools put on being "on task" and busy is so stressful that students look for an easy way to show that they are producing results; hence, the excessive printing or downloaded dumps.

One "makeshift" strategy to discourage needless printouts is to limit the number of pages that a student can print, especially from an electronic encyclopedia. This forces the student to choose the most relevant portion of the entry.

Sometimes students feel successful when they have generated a bibliography from their computer search until they realize the library does not own a single one of the sources. They have shortcut the thinking process, but this will eventually cost them more time and effort. How much more successful they could be if we taught them how to assess the usefulness of a record by reading abstracts and checking the list of library holdings first.

Taking Time To Think

Our message to students should be that critical thinking is more important than a push-button printout. Thinking should somehow be documented; the act of composing, with pencil or word processing, makes ideas "real." Seeing the student's information search in writing also helps us understand where the student is coming from, and enables us to direct the student toward success.

Time should also be allotted to talking about information. At some time during each research session, students need to discuss their progress and problems. Students can share their findings with a partner to compare results and processes—and frustrations or obstacles. The class as a whole can list the most and least effective strategies and sources, stating why they did or didn't work. These quick assessments reinforce the idea that information worth getting is worth thinking about. Being busy is not enough. Moreover, such reflective processing makes the life of the librarian easier because we can tailor library skills instruction to fit the specific needs of the students.

Process over Product

At the most basic level, librarians help students figure out what type of resource is most appropriate for a given topic: magazine articles for current events, online resources for ground-breaking scientific discoveries, primary sources for first-hand witnesses to history, encyclopedias for basic background information, almanacs for quick statistics, monographs for in-depth analysis. But this is just the start.

Many librarians go the next step by showing students techniques to determine if a resource will be useful to the research subject at hand. Looking at a book's table of contents and index, reading a chapter's or article's introduction and subheadings, examining a CD-ROM's main screens—each is a skill students should know.

The next key step, which sometimes gets overlooked, is the critical look at the specific content of a source. What is the publication date? What is the author's background and perspective? Is the information fact or opinion? How does the author justify his or her stance? What is the depth of the information?

Lesley S.J. Farmer is the Library Media Teacher at Redwood High School in Lakespur, California. She is the author of three books in the Professional Growth Series (Linworth Publishing), Creative Partnerships, Leadership within the School Library & Beyond *and* Workshops for Teachers: Becoming Partners for Information Literacy.

Information Literacy...

Librarians need to help the student become engaged with the information, and dialogue with it.

One easy way is for the students to record their responses, whether on paper or tape, to the information found. They might comment on an idea, say the author is all wet on some point, or draw a picture of something the author described. Students can be encouraged to copy down "golden phrases": something that strikes them personally or impresses them. Requiring students to hand in five golden statements forces them to pick out points and make judicious use of quotations.

I-Search Papers

In the student research method known as I-Search, students write down their processes as well as their products. They record how they found—or did not find—information and how they feel about their strategies. They note how they choose/reject and evaluate sources. They mention their reactions to the process of synthesizing and organizing what they find.

The value of the I-Search paper depends on how the teacher and librarian use the papers. If they add comments and suggestions, students get needed feedback to guide their future efforts. Peer comments along the way also validate the process and help the searcher.

On a more global level, the teacher and librarian can look for trends or search patterns among students and offer ways to expand their skills. In that way, I-Search papers act as a diagnostic assessment that can help further customize information literacy instruction. Such metacognitive evaluation also reinforces librarian-teacher planning and ongoing teaching.

Beyond the Research Paper

One of the "enablers" of the mechanical approach to push-button, mindless information gathering is the traditional research paper, such as five pages on a state or a person. Not only are these usually boring for the students (and for the teacher grading them) but encyclopedias, whether in print or electronic form, generally are arranged in traditional report order and, hence, conducive to copying. In addition, the new sources are being written in an uncomplicated style that a teacher could mistake for students' words. (Some students will use a spell checker to globally misspell words on a downloaded article so the teacher will think it's student work.)

Appealing to the student's sense of right and wrong does not eliminate the problem of copying. Students obviously need to understand the issues behind plagiarism and copyright, but they will always be tempted when they see exactly what the teacher wants ready-made in print or printout and know they can't equal it, especially under a short deadline.

One way to encourage reflective processing is to change the report format so students cannot hand in copied (and plagiarized) information that requires no thought. Any topic worth researching is worth reporting meaningfully and creatively. In some way, information should be transformed into an original product. For example, if students have to develop a skit about immigrant experiences, they will be encouraged to use their own words and make their own interpretations. Here are some other formats that facilitate original thinking and processing:

- debates
- letters and journals
- games
- videos
- hypertext stacks
- slide shows
- simulations
- poetry
- scripts
- case studies

Doing a substantial research paper can be a valuable experience, but it needs to be structured to guarantee information transformation. For example, students can be given scenarios to respond to in writing, justifying their stance through research: "The Japanese government has decided to establish extremely high tariffs on American products. What would be the predicted policy of California's and Michigan's congressional representatives?" or "Is the earth warming or cooling? Why and what can you do about it?" Similarly, a class could hold a mock summit on a controversial topic such as environmental protection, with each student or small group representing a country; the research paper would be a policy statement or "white paper" on the issue.

Partnerships for Learning

One covert message runs through this approach to information and knowledge: librarians and teachers need to work more closely than ever before. At a minimum, they need to design meaningful activities, to incorporate thoughtful processing time throughout the experience, and to modify their instruction to meet the needs of their now-reflective students.

In a way, this approach means more work for the librarian and the teacher, but the work can be more intellectually stimulating for them as well as the students. Learning can be richer and more original. Real knowledge is to be gained. And no one need ever grade a dull, mechanical paper again!

FOR MORE INFORMATION

SEE TECHNOLOGY CONNECTION: The Magazine For School Media and Technology Specialists for a series on conducting research with electronic sources, The Great Hunt series by Jamieson McKenzie (April – November issues). He discusses framing "essentials" questions, sifting data, and presenting multimedia reports.

Media Literacy: From Viewing to Doing

By Joan Collins

"Media Literacy From Viewing to Doing" was a collaborative, interdisciplinary 10-week project that addressed improving students' critical thinking and information skills, culminating in a published school Web site. Because our school (John Glenn Middle School, Bedford, MA) is rich in technology and almost all our computers are Internet-connected, we wanted kids to analyze media messages, not only on television and in print ads, but specifically on the World Wide Web. A team of four teachers—two English teachers, a library media specialist, and a computer teacher—designed and implemented the pilot project, which involved about 75 sixth grade students. Using a variety of activities, they learned to read media messages in preparation for the creation of a school Web site designed for incoming sixth graders.

Teachers met during the summer to set goals and assess technology needs. The team contracted with Bill Plante of New Media Associates to help keep the project on track and to mark our progress with special events. We wanted Bill to provide several big events and to validate and evaluate the students' work with his professional eye. We also bundled the home page designs and mailed them to him to select a winner.

Preparing for the technological task, students learned to think critically about advertising. They examined magazine ads and viewed television commercials. Bill began by showing a "Surge" ad that has over 30 cuts. He slowed down the ad so the kids could analyze it. The teachers wanted students to learn advertising techniques and jargon such as "jumping on the bandwagon" and "come-ons." Students kept a log of TV commercials and noted that shows were geared to certain audiences and ads were targeted to the same groups. They would recall this information when creating their own products. During this process, students considered target audience, product name, and advertising strategy. With this knowledge, they created their own advertising copy for a new product. Just prior to Hershey's introduction of a new candy bar in February, the kids planned an ad campaign. The product was 1.5 ounces and had two wafer bars with peanut butter and milk chocolate. The students had to utilize their knowledge of advertising techniques to create a print ad for their designated audience: young children, teenagers, or adults.

Students then took their knowledge of media to the World Wide Web. They began research by reviewing selected Web sites appealing to kids, focusing on such elements as audience, purpose, message, content validity, and ease of navigation. They evaluated school sites in order to envision their own future school Web site. They wanted to give information that would answer current fifth graders' questions about daily life in the middle school.

In order to prepare for production, students actively competed for a winning home page design. Students decided a show would walk the viewer through their Web site. Bill Plante selected the winning sketch, a very patriotic sneaker, from the competition.

At this point, the students were in the hands of our very capable computer teacher, Mike Rinaldi. He asked them to fill out employment applications for "techie jobs" as graphic designers, animators, photographers, and editors. Once these jobs were awarded to the kids, they worked in teams at the computer lab.

Students used *Netscape Communicator* to create Web pages, and *Truespace 2* and *Director 4* to do animation. A scanner converted photographs and student designs into graphics, while a digital camera captured school activities. The project developed a life of its own by allowing all students to participate, from novice to expert. Teachers were the guides, and students were the experts, especially when using advanced technology. Kids learned independently but worked in groups. They constructed meaning from information research while understanding media's hidden messages.

The students evaluated advertising on the Web. They followed click streams and sketched out placement of advertising on various sites on the Web. They knew that every form of communication has a purpose or agenda. Every message is information with a purpose. By creating their own Web site, our sixth graders delivered information to the fifth grade in a spectacular package that was full of animation, color, design, and motion. Students didn't want their Web site to be dull. And it wasn't.

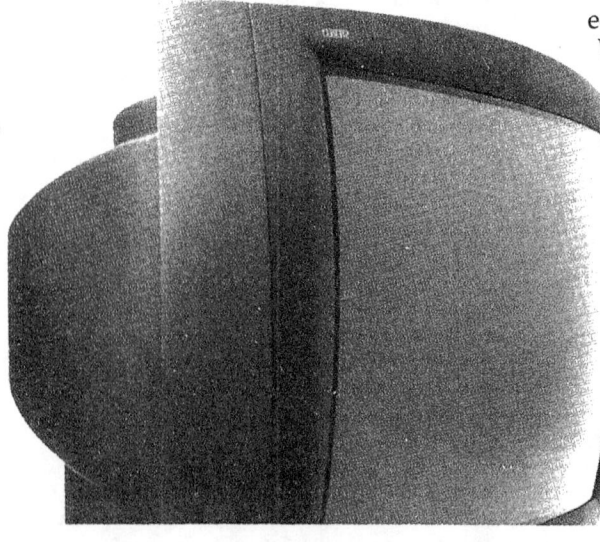

Students published a quality product on the Web for their intended audience, the fifth grade. They researched, acquired, organized, processed, and transformed information into knowledge, communicating what they learned. Bedford's media literacy project was a collaborative curriculum project that involved students, language arts teachers, a media specialist, and an instructional technology teacher.

Students expressed enthusiasm when they evaluated this project. One student wrote, "I greatly enjoyed this project for the creativity and people skills necessary to succeed. . . . Thank you for giving us the challenge of creating this page. Another wrote, "The whole experience of this has been new and exciting." And yet another wrote candidly on how each member of her team systematically problem-solved, but all kids felt success.

"Everyone in this project has been having a good time; therefore, I think that the Web site is not only a success but a fun project too."

The Web site may be viewed at <www.bedford.k12.ma.us/jgms/5thwebsite/5thgrade/5thpages/intro.html>. 🅱🆁

Joan Collins is a library media specialist at the John Glenn Middle School in Bedford, Massachusetts.

Notes

Policies and Standards: How Important Are All Those Acronyms?

KEEPING THE AHHH! ALIVE
THE EXCITEMENT OF DOING LIBRARY "SCIENCE"

By Terrence E. Young, Jr.

[We must] be more expansive in our approach to working with both teachers and students, to be willing to design programs to accommodate the real needs of the teachers and students rather than their desires or our preconceptions of what is best for them.

Children are natural-born scientists. They are curious, inquisitive, and full of vim and vigor in the exploration of their world. Children want to know everything, and once the questions begin they seemingly never end. Why is the sky blue? How do rockets get into space? What makes a fire burn? How do plants grow? Where does rain come from? When children start school, most have an innate curiosity that seems perfectly suited to learning about the wonders of science. As educators we must continue to convey the joys of science by keeping the "Ahhh!" alive–the excitement of doing science.

It is essential that everyone involved in science education provide an opportunity for all students to become scientifically literate. Students must be prepared to live in an information rich and ever-changing global society. Due to the rapid growth of technology, the amount of information available is accelerating so quickly that teachers are no longer able to impart a complete knowledge base in a subject area. In addition, students entering the workforce must know how to access information, solve problems, make decisions, and work as part of a team. Therefore, information literacy—the ability to find and use information—is both a keystone of lifelong learning and a basic skill essential to the 21st century workplace and home.

In 1996, the *National Science Education Standards* were published and posted on the Internet<www.nap.edu/readingroom/books/nses/html>. The publication describes exemplary teaching practices that provide students with experiences that enable them to achieve scientific literacy. The Standards urge educators to replace traditional teaching methods with stimulating learning experiences that mirror the excitement of the scientific process itself. As students' interest levels increase, so will their levels of learning. The science content standards provide indicators for what students should know, understand, and be able to do from kindergarten through high school. They promote and develop thinking processes which students will use in both classroom and real-world situations. The Standards are organized into seven chapters. Librarians will be most interested in the content standards for students, found in Chapter 6 and organized by K-4, 5-8, and 9-12 grade levels. The Web site is a fully linked table of contents which allows easy navigation of the document and the standards by grade level. These science standards can also be found at the Developing Educational Standards site, <putwest.boces.org/Standards.html>, which includes an annotated list of Internet sites with K-12 educational standards and curriculum framework documents. While *Information Power: Building Partnerships for Learning* provides "Examples of Content-Area Standards," this site provides the complete standards for all curriculum areas.

The *National Science Education Standards* (pg. 52) envision change throughout the system. The teaching standards encompass changes in emphases as seen in table on page 10.

Since the publication of the *National Science Education Standards* and the endorsement of the standards in general, at both the state and national levels, the time has come to pay full attention to the task that is even more difficult than setting standards: implementing them. Standards on paper are useless without actual changes at all levels–and changes begin with instructional personnel.

Among us are those who understand the needs of science teachers and who are cognizant of the kind of background teachers must possess to be able to teach to the *National Science Education Standards*. In our ranks are those who understand the climate of the schools and what is feasible to implement in them. We also have those who understand the problems of assessment and how to design and employ new assessment protocols. Moreover,

we have those who know how to use technology to further educational goals. Finally, we have those in our ranks who are splendid communicators, who understand the content of today's curriculum and how to teach to exacting content and pedagogical standards.

But no matter what the course is, the key component is the teacher, and we must recognize the importance of having a class led by a teacher. The interactions that can occur are unique with that teacher at that time with that group of students. This will require us to be more expansive in our approach to working with both teachers and students, to be willing to design programs to accommodate the real needs of the teachers and students rather than their desires or our preconceptions of what is best for them. School library media specialists should employ a variety of strategies such as discovery learning, use of manipulatives, simulations, cooperative learning, differentiated instruction, and technology when designing programs to meet these needs.

Information Literacy Standards for Student Learning, prepared by the American Association of School Librarians and the Association for Educational Communications and Technology, guides school library media specialists and others within the K-12 education profession as they cultivate and refine their students' information literacy skills. When coupled with the *National Science Education Standards*, we acknowledge this as a powerful tool for ensuring the success of American students in the field of science.

The *National Science Education Standards* states that as a result of activities in grades K-4, students should develop the abilities necessary to do scientific inquiry and to understand the process of scientific inquiry. Science investigations and reading are information-processing procedures that have many skills in common. Students and teachers bring the basic skills of communication, problem solving, resource access and utilization, and linking and generating knowledge into both the classroom and school library media center. These basic skills are tightly woven into the scientific method. When students identify a problem and attempt to reach a solution, communication skills allow them to create and share information through the use of reading, writing, speaking, listening, viewing, and visually representing. Resource access and utilization skills are fundamental if students are to identify, locate, select, and use resource tools to help in analyzing, synthesizing, communicating information, and forming a valid conclusion to their problem. Resource tools include pen, pencil, and paper; audio/video material; and word processors, computers, interactive devices, telecommunication, and other emerging technologies. Linking and generating knowledge across the disciplines and in a variety of contexts is the essence of education. It is the responsibility of all persons involved in the instructional process to build on these basic skills in order to achieve the success levels mandated by both the national information literacy standards and science content standards.

Information literacy skills must not be taught in isolation; they must be integrated across all content areas, utilizing fully the resources of the classroom, the school library media center, and the community. To effectively implement both the national science standards and information literacy standards, we must alter our perspective. Instead of seeing our classrooms as being full of information sources that are used to answer factual questions, we must see them as access stations where we ask more questions in response to both the information retrieved and the problem that faces us.

Putting the standards into practice involves all the resources of the school media center—engaging literature, "hands-on" activities, interactive displays, reference sources, and projects for specific scientific concepts. The literature component includes not only science trade books but also biographies, government documents, atlases, periodicals, CDs, online databases, and Web pages. Most activities can be modified for use by individuals, small groups, large groups, or as a whole-class activity.

The role of the elementary school library media specialist is to guide both teachers and students in researching and/or developing activities based on classroom dynamics and teaching/learning styles. The school library media center must provide a challenging learning environment that will arouse a student's imagination and curiosity and help students view science as a process of discovery and exploration rather than of memorization and regurgitation. This "hands-on/minds-on/get-active" process allows students to draw realistic parallels between their learning experiences and aids in their understanding of the relevance of science to their everyday lives.

Remembering that every child is a natural-born scientist, I invite you and your students to pick one or more of the sciences and explore to your hearts' content! The interest you spark in a student today may just kindle a lifelong love of science tomorrow.

To get you started on your science adventuring, here are some "off-the-top-of-my-head activities" and a brief bibliography. The activities on animals and the human body can be adapted to a variety of library research projects and topics.

ANIMALS

■ Each student researches the habitat and behavior of a selected animal. After completing the research, the student writes a diary entry of a day in the life of that animal.

■ Compare the information in books with the information presented in a video. What did they learn in the

LESS EMPHASIS ON	MORE EMPHASIS ON
Treating all students alike and responding to the group as a whole	Understanding and responding to individual student's interest, strengths, experiences, and needs
Rigidly following curriculum	Selecting and adapting curriculum
Focusing on student acquisition of information	Focusing on student understanding and use of scientific knowledge, ideas, and inquiry processes
Presenting scientific knowledge through lecture, text, and demonstration	Guiding students in active and extended scientific inquiry
Asking for recitation of acquired knowledge	Providing opportunities for scientific discussion and debate among students
Testing students for factual information at the end of the unit or chapter	Continuously assessing student understanding
Maintaining responsibility and authority	Sharing responsibility for learning with students
Supporting competition	Supporting a classroom community with cooperation, shared responsibility, and respect
Working alone	Working with other teachers to enhance the science program

book that wasn't in the video, and vice versa? Can the facts be verified in other sources of information?

- If the animal is on the endangered list, the class or school can adopt an animal by contacting the American Association of Zoological Parks and Aquariums (4550 Montgomery Ave., Suite 940N, Bethesda, MD 20814).
- Invite the local SPCA or Humane Society or zoologist to give a presentation.
- Invite students to create the ideal animal.
- Have a group discussion on what types of animals the world could do without.
- Recent estimates of the price of alligator hide run about $85 per square foot. How much hide would it take to make a belt, a purse, or a pair of shoes or boots? Estimate the price of a complete hide from an average-size alligator.
- A significant amount of public money is spent on protecting the whooping crane population. Decide whether the expenditure is worth it. Organize a group discussion that presents both sides.
- The eagle is a symbol of the United States of America. Find out the many ways in which the eagle is used, for example, on the Great Seal, on money, and so forth. Prepare a bulletin board that displays the use of the symbol, as well as appropriate magazine and newspaper articles.
- There is a lot of folklore information about owls. Become familiar with some of it and then make up your own myths and legends about owls; for example, how the owl can turn its head almost in a complete circle; why the owl looks like a cat, etc.

HUMAN BODY

- Discuss or write a story from the viewpoint of a body organ, such as the brain, heart, or stomach.
- Create a commercial about "My Favorite Body Part."
- Invite a guest speaker from the local blood bank to talk about the nation's blood supply and how it is collected, measured, stored, and preserved. How much blood is colected daily? Is it all used?
- "What if..." questions about essential body parts. "What if we had no skin?" "What if we didn't have bones?"
- Borrow a human skeleton from a doctor's office and X-rays from a hospital. Can your students identify the bones in the X-ray with those of the skeleton?
- Each student keeps a record of all foods eaten. At the end of the week, categorize the foods into the essential food groups. Ask the question: Are you a healthy eater?

An excellent example of the integration of books and Internet resources can be found at the Bubbles and Balloons; Resources for Primary Cluster Science Choices Web page bibliography at <www.nueva.pvt.k12.ca.us/~debbie/library/research/bib/bubbles&balloons.html>.

Bibliography

Once Upon a GEMS Guide: Connecting Young People's Literature to Great Explorations in Math and Science. Berkeley, CA: Lawrence Hall of Science, 1993. 0-912511-78-8

Teaching Chemistry With Toys: Activities for Grades K-9. New York, NY: McGraw-Hill Children's Press, 1995. 0-07-064722-4

Teaching Physical Science Through Children's Literature: 20 Complete Lessons for Elementary Grades. New York, NY: McGraw-Hill Children's Books, 1996. 0-07-064723-2

Butzow, Carol and John. Intermediate Science Through Children's Literature: Over Land and Sea. Englewood, CO: Libraries Unlimited, 1995. 0-87287-946-1

——. More Science Through Children's Literature: An Integrated Approach. Englewood, CO: Libraries Unlimited, 1998. 1-56308-266-7

——. Science Through Children's Literature: An Integrated Approach. Englewood, CO: Libraries Unlimited, 1989. 0-87287-667-5

Cooper, Kay. Too Many Rabbits and Other Fingerplays About Animals, Nature, Weather and the Universe. New York, NY: Scholastic, 1995. 0-590-45564-8

Fredericks, Anthony D. Science Adventures With Children's Literature: A Thematic Approach. Englewood, CO: Libraries Unlimited, 1998. 1-56308-417-1

Gath, Tracy and Maria Sosa. Best Books for Children, 1992-1995. Washington, DC: American Association for the Advancement of Science, 1996. 0-87168-586-8

Hefner, Christine and Kathryn R. Lewis. Literature-Based Science: Children's Books and Activities to Enrich the K-5 Curriculum. Phoenix, AZ: Oryx Press, 1995. 0-89774-741-0

National Research Council. National Science Education Standards. Washington, DC: National Academy Press, 1996. 0-309-05326-9

Phelan, Carolyn. Science For Young People. Chicago, IL: American Library Assocation, 1996. 0-8359-7837-1

Sosa, Maria and Jerry Bell. Inquiry in the Library. Washington, DC: American Association for the Advancement of Science, 1997. 0-87168-593-0

Young, Terrence E. Jr., and Coleen Salley. "Meeting the Standards With K-8 Science Tradebooks." Science Books & Films 33.6 (1997).

Terrence E. Young, Jr. is a School Library Media Specialist at West Jefferson High School in Harvey, Louisiana, and is the editor of the NetWorth column in Knowledge Quest. *Contact him at bestman@worldnet.att.net.*

> To effectively implement both the national science standards and information literacy standards, we must alter our perspective. Instead of seeing our classrooms as being full of information sources that are used to answer factual questions, we must see them as access stations where we ask more questions in response to both the information retrieved and the problem that faces us.

Information Literacy
FACING THE CHALLENGE

By Kathleen L. Spitzer

With the publication of the new Information Literacy Standards for Student Learning in *Information Power: Building Partnerships for Learning*, library media specialists face the challenge of implementing these standards in our own schools and school districts. At a time when the educational spotlight is on standards—both nationally, in the form of content area standards, and locally, in the form of state standards—we are in the right place at the right time to help students become information literate. How do we proceed?

KNOW THE BACKGROUND

As a first step, we need to understand the standards thoroughly. We can achieve this by reading *Information Power*, reflecting on how implementing the standards will empower students, and discussing the standards with others in our profession. In addition, we should familiarize ourselves with the history and development of the concept of information literacy. Some of the resources that can help in this endeavor are:

- "Information Literacy for Lifelong Learning" by Vicki Hancock (<www.ed.gov/databases/ERIC_Digests/ed358870.html>) provides a definition of information literacy, examines shifts in learning and teaching, and details the benefits of information literacy for students, citizens, and workers.
- The "American Library Association Presidential Committee on Information Literacy: Final Report" (available at <www.ala.org/acrl/nili/ilit1st.html>) is a fundamental document we all need to be familiar with.
- "A Progress Report on Information Literacy: An Update on the American Library Association Presidential Committee on Information Literacy: Final Report" (available at <www.ala.org/acrl/nili/nili.html>), published in March of 1998, gives a concise summary of progress made toward achieving the six original recommendations and details five recommendations for future action.
- The National Forum on Information Literacy (NFIL) Web site (<www.infolit.org/>) provides details about the NFIL, a coalition of more than 65 education, business, and governmental organizations working to promote a national awareness of the need for information literacy.
- *Information Literacy: Educating Children for the 21st Century* (National Education Association, ISBN 0810629755), by Patricia Senn Breivik and J. A. Senn, discusses how to work with administrators and teachers to develop a resource-based curriculum to promote information literacy.
- Information Literacy: Essential Skills for the Information Age (available from the ERIC Clearinghouse on Information Technology at <ericir.syr.edu/ithome/pubs.htm> or 800-464-9107), by Kathleen L. Spitzer, Michael B. Eisenberg, and Carrie A. Lowe, examines the development of the concept and its research base, provides examples of implementation at the K-12 and higher education levels, discusses the economic implications of information literacy, and explores technology literacy in terms of information literacy.

It is important that library media specialists be able to make the connection between technology literacy and information literacy. The National Educational Technology Standards (NETS, <www.cnets.iste.org/>), recently published by the International Society for Technology in Education, were a collaborative effort of many professional organizations, including the American Association of School Librarians. The NET Standards certainly provide food for thought for library media specialists who are wondering how technology literacy and information literacy fit together. There is also an excellent ERIC Digest on this topic, *Computer Skills for Information Problem-Solving: Learning and Teaching Technology in Context*, by Michael B. Eisenberg and Doug

LEARN ABOUT LOCAL AND STATE STANDARDS

Some states already have information literacy standards, as well as subject area standards, in place. Contact your state education department or check its Web site to locate the relevant standards. Next, determine if your district is developing or has already developed subject area standards. Consider becoming involved with the formulation of standards on the local level. For example, in one local school district, standards were being developed for all of the subject areas, including career education, but no standards were being created for information literacy. The library media specialists in the district wrote a proposal examining the subject area standards and demonstrating how information literacy would be integrated with each. They demonstrated this integration with a chart comparing each particular subject area standard with the Information Literacy Standards for Student Learning.

CREATE A PLAN

Collaborate with library media specialists and other educators in your district to create a plan to integrate information literacy with the curriculum. It would be helpful to engage the services of a process consultant to help your group work through these issues:
1) What is the definition of information literacy?
2) Should implementing the Information Literacy Standards for Student Learning be a district goal?
3) What subject area standards have been or are being developed by the district?
4) How can these subject area standards (or in their absence, the curriculum) be analyzed to show the integration of the Information Literacy Standards for Student Learning?
5) What plans can be made for the systematic integration of information literacy with the curriculum? For example, could a committee create a skills-by-grade matrix?
6) How will the concept of information literacy be disseminated to teachers, parents, and administrators?

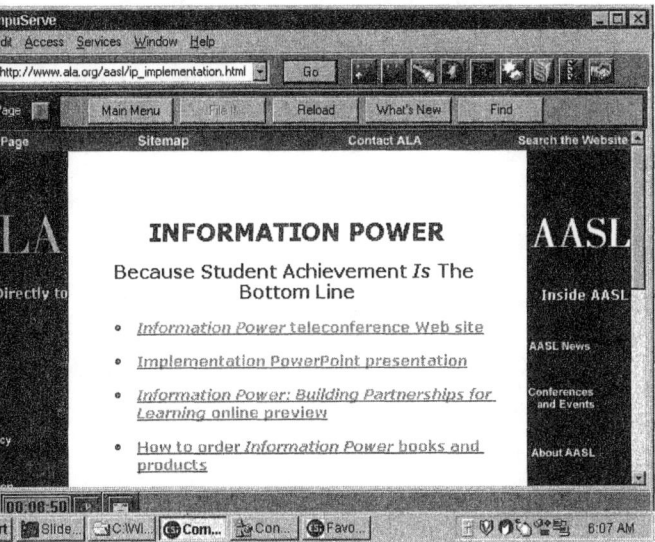

Used with permission by the American Association of School Librarians, a division of the American Library Association

Johnson (<www.ed.gov/databases/ERIC_Digests/ed392463.html>).

Library media specialists should also know how information literacy is being implemented in higher education. The Institute for Information Literacy (IIL), founded in 1997, is an organization that focuses on supporting information literacy efforts in higher education. The IIL Web site (<www.ala.org/acrl/nili/nilihp.html>) features resources that explain how higher education institutions are integrating information literacy with the curriculum and how information competencies are being developed. Finally, to stay informed about national and state efforts, check the American Association of School Librarians Implementing Information Power Web page (<www.ala.org/aasl/ip_implementation.html>). This site includes up-to-date information and the latest news about our professional organizations' implementation strategies, as well as the name of each state's Implementing Information Power coordinator.

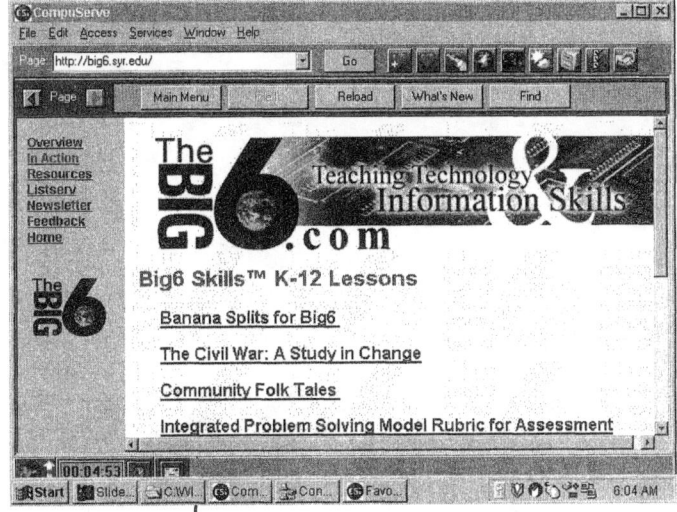

INDIVIDUAL EFFORTS

While working with others to create a plan, library media specialists may individually integrate information literacy skills with the curriculum at the building level. We can help spread the word to other educators by using the terminology and raising awareness of what information literacy is and why it is important. We know that the day-to-day assignments and projects that students need to complete provide us with ripe territory for integration. Consult with teachers to identify the particular information literacy skills that will help students with these day-to-day endeavors and create lessons specific to these skills. Where to find lesson ideas? Check the Learning Through the Library Web site (<www.ala.org/aasl/learning/>) and browse through the best practices section; visit the In Action section of the Big6 Web site (<www.Big6.com>), and review past issues of THE BOOK REPORT or read *The Big6 Newsletter* for ideas.

At a time when the educational spotlight is on standards, we are in the right place at the right time to help students become information literate.

CONCLUSION

Certainly, there is a great deal of work to be done to plan for the integration of information literacy with the curriculum. However, with support from other library media specialists, educators, and our professional organizations, we will be able to make a difference for our students. BR

Kathleen L. Spitzer received her MLS from the Syracuse University School of Information Studies in 1991 and is a member of Beta Phi Mu, the National Library Honor Society. She has been a library media specialist with the North Syracuse (New York) Central School District for seven years. She has written many articles on the topic of information skills and frequently makes presentations to professional organizations.

Notes

Orientation and Using Traditional Resources

It's the nature of schools: Every year we get new students. And while instruction in the use of library resources in conjunction with research assignments is important, our students need some basics early in the year, perhaps before any assignments are given. They need to orient themselves: What is in the library media center and where are the various resources located (including the "fun stuff" like paperbacks and popular magazines)? Students come from a variety of feeder schools and may have widely dissimilar backgrounds in library use. To ensure that all students are starting on the same page, an introduction to the library media center is a good idea. A questionnaire or quiz (preferably hands-on) at the beginning of the year indicates what skills students have mastered, what they may have encountered but not really worked with, and what skills need to be reinforced or taught. The quiz offered here, "What Do Your Students Know and When Do They Know It?" can be adapted and revised for many uses.

An introduction to the library media center can range from a tour, to a slide or PowerPoint show for an entire class, to a series of worksheets and hands-on lessons covering print and electronic resources available at stations around the center for individual students on a drop-in basis.

Not every school library media center is technology-rich. Not every public library our students will use after school, or after they graduate, will offer the variety of CD-ROM and Internet resources some will have been accustomed to accessing in school. Many smaller, older facilities still rely on the traditional stand-bys of the trade: the card catalog,

Readers' Guide to Periodical Literature, print biography series. Also, I have seen students quite puzzled when faced with a "decades" assignment that requires locating and examining a contemporary magazine because the CD-ROM or online index may not go back to the 1940s, and the concept of having to check different print index volumes for different years strikes the online generation as primitive. Some students walked away when I began explaining how to search the *Readers' Guide*. Those who tried were delighted to find old, bound issues of *Time* or *Life* at the public library, period advertising intact (something you don't get with full-text).

We deny our students a rich, challenging, and even f*un* piece of the research puzzle if we ignore the traditional print resources and concentrate entirely on searching electronic formats. We tend to get so involved in Internet search instruction that we may not see that some students-yes, even middle and high school students, and even adults-haven't quite figured out something as basic-to *us*-as the Dewey Decimal System. Our students may dazzle us with their computer skills, but we should never take broader research knowledge for granted.

Games present a painless way of having students put library skills into practice, and some ideas along these lines are included in this chapter. In every school where I have taught, I have posted trivia questions, and the students love them. When carefully selected, these questions can be applications of skills the students are expected to have mastered. It involves a lot more work, but "Stump the Librarian" days are also fun *and* educational-- for the librarian as much as for the students! In such an activity, students need to word their questions unambiguously, and I require them to produce proof of contested information, sometimes in the form of a citation from an acknowledged source *other than* a questionable Internet site. Many youngsters delve into some pretty obscure sources to come up with a stumper, discovering new tools and learning to use them. And they always come out of the activity with a newfound sense of ownership and pride in *their* library, which contains more good stuff than they ever realized!

☐ URL UPDATES

The Influence of Infoquest: Ask Learning Network:

www.ala.org/iconn/askkc.html

Mad Scientist Network
www.madsci.org/

Research & Web Citations from Nueva School
http://<nueva.pvt.k12.ca.us/~debbie/library/research.htmp>

Yahooligans! School Bell: Homework Answers
<www.yahooligans.com/school_bell/homework_answers/>

Surviving the "New" Library Skills Curriculum

Linda R. Skeele

A few years ago, I was the editor for a book on teaching elementary school children how to use electronic resources in the media center. When the book, *Teaching Information Literacy Using Electronic Resources Grades K-6* (Linworth), was published in 1996, I wrote an article for LIBRARY TALK on my approach to teaching reference skills at Western Elementary School in Georgetown, Kentucky. Over a year later, that article still elicits phone calls and letters from media specialists across the country, all asking the same questions: How do you find time to teach all those skills? How do you get every student to the computer if you have only one computer in the media center?

I suspect we would have received even more questions if it had been clear to readers that we also teach keyboarding and basic word processing in the media center.

Since we continue to receive inquiries two years after the original article, it appears that scheduling computer skills is a question of broad interest. What follows is an expanded version of letters that have been written to LIBRARY TALK readers on this topic.

Oddly enough, the key to incorporating electronic information skills in our media center curriculum may be the fact that we do not follow a flexible schedule. I consider my contribution to the students' learning so essential that I must have scheduled time with every class every week. Like the vast majority of media specialists, I am providing the sacred planning periods for teachers.

If I could create my perfect schedule, it would call for each class to visit the media center once a week all year with one grading period where the students came three or four times a week. This would allow us to concentrate on computer and keyboarding skills. Reality is quite another thing, so we learn to live with less-than-ideal schedules.

> **Oddly enough, the key to incorporating electronic information skills in our media center curriculum may be the fact that we do not follow a flexible schedule.**

Finding Time

To fit new responsibilities into an existing schedule, I suggest that you first look for something to cut out. We are all inclined to add new tasks without eliminating any of the old.

I look for some minutes in each class that can be diverted to teaching children how to use new electronic resources. I found one chunk of time during book checkouts. Instead of allowing all the children in a class to line up for 20 minutes of checking out books, I break each class into groups. In our media center, four to seven students are seated at five tables. These "tables" have become groups. When the first table finishes checkout and has 15 minutes of "free time," that group of four or five children goes to the computer to practice with the electronic program introduced in the last lesson. The "carrot" of time on the computer even speeds up check-out time. In a 15-minute practice session, four or five students should each have two or three turns at the computer. And, of course, groups rotate being first.

Other practice time has been carved out of normal class routines. For example, at the end of a class, I may send a group to the computer while the rest of the class puts materials away and other "housekeeping" chores. If I finish reading a story before the class period ends, I will send a group to the computer while the rest of the class has free time to read. Sometimes I will have only half of a class take part in storytime activities while the other half works on computers.

Management of Students & Time

I find that the maximum number of children to assign to one computer is five. If the number is larger, there is too much time between turns and attention wanes. Children will not tolerate more than 20 minutes of waiting before they begin looking for diversions. If the children know that their practice time is limited, they tend to stay on task.

Because there will be a great deal of waiting and taking turns, I set the ground rules for unsupervised time on the first day. Those who misbehave lose their turn at the computer.

To make the best use of their limited computer time, I am careful to tell the children exactly what they are expected to learn to do on the computer. If we are studying how to use the electronic atlas, I might tell the children that they will be expected to demonstrate how to find the capital of a state.

Another way to help students stay on task while you are working with other students is to place written "helps" at the computer. If a child has problems with the sequence of commands, he can look them up without interrupting the media specialist or waiting for attention.

Another timesaver is to give students some clues to subjects they might look up when they have computer time. Too many children will wait until they are seated at the keyboard before they begin to think about what they will do. I write examples of topics on cards, which I stack beside the computers. These are the same topics students will be tested on, and they know this. The cards are an incentive for children to use their computer time wisely. However, the main purpose of the cards is to cut down on the time individual students take at the computer.

If you teach the print and electronic tools at the same time, you can structure your assignments so that most children are working with print tools while others are at the computer. I switch groups every 15 minutes. In three class sessions, every group has been to the computer and also worked with print materials.

Testing

If there is only one computer in the media center, testing must be highly structured. Usually I give the class its instructions for the test during the session before the test. When students arrive, they know what they are expected to do.

For example, in the testing session for a unit on atlases, I place print atlases on every table along with a stack of worksheets. Completing the worksheet should take about 20 minutes. Students know to take one of the worksheets and use the print atlases to answer questions until I call one of the tables to line up in front of the computer with the electronic atlas. The children already know the instructions for the test, so I call one student and give him one of the cards from the stack. I begin timing when the children's fingers touch the keys. In this case the test is no more than timing how long it took the child to locate the information and recording a comment such as "needs more practice," or "very good." Most students take less than a minute to locate their information.

For testing purposes I select a fairly basic search skill that every child should have mastered, not one of the higher-level skills requiring analysis and interpretation of data. What I am trying to determine is how many students can independently and quickly access the information they need.

For my purposes only, I maintain a grade book that indicates level of mastery. I keep these grade books from year to year so that I can track students' progress. In the grade book, I record the child's time in seconds and make notes of problems, such as "can't alphabetize," "can't read," or "needs additional practice." After testing all class members, I calculate an average time and tell the students. In future sessions, the top scorers will work with the few students who score poorly.

This process of teaching and then testing a skill works fine with the youngest

Notes

elementary grades or when you are teaching only one or two electronic tools at a time. When you must teach eight to ten different tools in a relatively short amount of time, other ways have to be considered.

Keyboarding and Word Processing

Although in some Kentucky districts the school librarians teach keyboarding and basic word processing, I do not directly teach these skills. Our technology coordinator is not certified so she cannot officially teach classes, but she can work under my direction. We arrange our schedules so that both are working with the same students at the same time. You, too, may be able to team up with a special teacher or other school employee so that you can split up classes or block out time for intensive instruction. The technology coordinator and I feel we have refined time allocation and student grouping to a skill in itself.

Fourth- and fifth-grade classes come to the media center three times a week for 30-minute sessions. We have split each class into two groups of 12 students. Group A always goes to the computer lab for 15 minutes of keyboarding and word processing, while Group B comes to the media center for electronic reference instruction. At the end of 15 minutes, the groups exchange places.

For the last couple of years we have spent the first two months of the school year teaching keyboarding and reference skills to fourth and fifth graders. The rest of the year we expect students to use these skills in their research and reporting.

Twelve to 20 minutes is an optimum length for keyboarding instruction for our students. The class moves fast and the students know that there is no playing around. In the media center, I can introduce the important features of a new electronic resource in 15 minutes and still answer questions. In another 15 minutes all of the group can have one turn practicing the new skill.

Although we use the same techniques in teaching keyboarding to all students, primary classes usually spend four weeks in the lab. Again we split the classes in half, with half in the media center studying new programs while half learns keyboarding in the lab. Grouping for primary classes is roughly by age because we have multiage classes. There could be three grades in a single primary classroom.

Reference Programs

In introducing a new reference program, I determine what is the most important feature, or features, to know about it. For an encyclopedia, the basic skill is ability to locate an article quickly. I go over the special features of each type of encyclopedia, but I stress that students must learn how to find an article. Students know that they will be asked to demonstrate only one feature.

Among the skills tested are: ability to open and close a program; finding the definition of a word; locating a magazine or encyclopedia article about an animal; finding the name of the currency in a certain country; or playing the bird call of a robin.

Multiple Workstations in the Center

If you have several computer workstations available in the media center, you should consider installing a familiar reference program on some computers and a new one on others. The groups could switch from familiar to new, or individual students could go back to an old program they need more practice on. I often have as many as six computers, each with a different reference program, going at the same time. The key is to carefully assign children to permanent small groups and always rotate the groups in the same order.

The person who taught me the "stations technique" kept charts as records of what experiences groups had and where they needed to go at future sessions. Since I always move groups in a clockwise pattern, my students and I know where they are in the rotations. If students came to the media center only once a week, a chart would probably help them. I establish groups and a seating chart at the beginning of the year. A group is four to six students at an assigned table.

When it is time to test students in a center with multiple stations and rotating groups, I simply remove one computer from the rotation and call one group at a time for testing. The rest of the class goes on with its practice sessions. Incidentally, I do not test students on every program they learn.

Computer Reports

We send a summary of electronic tools mastered and the average keyboarding speed of the classroom to the children's parents. Last year we made small cards (about the size of a credit card) listing all electronic reference tools available in the media center and checked each tool the child could use independently. Card carriers could come to the media center anytime to work with that program. The cards also told teachers what reference tools children could use independently. This way, the teacher could send a child to the media center for unscheduled time with the expectation that the child would not need to ask for help or interrupt the media center schedule.

In short, the key to working with a limited number of computers, or teaching a number of electronic reference tools, is careful planning to use every minute to the fullest. A couple of minutes here and a couple there translates into an extra class over several weeks. This is time we must capture if we are to teach our children another set of information skills.

Linda R. Skeele is the Library Media Specialist at Western Elementary School in Georgetown, Kentucky. She writes the Software column for this magazine and is a reviewer for TECHNOLOGY CONNECTION.

A Model for Library Instruction

By Paul Rux

Recognizing that teachers must be involved in library skills instruction, this librarian has written a course of study to share with the staff.

Like love and marriage, horse and carriage, library use correlates with lessons on how to use a library. You likely won't get one without the other.

Use is the bottom-line measure of our professional effectiveness. We are not archivists, who embalm and dust off the bygone. Come in, get your hands on whatever interest you, and check it out! That's librarianship; instruction in library use is one sure-fire way to do our jobs and boost circulation.

At The Masters School, a boarding and day school for 270 girls in grades 6-12, we have developed a sequence of lessons to promote library use: "Library Literacy: Some First Steps." Since other school librarians wrestle with the same problem, we would like to share a brief overview of our approach to library instruction. You can adapt the model to fit your situation, or let it catalyze reflection on how you might improve your own library instruction schema.

However, please remember two things:

One, we deliver library instruction primarily through our language arts curriculum and faculty. This

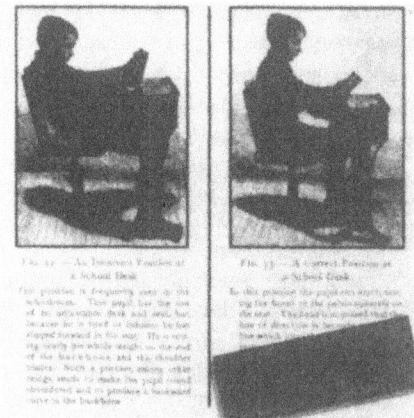

specifically includes ESL (English as a second language) teachers, who care for the roughly one-quarter of our students from 19 foreign countries whose native tongue is not English. Materials appropriate for our grades 6-8 do excellent double duty with our ESL students; we designed our model to cover such special needs. To help faculty select lessons appropriate for various need levels, we have developed a skill lesson-matching matrix (see below.)

Two, our commitment is to getting students ready for the next level of library service and skill. Ultimately, this means preparation for library environments beyond the school. We are a springboard, a catapult, a runway. Our best successes will occur beyond our ken.

The two caveats above ought to better focus our approach to library instruction as outlined in the packet reproduced below. This packet is given to the department heads. I am able monitor the use of the packet in several ways: Teachers come to the library to check out the kits and computer disks used in the more advanced sections. At the beginning section, teachers bring their classes to the library. Also, I am often asked to teach these sections.

Just becoming aware of what is in the library is the first step to library skills instruction. Only after the students have found out what's available in the library can they be

Library Literacy Matrix

Groups	Section 2 Orientation	Section 3 Skills Lesson	Section 4 Advanced Orientation and Skills	Section 4 *Readers' Guide*	Section 4 Reference	Section 4 *Britannica*	Section 6 Elementary Computer-assisted Instruction	Section 6 Secondary Computer-assisted Instruction	Section 7 Online Searches	Section 8 Field Labs
Middle School	x	x	?	?			x	?		
Upper School	x		x	x	x	x		x	x	x
ESL	x	x	?	?			x	?		

x = fit   ? = possible fit
Sections refer to those listed in the packet "Library Literacy: Some First Steps"
Section 5: Enrichment is not listed since it applies to each student group.

expected to make use of the library's resources.

(packet)
Library Literacy: Some First Steps

Section 1. Introduction-Rationale

The library skills lessons in this series are only a beginning. They are a starting point. First, they provide a foundation for a systematic grounding in library skills. Second, they afford ad hoc tutoring in specific skills on a needs basis. Three, they offer enrichment opportunities to learning activities already in place. Together as a series or alone as polishing of specific skills, these lessons are a first step in our quest for library literacy among our students and staff.

Skills are arranged from simple to complex. Skill sets are repeated at different levels of difficulty in the series. Jerome Bruner's "spiral curriculum" is the guiding paradigm behind the lessons (see Bruner's *Process of Education*, Harvard Univ. Press, 1960).

Section 2. Orientation-Basic

In a grocery store, we often ask for the aisle location of a specific product. "Where's the cat food?" "In aisle 6," snorts the cashier.

The same logic applies to our library. First, we must be aware of the existence and location of materials before we can use them. This is the idea behind the library floor plan exercises. We need to know where we are before we can take advantage of what's available.

Hand-out: Floor plan of the library

Exercise:

Locate and label the following features of the library. Answer the questions.

1. Card catalog. What is it?
2. Periodicals. Where are the old ones?
3. *Readers' Guide*. What is it?
4. Daily and Sunday *New York Times*.
5. *New York Times Index*.
6. Vertical file. What is it?
7. *Horizon* collection. What is it?
8. The Masters School art collection of research material. What is it?
9. Books by graduates of the school. Cite an author and title of interest to you.
10. Books about college and career choice. Cite a title of interest to you.
11. Books about teaching. What in their call number designates them a special collection item?
12. Map case. Cite a title of an atlas.
13. Books 709-799. What is the subject?
14. Books 500-599. What is the subject?
15. Books 800-822. What is the subject?
16. Fiction books. How are they arranged?
17. Special foreign language book collections. What languages are represented?
18. *Harvard Classics*. What are they?
19. Reference books. What is a reference book?
20. New book display. Cite an author and title of interest to you.
21. Talking books. How do you borrow them?
22. Microfilm and microform readers. How many do we have?
23. Books on history. The call numbers range from _ to _.
24. Microfilm room. What is kept here?
25. Largest dictionary in the school. What's its name?
26. Circulation desk. How do you check out a book?
27. What part of the library do you expect to use most and why?
28. What part of this tour surprised you the most and why?
29. How much does the average book in our library cost?
30. What does the cost of the book tell you about returning library books?

Section 3. Skills-Basic

Lessons are provided for middle school and ESL students in classification and use of the card catalog, *Readers' Guide*, and reference books.

No students ought to use the library for class research until they are prepared in these four skills. (See *Basic Library Skills* by Nancy Polette, Milliken, 1971.)

Section 4. Orientation and Skills-Advanced

A blend of audiovisual and printed materials are used to build on fundamental concepts of library use. The key skills in this unit are: use of the card catalog, *Readers' Guide*, and reference books.

Because reference use is considered the traditional heart of academic library skills, five fundamental reference lessons are provided. They progress from general orientation to reference to detailed exercises in literature and social sciences.

Kits: *How to Survive in School* and *Using Library Resources and Reference Materials* (Center for the Humanities) and *Using Today's Library* (Eye-Gate).

Paul Rux is the Library Director at Masters School in Dobbs Ferry, New York. Paul's article on curriculum involvement appeared in the first issue of THE BOOK REPORT.

Section 5. Enrichment

The library staff is ready to develop special units with teachers in all subject areas. Lessons in this section are examples of what can be done with some cooperation and imagination. (See *Dear Faculty, A Discovery Method Guidebook to the High School Library* by JoAnne Nordling, Faxon, 1976.)

Section 6. Computer-Assisted Instruction

The library has interactive software programs for instruction in the use of almanacs, dictionaries, atlases and so forth. The disks can also be used as class activities.

Resources: *Right On!*, library instruction software series (Right On Programs, 755 New York Avenue, Huntington, NY 11743)

Section 7. Field Labs

The library staff believes we ought to get our students ready for the next level of library services: college and university libraries. We believe the curricular areas in the school ought to work with the library staff to develop interactive lab experiences—not tours—with collections in nearby university and college libraries. (This may include sophisticated public and community college libraries.) Such field labs would be the culmination of preliminary research begun in our library, and would prepare our students for effective use of library services at the next level of education.

Section 8. Database Searching

The library is committed to developing lessons for students in this area. From our computer we can access two major reference databases, *Dialog* and *Wilsonline*. After students become familiar with fundamental library resources, concepts and skills through print and audiovisual lessons, they should cap their library literacy efforts with database searching experiences.

Wired for Learning New Library Skills

By Shelley Glantz

Before our library acquired its electronic research lab, the library orientation program for freshmen required one class period. During a scheduled English class, the students reviewed basic search skills and were introduced to resources, such as SIRS volumes, that were available only at the high school.

When we first subscribed to *Dialog Classmate,* an online database, we scheduled introductory sessions for upperclassmen and teachers. Teachers took to the product so enthusiastically that they began requiring at least one online source in all student bibliographies. By the second year we needed to introduce the freshmen to *Classmate,* and we needed a second orientation period. We were able to schedule this second class period in the English classrooms rather than in the library.

With the addition of more computer-based programs and CD-ROMs, it became obvious that these sources would have to be a significant part of the freshmen orientation. To avoid adding yet a third class period, we decided to revise the format of our traditional orientation. Half of each English class is scheduled in the electronic research lab while the other half watches a slide and tape program on policies, staff, and print resources available. The slide presentation is designed to last as long as the research lab activities and is updated annually.

Students in the electronic research lab were further divided into groups of two to three students who rotated through such resources as *Compton's Multimedia Encyclopedia, PC Globe, TOM* magazine index, *Book of Mammals, Discovering Authors,* and *BookWhiz.* The small groups averaged five minutes at each workstation, admittedly only a brief taste of the resources but enough to whet their appetite to return on their own time.

One of the English teachers who

found that the freshmen students were enthusiastic about their new knowledge of electronic searching and the high school library wanted to follow up with another activity. We devised an information search in three versions, to avoid logjams at any source, and used another class period. Each search consisted of ten questions, which touched on facts students would encounter in their English and social studies classes. Students worked in teams of two and were required to use a different print or electronic source for each question and to state the source. Prizes were given to the first three teams with correct answers.

I believe this group, with its follow-up activity, has been more proficient and more comfortable in using the library resources than other freshman classes.

Shelley Glantz is the Library Media Specialist at Arlington High School in Arlington, Massachusetts. She is a reviewer and feature article writer for THE BOOK REPORT *and several other professional journals. She won the 1992 Microcomputer in the Media Center Award, sponsored by the American Association of School Librarians and Follett Software Company.*

Notes

Library Instruction Test

What Do Your Students Know and When Do They Know It?

Mark Baker gives the following quiz to seventh graders before they receive instruction in library use and to eighth graders before they leave the school.

(1.) Books which are used mainly for looking up facts and information quickly are called
  a. fiction
  b. autobiographies
  c. reference books

(2.) The person who writes a book is called the
  a. publisher
  b. author
  c. editor

(3.) A book about the writer's own life is
  a. an autobiography
  b. a biography
  c. a bibliography

(4.) You can find a listing of all books in the resource center by looking in the
  a. vertical file
  b. card catalog
  c. book depository

(5.) A _____ prints and distributes books.
  a. publisher
  b. author
  c. editor

(6.) The _____ lists a book's chapters in order and appears after the title page.
  a. index
  b. preface
  c. table of contents

(7.) Books which are created from an author's imagination are called
  a. fiction
  b. nonfiction
  c. biography

(8.) Books dealing with factual information are called
  a. fiction
  b. nonfiction
  c. biography

(9.) The _____ tells you when a book was published
  a. index
  b. copyright date
  c. table of contents

(10.) A list of books on a subject is called a
  a. bibliography
  b. biography
  c. novel

(11.) A book about a person's life written by someone else is called
  a. a bibliography
  b. a biography
  c. an autobiography

(12.) The classification number and author letter found on the spine of a book and in the upper left hand corner of the catalog card is called the
  a. index
  b. call number
  c. copyright date

(13.) A book with the call number 796.3N is a
  a. fiction book
  b. nonfiction book
  c. biography

(14.) A book with the call number 920 L is a
  a. fiction book
  b. story collection
  c. collective biography

Answer questions 15-24 by using these sample catalog cards.

(CARD A)
MONSTERS
001.9 Baumann, Elwood D.
B   Bigfoot; Abominable Snowman
         Watts, 1985.
         107 p. illus.

(CARD B)
001.9 Baumann, Elwood D.
B   Bigfoot; Abominable Snowman
         Watts, 1985.
         107 p. illus.

(CARD C)
Bigfoot; Abominable Snowman
001.9 Baumann, Elwood D.
B   Bigfoot; Abominable Snowman
         Watts, 1985.
         107 p. illus.

(15.) Card A is an example of a(n) _____ card.
  a. author
  b. title
  c. subject

(16.) Card B is an example of a(n) _____ card.
  a. author
  b. title
  c. subject

(17.) Card C is an example of a(n) _____ card.
  a. author
  b. title
  c. subject

(18.) The title of the book is
  a. Monsters
  b. Bigfoot; Abominable Snowman
  c. Elwood D. Baumann

(19.) The author of the book is
  a. Monsters
  b. Bigfoot; Abominable Snowman
  c. Elwood D. Baumann

(20.) The subject of the book is
  a. Monsters
  b. Bigfoot; Abominable Snowman
  c. Elwood D. Baumann

(21.) The book has _____ pages.
  a. 1985
  b. 107
  c. 001.9
     B

(22.) The publisher of the book is
  a. Elwood D. Baumann
  b. Watts
  c. Illus.

(23.) The copyright date of the book is
  a. 1985
  b. 107
  c. 001.9
     B

(24.) The call number of the book is
  a. 1985

b. 107
c. 001.9
B

(25.) To find the current population of Illinois, the best source is an
  a. almanac
  b. encyclopedia
  c. atlas

(26.) A book which contains the life stories of more than one person is called a(n)
  a. individual biography
  b. collective biography
  c. bibliography

(27.) A book which contains the life story of one person is called a(n)
  a. individual biography
  b. collective biography
  c. bibliography

(28.) The introduction to a book is called the
  a. title page
  b. preface
  c. glossary

(29.) An alphabetical list of special or unusual words used in a book is called a
  a. text
  b. preface
  c. glossary

(30.) The first page of a book which tells the title, author, illustrator and publisher is called the
  a. glossary
  b. title page
  c. text

(31.) An alphabetical list of topics and their page numbers placed at the end of a book is called
  a. an index
  b. a table of contents
  c. a bibliography

(32.) Biographies are arranged on the shelves in alphabetical order according to the
  a. last name of the author
  b. last name of the person the book is about
  c. title of the book

(33.) Books that have the same Dewey classification number, such as 973, would be placed in order on the shelf first by the Dewey classification number and then
  a. by size of the book
  b. by the author's last name
  c. by the color of the book

(34.) Fiction books are arranged on the shelves in alphabetical order according to
  a. the last name of the author
  b. the last name of the person the book is about
  c. the title of the book

(35.) A *cross reference* in a book, in a set of books, or in the card catalog indicates that there is
  a. more information on the topic under another heading
  b. no information to be found in that source
  c. information to be found in some other source

(36.) Under the Dewey Decimal System
  a. books on the same subject are grouped together
  b. no two books can have the same number
  c. only letters and no numbers are used

(37.) When looking up the book *The Outsiders* in the card catalog, look under
  a. T
  b. O
  c. the author's first name

(38.) If the title of a book begins with *A, An,* or *The,* you would look for the book in the card catalog under
  a. the author's last name
  b. the second word in the title
  c. "a," "and" or "the"

(39.) The *Readers' Guide to Periodical Literature* is an index to
  a. all of the materials in the resource center
  b. all of the stories and articles published in over 100 different magazines
  c. all of the newspapers published in the United States

(40.) The *Readers' Guide to Periodical Literature* is useful because it helps you find
  a. current information in magazines
  b. information on literary works
  c. reference to all of the materials in the library

(41.) What are some different methods to present your research report to your teacher and classmates?

(42.) Name some sources outside the school library where you could find information on a research topic.

(43.) What source do you go to first when you begin looking for information on a topic? Why?

(44.) What type of information (single fact, general information, or indepth information) is found in the following sources?
  encyclopedia
  almanac
  atlas
  nonfiction books
  vertical file
  special reference books
  magazines
  newspapers

(45.) What is meant by single-fact information? Give some examples and sources to use when doing research.

(46.) What is meant by general information? Give some examples and sources to use when doing research.

(47.) What is meant by in-depth information? Give some examples and sources to use when doing research.

(48.) What is retrospective information? Give some examples and sources to use when doing research.

(49.) What is contemporary information? Give some examples and sources to use when doing research.

(50.) What is the first thing you do when you begin a research project?

(51.) What are some benefits of using a word-processing program?

(52.) Name some types of sources you would use to find information on the effect of abortions on the male parents. Why would you use them?

(53.) Name some specific sources you would use to find information on Oliver North's trial in 1989. Why would you use them?

(54.) Name some specific sources you would use to find out more about the life and career of baseball great Babe Ruth. Why would you use them?

(55.) When you cannot find a needed reference book, what do you do?

(56.) What are the benefits of using the card catalog?

(57.) How many sources should you use when doing research on a topic?

(58.) What are three questions you should ask yourself about a research topic before you begin to look for information?

(59.) Name someone you could talk to, outside of the school library, to find information on the following topics:
  a. flu virus
  b. inflation
  c. life in Utah
  d. drug testing of athletes

(60.) When should you use the following sources in a research project? (When looking for single facts, for general information, or for indepth information?)
  a. almanac
  b. encyclopedia
  c. nonfiction book
  d. special reference book
  e. vertical file
  f. magazine

Biography Research

By Marilee Norris

To provide practice in using some of the reference books that are confusing to students, I devised a two-day unit on four books: *Current Biography, Contemporary Authors, Something About the Author,* and *Contemporary Literary Criticism.*

The assignment was:

1. Use each of four reference books to research one author.

2. Report biographical and other information as directed.

3. Use the card catalog to find one book by the author.

I introduce this unit by using transparencies to explain how to decode the information listed in the cumulative indexes in *Contemporary Authors* and *Current Biography*. On the first transparency I wrote information that might be found in the cumulative index to *Contemporary Authors*. For example,

```
Author, Bd-Dd..............CAP2
obituary..................25-28R
earlier sketch............CA 19-20
See Also..................CLC 11
See Also..................SATA 19
```

Other transparencies give examples from the *Current Biography Cumulative Index* and explanations of abbreviations found in the four references. I plan to adapt this unit to other reference books, such as the Wilson Author Series.

The worksheets give the students a list of authors from which they choose one to research in the four reference books. The format for reporting the research is

1. *Current Biography*
a. Volume used (year) _____
b. Name of author as listed
c. Birth date _____ Death date _____
d. Place of birth _____
e. Two details about the author's life

As the student researches in the additional reference books, the worksheets asks for additional information. For example, from *Contemporary Authors*, the students must give the information above plus list three books by the author. In the worksheet on *Something About the Author*, the assignment goes another step further and requests

Two details about the author's life that are different from those listed on your worksheets for *Contemporary Authors* and *Current Biography*.

Three books written by the author in addition to those listed on the *Contemporary Authors* worksheet.

In *Contemporary Literary Criticism*, the additional information required is

Name of reviewer _____

Two details from the critical analysis of the author's writing style.

Two other details that you could use to discuss this author's writings.

Marilee Norris is the Librarian at Tecumseh High School in Tecumseh, Michigan.

Notes

The Relevance of Vertical Files in the Modern Library Media Center

By Pat McAbee

When a devastating fire gutted Princess Anne High School in Virginia Beach, Virginia, on September 1, 1995, much of the school lay in ruin. Built in 1954, the oldest high school in Virginia Beach lost 27 classrooms, the cafeteria, administrative offices, and the newly remodeled library media center (LMC). A combination of fire, smoke, and water destroyed the entire library collection.

Rebuilding the collection presented the library staff with unique opportunities as well as overwhelming challenges. While most school libraries are slowly making the transition from a traditional setting to an increasingly technologically advanced media center, the Princess Anne library was thrust into the 21st century overnight.

Although deciding to replace outdated or unused equipment and books (no more 16mm film projectors and 1940 copyrighted books!) wasn't difficult, other considerations, such as whether to invest in the enormous effort of rebuilding the vertical files, were not so simple.

The Rationale for Vertical Files

Before the fire, more than 300 vertical, or information, files filled four large file cabinets. National, state, and local issues were covered, arranged alphabetically by subject. If students needed information on freedom of speech, they could find it in the "Censorship" file. Charter schools? Check the "Education" file. PETA issues? See "Animal Rights." Embassy bombings? Try the "Terrorism" file. Even body piercing (yes, a student asked)3/4look in "Fads."

With the amount of new technology currently available for research, why keep the vertical files? With hundreds of databases from which to choose, accessibility to the Internet, and newspapers and magazine indexes on CD-ROM, is it worth the time to maintain these files?

Even with multiple electronic sources, the vertical files are an indispensable reference tool for the following reasons:

Student accessibility. Students who are assigned to do research on current issues may be limited by the number and availability of computers. Although other sources may be available, our library has only six computers with Internet access, so most of the students in a class of 30 would have to wait for computer access if we did away with the vertical files. They provide an opportunity for many students to do research simultaneously.

Supplement to the school curricula. The library media specialist can save valuable time by keeping files on topics that teachers assign year after year. Our science curriculum, for example, includes a unit on genetic diseases, so a corresponding vertical file was created, full of current research that supplements our print sources. Also, as new textbooks are regularly adopted by schools, it isn't possible for the library collection to keep pace with the most current curriculum needs. The vertical files are a valuable supplement until funds become available to update the book collection to meet new and constantly changing curriculum requirements.

Local topics. Students researching local and regional issues may be frustrated by the lack of information found on even the most advanced technology in the LMC. Often the only sources on issues such as school board decisions, a proposal for a national sports arena in a nearby town, crimes committed in our city, or local politics may be the vertical files.

Limited financial resources. As costs continue to rise and local library funds decrease, every penny counts. Library media specialists must be more and more resourceful in spending money. Vertical files include clipped newspaper articles, brochures, pamphlets, and other free print materials, leaving library funds for other needed purchases.

Vertical File Guidelines

In the process of rebuilding the vertical files, the following guidelines evolved for maintaining a useful and current file collection. These suggestions may prove helpful as you begin, weed, or add to your own files:

1. **Keep the files current**. Files should be weeded when they are no longer relevant. Outdated or wrong information is worse than none, as students will assume the material contained in the files is current and accurate. Maintaining obsolete files takes up needed space and valuable time. While files on the Exxon oil spill and the O. J. Simpson trial should be kept as historical resources, new files on Election 2000, the Y2K problem, and cloning should be added. In addition, articles within each file should be reviewed periodically. Is the list of animals in the "Endangered Species" file still current? Does the "AIDS" file reflect

the latest research findings?

2. **Maintain a balance**. Both sides of controversial issues should be represented. Strive to maintain balanced views on provocative issues such as gun control, the death penalty, and school prayer. Personal political, social, or religious views of the library staff should not be evident from the vertical files.

3. **Be selective**. Topics easily found in other sources should not be included in the vertical files. Is there really a need for a voluminous file on the Clinton administration when so much information is readily available? On the other hand, don't create a file if there isn't enough justification for it. A list of hurricanes names through the year 2002 (which I found) may be interesting, but I would not create a "Hurricane" file to accommodate it. Start a "Miscellaneous" file for odds and ends.

4. **Consolidate/divide subjects**. Smaller, related topics can often be grouped in one file, saving space and providing easier access for students. Anorexia, bulimia, binge eating, and dieting can all be combined in an "Eating Disorders" file. Conversely, if there is enough information on a subject to fill several files, subdivide them into smaller ones for a more narrowly defined search within a broader topic. For example, "Environment" can be divided into "Environmental Pollution," "Environmental Organizations," "Environmental Policy," and "Environmental Activists." In our library, the Chesapeake Bay is a popular and often researched topic, reflected in our rather extensive (13) subdivided files.

5. **Keep a current subject index**. Frequently updated lists of all files should be kept within easy reach, allowing students to scan and locate subjects quickly. Topics are easily added or deleted if the print information is also saved to a disk. Vertical file topics can also be added to the automated catalog database, where they can be accessed by subject or keyword.

6. **Use "See" and "See also" references**. Cross references are useful to students as they search the subject index and files. A student may be unaware that information on the death penalty is located in the "Capital Punishment" file, an article on smoking is under "Tobacco Industry," and birth control facts are in "Family Planning." Students may not ask for help, leaving the library without needed information if not for the "see" and "see also" clues to lead them to their topic. A student researching AIDS may be directed by a "see also" reference to the "Sexually Transmitted Diseases" file, finding even more information for research.

7. **Rotate the responsibility for maintaining the files**. The staff member responsible for maintaining the vertical files will usually be the most informed about them and therefore most able to help students find what they need. Rotating this job is a good idea, as each library media specialist will influence the size, scope, and content of the files, resulting in a more balanced and comprehensive collection.

8. **Create a uniform labeling system**. Having the file name, source, date, and school name on each piece of information makes for easy checkout to students and easy refiling. Labeling each piece of material in red ink and purchasing a preprinted "Vertical files" stamp is useful. Don't forget that student and adult library volunteers can be trained to label and stamp materials, keep the files in alphabetical order, and refile.

9. **Designate a collection location**. Although collecting, organizing, labeling, weeding, and filing materials on a weekly basis is the ideal, it isn't always possible. As you gather bits and pieces of information, keep a box or basket on your desk to store items for later processing. Then, when useful material is found by any staff member, it can be added to the growing pile.

10. **Always be on the lookout for information**. From medical pamphlets donated by the public health department to reprints of journal articles to free government publications, collect material from a variety of sources. In addition to local and national newspapers, maps, posters, and newsletters, I regularly cull material from my home issues of Life, Reader's Digest, and Southern Living. Solicit brochures from businesses and nonprofit organizations, gather pamphlets and handouts from conferences, and request free materials whenever possible.

Vertical files continue to serve a useful purpose in the modern LMC, addressing specific curriculum needs, supplementing existing reference sources, and further stretching limited library funds. With time-saving tips and organizational guidelines, maintaining files that are current, balanced, and easily accessible to students are well worth the effort.

Pat McAbee is a Library Media Specialist at Princess Anne High School in Virginia Beach, Virginia.

Notes

THE INFLUENCE OF "INFOQUEST"

Building Influence in the School Library

By Peggy Milam

How influential can a small school library be? Plenty! For our school, the key to building influence for the school library media center began with a game. Mt. Vernon Presbyterian School is a private school that serves 500 students in grades PS–8. We have an outstanding faculty and staff, supportive parents, a low student-teacher ratio, and high-achieving students.

Sounds idyllic, right? It is in many respects, but recently, we had one serious problem — our school library media center. The school library media center was located in a long, narrow room. Circling the walls were musty bookshelves creaking under the load of too many books in too little space. Our school desperately needed to give the media center an overhaul, and it did. The center was moved to a wider, lighter room. Bright new shelves were built and a woodsy wall mural was painted in the story corner. A new computer workstation was outfitted with networked Macintosh computers. It was a cheery, inviting atmosphere, all ready for the children to visit. But they didn't. Outside of the dutifully scheduled classes, children rarely came in at all. Being left alone in the media center gave me time to ponder the situation, to wonder, and to dream. Obviously, we needed more than a facelift to attract the students. We needed a magnet! I thought, what if the media center was a fun place to visit? What if gathering information was a sort of game, with prizes? What if we made up challenging questions and encouraged the children to come on their own to find the answers? Bingo! "Infoquest" was born.

INFORMATION LITERACY SKILLS: GRADES 7–12, 3RD EDITION   37

INFOQUEST MASTER LIST OF QUESTIONS AND ANSWERS

1. **What is the last word in the Declaration of Independence?** honor, *Webster's*, p. 1005

2. **What does DTP stand for?** Desktop publishing, computer glossary, *Webster's*

3. **What was Christopher Carson's nickname?** Kit, *Webster's Biographical Dictionary*

4. **What pen name did Emily Brontë use?** Ellis Bell, *Webster's Biographical Dictionary*

5. **Which amendment to the Constitution gave 18-year-olds the right to vote?** 26th, *Webster's*, p. 1008

6. **What is an erg?** Unit for measuring work or energy, *Science Dictionary*

7. **What part of a spider is a protein?** Silky liquid used to spin the web, *Dictionary of Nature*

8. **Name three legumes.** Peas, beans, soybeans, *Science Dictionary*

9. **Who was Rachel Carson?** Scientist, author, conservationist, *Dictionary of Nature*

10. **What is a tufa?** A powdery rock, *Science Dictionary*

11. **What is unusual about a male seahorse?** It has a pouch for young, *1,000 Q & A*

12. **What is the smallest mammal?** Kittis hog-nosed bat, *1,000 Q & A*

13. **Which cats are bigger, lions or tigers?** Tigers, *1,000 Q & A*

14. **Which creature is larger, a sperm whale or a giant squid?** Sperm whale, *1,000 Q & A*

15. **What is a female fox called?** A vixen, *1,000 Q & A*

16. **Why do glowworms glow?** To attract a mate, *1,000 Q & A*

17. **Which bird has the most feathers?** A tundra swan, *1,000 Q & A*

18. **Who has more bones, a child or an adult?** A child, *1,000 Q & A*

19. **What was ENIAC?** First computer, *1,000 Q & A*

20. **What and where is the Globe Theater?** Shakespeare's theater, Southwark, London, *1,000 Q & A*

21. **What is a stupa?** A mound covering a sacred object on a Buddhist shrine, *Q & A quiz book*

22. **Which famous bicycle race takes place in France each year?** Tour de France, *Q & A quiz book*

23. **What is a mermaid's purse?** A rubbery case containing eggs laid by a shark or ray, *Q & A quiz book*

24. **What nocturnal animal lives in a sett?** A badger, *Q & A quiz book*

25. **Where did a black widow spider get its name?** After mating it sometimes kills its mate, becoming a widow, *Q & A quiz book*

26. **If an earthquake occurs at the bottom of the ocean, what happens?** A tsunami, *Q & A quiz book*

27. **Who is Kim Campbell?** Prime minister of Canada, *20th Century Biographies*

28. **Who is D.W. Griffith?** Director, *20th Century Biographies*

29. **In what year did Lucille Ball of *I Love Lucy* die?** 1989, *20th Century Biographies*

30. **What type of dinosaur is a Dacentrurus?** A type of Stegosaurus found in Portugal and France, *Dictionary of Dinosaurs*

31. **What did Valdosaurus dinosaurs eat, plants or animals?** Plants, *Dictionary of Dinosaurs*

32. **The well-known writer Arthur Miller published two plays in 1991. What were they?** "Ride Down Mr. Morgan," "The Last Yankee," *Dictionary of American Authors*

33. **James Dickey, the poet and novelist, was born in what city?** Atlanta, *Dictionary of American Authors*

34. **Did Sinclair Lewis ever win a Nobel Prize for literature?** Yes — in 1930, *Dictionary of American Authors*

35. **Isaac Singer, the well-known American writer, was born in Poland. When did he die?** 1991, *Dictionary of American Authors*

36. **Who wrote the poem, "The Bells"?** Edgar Allen Poe, *Dictionary of American Authors*

37. **How much should you tip a strolling musician in a nice restaurant?** $1 request, $5 for several, none if no request, *Emily Post's tips for teens*

38. **Who (in the Bible) is Methuselah and how long did he live?** Grandfather of Noah, 969 years, *Bible Encyclopedia*

39. **Where was the first mortuary?** Collingwood Memorial, Toledo, Ohio, *Famous First Facts*

40. **In what reference book other than an encyclopedia can you find a biography of Edgar Allen Poe?** *Encyclopedia of World Authors*, *Encyclopedia of World Biography*.

41. **Who said, "Cogito ergo sum"?** Descartes, I think therefore I am, *Bartlett's Familiar Quotations*

42. **Where is Bora-Bora?** Island in French Polynesia, *Webster's Geographical Dictionary*

43. **Who said "Live and let live"?** Johann Christoph Friedrich Von Schiller, *Bartlett's Familiar Quotations*

44. **Did Benjamin Franklin sign the Declaration of Independence?** Yes, *Webster's*

"Infoquest" is a game of challenging research questions that can be answered in our school library media center. Each week a different question is posed on the intercom and students have all week to come into the media center to search for the answer. Younger children are given hints and much more guidance, but all ages are encouraged to participate. Prizes are distributed on Friday for the participants who have found the correct answer.

If a student is out of school when the question of the week is announced, each teacher can supply the question from her own master list. Additionally, a flip chart of questions is kept in the media center in a central location clipped open to the question of the week. (Questions are asked at random, so no one knows what the next question will be.) Students must come to the media center to answer the question, and even if they have found out the answer from another source, they must verify it in the resources we have available. Questions vary from week to week as do the resources used to locate the answer. By the end of the school year, students who have been regular participants will have used nearly every type of print or non-print resource available.

Response to the program has been tremendous. Parents became excited by the interest their children were showing in the program, and from the onset, they pledged $16,500 to purchase 1,000 new books for research. This pledge tripled our yearly funding. With their curiosity piqued by the weekly questions and with the exciting new books in our collection to choose from, children were even more eager to check out books. Our weekly circulation doubled. Teachers rushed in to try to find out the "Infoquest" answers ahead of their students, and many stayed and browsed the periodicals or checked out supplemental materials. Twenty-five percent more teachers became active patrons. Parental volunteerism went from 0 to 6 regulars as parents became intrigued with the new programs and purchases and volunteered to help out. Most important, student research skills became the focus of our program beginning in the first grade. All of these improvements are a direct result of our "Infoquest" program and simultaneously worked to build influence for the school library media center. In a nutshell, our influence grew from a game:

- we set a **G**oal to improve patronage
- we **A**ppealed to all ages
- we **M**otivated patrons to continue coming
- we **E**xcited the administration, parents, and teachers who support it

We find that "Infoquest" is as popular with eighth-graders as it is with the first-graders. Most students are happy just to find the answer to our research question, but the little prizes encourage continued participation and make the media center a rewarding place to visit. Our school library media center is a busy, active center of learning once again.

Print Sources of Questions and Answers

Bartlett, John. *Bartlett's Familiar Quotations*. Boston: Little, Brown, and Co., 1968.

Burnie, David. *Dictionary of Nature*. New York: Dorling Kindersley, 1994.

Comstock, Anna Botsford. *Handbook of Nature Study*. Ithaca, New York: Comstock Publishers, 1967.

Concise Dictionary of Great 20th Century Biographies. New York: Gramercy Books, 1997.

Encyclopedia of World Biography. New York: McGraw-Hill, 1973.

Guinness Book of World Records 1998. Stamford, CT: Guinness Media, Inc., 1997.

Kane, Joseph Nathan. *Famous First Facts* 3rd Edition. New York: H.W. Wilson Company, 1964.

Kingfisher Science Encyclopedia. New York: Kingfisher Books, 1991.

Lessem, Don and Donald F. Glut. *Dinosaur Encyclopedia*. New York: Dinosaur Society, 1993.

The New Webster's Encyclopedic Dictionary of the English Language. New York: Gramercy Books, 1997.

Northcutt, Cecil. *Bible Encyclopedia for Children*. Philadelphia, PA: Westminster Press, 1964.

1,001 Questions and Answers. New York: Dorling Kindersley, 1994.

Post, Elizabeth and Joan M. Coles. *Emily Post's Teen Etiquette*. New York: HarperPerennial, 1995.

Question and Answer Quiz Book. New York: Dorling Kindersley, 1994.

Simon, Seymour. *Science Dictionary*. New York: HarperCollins, 1994.

Twentieth Century Authors. New York: H.W. Wilson Company, 1995.

Webster's Biographical Dictionary. Springfield, MA: G & C Merriam Company, 1976.

Webster's Dictionary of American Authors. New York: Smithmark Publishing, 1996.

Webster's Geographical Dictionary. Springfield, MA: G & C Merriam Company, 1977.

World Almanac for Kids. Mahwah, New Jersey: World Almanac Books, 1997.

Internet Sources of Questions and Answers

Ask Learning Network Ericir.syr.edu Kidsconnect <www.ala.org/ICON/q&areferralservice>

Mad Scientist Network <medinfo.wusl.edu>

Math Forum's ask Dr. Math <forum.swarthmore.edu/dr.math>

Pitsco's Ask an Expert <www.askanexpert.com>

Research & Web Citations from Nueva School <www.nueva.pvt.k12.ca.us/~debbie/library/research>

Yahooligans! School Bell: Homework Answers <www.yahooligans.com/schoolbell/homeworkanswers/reference>

Peggy Milam is a Library Media Specialist at Mt. Vernon Presbyterian School in Atlanta, Georgia.

LOOK IT UP!

By Mary Northrup

HandsOn Handout

Noah Webster (1758-1843) liked to read, write, and talk. He wrote the first American English dictionary. He also wrote spelling, grammar, and reading books. He advised President Washington and lectured on language and education in all 13 states!

In addition to dictionaries, many other reference books help us. Draw a line between each question in Column 1 and the book in Column 2 that would provide the answer. Then match the book with its use in Column 3.

COLUMN 1
- Where is Belize?
- What should I see when I visit New York?
- What was going on the year I was born?
- What does "syzygy" mean?
- Who holds the record for the marathon?
- How do I repair a dripping faucet?
- I want to know about elephants.
- What's another word for "cool"?
- I'd like to write to my senator.

COLUMN 2
- dictionary
- encyclopedia
- almanac
- thesaurus
- atlas
- directory
- handbook
- Guidebook
- yearbook

COLUMN 3
- How to do something
- Another meaning for a word
- A subject (long article)
- How to find your way around
- What happened in that year
- Location of cities, countries
- The meaning of a word
- Names, addresses, phone numbers
- Lots of facts

SOLUTION

Where is Belize?	atlas	Location of cities, countries
What should I see when I visit New York?	guidebook	How to find your way around
What was going on the year I was born?	yearbook	What happened in that year
What does "syzygy" mean?	dictionary	The meaning of a word
Who holds the record for the marathon?	almanac	Lots of facts
How do I repair a dripping faucet?	handbook	How to do something
I want to know about elephants.	encyclopedia	A subject (long article)
What's another word for "cool"?	thesaurus	Another meaning for a word
I'd like to write to my senator.	directory	Names, addresses, phone

Linworth Publishing grants permission to duplicate this page for use within your building.

Mary Northrup is a Writer and Community College Librarian in Gladstone, Missouri.

Tips and Other Bright Ideas

Freshman Orientation Video

For several years, we used a professionally produced video for freshman orientation in the media center. Though it was very well made, the students did not seem to relate the information presented in it to our library. This year, I decided to make my own video of the library. My co-star came in the form of a six-foot cardboard cutout of Darth Vader that I had purchased from a catalog. When Darth wanted to check out his favorite book *Invaders of Earth*, he was sent to the office to get an ID card, and when he came back, of course, he had a library pass. Though I was afraid the students might think this was all too silly, they really did seem to enjoy watching the video. Some of the ninth-grade classes even gave it a round of applause. - *Elaine Chambless, Kendrick High School, Columbus, Georgia*

Mini-Course in Library Usage

Our school offers a week of "mini-courses" between semesters. I taught a two-hour course in library organization to two small groups. I reviewed the Dewey decimal system and the function of indexes. Each student was given a topic and searched for a book on the subject, an article in SIRS products, and an article in the *Readers' Guide Abstract* CD-ROM. Finally, I allowed enough time for the students to sample the variety of CD-ROMS available in the library. Written responses from the students indicated they now have a better understanding of how to locate information. - *Arlene Kachka, Holy Trinity High School, Chicago, Illinois*

The World Almanac & Jeopardy

When I used commercially prepared worksheets in teaching how to use the World Almanac, the Students pronounced them boring. To enliven this part of information skills teaching, I asked pairs of students to look through the book and find 10 facts dealing with a topic they were studying. Then they wrote a question to go with each fact. I used the questions and answers to devise a Jeopardy-like game board. -*Allison Trent Bernstein, Wayland (Massachusetts) High School*

Self-Directed Library Orientation

Through the years, I've tried different approaches to library orientation. Two years ago I began using self-directed learning with seventh graders. With the students I reviewed cooperative learning and established work groups. In each group, one student was named to record the member's answers to these questions:

What kind of information do you expect to learn about the library?
What do you need to know before you can effectively use this library?
If you were the librarian/teacher/tour guide, what would you teach?

After the small groups developed their lists, we met as a large group and shared the items on each group's list. (This gave me the opportunity to ascertain that the students were covering the important features of the library.) Students were then directed to find the answers to their specific questions, such as where are the periodicals housed and how long are books checked out? In a wrap up session, students told me what they had found. They could also ask about resources. I expect to continue using this technique and will refine it over the years to ensure that the experience is educationally sound. -*Sally Mortie, Peoples Academy, Morrisville, Vermont*

Research Lessons to Go

Whenever a class is ready to begin a long-range research project, I try to arrange an orientation session in the classroom. Usually this takes place on the day before the class's first scheduled period in the media center. Taking a book cart of reference materials, I present an overview of the research process, review bibliographic formats on the blackboard, and discuss topics, research shortcuts and anticipated problems. I try to involve the teacher in as much of my presentation as possible. This one-day, in-class visit lets students know that the teacher and I are working as a team. Students are assured that I understand their assignment, know what the teacher wants, and am in a position to help them track down the kind of information they need. Students tend to be more focused when they begin their research, and seem less reluctant to ask for help. Even a 15- or 20-minute overview seems to make an impression. -*Kathleen M. McBroom, Fordson High School, Dearborn, Michigan.*

Dewey Decimal Ball

Learning Dewey Decimal skills is more fun when students are playing Dewey Decimal Ball, a game that can be adapted to fit the sport of the season-baseball, football or basketball. Draw a picture of the playing field or court on the board. Hold up a book and read the title. If the student (or team) identifies the Dewey number by hundreds correctly, they move a base, get a first down, or make a basket, then get another turn. Who needs boring worksheets-*Janice Jones, Piedmont Hills High School, San Jose, California*

Having Fun with Dewey

When seventh graders are reviewing the Dewey Decimal System, one project involves writing fictional titles for books in each general category. Wacky ideas abound! This year I used the students' titles in a bulletin board display. Here are some examples: "Mrs. Zimmerman's Encyclopedia of 'Do It Right'" "from the 000s;" "Just Between You and Me" by Newt Gingrich's Mom; "Martian Math Made Easy" from the 500s; "Forces from Beyond the Cosmos: How A Microwave Really Works" from the 600s.-*Sherry Hoy, Tuscarora Junior High School, Mifflintown, Pennsylvania*

Packaged Answers to Project Questions

For those class projects in which all the students come to the library media center asking the same questions, I write a checklist of resources. Students can pick up the list and be more independent in their research. And, the staff doesn't begin to sound like a broken record, repeating and repeating the same answers-*Allison Bernstein, Wayland (Massachusetts) High School*

CHAPTER 3

Research Methods and Models

Once they wrote their last high school or college term paper, few young people in decades past were likely ever again to crack open *Readers' Guide* or the index to the *New York Times*. But in today's information society, adults often find themselves needing or wanting to find something out, for a continuing education course, for their jobs, for recreation, for health and consumer questions. By presenting students with real-life scenarios to research and solve, using all the tools available, rather than the standard term paper, we are preparing them for this future. Most of the current models for teaching information literacy skills operate from this real-life perspective.

Several of the articles I've included in this chapter purport to be about using the Internet, and particularly the World Wide Web, for research. But the methodology they describe, the steps they suggest, have far broader applications. Framing essential questions, developing a vocabulary base from which to search, narrowing the field, browsing critically, being open-minded, evaluating one's findings, discarding the irrelevant, encapsulating information as concisely as possible, presenting one's conclusions convincingly-these skills are as useful for someone using a travel guide or a consumer magazine as they are for an Internet researcher.

There are a number of popular paradigms or models for research. The Big Six is discussed here, as is the more colloquial FLIP IT. Both models consider essential questions (What do I know? What do I need to know?), a search for relevant information in appropriate sources, a synthesis of that information, a presentation in appropriate format, and evaluation of the product and the process. While the numbers, acronyms, and bullet points are convenient mnemonics, it's not what we *call* our method that's important; it's the step-by-step meat of that method, whichever variation we choose, that needs to become second nature for students.

Students-and even some teachers and administrators-might question *why* we stress the process of doing research or the development of broad information literacy skills. Isn't it enough to hunt and peck, find a few facts, and be satisfied, perhaps relying on a helpful librarian, in the process picking up just enough familiarity with technology or print sources to get by for the current assignment? No. Today, it's *not* enough. There's a real world out there, full of questions and puzzles and choices, and the skills we teach are *survival* skills for that world.

URL UPDATES

Effective Searching Buys Time to Reflect, Ponder & Analyze:
>The Kincheloe Class
>Murder Mystery Project
>http://dewey.chs.chico.k12.ca.us/kin.html

>Chico High School Library
>http://dewey.chs.chico.k12.ca.us/

Library Technology Adds Immediacy to Research Assignments:
>Project Summaries on the Internet
>www.fcps_k12_va.us/mtvernonhs/index.html

Notes

Survival Skills for the Future

Linda R. Skeele

FOR THE LAST TWO YEARS I have been editing a collection of lesson plans using computers and other new technologies. As we publish *Teaching Information Literacy Using Electronic Resources K-6* (Fall 1995, Linworth Publishing), I have been asked to put down my thoughts on the state of and place of library skills in today's media center curriculum.

First is a question that is raised frequently: Why bother teaching library skills? My concern is that, in the rush to flexible scheduling and teaching reference skills at the point of need, we may be missing a golden opportunity. If we wait until a classroom assignment calls for research skills, we may be too late to do the child any good. Far too many teachers ask us to give a 20-minute lesson on the encyclopedia, atlas, and *Readers' Guide* and expect the children to use these tools successfully the next week when they are scheduled for a 30-minute library period researching the states.

While the 20-minute lesson may address the immediate needs of the child in some fashion, we cannot teach that many tools in that time frame and expect the child to locate the information he needs efficiently and easily. The searching skills need to be taught before research is attempted. It is no different from giving a lesson on cursive writing one day and expecting students to write a page in a nice cursive hand the next.

This philosophy of waiting until the student (*read* teacher) has a need for research skills also ignores one of education's dirty little secrets: some teachers will never get around to making time for these skills. There are teachers who consider learning to access databases nothing more than a waste of valuable instructional time. Often they themselves do not have these skills, so why should they take time away from the classroom? Oh yes, these teachers believe that students should learn to use a dictionary and an encyclopedia and perhaps an atlas, but they can teach these skills in their classrooms as part of the regular curriculum.

The results in a school with this philosophy are a hodgepodge of instruction. One teacher strives to teach information skills, another gives only lip service to the idea. Teachers in the upper grades are frustrated when some students in an in-coming class can use the Internet and others have never turned on a computer.

This problem has already arisen in our district where the elementary schools use technology in different ways. When students from different schools come together in middle school classes, teachers find that there is no commonality of experience.

Worse yet, among the children the technology "haves" are resented by the "have nots." The have-nots' school may have been well supplied with computers and other technology, but the students did not learn how to use these tools. When students and their parents realize that others have made far more use of the information technology, they become resentful.

Given the wide disparity in access to technology, it would be unreasonable to say that computer skill X should be mastered by third grade. Never will every child in a district, even in the same school, have the same learning experiences in information skills, but media specialists can ensure that all children have certain basic skills. In short, we need a plan of action that ensures that every child has mastered certain essential skills by the end of elementary school.

This is where technology makes our task much easier. Now we can teach fairly sophisticated search techniques to quite young children. We do not have to wait until children can alphabetize before we teach them to use an encyclopedia. In fact, nonreaders can locate information in an electronic encyclopedia such as *First Connections* (Hartley), and listen to it being read aloud.

Before electronic resources were available in school libraries, there was general agreement that every child should be able to use a dictionary, an encyclopedia, an atlas, the card catalog, and perhaps a simplified *Readers' Guide* before leaving the elementary grades. Some children might learn to use other reference books, but we librarians considered ourselves lucky if most of the fifth graders could find a subject in the encyclopedia in ten minutes. Teaching any searching skills before the third grade was a waste of time because students had not learned alphabetizing skills.

I now teach every first grader to locate simple subjects like "birds," "trees," "dinosaurs," and "elephants" in an electronic encyclopedia. Most can do it in record time, which for some is ten seconds or less and seldom over 30 seconds. They know how to navigate through articles by using the "contents" feature and how to activate the picture, sound, and animation icons. And they love to do it.

> *Before reference books were available on CD-ROMs, I would never have attempted to teach a first grader to find the currency of Thailand. Now the children and I think this is a perfectly normal task....*

Today's first graders can be successful at a skill that, a couple of years ago, some fifth graders never mastered because they were not able to alphabetize. (Remember the frustration of finding that some students were spending an entire research period looking for Indiana in the "I" volume of the encyclopedia because they were unable to comprehend searching by the second or third letters in the word. As a result they "searched" page by page from the first page.)

I have just completed a unit on the *Picture Atlas of the World* (National Geographic) with all of the primary students. Every child learned how to locate a country and four facts about that country. The facts were chosen not just because they were easy to find but because they happen to be the most commonly needed pieces of information for country reports. The lesson required the children to first find the Country Menu and then locate the area information. Average time for the entire task? About 35 seconds for most children, with many under 15 seconds.

Before reference books were available on CD-ROMs, I would never have attempted to teach a first grader to find the currency of Thailand. Now the children and I think this is a perfectly normal task for a first grader. Indeed, many of the reference tools remind children of computer games; we would be foolish not to take advantage of this. In the days of print only, few students ever begged to look up subjects in the encyclopedia. Now they do because it is fun to use the CD-ROM encyclopedias.

When I teach any information resource to a class, I plan some method of determining if every child has mastered it. For the electronic encyclopedia and atlas, I have every student in the school locate a subject. While I take notes about how they are doing, the students think only in terms of speed. Recognition is given to those students who correctly locate the information in the fastest times. Right now there is a banner in the entry hall of the school that lists students with the fastest times. An award is given to the class with the best overall skill. What is interesting about this testing is that other achievement levels are not a good predictor of search skills. Prior computer skills do make a big difference, but some of our speed demons are not the best academic students.

Today's children will live their adult lives in an information-rich world. It's probable that the reference skills that I'm teaching now will be swept away by something newer, faster, and easier to use. But for now, the search strategies I'm teaching will prepare them to take full advantage of whatever new form research will take.

Linda R. Skeele is the Library Media Specialist at Western Elementary School in Georgetown, Kentucky. She writes the Software column for this magazine, is an editorial consultant for TECHNOLOGY CONNECTION, *and mostly recently served as the editor for the new book* Teaching Information Literacy Using Electronic Resources K-6 *(from the Professional Growth Series, Linworth Publishing).*

Notes

Getting Off to a Solid Start

Wise use of media technology by sixth graders prepares them for middle school and beyond.

Mary Alice Anderson

ANOTHER SCHOOL YEAR is half over; by now all of the 350 sixth graders at Winona Middle School have searched the Internet, used online and CD-ROM databases like *Computer Cat* (Winnebago), *Magazine Article Summaries* (EBSCO), and *Biology Digest* (NewsBank). They have used word processing software for social studies, science and language arts papers and included graphics and graphs in many papers.

Students simultaneously use the *World Book Multimedia Encyclopedia* to gather information and a multimedia authoring program to create a presentation. Several have made slide shows using *ClarisWorks* or *HyperStudio* (Wagner) and presented them "adult style" in our distance learning facilities using computers, television monitors, and other projection devices. They are getting better about not printing everything in sight, remembering to copy and save or print just what they need.

Music classes use technology to study music theory and compose songs. They study topics such as holography, electronics, and robotics in a high tech modular lab for industrial technology classes. Science students build and experiment with lego/logo to study mechanical processes. Others are busy learning to use the scanner, send e-mail, or make their own Web pages. One sixth-grade team of 100 students participates in *CU-See Me* video conferences.

As we do every year, teachers and I comment on how advanced the incoming sixth-grade kids are compared to last year's. What students used to do in five days now takes two; what they used to learn to do in the winter or spring they now do in the fall. The word "game" has all but disappeared from their computer vocabulary. When they use the school computers before or after school, they use the technology primarily for productivity or information gathering. And, it is significant that all of our students have opportunities to use the same technologies and in a wide range of classes. Technology access, use, and learning are equitable.

The elementary schools from which sixth-grade students enter the middle school vary in the levels of technology available. Elementary media centers range from small and traditional programs to fully automated centers with multiple electronic resources. Elementary school Internet access and network connectivity have only recently become available. All elementary classrooms have Macintosh computers but curriculum integration is uneven although there are board-approved learner outcomes for technology. Yet, the middle school staff expects all sixth graders to use the resources of our state-of-the-art media center. And, they all do.

How do we get to this point? Immersion is a significant factor in what our students achieve. There is no escaping the media center or technology! The students begin using the media center and its resources immediately in the new school year, in most cases during the first week of school. Technology is immediately and continuously integrated into the curriculum. Projects involving technology may be in conjunction with language arts, science, or social studies assignments.

We limit our instruction in using the center's technology to what is needed for a student task. We never use worksheets. As I stress to the students, the only way to learn this is to do it as needed for the assignment. We do not worry about all of the students learning to use all of the key resources at the same time; for us, the important thing is that students learn transferable skills and concepts.

Formal classes run contrary to our philosophy: All technology instruction is integrated into the regular curriculum and technology is viewed as an information tool.

This past fall a teacher who often wanted to wait until the students "matured a bit" before she introduced them to media center technology started a major project—a study of local environmental issues—the second week of school. Her attitude has become "well, they have to use the technology sooner or later; we might as well get started."

Staff development and teaching teachers how to help students are important factors in student success. Sixth-grade teachers especially are encouraged to attend technology classes offered by the media center in the summer and during the school year. Encouragement takes the form of a letter from our principal and special meetings with sixth-grade teachers. The past two years we have held media program orientation just for the sixth-grade teachers. Special education staff and paraprofessionals are also invited.

Teachers learn about new materials and an assortment of concepts that they should reinforce with their students. We stress that the technology is new to the students too.

With over 1,000 students and 300

Common Learner Outcomes for Media/Technology

Winona Middle School
Independent School District 861
Winona, Minnesota

Students will be able to:

■ Locate information in resources appropriate to their needs by using electronic indexing and catalog tools including—

Computer Cat (online catalog)
Biology Digest
Magazine Article Summaries
and other appropriate CD-ROMs and databases.

■ Determine the value and appropriateness of resources (currency and reliability).

■ Apply appropriate and correct search strategies to indexes, Boolean searching, and hypertext searching.

■ Identify and demonstrate proper care of facilities, hardware and software. (Keep materials in their proper place, understand when to turn equipment off and on, and keep disks in protective cases.)

■ Transfer skills and concepts between technologies and between curriculum areas.

■ Communicate information in a way appropriate to the topic and audience, using word processing software, graphs, graphics, and multimedia presentations.

■ Show respect for the copyright law. Maintain a list of resources used and give proper credit to print and electronic sources used.

■ Use copyrighted software properly.

■ Work cooperatively with others (with a partner or in a small group).

■

Please visit our Web site (http://wms.luminet.net) to find more about our school's media/technology program.

Notes

computers in our school, I cannot reach or teach all of the students, but I can teach all of the teachers. The results are teachers and students learning together and teachers taking an active part in the resource-based learning projects.

The middle school is organized in teams of three to five teachers and 75-130 students, called houses. This concept is ideally suited for making sure all students have opportunities. It is easy to monitor what experiences houses have had and what competencies they have reached. Occasionally an entire house will participate in a week-long multi-disciplinary project. During the week, the students spend a major portion of their time in the media center and labs. While not quite 100% of our teachers integrate technology into the classroom to the degree desired, in each house there is at least one teacher who does.

District policy stipulates that a media specialist should serve on each curriculum writing team. As a result, specific examples of media/technology materials, projects, and outcomes for students are often part of the written curriculum. The common learner outcomes we developed during one summer curriculum writing/ staff development project appears on page 5. The outcomes are generic and serve as a core for curriculum writing and planning.

We are often asked if we have formal computer classes and what age the students are taught keyboarding. Our answer to formal classes is a firm "no." Formal classes run contrary to our philosophy: All technology instruction is integrated into the regular curriculum and technology is viewed as an information tool. Students learn through experience and doing.

Keyboarding is formally taught beginning in grade 4, but it is taught unevenly throughout the elementary schools. Yet, somehow the students do very well although not to the degree a business education teacher might like. We have observed that simply reminding students of proper keyboarding techniques is about all it takes to have them use proper procedures.

And just what should sixth-grade students be able to do? What do we expect of them? Basically, we expect them to do most of the things mentioned in the opening paragraph. We also expect them to have an open and positive attitude toward new tools and new experiences and to go beyond the expectations if they desire. Extended media center hours four days a week help provide opportunities for exploration beyond the classroom.

For our sixth-grade students, technology is a way of life and learning. They have a high degree of access to computers in their classrooms, in labs, and in the media center. Use is generally equitable for all students and throughout most of their curriculum areas. It is not a once-in-a-while situation; our students participate in numerous projects requiring electronic resources during the course of a school year. Many of the projects are simultaneous.

We see students enjoying learning, eager to use the media center, and certainly more motivated than in the past. One of my fondest memories will always be that of a student who came to the media center the last day of school and said, "Thank you for all you've taught me this year." He was just one of many who had grown tremendously that year.

Mary Alice Anderson is the Media Specialist at Winona Middle School in Winona, Minnesota. She is an editorial consultant for TECHNOLOGY CONNECTION: The Magazine for School Media and Technology Specialists. *She edited* Teaching Information Literacy Using Electronic Resources for Grades 6-8 *(Linworth, 1996).*

Notes

THE BIG SIX & ELECTRONIC RESOURCES:

A Natural Fit

By Michael Eisenberg & Robert E. Berkowitz

The Big Six Skills model, long a mainstay of school librarians' instruction, proves a perfect match to the influx of technology in student research. The model's authors show us how.

THE BIG SIX SKILLS model is an information literacy curriculum, an information problem-solving process, and a set of skills that provides a strategy for effectively and efficiently meeting information needs. It has been adopted by hundreds of schools as the basis for their information and technology skills programs.

The Big Six Skills approach can be used whenever students are in a situation, academic or personal, which requires information to solve a problem, make a decision or complete a task. When taught collaboratively by librarians and content-area teachers in concert with content-area objectives, it serves to ensure that students are information literate.

Over the past 20 years, many library media specialists and classroom teachers have worked hard to move away from teaching "library skills" in isolation from the content curriculum. Effective integration of information and technology skills teaching has two requirements: (1) the skills must directly relate to classroom assignments, and (2) the skills themselves need to be tied together in a logical information- process model.

The same trend is taking place in relation to teaching computer skills. Schools are seeking to move from teaching isolated "computer skills" to teaching integrated technology skills. Students need to be able to use computers flexibly, creatively and purposefully. Individual computer skills take on a new meaning when they are integrated within the information problem-solving process.

Technology skills are easily integrated into the Big Six Skills model. For example, word processing, desktop publishing, and presentation software programs are used for synthesis (to organize and present). Word processing is also important for use of information (note-taking). Online databases, CD-ROM encyclopedias, and other electronic resources provide location and access capabilities. Internet capabilities are also included in information problem-solving. E-mail is useful for linking students with their teachers or with each other for task definition activities and later for evaluation. Web browsers and search engines are used in information-seeking strategies and as tools for location and access. File transfer protocols help students use information.

Technology offers powerful information tools to students. Here are two typical assignments that focus the Big Six perspective on the integration of technology into information skills instruction.

Assignment 1
Students will
compare the Constitution of the United States to that of another country
by
using a WWW search engine such as *Alta Vista, Webcrawler* or *Yahoo!* to find the constitutions
in order to
list and compare the basic rights granted to citizens
to be shared
in the form of a data chart.

The Big Six approach to technology in this example includes the use of the Internet to find (Big Six Skill # 3—Location & Access), as well as to download information for review and analysis (Big Six Skill #4—Information Use) and present information in a data chart using a word-processing or spreadsheet program (Big Six Skill #5—Synthesis).

Assignment 2
Students will
interview a zoo employee, using a series of 10 questions via e-mail
by
locating the e-mail addresses of zoo experts using a WWW search engine

---

The Big Six Model of Information Problem-Solving

(Eisenberg/Berkowitz, Copyright 1988)

1 Task Definition
  1.1 Define the task (the information problem)
  1.2 Identify information needed in order to complete the task (to solve the information problem)

2 Information Seeking Strategies
  2.1 Brainstorm all possible sources
  2.2 Select the best sources

3 Location and Access
  3.1 Locate sources
  3.2 Find information within the source

4 Use of Information
  4.1 Engage in the source (read, hear, view, touch)
  4.2 Extract relevant information

5 Synthesis
  5.1 Organize information from multiple sources
  5.2 Present the information

6 Evaluation
  6.1 Judge the process (efficiency)
  6.2 Judge the product (effectiveness)

Notes

in order to
get information necessary to create a quality zoo exhibit for their chosen animal

to be shared
as part of their final assignment to prepare a zoo tour using multimedia presentation software.

Technologies incorporated in this example include a word-processing program to prepare the interview questions (Big Six Skill #5—Synthesis), a search engine to locate and access e-mail addresses (Big Six Skill # 3—Location & Access), e-mail to send and receive the interview (Big Six Skill #4—Information Use), and multimedia presentation software (Big Six Skill #5—Synthesis).

When we reflect on integrating technology skills into teaching and learning, we realize that it is not necessary to change the fundamentals of quality instruction or the information problem-solving perspective that is at the heart of the Big Six Skills approach. The implementation of the Big Six approach develops students' problem-solving, complex thinking and information management abilities. It also enables students to become comfortable with technology and understand that technology is simply a tool to help them perform their work.

The Big Six approach allows library media specialists and classroom teachers to collaboratively design challenging and exciting learning experiences. Such opportunities expand the scope of technology use in schools.

Michael Eisenberg is a Professor in the School of Information Studies and Director of the ERIC Clearinghouse on Information & Technology at Syracuse University, Syracuse, New York. Robert Berkowitz is an adjunct instructor at the University. They are the authors of Information Problem-Solving: The Big Six Skills Approach to Library and Information Skills Instruction *(Ablex, 1990). Their new bimonthly publication,* The Big6 Newsletter: Teaching Technology & Information Skills, *is "wrapped" with this issue of* THE BOOK REPORT *and other Linworth magazines. For subscription information and other details, see the ad on page 39 or the complimentary examination copy.*

FLIP IT!
For Information Skills Strategies

By Alice H. Yucht

With the help of seventh graders, the author devised a four-step program for young researchers— and all others who have problems to solve.

WE'VE ALL SEEN IT happen: a kid comes into the library in search of information, and then stands there, seemingly stumped, and expects us to take him by the hand and lead him to exactly what he needs. Meanwhile, we know that we've already taught this kid the skills he needs to use, and wonder why he can't or won't use what he should have learned! How do we get past this spoon-feed vs. self-sufficient seesaw and help kids become independent information consumers?

In 1988 I developed an information-skills strategy (or conceptual framework) to help students work their way through any kind of problem-solving situation. Actually, the framework itself was developed as part of an information problem that I posed to a group of seventh graders: Could we develop a generic process to help them keep themselves on track throughout the research process? I was not looking for a teacher-driven procedure; I wanted to find some way for the kids to know how to be independent problem-solvers. What we finally came up with was FLIP IT!, a four-stage strategy that can be used for all kinds of educational, personal, and even professional problem-solving.

Student-centered, FLIP IT! is based on the question "What do I already know that will help me here?" Used as a mnemonic to keep the thinker on task, FLIP IT! can be applied to any form of information problem-solving, whether it is a simple reference question, a complex research project, a lab report, or a math problem. Each step, or signpost, will lead the searcher from the initial questions to the final answers by following a logical progression of critical thinking skills.

In classroom situations, the student already knows what form the final product of his search must take, but he may not have thought through the process he should use in solving the problem. FLIP IT! supports a basic structure for the process. The student can develop a plan of attack that will bring about the needed solution/final product.

Once a student understands the process and how to use it, she can independently apply it to all kinds of learning situations by asking herself the questions in the four basic steps:

FOCUS (guideposts for the quest).

▲ What is the specific quest I'm on? What problem am I trying to resolve?
▲ How can I best narrow my target, to save time and effort?
▲ What are the basic questions/issues I need to focus on, in order to stay on task?
▲ What kinds of facts do I really need to find?

LINKS
(connections to help me proceed).

▲ What "prior knowledge" (about this subject or process) can I use to help me identify
  • likely resources?
  • a logical way to proceed?
  • the layout of a broader topic?
▲ Where/how can I look for the best or most information to use?
▲ How can I use these connections most efficiently?

INPUT *(putting to use the information I've gathered).*

▲ What kinds of information do I need to gather? Why?
▲ How do I interpret the information I acquire?
▲ How should I prioritize/categorize/organize what I've just learned?
▲ How should I record and acknowledge what I've got?
▲ Do I have all the information I need?
▲ What additional information do I need?
▲ What inferences can I make? What new ideas do I now have to consider?

PAYOFF *(putting it all together— for a profitable solution!).*

▲ Do I have a solution to my original problem?
▲ How can I communicate/present what I've learned/accomplished?
▲ What kind of product is required? How do I produce what was asked for?
▲ Have I proved my ability to demonstrate my new understanding?
▲ What kind of "profit" do I think I can earn from these efforts?
▲ What predictions/prognostications/

additional possibilities might I now consider?
▲ IT! (intelligent thinking).
▲ How did I demonstrate Intelligent Thinking throughout the process?

Each step of the process actually uses all four of the steps within itself, either intrinsically or as an external set of checkpoints. For example, in order to take effective notes (Input), you still have to keep your Focus questions in mind, cite the sources you used (as part of the Link to a broader sphere of information), decide how to categorize (Implement) the information for most effective use, and then present the results (Payoff).

In using FLIP IT! with many different groups, I have found some practices that seem to guarantee success: I *never* teach FLIP IT! as an isolated strategy. Instead, I teach it as part of a genuine information need or an already assigned problem. Only after we have used the process several times do I point out that this is a generic strategy that can be used for all kinds of problems. I display posters that say: "FLIP IT! for successful problem-solving." I will often remind kids (who have already used the process) to FLIP IT! when they are "stuck" at some stage of a problem.

You cannot just say to kids "here's a process, go use it." You have to first model it and then walk through it with the students (guided practice) before you can expect them to use it on their own (independent practice).

Constant, ongoing self-evaluation is an integral part of the process. At each step, the learner needs to re-focus on the original concerns to make sure that the target questions are being answered and acted upon. (This is part of stressing time on task.) Each step, therefore, leads naturally and reasonably to the next step and back to the beginning. If you try to teach only parts of the process, without showing how each element is part of a unified process, kids won't see the point. It's like teaching someone how to tie shoelaces by only paying attention to the "make-a-loop" part.

The question "What do I already know that will help me figure out what I now need to know?" is constantly reiterated. In my opinion, other strategies do not put enough emphasis on the students' base of prior knowledge. You can't start this process out of nowhere; you have to build on what is already there. As with any other abstract and multiple-stage strategies, FLIP IT! should be teacher-guided up through grade 4, when most 10 year olds are starting to master independent use of a complex conceptual framework.

FLIP IT! uses kids' language. Yes, the process does involve task definition, search strategies, information assessment, and even synthesis and evaluation, but I've never heard a kid use those words in his own discourse. Focus, Link, Input and Payoff—those are words that most kids do understand, both concretely and abstractly. The original mnemonic—Focus, Locations, Information Implementation, and Product—was created by that first group of seventh graders.

Over the years, I have also taught this process to inner-city teens as a lifetime learning/coping strategy. Many of them commented that they liked the name FLIP IT! because it didn't sound formal and teacher-like.

I know that many of you have been exposed to the Big Six Skills strategy for information problem-solving (*Curriculum Initiative* by Michael B. Eisenberg and Robert E. Berkowitz, Ablex Publishing). Think of this as the Fab Four, if you will, and give it a try. I'm working on the book about FLIP IT!, complete with worksheets and outlines right now, to be published this year. I'd love to get input from anyone who tries this strategy in his library or classroom. And yes, I am available for workshops and presentations to schools and associations.

After many years working in middle schools in New Jersey, Alice H. Yucht is now writing two books and conducting workshops around the country. Her e-mail address is Aliceinfo@aol.com. She can be reached by U.S. mail at 141 North 7th Avenue, Highland Park, New Jersey 08904. Yucht is a member of the Advisory Board for Linworth Publishing, Inc.

FILED ABOVE THE ROD

FLIP IT as a Planning Strategy

Alice H. Yucht

In my September column on "new school year" resolutions, I mentioned the need to develop a simple, standardized format for planning collaborative activities with teachers. Judging by the comments and responses I've gotten from readers, simple, standardized forms are what everyone needs, for a variety of purposes.

All of the forms I use are based on my FLIP IT framework (see article in November 1996 LIBRARY TALK and book now available from Linworth). FLIP IT stands for Focus—Links—Input—Product, a four-step strategy that can be used for all kinds of problem-solving activities. IT is shorthand for If—Then, the formula for most deductive problem-solving. FLIP IT is a nonlinear process that's easy to learn and use across all grade levels and curricular areas. In simplest terms, here's how it works:

Focus on the real question. What is the problem I need to work on at this time? Find *Links*. What "connections" can I use to make this activity as efficient as possible? *Input* is implementation—searching, sorting, sifting, and storing. What really needs to get done? How does it need to be accomplished? The *Product* is the sharing of results. What should the final results be? Finally, *If* A is true, *Then* B must follow. IT is the classic premise-conclusion formula that underlies every other decision and activity in this process.

FLIP IT works particularly well as a framework for developing collaborative resource-based activities. The framework outlines the interrelationships of all the specific skills and information that you will need to utilize in order to complete the project. Using this kind of formula to gather and organize input from both the teacher and the librarian helps insure that:

Necessary library and subject skills and library and subject content will be introduced, reinforced, or reviewed, as necessary;

Ample and appropriate resources are available;

Teacher and librarian both have clearly defined roles and responsibilities for each element of the project;

Strategies for critical thinking are an integral part of the learning activities;

Students will have a clear understanding of what is expected of them; and

Specific time frames will be established and scheduled as needed.

Here's a detailed explanation of each of the elements I use in my library activity planning guide (described in the November/December column) when teachers and I plan a project. Once the teacher and I have discussed these elements and agreed on dates, I make duplicate copies for both of us, so there are no surprises later on.

First we **focus** on what the students will be investigating—what topic or topics as part of what unit of study. We answer questions such as these: Does the library have enough material available and appropriate for this grade level? How many students will be working on the project? What types of information are needed? Finally, what are the desired student behavioral outcomes?

We search for **links**, considering content, resources, and constraints.

Content:

What terms are students familiar with from classwork?

What subtopics, descriptors, and subject headings does the teacher recommend?

What other terms or descriptors are used by resource materials for this topic?

How much do students already know about this topic?

How much do students already know about using the necessary resources?

What skills will students need to use? What skills does the teacher assume that students have already mastered? Why?

Resources:

What resources (print, online) does the teacher expect to be available?

What other resources does the librarian think appropriate?

What else might be needed? Why?

What does the teacher or librarian *not* want students to use? Why?

How will restrictions be handled and reinforced?

Constraints:

How much time is needed and how much time is available for coverage of subject content? For pre-search (including skills instruction), research, and post-search activities? In the classroom? In the library?

What other facilities or set-ups are needed (computer lab, art room, printing, display)?

Input includes searching, sorting, sifting, and storing both content and process information.

Content:

What kinds of information are needed? How much detail and depth are expected of the students? Why?

What additional formats, such as pictures, might be required?

Process:

What specific library information skills and materials will need to be introduced, developed, and reviewed?

What is the best delivery format?

Are context, strategies, and activities necessary?

What are the time constraints? What support, supervision, and evaluation will be necessary?

As we plan thinking and writing activities, I ask: What note-taking procedures and formats are to be used? What context, strategies, and activities will be necessary? What materials are needed? Who are they to be provided by? Again, I consider time constraints and support, supervision, and evaluation needs.

Finally, the **product**. What is the format? What are the requirements? I consider examples, possibilities, reasons for the choice, as well as assessment rubrics and grading concerns.

Planning includes the assignment time line. What are the dates? Is it part of a master calendar? Who is responsible for the introduction? Will it be made in class or in the library? What library work, search strategies, and note taking does the project require? Are there forms to follow? Checkpoints for additional help needed?

I note due dates for phases of the project: notes, work in progress, related activities, bibliography, final product. Are there due dates for evaluation, presentations, or displays?

I make a simple form of this FLIP IT formula as a notetaking guide as soon as a teacher mentions scheduling any kind of library activity. As we talk, I ask questions and take notes on all the nitty-gritty issues. Then I write up the more detailed version, based on my notes, and share it with the teacher. Even though revisions will inevitably be needed throughout the actual activity, this working guide now serves as both reminder and outline for each of us, clarifying and specifying exactly what activities are involved at every stage of the process.

When dealing with teachers who balk at discussing and planning in advance, I usually explain that this paperwork is necessary in order "to help document the library's program and statistics for administrative reports." Think of it as "portfolio assessment" for professionals, I say, and we both grimace and get on with it.

When the kids are ready to start their research, we start with a "scouting expedition," walking and talking our way through the information possibilities. Students take notes on a project checklist, which also uses the FLIP IT framework, as we discuss and identify:

Focus: Specific topics, and keywords and search terms to use.

Links: Likely resources and their call numbers or access points, related topics that might also provide useful information.

Input: Kinds of information needed, the proper ways to cite the resources used, notetaking formats to be used.

Product: Requirements, rubrics, deadlines.

Since many of these projects become annual events, this kind of paperwork also makes it much easier to see what works and doesn't work from year to year. By now some of these projects have developed extensive files of their own. In one school the fifth grade's annual "Countries Project" now fills a two-inch binder, with the following sections:

Focus: Curriculum objectives, activity guidelines.

Links: Resources to be used, including classroom and library materials, community resources, Web sites, addresses for embassies.

Input: Schedule and calendar of activities, lesson plans, study sheets and handouts.

Product: Formats to be used (changes from year to year), rubrics, group evaluations of activity.

Planning and discussing all the details in advance means that both teacher and librarian have an equal stake in the process and the final product. Working together this way also helps reinforce the librarian's role in the total educational program. This is an important issue for program advocacy, especially as we hear more and more about how "Internet access will eliminate the need for school libraries and librarians."

Few teachers have the time to keep up with all the new resources that could be used to complement and extend their curriculum's content. Nor will most teachers develop the "information navigation" expertise that librarians must maintain as part of their professional responsibilities.

Discussing projects in advance with teachers and being part of the total planning process are the ideal way to insure that resource-based activities will require more than just copying of information. Here's the best time to suggest alternatives to standard report formats, by showing teachers that:

When students have to "restructure" and "repackage" the information they've acquired, they will be forced to think more critically and creatively (see the book on FLIP IT for a variety of examples);

A variety of format possibilities engenders more enthusiasm for the project;

"Authentic" presentations develop greater understanding of real-life skills;

Collaborative planning increases the likelihood of student success with the assignment; and

Carefully planned and designed project requirements make assessment much easier.

Collaborative planning is also beneficial for demonstrating the role of the library program in the total educational infrastructure:

Focus: Librarians can demonstrate the value of lifelong learning skills to both students and adults. Since information formats change so quickly these days, we have to keep learning in order to master the new technology skills.

Links: Teachers see librarians as equal instructional partners, as allies rather than support staff, and parents see that librarians are also professional educators.

Input: Success breeds success. One joint effort usually leads to more possibilities, as other teachers notice the results of these cooperative ventures.

Product: Administrators see more value in the library budget. Expensive resources are being used more, justifying their initial expense. Increased collection use as a result of greater curricular involvement is the best way to substantiate requests for additional budget funds.

If we use the opportunity to collaborate on resource-based activities whenever possible, **then,** we're working for everyone's ultimate benefit.

Alice H. Yucht is the School Librarian at Heritage Middle School in Livingston, New Jersey. Her book FLIP IT! An Information Skills Strategy for Student Researchers *was recently published by Linworth Publishing.*

Notes

FLIP it! Worksheet Formats

By Alice Yucht

"Four-boxers?" the kids ask as their class enters the library. I nod, and each student picks up a few sheets of paper (lined or unlined—their preference) as they make their way to the tables. Once seated, they fold their papers in half, then in half again to make four equal boxes, then check to see which FLIP it!™ worksheet format I've displayed. Here's a simple diagram of the basic elements of FLIP it!:

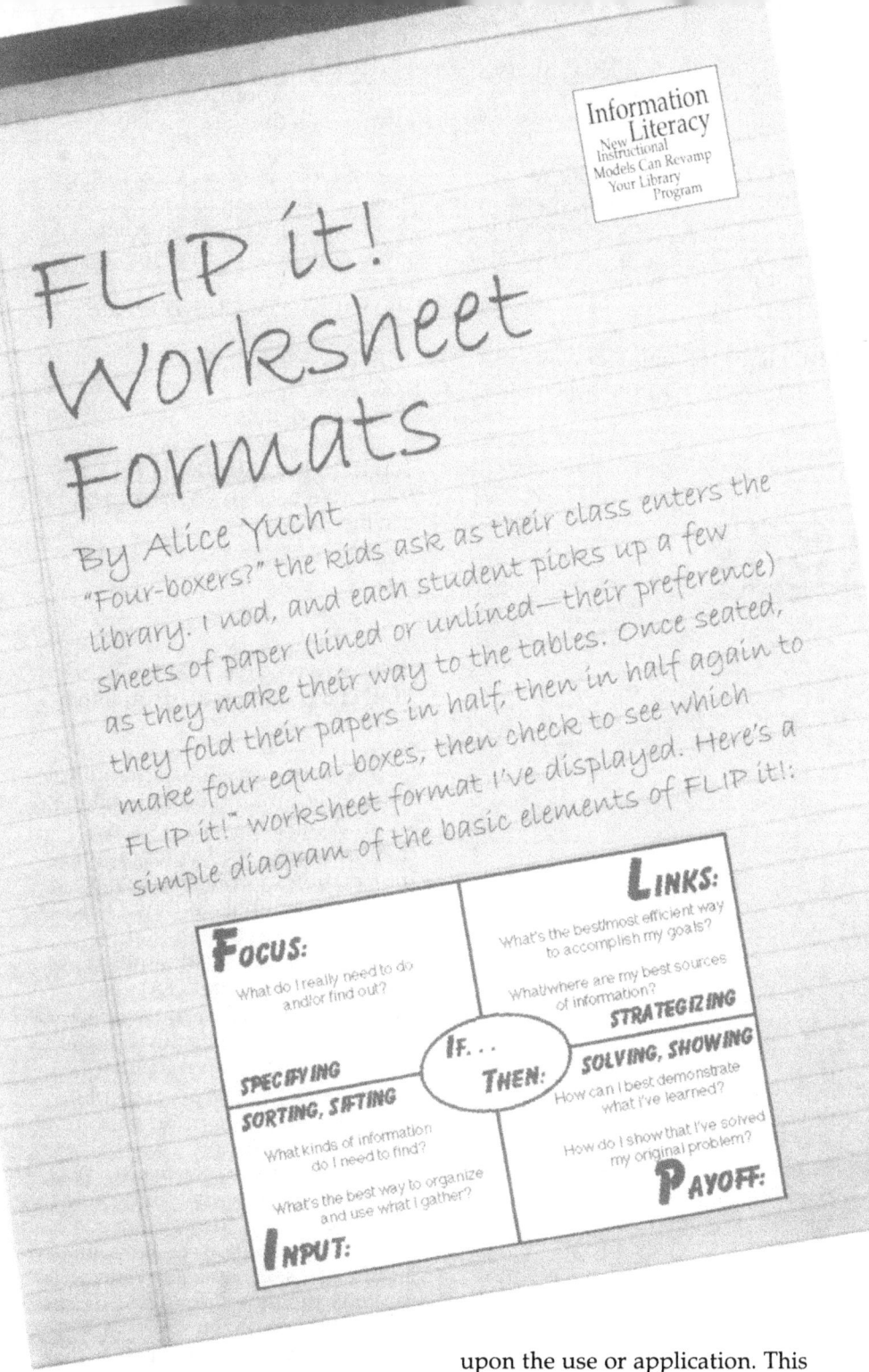

Information Literacy: New Instructional Models Can Revamp Your Library Program

These students are very comfortable using FLIP it! for all kinds of learning activities, because their school has been using this cognitive framework for student learning and classroom management for several years. Although the initials and basic concepts for each stage in the framework stay the same, the words in the mnemonic often change, depending upon the use or application. This week's library/research project will use FLIP it! as the foundation for several graphic organizer worksheets.

Right now, this class and I are using FLIP it! to plan the students' Explorers Posters project, which will be hung in the main hallway when completed. As we talk about the project, the students write their ideas in the appropriate "boxes," or sections, on their own papers, discussing possibilities as the teacher notes them on the whiteboard, and then adding or crossing out ideas as we make our final decisions. For this Project Planner form, they label the outside margins of the boxes like so:

Top left box: **FOCUS TOPICS**

Top right box: **LIKELY RESOURCES** (Links)

Bottom left box: **INFO NEEDED** (Input)

Bottom right box: **PRODUCT FORMAT** (Payoff)

In the center of the paper, where the folds cross, they write the words **IF/THEN** inside a small circle.

Our discussion proceeds:

FOCUS: What's our topic? European Explorers, 1100-1600. Each student is researching a different (preassigned) explorer. What's the basic/most important information we need to find out about each explorer: Who was he? Where did he go? Why did he go there? How did he go? Hmm. . . IF that's the kind of information we think is important, THEN what should be on the posters?

PRODUCT FORMAT: A 24" x 36" oaktag poster. Personal information will be placed at the top; a map of the explorer's travels will go in the middle, and an explanatory paragraph about how, where, and why he went where he did will go at the bottom. A simple bibliography (using a minimum of three resources) will be listed on the back of the poster.

Now we need to decide what specific pieces of INFO will be needed, and then where to find them. We brainstorm which LIKELY RESOURCES will provide the necessary information. Notice that in this case, "Input" determines what "Links" are used, as in: "IF I need to have a map of his route, THEN I will need to use an atlas." A boy asks, "Can I have pictures of my explorer's ships on my poster?" Well, does that reflect back to the Focus and Input questions? IF it

INFORMATION LITERACY SKILLS: GRADES 7-12, 3RD EDITION 57

does, THEN, yes, put the ships on the map!

We turn the Project Planner page over, and briefly review the following effective research strategies and library behavior, taking notes if necessary:

FOCUS: Key words and search terms to use (and how they are spelled).

LINKS: Locations and call numbers of likely resources, related topics that might also provide useful information, etc.

INPUT: Kinds of information needed. Note-taking strategies: write only words and phrases, not whole sentences. Copy bibliographic information carefully and accurately.

PROPRIETIES (students love this "fancy" word for proper behavior): Use a variety of resources. Share materials as appropriate. Put stuff away when finished with it!

The kids are now ready to start their actual research, so we set up another "four-boxer" on a new piece of paper, the Research Record form:

Top left box: **FOCUS TOPICS:**
   A. Personal life
   B. Places explored
   C. Reasons
   D. Trip details

Top right box: **LOOKED IN** (resources used, each listed next to a symbol):
   #
   $
   *

Bottom two boxes: **IMPORTANT POINTS** (numbered 1-5 on left, 6-10 on right)

The students will use this simple worksheet for all their note taking. As students explore a resource, they will write the bibliographic information for that source next to one of the symbols in the LOOKED IN box. Each informational note/fact will be written next to a number in the IMPORTANT POINTS boxes. Next to each fact the student identifies the topic letter and source symbol for that fact. Using Columbus as an example, #3(fact): Isabella of Spain paid him to find a route to India [C. (subtopic), # (resource used)]. With this system, students will be able to see which topics they still need more information on as they are taking notes. Because they are writing only the most important/necessary words or phrases, they are also learning how to extract, rather than just copy information. (And no note cards get lost in the shuffle!)

While the kids are doing their preliminary research, the teacher prepares and makes copies of the Project Guidelines reminder/Checklist for the students to put in their Assignment books. Designed as another "four-boxer," it includes:

Top right box: **FOCUS:**
   European Explorers
   Age of Exploration
   History/Map Skills/Research Skills/Writing Skills

Notes

Notes

Top left box: **LAYOUT:**
Poster, 24" x 36" oaktag, hung on wire hanger.
  Explorer's name at BOTTOM of poster, in two-inch letters.
    Side 1: Personal info
      Map of voyages
      Reasons for explorations
      Impact on history/society
    Side 2: Bibliography of resources used

Bottom right box: **INPUT:**
  Minimum of 10 facts needed
  Minimum of three resources to be used
  Map must include longitude and latitude of all places listed

Bottom left box:
PAY ATTENTION TO:
  Spelling
  Punctuation on bibliography
  Sentence structure
  Neatness and accuracy

DUE ON:
  By the way, the students already know that their grade on this project will be based on the following evaluation rubric, which they helped to develop.

FOCUS:
  Provides answers to the target questions; 25 points
  Provides clearly marked map information; 10 points

LOGISTICS:
  Presents information in an organized and logical order, in a way that makes sense to the reader/viewer, including:
    Introduction/attention-grabber; 5 points
    Development of important details; 5 points
    Conclusion/summary; 5 points

INFORMATION CONTENT:
  Demonstrates use of a variety of resources and viewpoints; 5 points
  Answers the target questions with specific facts and supporting details; 10 points
  Is both meaningful and interesting to other readers/viewers; 5 points
  Presents accurate and documented information; 10 points

PRESENTATION:
  Meets recognized standards of writing/presentation mechanics; 10 points
  Identifies and credits other "authors" when their work is quoted; 5 points
  Presentation methods are relevant and appropriate to content; 5 points

IT (innovative thinking):
  Extra credit for presentation creativity above and beyond the requirements, but still relevant to the intent of the assignment; 10 points

Using FLIP it! frameworks in so many ways has helped the students internalize it as a generic thinking strategy. FLIP it! serves as a guide as they develop the skills they need to become effective learners, thinkers, and problem-solvers who are:
- Goal-oriented (WHAT do I need to accomplish?)
- Purposeful and Productive (WHY do I need to do this?)
- Strategic and Self-Evaluative (HOW will I know what to do/HOW well did I succeed?)

By now, given any kind of information problem-solving activity, their first step is inevitably to "FLIP it!" in order to know what to do, as effectively and efficiently as possible. ■

For more information about how FLIP it!™ works as an effective cognitive framework for information problem-solving across all subject areas, see the earlier articles in the November/December '96 and January/February '98 issues of LIBRARY TALK, and the book *FLIP it! An Information Skills Strategy for Student Researchers* from Linworth Publishing.

Alice Yucht is a Librarian at Heritage Middle School in Livingston, New Jersey.

Introducing a Problem-Solving Method and Library Resources in a Science Class Research Assignment

By Robert Kirsch & James Bradley

Many examples of integrating library skills teaching and library resources into the curriculum can be found in the series of books from our Professional Growth Series titled: Skills for Life: Library Information Literacy. *One of them is reprinted here. It was developed by a high school librarian and a science teacher.*

Lesson Plan

Introduction
Scientific information can be found in many of the general reference sources and databases in the library. Researching it has much carryover for students when they are researching in other disciplines. Newspapers, magazines, pamphlets, science and general encyclopedias, the card catalog, and more are typically included in this unit.

Grade Level
Ninth Grade

Time Required
Two to three weeks with one day of library research. Assignments are generally expected to be completed outside of class.

Objectives
After completing the assignment, the student will be able to:
• Evaluate resources in the library to find the most appropriate for his research topic.
• Use the electronic databases in the library effectively.
• Develop scientific research ideas and narrow the focus of this research through critical thinking.
• Construct a topic outline.
• Write a bibliography using the format approved by the teacher.

Materials Needed
Work sheet for the "DECIDE" approach to problem-solving (see below)
Sample science questions work sheet (see below)
Electronic databases

Procedure
The classroom teacher discusses problem-solving methods in the class and explains how library resources are used in the process. In the library, students are given an assignment sheet of questions to be answered using both electronic and print resources. The librarian should point out that the purpose of the exercise is to acquaint students with reference works they will use in writing a research paper.

Robert Kirsch is the Librarian at Lake Forest High School in Lake Forest, Illinois. James Bradley is a Science Teacher at the same school.

DECIDE Work Sheet

The DECIDE approach, which employs the six key steps to solving a problem, can save time and effort.

1. Define the problem by writing a description of the general nature of the research or problem. If you find it difficult to describe or refine, consider the following:
   Consult a thesaurus.
   Look up definitions in a dictionary.
   Talk over the topic or problem with others—a friend, a student, the teacher, the librarian, or an expert on the topic.

   If you have difficulty with this step, move to step two or three. With more information perhaps the topic or problem will be more clear.

2. Explore possible sources of information.
   Use a general encyclopedia to find an article on the topic.
   Make keyword searches on electronic databases to find general and specific materials, including books, magazines and videotapes.
   Think about unique local sources— the newspaper, your friends, relatives and acquaintances.
   Remember the power of electronic searching and use these CD-ROMs early on in your search—*Readers' Guide, Newsbank Index,* and SIRS *Combined Text & Index* CD-ROM.
   When in doubt about resources, consult the librarian.

Compile a list of sources (bibliography) and keywords useful for your topic.

Use 3-x-5 note cards to list sources, one source per note card.

3. Compile keywords in categories so that you can narrow your search by using the Boolean connectors (and, or, not).

4. Investigate the resources by taking notes on print sources and printing out the citations from CD-ROM databases.

Take notes on 4-x-6 cards. (Remember to paraphrase but use quotation marks when you copy word for word from the source.)

Give each note card a subtopic heading so that you can organize the cards by subtopic later.

5. Develop a thesis statement and organize the information you found.

Organize the note cards by putting like parts of the topic together.

Write the first draft of your paper. Be careful to use your own words. Use footnotes for direct quotes.

6. Evaluate your effort. While the teacher will evaluate the assignment, your ability to analyze your strengths and weaknesses will lead to self-improvement. Check each step and give yourself a "grade."

Sample Science Questions Work Sheet

1. Use the card catalog to find out if this library has the book *Great Experiments in Biology*.
___No ___Yes   If yes, the call number is _____

2. Using *Readers' Guide Abstracts*, find a magazine article on the subject "Biology in Art." Attach the printout of the citation to this work sheet.

3. In the *World Book Information Finder*, find the one-page article on Sir Isaac Newton. Print it and attach it to this work sheet.

4. Using the SIRS *Index* CD-ROM, find the article on plants that are resistant to pollution, published under the title "Street-Smart Plants." Attach the citation to this work sheet.

5. SIRS *Researcher* CD-ROM is a full-text database. Find an article on drought in the United States and attach a printout of the source only to this work sheet.

6. Select the *Chicago Tribune* database, 1991-92. Find a newspaper article on Fermilabl and write the title, date and page number.

Title
_____
_____

Date
_____

Page number
_____

7. In the 1991 *Chicago Tribune*, find an article on Argonne Laboratory written by Suzanne Hlotke. What is the title of the article?

8. Using the *Newsbank Index* on microfiche (1988-), find an article on the problem of pollution from rain in the state of South Carolina. Print the citation and attach it to this work sheet.

9. Using the *Newsbank Index* on CD-ROM from 1992, find a newspaper article on pollution in the Amazon River. What is the source of this article?

10. Using *Grzimek's Animal Life Encyclopedia*, find the answer to this question: How fast can penguins swim underwater?

11. Using the *Dictionary of Scientific Biology*, find out what famous scientist Arthur Edwin Dennelly was associated with.

Notes

Effective Searching Buys Time to Reflect, Ponder & Analyze

By Peter Milbury

*The time is out of joint: O cursed spite,
That ever I was born to set it right!*
—*Hamlet*

TIME SEEMS TO have sharply quickened its pace here in the last decade of the 20th Century! This is especially true of what I call "info-time," the time that it takes to locate and obtain information. Indeed, it is hard not to notice how the time for obtaining information has remarkably shortened.

Faster info-time can be a blessing or a curse. Students are now able to use far more of their available time to ponder, analyze, reflect, and synthesize the information they have found. But info-time is only available if the student knows how to sort through the immense amount of information at his command. It is up to the librarian to assure that this occurs.

When I was a high school student in the late 1950s, I spent hours plodding through volume after volume of periodical indexes, scribbling down the titles of possible sources, filling out the request slips, and waiting for the magazines to be brought to the counter—those that were available anyway!

Using CD-ROM and Internet magazine and newspaper database archives, we can quickly pull up huge amounts of information related to a topic. If a student asks for sources of news about current U.S. economic policy, I can take her to a computer terminal, call up a periodical index on the Web, and in a less than a minute retrieve a list of over 800 magazine and newspaper articles on President Clinton's policy— showing the most recent articles at the top. With another few clicks of the keys I can scan down the list, mark those that appear pertinent, and display the full text in most cases.

Notice that I used the first- person singular—I, the librarian, trained for such electronic searching, sorting and selecting. The question is, how do we guide our students to the right information without doing their work for them? How do we provide them with vast resources without overloading them with poor quality information, which is even more burdensome to work through than multiple volumes of periodical indexes?

> *But info-time is only available if the student knows how to sort through the immense amount of information at his command.*

Effective Use of Electronic Resources

There are several aspects to effective use of electronic resources. One is the proper application of information literacy concepts. Fortunately, effective processes developed by experts, such as Eisenberg and Berkowitz (The Big Six Skills for Information Problem Solving), offer a great deal of support in this area. The Big Six Skills model helps students deal with large amounts of information. But this doesn't absolve school librarians of their responsibility to make information available in an effective and well-organized manner.

We now must also develop effective management tools to deal with this rapidly increasing flow of information. We need to organize our resources so students may make better use of their info-time. The World Wide Web offers an excellent tool to accomplish this. Many school librarians have created Web pages to guide students to useful information. (See "School Libraries and Librarians on the Web: Online Models for Effective K-12 Internet Use" TECHNOLOGY CONNECTION. November 1996, and School Librarian Web Pages at http://www.cusd.chico.k12.ca.us/~pmilbury/lib.html.)

At the Chico High School Library, we have created a Web site with direct links to hundreds of resources organized by subjects in our curriculum. Our site also has links to two powerful commercial periodical databases. This organization is effective because it reflects how most of our students use our library. They first come to the library as a class and return later to do follow-up research on their assignments.

When I first started to create a library Web site, I had already gathered a file of links to resources that I thought our students and teachers would find helpful. Using *Netscape's* bookmarks file organizer, it was a relatively easy matter to create folders for each curriculum area and transform the folders into a Web page called "Helpful Bookmarks." (I also gathered resource links that would be of interest to teachers who wanted to learn how to use the Internet in their teaching.)

That was several years ago, and those links have been updated, reorganized, and more closely aligned with the curriculum and classes taught at our high school. I have done this with the close cooperation of the teachers who bring their classes to the library for research and study.

Outreach, Training and Planning Interview

The three major components of the organization of our electronic resources have been the use of outreach, training, and planning interviews. This "web" of resource development activities has allowed for the creation of an electronic collection that is effectively used by students and teachers.

Outreach is a natural activity for school librarians. We love to share new books, materials, and ideas with teachers. Internet resources, whether useful lists of titles from LM_NET postings or primary sources from the Library of Congress American Memory Web site, are easy to print out and stick in a teacher's mailbox. Better yet, pop by the teachers' rooms and hand the printouts to them. Either way, it is important to establish your presence as someone who is familiar with electronic resources.

Training is an opportunity to extend your expertise, and to discover the information needs of teachers. Even if someone else on the staff is responsible for technology training, most teachers will sooner or later want to use their technology more effectively. In the school setting, the librarian is the expert in effective and efficient information retrieval.

It is important that school librarians be included in planning and giving staff development. At Chico High School, the librarian is included on the instructional council and the technology and staff development committees. This has helped to assure that the library program is at the center of the curriculum because teachers are trained, coached and encouraged to take advantage of all our resources.

The planning interview is one of the most critical components of this triad. Due to the high demand by teachers to bring their classes to the library for research, it is mandatory that all teachers are interviewed before their classes can be scheduled. This is a firm rule supported by the administration. Though often brief, the interview gives a chance for the librarian to query the teacher about the information needs of the assignment. Even better, it often becomes an opportunity for collaboration for instructional development. Many of the subsections of the Helpful Bookmarks Web page have been created as a result of a brief planning interview.

Kincheloe Class Murder Mystery

During a planning interview this past year, an English teacher, Mr. Kincheloe, wanted to duplicate a class assignment that he had found in a highly respected book of projects for English teachers. It required access to a collection of 19th-century newspapers. Unfortunately, we did not have them. However, when I learned that he planned to use old newspaper articles about murder trials to stimulate research and writing skills, I felt that the Internet might give us the resources he needed.

Many newspapers are now available on the Web although few have archived significant numbers of back issues. It took several hours of Web exploration, but I located 25 online daily news sources (newspapers and TV news programs) on the Web that yielded more than 60 murder trials. Then I created a Web page where students could access these full-text online news sources—"The Kincheloe Class Murder Mystery Project" at http://www.chs.chico.k12.ca.us/libr/webres/kin.html. The page also includes seven links to information about the justice system and trial procedures, a link to maps for illustrating the crime sites, and a link to research and writing tips.

This page helped focus the student use of the Web, avoiding countless wasted hours on general search engines. In the process of using these "webbed" electronic resources, Mr. Kincheloe's students learned to use a variety of search engines and became familiar with a wide range of resources that are available to them in other classes as well.

Other Considerations

At the Chico High School Library, our program is always in development. But without the solid foundation of outreach, training, and planning interviews, it would be far less effective. For example, now we are considering adding an orientation program and making changes in the physical location of the terminals and other technology.

We are constantly moving the furniture and hardware around the library. This summer we are having a wall removed to take advantage of a former textbook storage room that has been converted to a library computer lab. The new, open space will allow us to have better supervision as well as offer better assistance to students and teachers while they work at the terminals.

An LCD panel and overhead projector are frequently used for orientations at the start of a new unit of study. Rather than giving a series of long orientation sessions at the beginning of the school year, we have moved to a single introductory exploration activity, which gives the freshmen a feel for the layout of the library. This is regularly reinforced by short lessons focused on the information sources related to an assignment. These lessons are greatly appreciated by the students and by the librarian as well!

Please make an online visit to the Chico High School Library and take advantage of any ideas that may be helpful to your program. We are located at http://www.chs.chico.k12.ca.us/libr/webres/helpful.html

---

Peter Milbury is Librarian and Library Webmaster at Chico High School in Chico, California. He is also a co-founder and moderator of LM_NET, the online discussion group for school library media specialists, and an editorial consultant for TECHNOLOGY CONNECTION.

Get Student Researchers on Target

by Shelley Glantz

From narrowing topics to creating smashing presentations, technology gets top marks from students and teachers

Often, students have little or no concept of their topics when they begin their research assignments. They usually have been given their choice of topics or they have been assigned a broad subject area and need to narrow it. In the past, students at my school responded in one of two ways; either they wandered around with a glazed look—clueless about how to begin—or they leafed aimlessly through the first print encyclopedia volume they touched. Neither method was very successful, and many reluctant researchers were turned off before they had even begun.

Fortunately, those strategies—if they can be called that—have become obsolete. Now, students looking for research topics use one of our electronic encyclopedias, *Encarta '95* (Microsoft, 1995) or the *New Grolier Multimedia Encyclopedia* (Grolier, 1994), to select a topic or to narrow a subject that interests them. Students choose topics on *Encarta* by going through the Area of Interest feature, picking a branch of that subject (for example, Anthropology, Economics, Psychology, or other branches found under social sciences). They then use the Pinpointer feature for specific articles. The electronic encyclopedia enables students to define their research preference and begin researching the articles they've been directed toward.

Once students have their direction, they go to the card catalog and do a subject search for materials that can be used at home or in class. If their topic was derived from an electronic encyclopedia, it is probably under the same subject heading as that found in the catalog. Students are then directed to the appropriate books, vertical file materials, videos, and other resources.

Audiovisual Materials Are Excellent References

Using audiovisual materials such as videocassettes, videodiscs, or audiocassettes for research is a skill which most students do not possess. When faced with these devices, few students—even the most technologically literate—remember to pause or rewind when they see or hear noteworthy information. They need to be taught to render visual or oral information into written notes. They can learn to do this by taking notes while watching videos in class.

Once they develop the skill of extrapolating information from audiovisual sources, students get a new perspective, which cannot be found in books. They can bring their subjects alive through pictures as well as words. Often, audiovisual resources offer primary source materials not found elsewhere. Students who do not read or process the written word well can become successful researchers using nonprint sources.

Students researching current events are quick to use the CD-ROM or online periodical indexes. Those concentrating on historical topics rarely think of these sources as relevant to their research. It should be emphasized to these students that many magazine and newspaper databases contain historical publications, and that past events can again become newsworthy because of an anniversary or comparable news story. For example, World War II was in the news often in 1995 because of the 50th commemoration of significant battles and other events. The unveiling of the Korean War memorial in Washington is a current event that has stimulated recent news coverage of that war.

Other historical CD-ROM and software titles are also popular in our school. They include *The Story of Civilization* (World Library, 1994), based on the Durants' history of the world from prehistory to the mid-19th century, and *Beyond Planet Earth* (Discovery Communications, 1994), which offers information on the solar system and space exploration. Other titles such as *The Holocaust* (Quanta Press, 1994) and *The Electronic Encyclopedia of World War II* (Marshall Cavendish, 1993), which covers the Second World War only, and *From Alice to Ocean* (Claris Clear Choice, 1993), about Australia, are of a narrower focus.

Popular Titles Are Useful, Too

The relevance of some titles to students' research is not at first clear—it requires creative thinking to see the connection. A good example of this is *Cinemania '95* (Microsoft, 1995). Students are often interested in the media and pop culture, and look for ways to connect these to their research topic. By specifying a genre or subject, students get a list of movies and can then access story lines or reviews reflecting the medium's interpretation of a particular event. Many of my students have used this approach for research on topics like the Vietnam War or a survey, covering several decades, of the portrayal of African Americans in film.

Another useful title for student research, though not produced for that purpose, is *Sneak Previews Plus* (Follett Software Company). Originally designed as a selection tool for library collection development, it offers students biographical and bibliographical material on children's and young adult authors.

Online Searches Are Last Step in Process

At school, students go online to do the final pieces of their research. They have access to the Internet and Dialog CIP databases (Knight-Ridder Information). I recommend these resources after students have gathered material from other available references for two reasons. One reason is financial, specifically in the case of Dialog, where we pay for connect time. The other, more important reason is that students are able to conduct the most efficient and effective online searches only after they have become familiar with the topic. They are able to narrow their search and input the best keywords or search terms because they know enough about their topics to do so.

The most commonly used Dialog databases are the full-text newspapers and those containing abstracts of science topics. Because the material comes from scientific journals, students can glean more than enough understandable information from the abstract. They search newspapers for current social issues or contemporary events. Students will often compare coverage of a news story by papers from different parts of the country.

When students use the Internet, they often search the catalogs of the libraries in our local public library network, local academic libraries, or libraries from around the world. If they need information from other sources, we try to find the URL addresses of specific locations. I obtain the addresses from several sources including Classroom Connect (Wentworth) and LM_NET. I store them in a three-ring binder along with a description of the type of information provided. The notebook also contains lists of resources.

During these online searches, the need for familiarity with terms associated with the research becomes obvious. Students become frustrated if their searches are lengthy and yield irrelevant hits. To avoid wasting time and money online, students are required to complete a written search plan beforehand. All searching is done by students, but a staff member sits beside them to answer questions and keep them on task. We have only one workstation with a modem so online searches must be efficient.

After researchers have gathered their information, they put their material into the appropriate format for presentation to the teacher or their classmates. In my high school, many teachers require both written and visual or oral offerings. Previously, the format of choice was an oral summary of their paper accompanied by a poster. Now students are producing their own videos, using clips from commercially produced videos, or creating audiocassette presentations. Others are writing their own computer programs. Students are using desktop publishing software to create more interesting and eye-appealing handouts. In other schools students are creating multimedia presentations. The options are endless.

Students and Teachers Both Like the Results

Our teachers are excited by these approaches because they are seeing positive responses from both presenters and audiences. Students who become proficient at using computers, video, and other technologies to gather information have more time left to actually write interdisciplinary connections between their research and the world, and their classmates are paying attention to the material being presented. All the multiple intelligences described by Howard Gardner—linguistic, logical-mathematical, spatial, bodily-kinesthetic, musical, interpersonal, and intrapersonal—are addressed by students' presentations which include various teaching styles and teaching materials.

Students' use of technology to research and present information clearly makes use of a variety of these intelligences. The student who does not learn linguistically by reading or writing may be stronger spatially or musically and prefer working with video or multimedia. Students using the new technologies for research can either work independently or cooperatively.

Finally, at my school, reluctant researchers with glazed eyes have become enthusiastic about their topics and, thanks to technology, they are more willing to also investigate traditional print sources.

Shelley Glantz is a Media Specialist at Arlington (Massachusetts) High School and Reviews Editor of Technology Connection. *Her e-mail address is glantzs@meol.mass.edu.*

6 Steps to Simplifying Student Searches

By Joyce Valenza

Databases are multiplying by the minute and mastering research skills is becoming as fundamental to students' success as learning to read and write. Online searching can be intimidating, however, so we must break down these skills so they can be taught logically. I use the following six steps as a model for simplifying the thinking steps needed for seeking and retrieving online information.

I introduce this process one step at a time at ninth grade orientation, using five to ten minute mini-lessons and reinforcing these sessions as I walk around and peek over shoulders. I have developed a worksheet which includes "or" and "and" fill-ins and the steps described in this model. If you have any suggestions for improving it, please send e-mail to jvalenza@mciunix.

1 Identify the problem.

I'm surprised at how many students dive into their research before they even think about their problem. That's why we librarians are always asking the types of questions we hope students will eventually internalize and ask themselves. What type of information do you really need? How much information do you need? Do you need an overview or perhaps a point of view, for a debate or persuasive speech?

2 Select the appropriate database.

This decision could be a big one—especially online. DIALOG, for instance, offers hundreds of choices. Even offline, on CD-ROM, students need to choose thoughtfully. Subject is certainly the main consideration, but the student also needs to consider scope of coverage in terms of date and types of journals indexed. If the database is not full text, are journals available physically? Are available journals too difficult for students to comprehend? If they can't make sense of the title or abstract, odds are students won't be able to make any sense of the actual article. You must help students make a number of basic CD-ROM choices as well. Would the best choice be a newspaper, magazine, encyclopedia or other specialized database?

3 Brainstorm keywords.

Now is the time to map out synonyms and related terms ("ors") in columns and link them to additional words, phrases or concepts using "ands" in other columns. How shall we handle plurals, variant spellings or other word forms if we are searching by keyword? How will our strategy be affected by wildcards or truncation devices? How should proper names be handled? Will the strategy be different if the database is full text? Consider which databases you will be searching. If you are in a sports database, the word "sports" would be meaningless. It is best to have this all mapped out on paper to avoid the dreaded "freaking out online" syndrome.

4 Search by subject or keyword.

Almost every CD-ROM database a student approaches poses the initial question: Do you want to search by subject or keyword? The answer will take into account a number of factors, and in some cases the user may need to try both approaches. This one decision is crucial to conducting a successful search, so put special emphasis on it. Generally, when more than one concept is being searched and flexibility is needed, keyword searching should be the first choice. If you are browsing for an appropriate manageable topic for a paper, Subject/Topic searching is best. If you are unsure of spelling, topic searching functions as a type of thesaurus if you can get the first three letters right.

5 Refine your search (online).

Here, I emphasize to students that searching is an interactive process. If your plan is in front of you, you can easily refer to other words and concepts when the first approach falls flat. Clues are all over the database. Choose your very best hit as a "guinea pig." Examine the descriptor/subject field. Look for related proper nouns that keep surfacing. In a search about euthanasia, for example, the name "Kervorkian" might provide many additional hits. If your subject begins to seem unworkable, note related topics for which more information is available. When you're exploring, there are no mistakes! Even the most experienced searchers must re-evaluate and refine their searches.

Some simple things to consider at this point: Were your initial keywords spelled correctly? Is there an online word list that might offer some spelling help? Very important: Consider the number of hits! Is there too much or too little material? Should you add additional keywords to narrow your search, or think of broader terms to enlarge it?

Evaluate your search. Plan another attack.

This is the "what if?" step when you analyze the printout to separate the important from the trivial and identify the strengths and weaknesses of a search strategy. Ask yourself whether your search met your needs. Online time is costly, and students need to learn to use it wisely. Even with CD-ROMs, they have limited access to workstations during class periods and consequently should be thinking about their problems and successes offline.

Some good evaluation questions for students to ask themselves: Which part of my strategy worked well? Were there keywords I should have thought about? Are there descriptors on my printout I might be able to use next time? Did I select the best database? How available are the resources on my printout? Were the resulting hits relevant? Timely? Credible? Biased? Readable? What's my next step? Our goal is to train students to search efficiently and learn from previous experiences. Tc

Joyce Valenza is the media specialist at Wissahickon High School Library, Ambler, Pennsylvania.

Search Strategy Worksheet

1. What's my problem?
   Express in one sentence.

2. List appropriate databases:

3. Brainstorm keywords/topics:

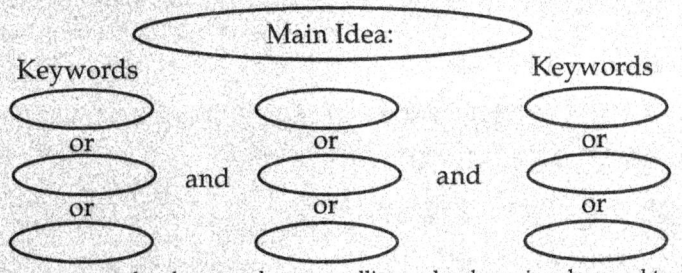

Consider synonyms, related terms, phrases, spellings, plurals or singulars, and truncation.

4. Topic vs. Keyword search:

5. Refining the search (online):
   Other usable keywords:
   Terms to narrow or broaden:
   Proper nouns to search:

6. Evaluation (offline)—What worked, what didn't:
   Ideas for the next search:

Technology Helps Students Do More Research Better and Faster

By Patricia J. Hare

LIKE MANY OTHER SCHOOL districts, Northwest Local in Hamilton County, Ohio, entered the technology age after much discussion, visits to other schools, reading, and research. One of the tasks for the high school library was to "prove" to the board of education that automating the library and providing CD-ROM reference tools would be beneficial to students.

Our search for current studies that would provide "proof" yielded little on the benefits of electronic reference tools for high school students. We could find research to support positive effects in English, math, and general achievement (see below). Only one study had researched the effects of the availability of an online catalog and CD-ROMs (Margaret H. Birgham, "Results of Two Studies on the Benefits and Pitfalls of Technology-based Information Accessing," *T.H.E. Journal*, November 1992). Despite the lack of "hard data," the school board was convinced by visits to other schools and by surveys of our students and parents to automate the high school library and purchase computer-based technology.

The library serves 1,175 students and 85 staff members. Available to students for research are six networked computers and several standalone computer stations. The circulation and catalog are online using Follett's *Unison* software. Available on CD-ROM are the periodical indexes *ProQuest* (UMI), and *InfoTrac* (Information Access) and the newspaper index *NewsBank*. We also have *The Grolier Multimedia Encyclopedia*, *StatBank*, *Discovering Authors* (Gale), and *CIS for Windows* (a career information system).

GROUP	Number of Sources Found in Print	Number of Sources Found Online	Percent Increase
1	25	62	144%
2	23	97	317%
3	25	187	648%
4	29	111	283%
5	27	149	452%
6	22	64	191%
7	37	111	200%
8	20	148	635%
Total Sources Found	183	926	**406% Increase**

> The average increase in the number of resources found when the groups used technology was 359%. This translates to over five times more resources found with online and CD-ROM technology than with traditional research.

With the technology in place, we felt we could look for some proof that the students were benefiting. In cooperation with the teachers of a 10th-grade block class called "Sophomore History, Environmental Science, and Literature Learners," the library staff devised the "More, Better, Faster Experiment." The purpose of this study was to test the theory that research findings with the aid of computer technology would be "more" and would be done "better and faster" than research by traditional methods. The vehicle for the experiment was the "pathfinders" that students use to locate books, magazine articles, and other sources that may yield information on a research topic. It is used as a preliminary list or step before actual searches of the materials.

The tenth-graders were divided into eight groups. Each group used the pathfinder form to conduct searches for their topic in print resources, such as *Readers' Guide*, encyclopedias, vertical files, and publications from Facts on File and SIRS. They spent 20 minutes in this print search. Then the students were given a 20-minute train-

Patricia J. Hare is the Library Media Specialist at Northwest High School in Cincinnati, Ohio. Assisting her in the experiment described here were Jeff Davis, Science Teacher, and Johanna Arbaugh, English Teacher.

Notes

ing session on the CD-ROMs and the online catalog. Finally, students were given 20 minutes to research the same topic using the resources available on the computer network. Both pathfinders asked for the same information— books, magazine articles, newspapers, and other sources.

Forty-three students completed all three parts of the experiment: traditional searches, training on the new technology, and searches using the new technology. The average increase in the number of resources found when the groups used technology was 359%. This translates to over five times more resources found with online and CD-ROM technology than with traditional research (see box on previous page). Variations in the percentage of increase for the individual groups can be attributed to the differences in topics, comfort levels of the students using the technology, and student abilities.

We concluded from this study that students are able to find a significantly greater number of resources in a shorter amount of time when they search electronically. The variety and quality of the resources found are comparable to those from print sources and often are more up-to-date.

After the study, we asked the students if they felt comfortable using the new technology. Over half of the students felt comfortable in using the online computer programs after the 20-minute training session. It was also evident that most students preferred using the electronic resources. Many are convinced that their "better" grades were the result of finding "*more* information, *better* information, *faster*" using the new technology.

FOR MORE INFORMATION

In their search for studies of the impact of technology, Hare and her colleagues located these:

English Achievement

Robert A. Eliason, "The Effects of Word Processing Adjunct Programs on the Writing of High School Students," University of Florida, 1994.

Bernice A. Smhelz, "Implementation of an Integrated Learning System in a Tenth Grade Remedial English Course and Examination of Achievement, Attendance, Behavior, and Attitude (Computer-Assisted Instruction)," University of Miami, 1994.

Math Achievement

Donald E. Carter, "Effects of Computer Technology on Student Outcome for Low-Performing Ninth-Grade Students," University of La Verne, La Verne, California, 1994.

General Achievement

Jay Sivin-Kachala and Ellen Biala, "Proof Positive: Research Says Technology Makes a Difference," *Electronic Learning*, May/June, 1993.

―A BOOK REPORT THEME SECTION―

Library Technology Adds Immediacy to Research Assignments

By Terry McConnell & Others

Wanting to maintain the library's prominent role in research projects, but watching teachers turn to the computer as a report processing tool, this librarian developed a system for research projects that involves teachers, technology specialists and administrators.

How many educators does it take to to teach students to use technology to do library research? In the project described here, it took at least eight—a reading teacher, a social studies teacher, an English teacher, a business teacher, two librarians, an assistant principal, and a technology specialist.

What makes our research projects special—besides the fact that so many of us collaborate—is that the project, described here and called Major Views, goes beyond teaching research skills. It also teaches students to develop points of view about their subjects, and to use technology to communicate their views to classmates through cable TV and on a home page of the Internet. The Major Views format fosters discussion and debate on current issues and a level of excitement in the classroom that stimulates more student research.

The system can be applied to any class assignment that requires the resources of the library. For several years, before the computer became so much a part of the school scene, I had always worked with students in producing videos as part of their classwork. When a Macintosh lab was installed in our school, I felt the library was taking second place to the lab as "the place to do" research papers. In addition, I needed to learn more about the advances in technology. The best strategy, in my view, was to install a lab in the library. Not only could students do their research where the resources are housed, but I and their teachers could learn from each other. A number of donated computers (from businesses and the military) and close cooperation with the technology specialist as well as the cooperation of teachers made it possible.

The project described here started in the social studies department but the format is followed with adaptation by other departments for

---

Terry McConnell is the Librarian at Mount Vernon High School in Alexandria, Virginia. His co-authors and collaborators in the Major Views research projects are: Bernie Glaze, Social Studies Department Chairman; Harry Sprouse, Assistant Librarian; Betty Lindholm, Reading Teacher; Rob Sanders, Assistant Principal; Kelley Durham, Technology Specialist, Jan Mosher, English Teacher; and Toni Mason, Business Department Chair. McConnell can be contacted by e-mail at jmcconn@aol.com for more information.

students at all high school grade levels.

One advantage that we have in our school system is the employment of a technology specialist in each of the 24 high schools who is responsible for training the teachers in the feeder schools. This "pyramid" technology specialist is a computer expert. When the school district considered eliminating this position, the librarians banded together to protest—and were successful. While we librarians can and should come up with systems that make full use of the computer in research and reporting, classroom teachers need technical support and training if they are to incorporate technology in their assignments.

First, Students Define Their Theses

In the social studies department, this process begins in the classroom where the teacher encourages the students to identify topics of interest to them. One technique teachers use is journal keeping. In the context of the subject being studied in the classroom, the teachers ask students to write about what interests them most. The journal entry is the beginning of an "I Search" about a topic the student will research in the library.

To help students stay on track, we have devised what we call the "graphic organizer" (see next page). Before the search for facts begins, the student writes his or her thesis statement on the graphic organizer.

Orientation and Research Come Next

After students have written their theses statements in the classroom,

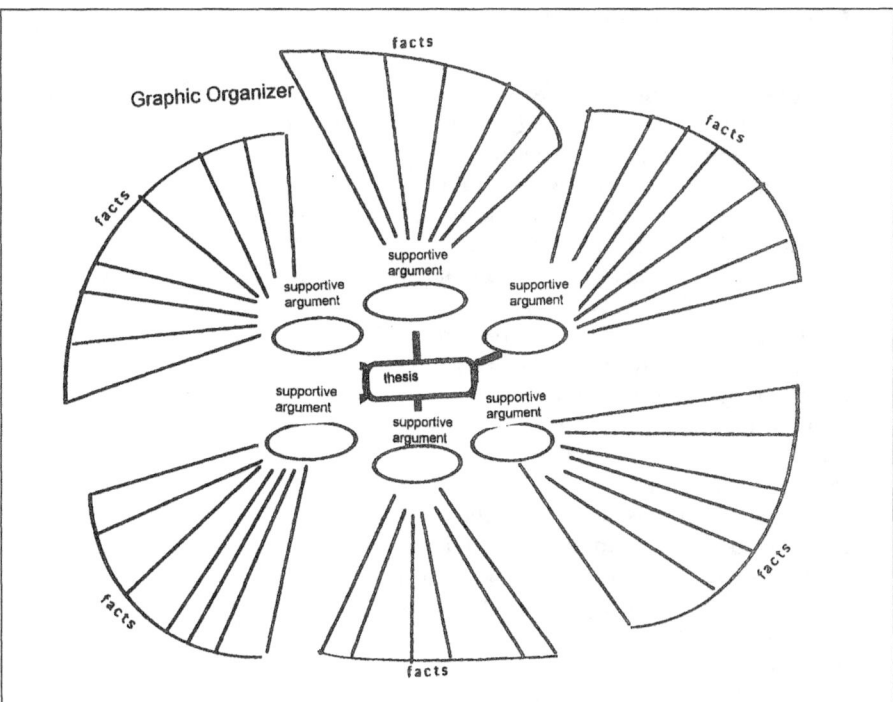

Graphic Organizer

HIGH-TECH RESOURCES FOR CURRENT RESEARCH

Students enjoy using high-tech resources to get up-to-date information. For example, events of the war in Bosnia during the past two months can easily be found using a reference tool like *Proquest Full Text USA Today* on CD-ROM. What makes this so great for student researchers is that a news article from an easy-to-read publication like *USA Today* can be accessed in a matter of minutes. If a student is researching actions against illegal immigration in Sacramento, California, he can go online to Dialog and pull up yesterday's local newspaper, the *Sacramento Bee.*

Is a magazine article needed for a specific point of view on welfare reform? Full-Text Proquest for magazines on CD-ROM with its offering of 100 magazines is sure to have a current article with either a liberal or conservative slant. Students who did a Major Views project on U.S. intervention in Haiti found that *SIRS Researcher* on CD-ROM provided great background information from various magazines and newspapers throughout the world.

Netscape software, has made it easy to browse the Internet. For interviews with Holocaust survivors, get on the Internet at Yahoo "http://www.yahoo.com" and go to the Cybrary at the Holocaust Museum in Washington, D.C. Locally, the online card catalog tells students what books on their topics are available in the school library and other local libraries. These high-tech sources make research projects exciting to students because the information needed can be obtained quickly and easily.

---

they come to the library in groups of four to six for library orientation. The groups are placed at various stations around the library, with one educator or a parent volunteer assigned to show each group how to operate the computerized card catalog, CD-ROM stations, and the Internet/Dialog station. The adults help each student determine what facts would be relevant to his thesis. Then students learn how to print information from the electronic sources. This small group approach to library orientation ensures that each student will be able to use the library's resources.

Next Stop: The Word Processing Center

Once a student has found her facts, she walks over to the word processing center in the library to begin hammering out her rough draft. Our high school has block scheduling so most class periods are 100 minutes long, which can allow students time to search resources and begin typing a rough draft in one class period. Armed with his graphic organizer, the student has an outline on which to base his paper. The printouts from information on CD-ROMs come in handy when students need specific information and direct quotes. We encourage the students to use markers to highlight the most important information they printed out. Student who need more time can either finish typing after school or take the disk home.

Scripts Are Prepared for In-School Cable TV

After students rewrite and polish their rough drafts, they choose which topics should be used in video scripts. At this point, students become highly motivated. Now they are not just writing for themselves and the teacher. They have a more important purpose—to communicate their findings over our in-school cable TV system. In deciding which topic will be shown on the cable system, students take into account which topics have good visual footage available from *CNN Newsroom*. CNN, the cable network, allows teachers to use CNN Newsroom footage in a student-produced video shown within a school.

Because the topics are often matters of current interest and controversy, a part of the TV production will be students' opinions on the issue. Once a student group has selected a topic, the members write survey questions to pose to their fellow students. Results of the "opinion polls," along with student interviews, and research information, are incorporated into a TV script. The script is shorter than the written paper.

While some students write the TV script, other teams or individuals are learning how to operate the camera,

Library Technology...

do video editing or find relevant visual material to edit into the show. This is the first video production experience for most youngsters. Our students have found the Panasonic cameras and editor VCRs like the AG-1970 are easy to use. This equipment uses the S-VHS format which guards against loss of quality when tapes are edited and duplicated. We shoot the anchor person's comments first and then edit in student interviews. Next we video insert the visual footage from CNN *Newsroom*.

Once the video is completed, the student body sees it on the in-school cable system. This is the heart of Major Views. Information is now important and newsworthy because our students are using it to make a point about a topic they care about. For example, one student wasn't interested in Haiti until he found out in the Major Views video that his best friend thought "our troops should get the heck out of there." This airing of views encourages more library research projects.

Project Summaries on the Internet
Some students write summaries of their Major Views projects, including their survey results. These summaries are published on our school's home page (http://pen.k12.va.us/Anthology/Div/Fairfax/Schools/MtVernon-HS/mtvernon.html). For an up-to-date description of current Major Views projects, select "Technology and Internet" on our home page.

Variations on the Theme
While Major Views emphasizes video production, similar projects have used other reporting techniques. For example, English students researching mythology created a "newspaper" in which the major figures' doings were reported. Each student was responsible for writing a news article and then groups of students were assigned to the sections of the paper.

A Chance to Shine
The Major Views project won first place in the 1995 Media General Cable Teacher Grant Competition and a $1,500 prize. Best yet, the Major Views format gives each student a chance to excel. The eight educators share in their excitement.

CONNECTING WITH  THE CURRICULUM

Perfect Partners
Technology and Integrated Instruction

by Nadine K. Hinton and Linda Orlich

How You Can Use Technology Across The Curricula

Technology has forever altered the way we receive and process information. As a result, our schools have the formidable responsibility for training our young people to use this technology productively. Fortunately, authentic assessment opportunities abound. And by providing students with wider access to information, we can help them recognize that not all information is equally useful and that they must think critically and creatively as they examine the merits of different sources.

Curricula reform in our district emphasizes that technology is an integral component of instruction—not an add-on or replacement. Even with this philosophical commitment and modest financial support, we as teachers have often found ourselves overwhelmed by the sheer volume of ever-changing information related to teaching the new technology. From our experience with integrated instruction (and partly in self-defense!), we scoured the courses of study for all references to uses of technology in instruction. The results were still overwhelming. We then decided to distill the lists to identify elements that emphasized the importance of technology across curricular areas. We hope that other teachers, media specialists, technology coordinators, curriculum coordinators, and administrators can use this information as they plan for effective use of technology in instruction and to strengthen their proposals for increased budgets for technology.

Technology should be viewed as a tool to help students construct knowledge and to help teachers provide opportunities for more effective, meaningful, integrated instruction. The time required to achieve these lofty goals and the dollars necessary to begin and maintain the system are substantial. However, we have found that incorporating technology into science, math, language arts, and social studies curricula is an outstanding use of both time and money.

Benefits of Integrating Technology:

Easier Searching

- Search nonprint sources to locate relevant information, including laser discs, CD-ROMs, and telecommunications.

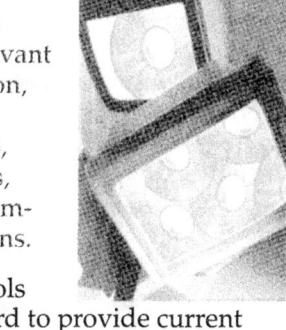

Many schools cannot afford to provide current print resources to all students. Laser discs and CD-ROMs offer an economical alternative for some references. Telecommunications, once modem connections and Internet links have been established, widen access to information, including access to towers of CD-ROMs available in many public libraries.

Increased Propriety

- Write, edit, revise, and publish written work in an electronic portfolio.
- Display and publish enhanced written work.
- Integrate sound and speaking skills into students' presentations.
- Produce correct spelling.
- Choose fonts that enhance meaning and voice.
- Search for information and maintain records of their work for enjoyment, evaluation, and sharing.

Students should have access to their own filing systems, either electronically or on paper. Electronic portfolios (with "At Ease," disk and tape backups) provide a useful network system for storing files while addressing security needs within the school.

Broader Appeal

- Extend senses.

Vicarious field trips enable students to experience sounds via electronic technology. They add depth to learning and portray a more realistic experience for the learner.

INFORMATION LITERACY SKILLS: GRADES 7-12, 3RD EDITION 73

Worldwide Collaboration

- Examine issues from diverse perspectives.
- Participate in individual and group projects, and simulations.
- Develop an understanding of the interdependence of a global society.
- Interact via telecommunications with others outside the classroom.

The global community is within reach. Technology can open doors that lead students to ever-changing sources of information.

Customized Information

- Collect, record, analyze, and synthesize information and numerical data.
- Quantify observations; create, organize, and interpret charts, tables, pictographs, and graphs.
- Use geometric shapes in drawing programs.

Production and manipulation of data internalizes learning. Using technology, students can process and reprocess information with ease, allowing opportunities to analyze which format best represents the intended message.

Horizontal Focus

- Develop critical thinking skills and evaluate information.
- Develop graphic organizers such as webs, outlines, charts, lists, and maps.

Word processing gives students the means to create a finished product and, for proficient typists, transforms the nature of the writing task that is so laborious for some students. Word processing also provides support in spelling and grammar. Students can produce clearly illustrated materials that can be easily manipulated to fit the space and purpose of the project, thus allowing more student time to be spent on content rather than on production skills.

Multi-disciplinary Applications

- Integrate information across disciplines.

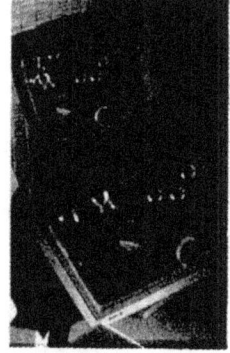

By integrating language arts, science, social studies, and math through the use of technologies, students can process and manipulate data and then prepare presentation materials quickly, professionally, and efficiently. Technology is integral to our instruction; it is not an addition to or replacement for current instruction.

Increased Retention

- Interact with text and graphics.

Computer programs such as *The Writing Center*, *HyperStudio*, *ClarisWorks*, and *Microsoft Works* enable students to combine their written text with clip art, reference graphics, student-generated art, or materials from level III laser discs, thus enhancing the appearance of the final product and more fully demonstrating mastery of the material.

Well-rounded Responses

- Make inferences based on information from various sources.
- Use logic to solve problems.

Information collection from reference materials such as CD-ROMs and laser discs can be combined with electronic conversation with experts via the Internet and the World Wide Web. These online connections also provide access to more varied databases. **TC**

Nadine K. Hinton is a teacher at Emerson Elementary School and Linda Orlich is a teacher at Central College Elementary Magnet School, both in the Westerville (Ohio) City School District.

Teaching the Research Process? Check Out *The Mind's Treasure Chest*!

By Robert Kirsch

A librarian reflects on his experiences in using this full-length motion picture to teach research skills.

IN THIS AGE OF EXPONENTIAL information growth, librarians and teachers are challenged to teach process versus memorization and facts. How to find information is a small part of our learning objectives for students. Our major task is to teach students to analyze, hypothesize, synthesize and develop the information they find so that a quality research product is created. Teaching the circular process of continuous revisions and rethinking is a formidable task.

The British economist John Maynard Keynes once observed that some learners are superficial and random in their research, much like water bugs that skim across the water barely touching the surface and showing no interest in anything below the water. How do we motivate students to go beyond the surface of the large lake of information, or to stop resting on the lilly pad long enough to make new discoveries? I found a partial answer in a relatively new tool to teach the process of research. *The Mind's Treasure Chest*, a full-length (90 min.) motion picture, lays out the research process as an "action adventure," to use the film industry's parlance. The specially produced film was developed by Learn TV and released by Follett Software Company in 1991.

Produced to professional standards, the film tells the story of a high school senior who thinks winning election to the student council will be easy for him. But the hero of the video, Jack, finds himself losing the race in the classroom, where his more intellectually inclined opponent shows him up. It's Jack's mad dash (and all night) to research for a class debate that is the "action" of the movie. While viewers will enjoy the humor of the story, they will also watch the hero use about 50 resources to develop his impressive presentation on the Cuban Missile Crisis.

In our school, American history teachers previewed and evaluated the film for possible use in their classes where a research paper is required. *The Mind's Treasure Chest* provided a comprehensive introduction for the follow-up research assignment in these classes. This assignment challenges the students to "be like Jack" by finding the latest research on interesting or controversial questions in American history.

Using the acronym DECIDE, I reviewed the six steps essential to successful research: (1) *D*efine the problem. (2) *E*xplore the library for resources. (3) *C*ompile sources and keyword possibilities. (4) *I*nvestigate and take notes from the best sources. (5) *D*o the assignment. (6) *E*valuate your total effort. We divided the class into research groups of three students each and gave them topics about which there are unanswered questions. In another presentation to the classes, I highlighted some key resources and referred back to the several techniques Jack used to find nontraditional information, such as his searches of newspapers and periodicals. The topics were:

The Lost Colony of Roanoke
The Boston Massacre
Custer and the Little Big Horn
The Death of Harding
The Sinking of the Lusitania
The Lindbergh Kidnapping
The Sinking of the Maine
Roosevelt and Pearl Harbor

Each group was required to develop three key questions and answers about their event and to show the research required to do it. Because of the speed and efficiency of CD-ROM databases, we expected students would have time to seek out the best and most relevant articles rather than settling for the first news articles they found. Students were made aware that the ease and time saved in accessing this data quickly should be applied to higher order thinking and analysis, which would lead them to an interesting series of questions, answers, and supporting annotated bibliography.

The movie proved to be an effective model for the student groups researching the eight topics. Most students were surprised by the number of magazine and newspaper articles applicable to their topics. Like Jack in the movie, most groups stumbled for a while in devising their key questions, but eventually they moved beyond "the water bug" approach, to full utilization of the research process.

What was the reaction of the students to the film? The history classes were asked to give the film a 1 to 5 star rating. Forty-five percent gave it three stars, 35% said it was a four-star

Continued on page 24.

Robert Kirsch is the Library Director at Lake Forest High School in Lake Forest, Illinois.

Jack, high-school hero of The Mind's Treasure Chest, *uses some 50 library resources in his all-night quest to become an expert on the Cuban Missile Crisis, thereby gaining credibility to win the school election.*

Treasure *continued from page 19.*

film and 15% gave it the highest rating, five stars. The film was definitely enjoyed. If one characteristic of the film stands out above all others, it is that Jack Paterson, the protagonist, is always asking questions and takes only yes for an answer. He asks questions of everyone—his fellow student Samantha, and the ever present librarian—as well as of every print and media source he examines. The flashbacks in the film always concern a question. This inquisitive nature of Jack as well as his enthusiasm for finding answers proved valuable in framing the assignment given after the students viewed the movie.

Teachers and librarians generally acknowledged that orientation to library sources is taught most effectively by relating it to a class assignment or a specific discipline. Connecting the activity to assignments identifies the librarian as a subject specialist who teams with the classroom teacher to achieve specific objectives. With a resource such as *The Mind's Treasure Chest*, the librarian can go beyond this and bring the power of a vicarious research experience to each student. Students may view librarians, libraries, and the nature of information in a new way after this experience.

Notes

Computer Skills

In some schools, the library media specialist also wears the hat of the computer teacher. In other schools, they are two people-but not always necessarily two *distinct* people. Frequently in my position, the computer teacher and I find ourselves discussing whether we're stepping on each other's toes in instruction of database creation and use, multimedia CD-ROM research, and Internet searching. Often the answer involves a team-teaching approach.

Not long ago, teaching computer skills encompassed keyboarding and simple programming. Many of us still remember our excitement at getting the tiny turtle on the screen to draw a circle, or seeing numbers flash in sequence from one to 10 as we learned all we'd probably ever know about BASIC. Perhaps in high school classes, with students sufficiently familiar with the keyboard, we introduced some applications: word processing, databases, spreadsheets.

With amazing speed, our expectations have changed. Programs that can process speech into text and text into speech are a thing of the present, not the future, reducing the emphasis on keyboarding. Not long ago, I postponed teaching a certain CD-ROM tool until fifth grade, because it utilized DOS commands that I could not expect younger students to master. Today, because of the Windows environment, that program is of the point-and-click variety, and second graders have no problem navigating around it. The Internet and presentation tools like PowerPoint and HyperStudio are creatures all their own, and will be discussed in other chapters.

Many students, especially on the secondary level, exhibit certain computer skills far greater than ours. Having used a variety of computers and programs at home, they are familiar with many of the CD-ROMs we present for research and presentation. Some have the disturbing ability to get into the machines' innards when our backs are turned. Sometimes the fruit of their labors is as innocuous as an unexpected screensaver; sometimes it's something serious enough to crash the system.

But a student's knowledge of how computers work or familiarity with a program does not preclude a need for instruction. Some of the youngsters most gifted in *working* the computers have the least solid grasp of how to do *research* using the computer. These students are certainly of great use as peer instructors when it comes to technicalities. We, however, are still the experts on how to compose a search (whether it uses print or electronic sources), how to amass and arrange notes, and how to turn those notes into the most appropriate product to answer the assignment. That product is still sometimes a typewritten or word-processed report.

As I repeat throughout this volume, all schools are not equal in the matter of technology, and all students do not come to us with similar computer backgrounds. As I discovered while teaching an adult workshop, our students need to be able to operate a mouse before they can get into the great stuff on a new CD-ROM. In our excitement to move on to the cutting edge, we may be leaving beginners behind, whether our school is just introducing technology or students are just discovering it.

So, after some exciting ideas in the first article about schools that *are* on the cutting edge, this chapter, with articles on CD-ROMs, computer labs, circulation programs, and applications, may seem tame to some. Remember: This still represents where some of us are. Also, a few of these articles are about elementary schools and young students. I have included them because they offer ideas that can be adapted easily for secondary schools or used with certain groups in those schools. A CD-ROM encyclopedia that incorporates more sight and sound than its "age-appropriate" competitors might be included in a high school's collection, for example, for use with non-English speakers or special education classes.

The computer revolution has been so rapid, and has come so far so quickly, that schools that hesitated initially may feel there is too much ground to make up at this point. These articles may offer reassurance that good things can be done with even one computer, and that exciting goals *are* attainable for anyone with the vision to begin.

☐ URL UPDATES

How Are We Using Computers in the Classroom?:

    Hyper Studio Network
    www.hsnetwork.com/

    The Nasa Space Shuttle Small
    Payloads Project
    http://sspp.gsfc.nasa.gov/index2.html

These teachers make the computer an integral part of classroom projects rather than just a report-writing tool.

by Sharron L. McElmeel

What exactly are educators and students doing with the computers in labs, libraries, and classrooms? I invited educators to share their computer experiences. Ideas came from Washington State to Texas to New Jersey and from primary schools to colleges. Equipment ranged from three Power Macs in a school to a fully-equipped computer magnet school. It quickly became clear that while hardware and software are necessary components, it is the determination and creativity of the educator that provides impetus for integrating computers into learning. The following activities are some of the best reported to me.

Investigating Celebrities and Classic Writers

Karla Walters (kwalters@whitecap.psesd.wednet.edu) teaches English and mathematics at Sumner Senior High School in Sumner, Washington. Sumner may seem unique in that it will soon move to a four-period day, but otherwise it is a traditional high school set in a small town (population 8,000). Computers are housed in classrooms, in the library media center, and in a separate lab. The school has an Internet policy that requires each student under the age of 18 to have a signed parental permission form on file.

Using one classroom computer with Internet access and also computers in the library media center, Walters' sophomore English classes research celebrities. Students are asked to gather information for oral presentations. The celebrity must be someone the student admires. After students generate a list of celebrity names, each student selects one. Past celebrities have included rock musicians, movie stars, and athletes.

The research usually begins with some preliminary research to locate an address for the celebrity. Biographical information is sought from the Internet, computer databases, and from traditional print sources. Databases on CD-ROM prove to be useful sources also, especially the *Seattle Times* and the *InfoTrac* periodical index.

Walters' senior English students research writers of the Romantic period. Each student's presentation includes a discussion of the writer's work and a time line of the writer's life relative to world events on two continents. The core of the presentation is the biographical information. Students must include an audio or visual component in their presentation. Most often, art or music from the period is included. The Internet is utilized for these presentations, and Walters makes available key print resources in her school's library media center. The CD-ROMs *Grolier's Multimedia Encyclopedia* (Grolier) and the *Infopedia* (ELO) are also used. Research and preparation is completed within a week, and another week is required for the presentations.

Computers to Go - HyperStudio on a Cart

A project at Mountain Way School in Morris Plains, New Jersey, exposes second graders to *HyperStudio* (Wagner). The three Power Macs in the school where Vicki Sweet (esweet@postoffice.ptd.net) is educational media specialist are used heavily. One computer is the library media center's circulation computer; the other two serve as student station and faculty resource. Sweet has managed to implement a "Have

Computer, Will Travel" program. She rolls two of the Macs into the second-grade classrooms for a language arts enrichment program. Research activities using traditional resources and activities result in the creation of *HyperStudio* stacks. Students work together to create the stacks. They draw, add clip art and graphics, add buttons and sounds. After they have learned to record their voices, they record the text within each stack. Those who need extra time to complete their stacks are encouraged to finish their work in the library media center. Parents are invited to an evening in the library media center to see students showcase their *HyperStudio* stacks.

Computer Use in a Magnet School

Terri Miller (TerrieM498@aol.com) teaches at Banneker Computers Unlimited Elementary School, a magnet school in Kansas City, Missouri. The school's staff strives to use computers in 50% or more of instructional time. Computers are in the classrooms, in the library media center, and in a lab separate from the media center. Banneker students participate in a variety of computer enhanced activities every day. The *AECT/ALA Space Project* was used to complete a science fair project. CD-ROMs and books were also used. The classroom teacher and the library media specialist collaborated on this activity, which culminated in an online chat with astronaut Guy Bluford.

Banneker's teachers use *Josten's Learning System* and a variety of networked software for enrichment activities. *Linkway Live* and *PowerPoint* (Macintosh) are used for classroom demonstrations.

> HyperStudio Network, a commercial Web site at http://hsn.anoka.k12.mn.us/HSN.html, features a link to HyperInternet that focuses on "the most successful way for staff and students to include Internet resources in their *HyperStudio* reports and presentations."

- The NASA Space Shuttle Small Payloads Project, another popular space project site, is available at http://sspp.gsfc.nasa.gov.ssp-phtml.html. It is one of many space projects located on the Internet with the aid of Internet search engines.
- International Read-In. The library media specialist facilitated this special online day during which students participated in a variety of reading activities. A highlight was an online chat with R.L. Stine, author of the popular *Goosebumps* horror stories.
- Campaign '96 - Fifth graders followed presidential candidates and their activities online through various Web pages. The students were able to participate in online votes. Students utilized Cable in the Classroom's CNN and C-SPAN coverage.

Another project funded by a federal grant through the McRel Corporation seeks to identify and construct a Web database of links and information for teachers working with youth at risk. A combination of desegregation and general operating funds from the State of Missouri and the school district have funded the computer-rich environment at Banneker. This school year the Kansas City School District will complete the final stages of installing a Wide-Area Network (WAN) that will provide Banneker with more access to online projects and create the potential for additional telecommunication expansion. The school will have access to a variety of Internet on-ramp sites and will begin using videoconferencing with the CU-SeeMe and Real Audio technology.

Literature Discussions

The idea of using computers to carry on interactive literature discussions came from a university project, in which university professors created interactive discussion groups for their students.

June Harris, an associate professor in the Department of Literature and Languages at East Texas State University, asks her students to write response logs for their introduction to literature class. She uses *Daedalus* (The Daedalus Group), an interactive program in which all students are able to read each other's logs as well as Harris's own prompts.

Linda Lamme at the University of Florida has a similar program for her students in children's literature, but she asks her students to utilize computers and the Internet in other ways as well. They make regular use of listservs to seek information about books and topics and to connect with authors, illustrators, and poets via the Web. Some of her students have book discussions with children regarding a book they have read. Others students discuss issues with students in other universities via e-mail or pre-arranged discussion listservs.

> Many news sources focusing on the 1996 Presidential Campaign are available on the Internet. These are some of the more popular sites:
> - CQ Alert's Campaign News (updated daily) – http://voter96.cqalert.com/news.watch.htm
> - Campaign News from Politics USA – http://politicsusa.com/PoliticsUSA/news/
> - AllPolitics – http://AllPolitics.com/index.html
> - CBS News Campaign96 Home Page – http://www.cbsnews.com/campaign96/home
> - *U.S. News & World Report*'s Election '96 page – http://www.USNews.com/usnews/wash/election.html
> - NBC News Decision 96 Home Page – http://www.decision96.msn.com/
> - ElectionLine – http://www.electionline.com
> - *Atlantic Monthly*'s Election Connection '96 – http://www.theAtlantic.com/atlantic/election/connection/
> - *Boston Globe* Campaign '96 Coverage – http://www.boston.com/globe/cgibin/globe.cgi?nat/glncamp96.htm
> - *Mother Jones*' Campaign News – http://www.mojones.com/election_96/hunt.html

HEAD FOR THE EDGE

Putting Computer Skills in Their Place

By Doug Johnson

What are the basic computer skills all high school students should master before graduation, and where, how, and by whom should those skills be taught? Can a student who operates a computer well enough to play *Doom* be considered computer literate? Will a student who has used computers in school only for running tutorials or an integrated learning system have the skills necessary to survive in college or in the work place?

One educational philosophy is that computer skills should not be taught in a separate "computer class," but should be integrated into the content areas. Yet to my knowledge, no comprehensive K-12 set of computer skills and model for integration exists. Too often computers are used only as electronic flash cards or worksheets while the productivity side of computer use is neglected or grossly underdeveloped. Productivity tools, such as word processors, databases, spreadsheets, graphics, and chart makers often are taught only in special classes like business or technology education—classes taken by a minority of students, despite the fact most of these applications could benefit all students.

However, many schools have successfully integrated information skills into the curriculum, with the best media programs being designed around cooperative projects jointly taught by the classroom teacher and the library media specialist. The inclusion of a comprehensive list of computer skills in an information literacy curriculum creates a model for a computer literacy curriculum, and eliminates the need for a separate computer curriculum.

Varieties of information literacy curricula can be found in several places, including the position paper on information literacy adopted by AASL, the Big Six information problem-solving models of Mike Eisenberg and Bob Berkowitz, and the Michigan State Board of Education information literacy model. In each of these models, the curriculum is a process divided into several steps, retaught at increasingly

Computer skills within an information processing curriculum need to be stated separately and clearly.

more sophisticated levels. One approach to integrating computer skills into the general curriculum is to revisit your school's current information processing model, and add specific computer literacy skills to supplement the more general information skills listed. Examples of such integration can be found in the ERIC document (EDO-IR-96-04), "Computer Skills for Information Problem-Solving: Learning and Teaching Technology in Context."

Computer skills within an information processing curriculum need to be stated separately and clearly for a number of reasons: Many districts already have some form of computer skills curriculum, and those skills that are valid should remain clearly stated. It is not realistic to expect most teachers and many media specialists to understand that information literacy automatically assumes computer literacy. Clearly stated computer skills help determine the resources needed to effectively teach a skill. If it is the expectation that information be communicated through a computer-generated graph, then the need for a certain number of computers, types of software, and level of teacher proficiency is more easily established. The business world, academic community and public are aware of the need for students to have computer skills, but the need for information skills may be less apparent. The inclusion of readily understood computer skills may increase the acceptance of the information literacy curriculum.

Listing computer skills within a process framework is only a first step in assuring that all our children become proficient information and technology users. A teacher-supported scope and sequence of skills, well designed projects, and effective assessments are also critical.

Many library media specialists will need to hone their own technology skills in order to remain effective information skills teachers. But such a curriculum holds tremendous opportunities for library media specialists to become indispensable staff members, and for all students to master the skills they will need to thrive in an information rich future. **TC**

Doug Johnson is the District Media Supervisor for the Mankato (Minnesota) Public Schools, and can be reached by e-mail at djohns1@west.isd77.k12.mn.us (or) palsdaj@vax1.mankato.msus.edu.

CAN INFORMATION SKILLS BE TAUGHT WITH ONE COMPUTER?

BY BETH FARRIS

What would you do to ensure maximum student access if your school had only one Macintosh computer with a CD-ROM drive? (Our other library media center computers are Apple IIes.) At our school, we devised a lesson that gives students a chance to compare and contrast information from a variety of CD-ROM and print resources. The lesson uses cooperative learning to address information skills by organizing students into small groups for a collaborative project.

Among our CD-ROM programs for use on our Macintosh LC575 are *The New Grolier Multimedia Encyclopedia; National Geographic Mammals: A Multimedia Encyclopedia;* and *The 1994 Guinness Multimedia Disc of Records.* Students have had some previous experience with each of the programs before beginning this activity, which compares and contrasts information found in these sources about the cheetah for a study unit on animals.

Explain and discuss with small groups the objective of obtaining information from these three sources, comparing and contrasting each source, and using further comparisons with data from print encyclopedias. A sub-group of two students will be assigned to research each CD-ROM program and the print encyclopedia(s), and complete an information form as they progress. To save time, students using the CD-ROM programs may print out the information they find and use the printout to complete their form, so that others may have quicker access to the computer.

Students may use these steps for the CD-ROM Programs:

The New Grolier Multimedia Encyclopedia

Under the **"Main Features"** category, click on "Title List," type in the word cheetah and click on "Go To" to find cheetah in the list. Click or press "return" to access the article on this animal. After the article is read, click on the cross-referenced picture, along with the picture caption. Print out the article, picture caption, and picture for further reference and for use in completing the information form.

National Geographic Mammals: A Multimedia Encyclopedia

Click the "A-Z" button at the top left of the window to see the list of mammals. Scroll down until you see cheetah in the list and click. Read and print out the information on the order, food, habits, status and species. Next click the "Text" button to read an essay about cheetahs. This essay may also be printed out. Then click the following: "Ruler" for information on size (this may be printed); "Globe" to see where the cheetah lives; "Movie Projector" to see a movie clip of the cheetah; and "Camera" to see still photographs of the cheetah.

Guinness Multimedia Disc of Records

Click on the "Word Search" category, type in the word cheetah to check on any possible records. View and print out the Mammals: Fastest on land information, then click on "Picture" to see a picture and its caption of the cheetah. Both picture and caption may be printed out. Also click on "Movie" to view a movie of the cheetah.

After they complete the information forms, have the total meet to discuss their findings and to compare and evaluate their information. Students will discuss consistencies and inconsistencies (if any) found in their research. Students may then want to make an oral presentation, using transparencies made from their information forms.

While the subject "animals" is the focus for this study, other topics in science or social studies and other CD-ROM programs could also be used with this same lesson framework, with small groups working together to research, compare, and report information on various topics.

Having only one computer with a CD-ROM drive does limit student access, but group projects and activities ensure involvement of the maximum number of students. It is a beginning! **TC**

Beth Farris holds a doctorate in education and is a Library Media Specialist at Cummings Elementary School in Memphis, Tennessee.

Information Fo
Information Source
Name of Animal
Classification
Habitat
Size
Other Characteristics (body covering, movements, communication)
Food
Status (endangered or threatened)
Other Interesting Facts
World records (if any)
Student Name
Grade

TECHNOLOGY AND AT-RISK STUDENTS

In Defense of Dabbling: The Case for DROP-IN SESSIONS

by Carmela Federico

If you aim to create a rich, diverse, and inspiring learning environment in your computer lab, you must encourage your students to dabble.

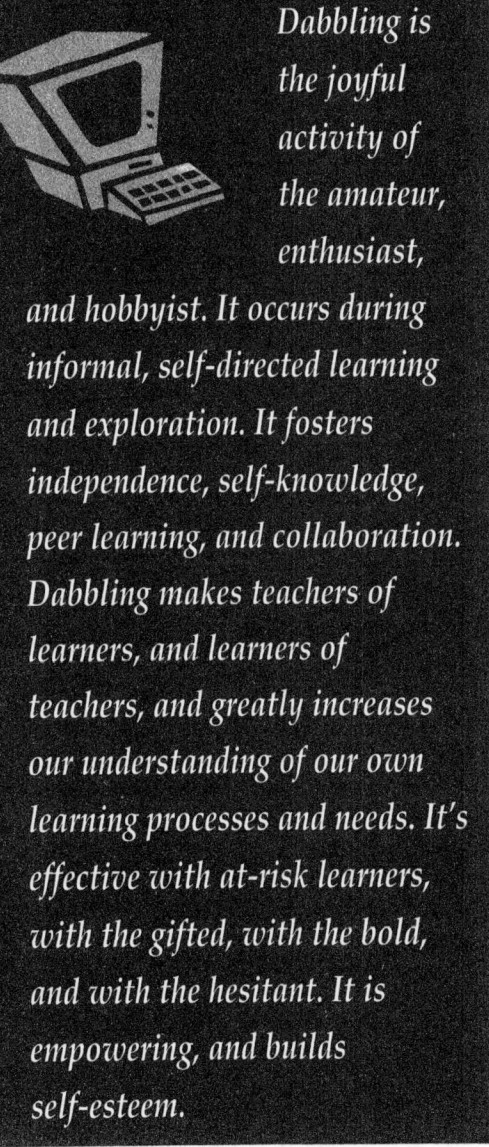

Dabbling is the joyful activity of the amateur, enthusiast, and hobbyist. It occurs during informal, self-directed learning and exploration. It fosters independence, self-knowledge, peer learning, and collaboration. Dabbling makes teachers of learners, and learners of teachers, and greatly increases our understanding of our own learning processes and needs. It's effective with at-risk learners, with the gifted, with the bold, and with the hesitant. It is empowering, and builds self-esteem.

Think back to the last time you learned a new computer activity. Did you sign up for a course before opening the cellophane wrapper on the box? I'll bet that you first independently explored the program's various toolboxes and menu bar commands. Perhaps you next asked an experienced colleague to share insights, shortcuts, and tips with you in a hands-on session. Maybe you ran a self-paced tutorial that came with the program. Perhaps, working at your own pace, you also consulted the manual or a separately purchased "how-to" book on the program. This self-paced, informal, collaborative means of learning is the essence of dabbling.

You probably choose to learn this way because you find it an extremely effective and psychologically satisfying approach to learning. Dabbling is inherently motivating; you learn on a need-to-know basis and you use the resources at your disposal (the books, the on-screen prompts, the colleague) to solve problems of immediate interest to you.

Your students deserve to have this same rewarding experience. To do so, they need to develop skills so that, like you, they can independently foster their own learning.

Dabbling is inherently motivating, because you learn on a need-to-know basis...

Promote Dabbling at "Drop-In" Sessions

Institute "drop-in sessions" in your computer lab—at lunch time, perhaps, or after school—to give students the opportunity to explore and produce freely. You can allow students total freedom to choose their activities, or you can try to focus their energies on various themes or group projects. Help and inspiration can come from staff, teen mentors, tutorials in various media (print, online, and video), and packets of imaginative challenges for students to browse and try.

Inspiration also may come from peppering the computer lab with successful student projects. You also can encourage peer evaluations of projects and have "show-and-tell" sessions. Show students how to create and maintain portfolios of their projects. Then periodically show off their dazzling results at open houses for parents and the community.

Make the Case for Dabbling to Your Colleagues

Excited? I hope so. Now you need to convince your community of educators. Depending on the structure and educational practices at your site, this may be a difficult campaign. Drop-in sessions are messy and unpredictable. Some will ask, "Why bother?" Others will fear that students will wreck the lab and mess up the computers. Some teachers will believe that allowing students to play with the programs used in formal school courses will wreak havoc with classes and curricula. You may encounter staff who believe that all students are going to do is play stupid games. Here are some objections and answers to them:

Objection:
Why Bother?

- **Drop-in sessions create a multifaceted resource for your site.**

Futurists agree that tomorrow's workers will need to think and solve problems independently, will need to be self-motivated, and will need the skills to research and follow through on projects. Because they enable students to choose and direct their own work, drop-in sessions at computer labs foster just these skills. Your job as coordinator, of course, is to create a lab environment that motivates students, inspires them with project ideas, and abounds with resources and pointers to off-lab sites of information and materials.

Student-directed activities at computer labs are constructivist, hands-on, and, by definition, relevant to the participants' interests and lives. They foster collaborative learning, cross-curricular group projects, and the use of multiple intelligences—computers can use graphics, sounds, animations, and words to communicate. Drop-in sessions at your computer lab can become a pedagogical model that enhances the prestige and fundability of your entire educational program.

Moreover, these sessions can become a source of revenue for students and for the school. Students can start entrepreneurial flyer- and pamphlet-making businesses; a portion of their earnings can be donated to help defray the computer lab's expenses. Skilled participants can, for a small fee, provide computer training to teachers, and can produce materials for other students and teachers. The fee can be split between the lab and the students. Your lab can become an income-generating resource for students, for the school, and for the greater community!

- **Drop-in sessions can help students with special needs.**

At-risk students, in particular, prosper in drop-in settings; they flourish within an environment with fewer rules and dictates, and often flower when allowed to research or present topics meaningful to them. Slower students have the time to try various approaches to difficult skills and materials. Gifted students can fly off on their own dazzling tangents. Students with low self-esteem can produce concrete achievements that can hang on the walls and draw smiles from loved ones.

- **A successful drop-in lab can help deter truancy.**

Drop-in sessions can enable artistic communication, the articulation and presentation of a student's world view, and can even (through modems and the Internet) foster global communication. Your lab can become a magnet that draws kids to school and keeps them there. Although harsh and immediate eviction of chronic truants from drop-in sessions isn't recommended, you can develop some motivating policy to link participation in drop-in sessions to attendance—perhaps limiting printouts or access to socializing on the Internet (via e-mail or chat) to students with good attendance records.

In short, drop-in sessions can benefit your students, your programs, and the world!

Objection:
Students will wreck the lab and mess up the computers.

Admittedly, drop-in sessions are logistical and maintenance uh..., challenges. You will indeed be introducing an element of disorder and unpredictability into your lab by scheduling student-directed dabbling. If not handled properly, these activities can indeed wreak havoc with your institution's other programs and with your software and equipment. The gains in student interest and competence are worth the risk, however, and damage can be minimized by taking the following steps:

- **Implement peer mentoring.**

Encourage responsible, experienced students to buy into your program and take responsibility for its proper functioning. Make sure these students commit to a regular schedule of availability at the lab. If your site requires volunteer service from students, make sure drop-in mentorships qualify. Student mentors will greatly spread the reach of the rules and principles you want for your program.

- **Require orientation sessions.**

Make sure students know the essentials of your operating system (for example, launching programs, opening/saving/printing work), and know who to ask and where to look for information, schedules, tutorials, and other essentials. Hold these sessions regularly, and issue cards and data disks to students who attend. Some of these sessions can be part of the general student orientation that takes place at your site. If it is difficult to schedule monthly orientation sessions, have them at least once a semester. Between sessions you can require new students to be given a tour by a peer mentor.

- **Backup from a file server.**

Back up all relevant programs, preference files, and .ini files onto a file server, or onto a portable tape backup or drive. Take time to organize this backup well, and schedule time each week (perhaps with student assistance) to make sure machines function properly.

- **Have students sign in at particular machines.**

Make an easy-to-use form to record students' use of particular machines. Keep these filed for future reference. This can help you later, if outright sabotage takes place.

- **Use software tools that limit student tampering.**

Several programs exist which do this; *At Ease* (Apple Computer, Inc.) for both Windows and the Mac is a popular choice. These flexible programs can go far in protecting your hard drives and settings. Students should, in general, save their work on floppies or (for large projects) Zip disks, Syquest cartridges, or other such media, leaving your hard drive protected. A password can give staff and other school classes access to the hard drives.

Be wary of two things, however. First, floppies are unreliable, and some student work will be lost. You can minimize lost work by checking the reliability of floppies before issuing them (a mammoth, beginning-of-the-year, student-assisted project), and by encouraging students to back up important projects onto several floppies. Also, have disk-repair utilities (e.g., *Norton Utilities*) on hand to save data when possible. Second, you need to make sure that students can access all the files they need from the hard drive. Students should be able, for example, to access templates, clip art, sample files, and tutorials. Using *At Ease* or some other access-limiting software, file-locking (to allow access but prevent changes), and other such security precautions can greatly help in protecting your lab from student maliciousness.

- **Develop Internet and shareware policies.**

If you are going to allow students free access to the Internet during drop-in sessions, your site needs to develop, with parents and participants, an Internet policy. You then need to enforce this policy strictly, banning and disciplining students who violate it. Unfortunately, many administrators and parents have been hypersensitized to the evils of the Internet through an extraordinary amount of media exaggeration; one prankster can destroy access to the Internet for everyone. Programs such as *Surf Watch*, which attempt to place certain controversial Internet sites off-limits, are not effective restrictors of Internet information.

Your site needs to develop an Internet policy based on a frank and open discussion of the pros and cons of access to the Internet. You need to be honest about both the advantages of Internet use during drop-in sessions and the limitations of overseeing student access. (If your lab has 20 stations, and you hope to teach occasionally during these drop-in sessions, you won't be able to monitor 100 percent of Internet access.) You will then need to abide by your site's Internet policy.

You will also want to develop a policy with regard to downloading shareware or freeware programs from BBSs or from the Internet. I recommend that only staff or teen mentors have permission to download software; only with an official seal of approval (and a thorough virus-check) should the software be available for use at the lab or at students' homes. If used in the lab, you of course will need to comply with the author's registration requirements; using shareware without registering it is piracy and is illegal, and will make your lab vulnerable to lawsuits. Subscribe to a virus protection service, which regularly updates your virus-protection software, to keep your machines free from viruses.

On a similar note, I strongly recommend forbidding students to bring software from home into the lab. You must protect your lab from illegal software copies and the legal liability of piracy, and you will wish to avoid confusing issues of ownership during the hustle and bustle of a drop-in session.

Objection:

Allowing students to play with the programs used in formal school courses will wreak havoc with classes and curricula.

Some teachers initially may object to allowing students free and haphazard access to programs they wish to formally present as part of a class. They may fear that such students will be bored and thus disruptive, or will tune out because they feel that they already "know it all." You can try to persuade these teachers that you are actually doing some prep work for them. They can require all students, regardless of prior exposure, to finish assignments. If dabblers finish early because of their expertise, they can be allowed to dabble further, have free time, or can be asked to help others and share their discoveries with the class. If their work is substandard because they didn't listen and thus failed to learn the necessary skills, their grades can reflect this—and can inspire them to listen and learn more in the future.

On the positive side, of course, students can use drop-in sessions to conceive of and complete class assignments. Additionally, the possibilities they glimpse through dabbling can motivate students to take a more in-depth course that will unlock the full possibilities of a program for them. Examples of "master" work displayed in the lab can further this inspirational process.

Objection:

All they're going to do is play stupid games.

This is a real risk: after a few weeks of cursory clicking, students can indeed settle down to a steady diet of simple, repetitive games, or to the nearest approximation of such, if available in your lab.
Here are some ways to avoid this outcome:

- **Make sure there is some educational value in all the software in your lab.**

Some of this software, of course, can be quite entertaining: witness *SimCity* (Maxis), the city construction kit, or *The Incredible Machine* (Sierra/Dynamix), which students use to construct delightful, imaginative Rube Goldberg-like mousetraps.

- **Inspire students with high-quality peer projects to keep them questing for higher-quality output.**

Be honest, however, about the time needed to produce these stellar works, and also provide suggestions for shorter, still-impressive projects.

- **Encourage completion of projects. Try lab contests**

(and participation in larger, national contests), bulletin board demonstrations of student work, complimentary notes added to a student's file or even report card, and exhibitions of student work.

How to Run Your Lab Efficiently

Now that I've convinced you to institute drop-in hours, and you've convinced those at your site to buy in to this new learning activity, here are some tips for successful, efficient, functioning:

- **Talk your school or institution into letting the supervising teacher count drop-in session supervision as a class.**

You may encounter resistance from supervisors who don't think that such an assignment should count as a teaching block. I would argue that supervising drop-in sessions is actually more difficult than teaching a traditional class. The challenge of working with numerous students simultaneously is great, as each student has his or her own agenda and needs, and each learner requires individual strategies for challenge, remediation, and achievement.

If you succeed in this, you will have sufficient, committed staff who take their responsibilities seriously and who have the resources to devote sufficient time to plan drop-in sessions and maintain the lab.

- **Have students write up challenges and interesting discoveries and share them with others.**

You can even keep digitized pictures of students on file, and prepare a form a student can quickly fill out with his or her achievement, attaching his or her digitized image to it.

- **Encourage peer learning from those who have already mastered the material.**

- **Generate impromptu group learning.**

Tell the group when a common problem or an interesting discovery arises by chance in the lab. Call students over so many can learn at once how to cope with this problem or benefit at once from this discovery.

- **Make sure everyone knows the basics and the underlying logic of software use.**

At the minimum, students should know the basics of mouse manipulation, how to launch and quit a program, how to save and print their work, how to access help, how to "parse" a computer screen for information, how to cancel a command (Undo, the Escape key, the Cancel button in a window), and how to hunt for a command in a menu bar. Cover these basics in orientation sessions.

I hope the above arguments and tips have convinced you that drop-in sessions can serve and inspire your entire learning community. My own experience as a dabbler and as a coordinator of drop-in sessions has convinced me that, with a little forethought, planning, and care, you can create a culture of skilled dabblers anxious to spread their technological expertise like ripples through a pond. **TC**

Carmela Federico is a teacher at Crossroads School in Santa Monica, California, and a community computing advocate. She welcomes comments at carmela@lightside.com.

You can write to Carmela Federico at (carmela@lightside.com) or to the folks at the Playing To Win Network (contact Andrea Kimmich Keyser, ptwny@igc.org, 7 Matilda Street, Ossining, New York 10562-3215) for further information about drop-in sessions. Or drop in yourself at Crossroads School between 12:20 and 1 p.m. (PT) to see a drop-in session in action!

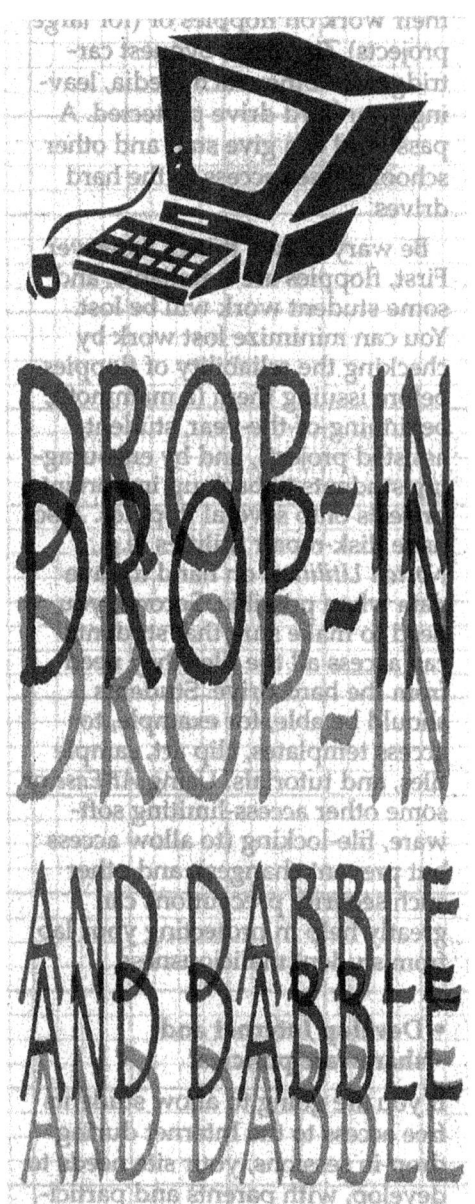

No, You Don't Have to Write Your Name Anymore

By Jacque Burkhalter

Elementary school youngsters learn how to use their circulation system.

The bar codes are in place and your computer is loaded with "items" and "patrons." At the front desk, the wand waits for its first customer. And just when you'd like to "start slow" and "feel your way along," children stream through the door in numbers that you've never seen before to check out books!

You suspect that one reason for this run on books is that every kid wants to see his or her name flash up on the computer screen. Nevertheless, you must have orientation activities ready when the circulation system is ready for its first use. Children need to learn how to use their new automated circulation system.

Orientation for Intermediate Grades. Students from grade 3 and up are eager to see how the circulation computer works. A good way to show the menu to a class is to connect the circulation station to an LCD projection panel, which allows the computer to work directly with an overhead projector. As you explain each step in the circulation procedure, the class can see the process on the LCD screen. (To hold the children's attention, I created some unusual patrons and book titles. For example, Garfield the cat checked out *Italian Cookery* and *How to Train Your Dog*, while Odie chose *Ways to Increase Your Brainpower*.)

If an LCD projection panel is not available, transparencies will work just as well. Check with your automation supplier for blackline masters of the computer screens. Start with a transparency of a blank screen and add overlays to simulate the data that appears in an actual check-out.

In addition to demonstrating the check-out process, take time to explain the features on the main circulation screen. Discuss the meaning of each item and encourage students to verify data about their own status, especially overdue books, when it appears on the screen. (Our students are trained to read the circulation data and will check on their overdues when the information comes up on the screen.)

Notes

I work with small groups (6-10 students) when I introduce the online catalog so that the children can easily ask questions. We identify the elements on the screens; browse through records by title, author, and call number; search for specific subjects; and experiment with key word searches. In a second session, students receive more indepth instruction on Boolean searching techniques.

I found it was important to follow these orientation sessions with some basic location-skills activities. Not all of the students who found books in a computer search knew how to find books on the shelves by call number.

Orientation for Primary Grades. When Alexandria, an automation system from Companion Corp., was installed in our library, I used the Disney character Mickey Mouse as a nonthreatening guide for the primary children. After storytime (a mouse story, of course), I excused myself . . . and returned in a Mickey Mouse shirt and hat. As Mickey, I explained that "Mrs. B." said it was time for everyone to find a book. Mickey quickly "found" the book he wanted: a big-book copy of *If you Give a Mouse a Cookie*, with an oversize circulation card temporarily pasted inside. The children took their guest to the circulation counter, where the library aide or a parent volunteer was ready to show "him" a new way to check out books. As Mickey, I made several calculated mistakes as the students watched. Then, they were given their new library cards so that they, too, could check out a book the "new" way.

As a follow-up to the skit, I created a set of picture cards to provide reminders of the circulation process and expected behavior. From "Choose your book" and "Find your patron card" to "Show your book at the door," the sequence of activities was discussed and then posted for several weeks. I continue to use the cards at the beginning of each school year.

Once is Not Enough. A few weeks after the initial orientation, you should review circulation procedures with students, allowing plenty of time for questions. After using the automated system for a while, students will be able to formulate questions. Listen carefully! These questions will give you valuable clues as to what students need to know. For older students, this review is a good time to introduce them to reserve and renewal procedures, fine schedules, and check-out limitations.

Create A Sense of Ownership. Throughout the first weeks, it is important to remind students that it's their automation system and everyone must use the new equipment with care. I told students that anyone "fooling" with the equipment would be banned from using it for a time. "Nailing" a few adventurous kids was all that was needed to set the standard for proper use.

Lastly, be aware of how easy it is get uptight when you're trying to teach something you're not completely familiar with. Somehow kids can always sense your uncertainty. My advice is to admit that "we're learning together." TC

Jacque Burkhalter is a K-6 librarian on Fidalgo Island in Anacortes, Washington. In her spare time she's a computer nerd. She is also a moderator for the Library Automation Division on Scholastic Network Online.

Notes

Notes

A Workbook for Accessing University Catalogs from Remote Terminals

By Nancy Everhart

Like many other large state university systems, Penn State University encourages residents to log-on to its catalogs, conduct searches, and check out materials if they live nearby. Our university's online catalog is known as LIAS (Library Information Access System). Along with records of books, maps, and audiovisual items, LIAS includes government documents, microforms, magazines and musical scores. Users can search by keyword and Boolean operators.

Even though these resources are available, high school students with no prior experience with online catalogs may be confused, or unable to use the catalog to its full potential. To remedy this, the Pennsylvania School Librarian's Association sponsored the research and development of a workbook for students. The association devoted its professional development award, which is funded by Brodart Corporation, to the project in 1993. The workbook is titled *Lion's PALS* (Public Access LIAS for Students).

The workbook takes a student through these processes: planning a search, connecting, choosing a library, searching by author, title, subject, and keyword, locating items on the shelves, and creating bibliographies from LIAS citations. High school students cannot send interlibrary loan requests via the online catalog, but they can determine if materials are available at a branch campus near them. If the high school has a borrowing agreement with the campus library, they may borrow items in person.

Like other residents, students can access the catalog from home computers using communications software. Instructions are given in the workbook for setting the software for home computers.

In writing the workbook, I worked with the university librarians as well as high school students. A group of students went to one of the campus libraries to field test the workbook. The 40-page booklet was printed in the summer of 1994.

Along with step-by-step instructions, the booklet gives practice sheets so students can put their knowledge to use with guidance.

Our goal was not to encourage students to use the college campuses in place of school and public libraries. However, many students will attend colleges that are part of the state system. Even if they go to other universities, they will find that the online catalogs are similar.

Nancy Everhart is an assistant professor of school library media at St. John's University in Jamaica, New York. She was formerly the librarian at Tamaqua Area Senior High School in Tamaqua, Pennsylvania.

THE PAPERLESS CLASSROOM

By Gene Pelowski

The paperless classroom represents one advantage of using the computer. When students in my Challenge American Government class finished reading *The Making of the President, 1960* by Teddy White, I assigned a project entitled The Making of the President 1996. By using their candidate's World Wide Web page and other related Internet sources, they were to tell the story of that candidate's attempt to capture the presidency. White's book would serve as a guide but students would add graphics and sound. Students also critiqued their candidate's WWW page for ease of use and political propaganda.

At no point in the assignment did students use paper. All data was copied to diskette or hard drive and then organized. This was the first assignment at Winona (Minnesota) Senior High School done entirely on the computer. It had several advantages. It taught students to use *Netscape* and *ClarisWorks*. It saved reams of paper and kept the limited number of printers free for other needs.

Periodically, I displayed students' drafts on the TV monitor in my classroom to illustrate how to pull together various elements of the project. This allowed students to explain how they wrapped text around a graphic or added sound. It also exposed them to the complete range of candidates.

For the assignment to be a success, the instructor must research the Web pages in advance and give the students the addresses. This keeps them on task when using the computer lab. Because there are many students and few computers, time must be used judiciously. It also prevents students from surfing into problem areas on the Internet.

The final product was turned in on diskette and corrected on my laptop computer. A corrected version of the project was saved in a separate file on the diskette and returned to the student. The results were impressive in substance and form. Most important, the assignment allowed each student to investigate a complex topic with the latest information from one access point and use his own creativity to evaluate his candidate. As one student noted, "When I began this project I supported this person; after reviewing his candidacy, I will not vote for him."

The students also found that White's observation of the presidency is as true in the age of the Internet and the paperless classroom as it was in 1960. "There is no one way of becoming President of the United States." **TC**

Gene Pelowski is a Minnesota State Legislator and Social Studies Instructor at Winona (Minnesota) Senior High School. He can be reached at Rep.Gene. Pelowski@House.leg.state.mn.us.

Notes

ALTERNATIVE EDUCATION

Synthesizing That Social Studies Unit Do It with a Database!

By Susan Monahan

Most of us think of a database as a useful way to organize information. We use databases to keep track of the many details of our students' educational lives, but we don't think of the database as a potentially powerful way for our students to pull together what they have learned or to look at their knowledge in a new way. My teaching partner and I used a *ClarisWorks* database with teams of fourth and fifth graders to reinforce a social studies unit on Native Americans of Texas.

My own experience using databases to keep student information gave me the idea to use databases in the classroom and show students how to organize what they learned the database way.

I had designed a *ClarisWorks* database early in the year called My Friends and I. I wanted to teach database vocabulary, such as *data*, *field*, and *record* and fundamentals such as *find*, *sort*, and *match records*. The fields centered around information about the students' appearance, preferences, and families (see illustration). The students were excited about using the database, which I customized using a new layout in *ClarisWorks*, making it

My own experience using databases to keep student information gave me the idea to use databases in the classroom.

large and colorful and illustrating it with clip art. The students enjoyed sorting alphabetically or in descending order by height in inches to see who was the tallest. Using

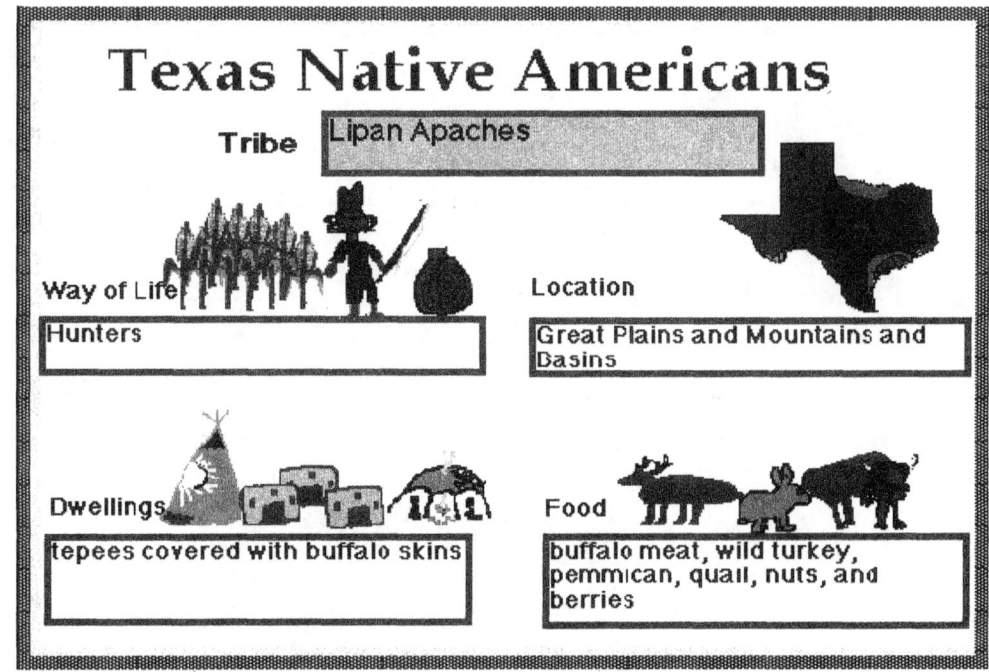

Find showed how many students had brown eyes, or said pizza was their favorite food.

After they had finished the Friends database project, we decided to have the students participate in the development and design of a curriculum-related database. We had worked for several weeks on a Native Americans of Texas unit. Resources included reference books, CDs, and literature books with Native American themes, and the students' tasks had been for two-person teams to research a tribe and then report on that tribe's location, ways of obtaining food, and customs.

We asked the students, "If we were going to make a database on Native Americans, what fields would we define for our database?" We drew a big web on chart paper with blank circles representing our fields. I was surprised at how readily they began to think in general attributes and categories because of their previous experience with the My Friends and I database. *Tribe Name* as a field was arrived at quickly, as was *Region*. Some students came up with examples of data that belonged in a field, such as tepee. When this happened I asked, "What is a word that tells what a tepee or a lean-to is?" and they were able to generate a category like *homes* or *dwellings* to use as a a field. After our web was filled in, we scanned Native American reports for information that could go into the fields. We asked, "Why would we want to make a database of our information when we already have your reports if we want to find something?" The students suggested that a database about Native Americans was another way (in addition to books and reports) that information could be organized and presented, but that a database allowed us to do something that books and reports could not—to find and sort quickly.

The students had not seen the *define fields* process before but were able to take turns completing the steps to creating the five fields we had decided on. *ClarisWorks* database makes a new layout easy. After choosing *Layout/Layout* from the menu you use the tools to create a rectangle background and change fonts, text color, and size of labels and fields. The students were guided through this process, with each team member doing part of arranging and rearranging field position, choosing fonts and text colors, and making decisions about the size of fonts.

The students illustrated their new layout with their own clip art which they created in *HyperStudio* and copied and pasted into *ClarisWorks*. (We find *HyperStudio*'s painting tools easier to use than *ClarisWorks* painting tools.) When the new layout was completed, students went back into *browse* and were ready to enter their data.

Our database teams took their project to the Texas Computers in Education Convention in Austin. They explained how their database was created and then demonstrated for the audience how it could be used to sort and find.

These two database projects proved to us that even elementary students not only can be taught to create and use databases but also can benefit from the inherent strengths of the database format. What's next? The students have an idea for a book review database where class members can complete a record about a book they have read.

We teachers would like to see another curriculum-related database—maybe something related to that ocean unit coming up. The possibilities are endless. **TC**

Susan Monahan is an Itinerant Teacher for the Auditorily Impaired at the Regional Day School for the Deaf in Austin, Texas.

> *Even elementary students not only can be taught to create and use databases but also can benefit from the inherent strengths of the database format.*

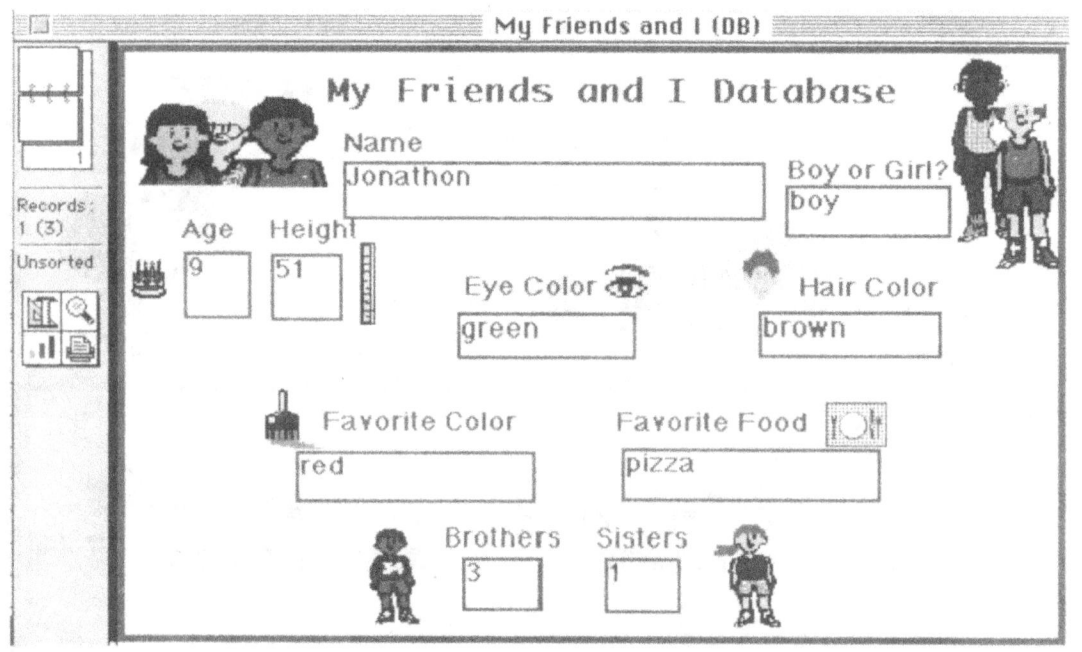

SKILLS

Generic Instructions for Electronic Resources

Marjorie Pappas

Electronic resources bring a new and different set of rules to students and teachers accustomed to using reference books. First, the information is organized in a nonlinear format, meaning there is no set pattern for accessing information. Second, electronic resources are dependent on hardware systems, which often have different and inconsistent features. Third, the software design is typically inconsistent from one resource to another.

Focus on Generic Features

I teach graduate and undergraduate students to use electronic resources in the process of gathering and using information. Like all school environments, the Educational Resource Center at Wright State University has limited electronic resources, so I am forced to be creative as I develop lessons. A typical lesson involves electronic encyclopedias, periodical databases, and clipping services; these electronic resources run on both DOS and Macintosh computers. Some of my students have a working knowledge of these computers while others have barely touched a computer prior to the class.

I have begun focusing on some generic or common features of electronic resources that can become a set of fundamental rules for dealing with new formats. Some of the generic features include: Help functions, menus, printing, browsing, searching, and cross references. Students need easy access to concise information about these generic features as they move from one resource to another. One way to provide this information is to develop a set of cards that can be placed at each workstation. Some examples follow.

Marjorie Pappas is Assistant Professor and Library Media Program Coordinator at Wright State University, Dayton, Ohio.

HELP

To get started with an electronic resource, look for some online Help instructions. This feature is often located as one of the major menu items, across the top or bottom of the screen. Once you have located Help, open the function and read the information that will enable you to get started. You may find there is too much information to absorb all at one time, so at the beginning concentrate on simply getting started. As you use the system, you may refer to Help for further assistance. Many Help functions have been designed to operate in-context. For example, if you are ready to print and have begun to use that function, but need help, go to the Help function, which should take you to the print instructions within Help.

MENUS

Menus act like a table of contents for the system. Some menus are located as a list on an opening screen, while others might appear across the top, bottom or side of the screen. Typically, there is a Main Menu, and each item on that Main Menu breaks down into submenu items when selected.

Menus, which appear across the top of the screen, are fairly common in systems, and these are usually pull-down menus. To select one of these menu items, press the key which represents the first letter of the menu item needed, and then press the first letter of the desired subset menu item as well. If a mouse is available, position the mouse cursor on that menu item, press the mouse button, and hold down. The subset of that menu will appear on the screen. To select an item, pull the mouse down through the list until the desired item is highlighted, then release the mouse button.

FUNCTION KEYS OR SPECIAL KEYS

Some systems operate with function keys, typically a set of keys located in the top row of the keyboard. The screen instructions refer to these as F# (i.e., F1, F2). For example, when you need to print, the screen instructions may tell you to press F4.

Keys which have special or unique functions are labeled as such for some systems. Follow the screen instructions and press the key which matches the label provided.

PRINTING

Electronic resources have a print feature which will let you print a portion or all of an article or citations. To begin this process, select Print from the menu, which is typically a submenu item under the file menu. Once you have done this, another menu or function box will appear. Typically, the system will ask you to input the pages you want to print, or ask if you want to print the entire article. Some electronic resources will only let you print a portion of a full text article. Be sure your printer is on and the paper is properly positioned. Then select Print and wait for your article to be printed.

BROWSE SEARCHING

The Browse function in electronic resources acts like an index for a book, listing subjects available in the system. This may be titled Browse or Index in the Main Menu. Select this and a box or line will appear where you can type in your search word. When you type a search word, the system shows a list of index words on the screen which are close alphabetically to this word. If the word appears, select it by pressing the Return (Enter) key. To use the mouse, position the cursor on the word and press the mouse button. The article text or periodical citations will appear on the screen.

Sometimes the search word is not included in the index, but other words which are close in meaning do appear. Use the arrow keys, or page-up/page-down keys to browse through the list. This is a good way to get ideas for potential search words.

Browsing is useful when you are unfamiliar with the electronic resource or are having difficulty deciding on search words.

SEARCH

The Search function enables a more analytical search process. To begin, select Search from the Main Menu or Menu Bar. Typically, this function brings up a different screen which includes the Boolean operators AND, OR, NOT. In the Search function, you can combine words using these Boolean operators. The electronic resource will search through text for this combination of words. This is a more complex search because the electronic resource is looking for multiple words and lets you explore relationships.

For example, you might input POLLUTION AND ECONOMICS, trying to find information about pollution which might relate to its impact on the economy. The electronic resource will search through the text looking for these two words in close proximity to each other. Then the system produces a list of article titles or periodical citations on the screen. Select the article or citation title by pressing the Return (Enter) key, or by pressing the mouse button. The article text or periodical citation will appear on the screen.

The use of the Boolean operator AND narrows the search because both words must be present in the article. The Boolean operator NOT can also be used to narrow a search. For example, using POLLUTION AND ECONOMICS, you can further narrow this search by adding NOT ACID RAIN, so your search phrase would be POLLUTION AND ECONOMICS NOT ACID RAIN.

To broaden a search, use the Boolean operator OR which means only one term or the other must be present in the article. For example, using the same search topic as above, if you input POLLUTION OR ECONOMICS the system will select articles which include either of these terms. They do not both have to be present in the article. This will produce a much longer list of articles. Use this when information is difficult to find.

CROSS REFERENCES

Electronic resources that are full text use a cross reference feature, which enables you to move quickly to other related information. Some electronic resources put cross reference words in upper case. Typically, you need only highlight this word (or phrase) and press the mouse button. The system will bring that article to the screen. In some systems, you will have to select Cross Reference from a menu and then input that word in the space provided.

Notes

How to Use Two New Multimedia Encyclopedias

By Marjorie Pappas

The producers of electronic resources are working at designing user-friendly software, but students will still encounter many differences as they move from one electronic resource to another. One way to help students is to provide information packets or guides at each workstation. Here are some guides that might help students work with two electronic encyclopedias.

Marjorie Pappas is Assistant Professor and Program Coordinator for Library Media at Wright State University in Dayton, Ohio.

Your Guide to CD-ROM Encyclopedias

Getting Started
Load the CD-ROM into the disk drive.

Double Click on Grolier: the opening screen shows the encyclopedia logo. Click on this logo to get to the next screen, which shows a menu bar across the top and a Tool Palette—both of which can perform many of the same functions. For example, to open the Timeline, you may select the Timeline icon (clock) from the Tool Palette or open the Search menu from the menu bar and then select Timeline.

Double Click on Encarta: the first screen that appears on Microsoft Encarta contains pictures showing the major functions of this encyclopedia. Moving the cursor over each picture produces a short description of each function. To begin using Encarta, click on Enter Encarta at the lower right corner of the screen. The next screen is divided into three sections with menu bars at the bottom of each section. The frame on the right side of the screen contains the article in text format. The frame on the top left is the Category frame; Gallery frame is on the lower left.

Browsing
A browse search is often the best way to begin if you are unclear about your topic or can't decide on a search term.

Grolier: the Browse Title Text feature provides a list of all articles. When you select Browse Titles, a box appears at the top of the screen. Type in a search word and press return or click on the Go To button. A list of articles will appear that may include one on the search word you used. Now you may select that title (click to open and read the article) or, if your search word failed to produce an article on your topic, browse through the list for related articles. If you want to browse after you've opened an article, highlight a word or phrase from the article and click on Hyperlink on the Tool Palette. A list of articles containing this word will appear on the screen. Hyperlinking will lead you to connections among articles and help you clarify your search.

Encarta: to begin a browse search, click on Contents from the Main Menu Bar to open a screen with an index-type list of articles. You may scroll through these or type a search word in the box at the top of the screen. To open an article related to your topic, click on the title. Click on Outline at the bottom of the Article frame to see an outline of an article. To produce a list of related articles, click onto See Also, which appears in the Menu Bar at the bottom of the Article frame. To continue browsing, return to the article list and select other titles. As you scroll through articles, watch for words in red type. They are connecting links to related articles that can be accessed by clicking on them.

Hierarchical Searching
A hierarchical search is useful when you are beginning with a broad concept, i.e., space, rather than with a specific topic, such as Neil Armstrong.

Grolier: a hierarchical search begins at the Knowledge Tree featuring six broad topics, each of which contains a number of subtopics. Begin by selecting a broad topic that might contain the concept you want to explore. For example, if you want to find out about diseases, you might select "Science" from the Knowledge Tree and then click on Expand. When subtopics appear, select Life Sciences and click on Expand. Continue in this manner until "diseases" appears in the subtopics list, then click on Linked Articles for a list of topics about diseases.

Encarta: click on Category Browser in the Menu Bar of the Category frame. This opens a window on the left with 9 broad areas of interest. You might choose "Physical Science and Technology" to look for information about space. The right side of the screen lists categories. Click a category that sounds space-related. The next screen shows a list of articles in that category; click to see the article.

Analytical Searching
An analytical search combines words or concepts with the Boolean operators AND, OR, and NOT. Often, using only one search word will produce a long list of articles. The Boolean operators narrow the search and make it more efficient.

Grolier: to begin an analytical search, select Word Search from the Tool Palette. A Search Template will appear with three boxes for search words. Always click on Reset to clear any previous searches before you begin. Next type a search word in the first box. For example, if you were looking for information on women astronauts, you would type "astronauts" in the first box and click on WITH. Then type "female" in the next box. Click on Search. When the search is finished, click on OK to see a list of the titles. Select a title that interests you, then click on Open.

Encarta: begin by clicking on Find at the top menu bar. When the word box appears, type in your search word and click on Find. The next screen will show a box of article titles in the lower left corner. Scroll through these, select one that interests you, and click to open. For tips on using a Boolean search, click on the Hints button or use the Wizard feature to guide you to other options that will help you narrow your search.

Consult Your Users' Guides
These products have dozens of wonderful features. For example, *Grolier* has an electronic bookmark that, with the touch of a key, lets you refer to articles you've marked. *Encarta* can provide automatic footnotes. Consult the users' guides of these CD-ROM products to learn more about the many exciting features of each.

— A BOOK REPORT THEME SECTION —

Observing Student Searches in an Electronic Encyclopedia

By Marjorie Pappas & Gayle Geitgey

These authors believe librarians and teachers should observe students in action at the CD-ROM encyclopedia in order to devise strategies for teaching new skills.

Teachers and students have accepted electronic encyclopedias as resources for their research assignments. As a result, their processes for accessing information have changed and the old strategies for teaching research skills no longer apply. What new strategies should take the place of the old ones? To find out we observed the actual searching activities in a high school media center where students used *The Grolier Multimedia Encyclopedia.*

We observed three sets of students: sophomores in two college-prep English classes; eighth-grade health students; and seniors in a job-oriented program. Three teachers cooperated with us in the observations.

In our observations we were seeking the answers to three questions:

• How do students use an electronic encyclopedia to gather information?

• What is the role of the teacher in the search process?

• What is the role of the library media specialist?

We saw the librarian playing a two-part role—instructor for both teachers and students in the use of the CD-ROM and facilitator of students' searches. The librarian taught how to access the encyclopedia and how to use its built-in search strategies. She developed a presearch worksheet on which the students could brainstorm with their teacher for synonyms and for larger or small topics that would serve as the key words for their research topic. Once key words were identified, word searches were executed more efficiently.

After the students and teachers comprehended how to access the electronic encyclopedia, Boolean logic and analytical search techniques were explained. At this point the library media specialist took on the second role—facilitator. As facilitator, the librarian helped students focus on their topics by asking questions that led to new key words. She also suggested resources that could generate

---

Marjorie Pappas is Assistant Professor and Program Coordinator for Library Media at Wright State University in Dayton, Ohio. She is a past president of the Ohio Educational Library Media Association and currently serves as Region 3 Director for the American Association of School Librarians. Gayle Geitgey is the District Media Specialist for Urbana City Schools in Urbana, Ohio.

---

search terms, such as the dictionary, thesaurus or *Sear's List of Subject Headings.*

The Teacher's Role in Electronic Searching

During our observations, three types of teachers became evident, which we called the no-help teacher, the basic-level-help teacher, and the fully trained, ready-to-help teacher. For all three types, prior instruction on the use of the electronic encyclopedia was important.

The no-help teacher had not learned how to use the electronic encyclopedia before his or her students came to the library. In the case of the no-help teacher, peer teaching by students became crucial to the search process. Often the librarian stepped in and trained some students who then taught others to use the encyclopedia.

The basic-level-help teacher was familiar with access to the encyclopedia and beginning a word search, and was willing to learn along with the students. (Many of the student searchers seemed pleased with themselves when they were able to teach their teacher.)

The fully trained, ready-to-help teacher had learned the encyclopedia and its various search options before she brought her classes to the media center. She sat with her students, making suggestions as their searches ran into dead ends. This teacher herself observed that if she helped too much the student became dependent on her. To encourage cooperative searching, she established a system of "runners, recorders and reporters." The runners conducted the search, the recorders took notes, and the reporters gave the information found in the search to the other class members.

Students' Use of Electronic Resources

Our observations of students using electronic encyclopedias suggest that their actions fall on a continuum from simple browsing to a more complex analytical strategy. Initially, students began with a browse approach, focusing on one-answer queries as if they were using a print encyclopedia. Browsing was found to be a useful strategy when students understood how a title or word index functioned. Entering a word or phrase brought up the section of the word index where the student's word or words fell. The student was then able to select the words that matched his search term or browse through related words. Although this strategy did not provide for combining terms, it did facilitate the discovery approach as students selected from the word list and opened articles that appealed to them. The discovery approach was further enabled by the cross-reference feature of the encyclopedia, which made connections from one article to another related topic. This approach was useful for students who were in the presearch mode and still needed to clarify concepts and terms.

Our observations of browsing students revealed that their search could be characterized as hit-and-run. They were looking for quick information and did not take time to do a presearch worksheet. There were several reasons for hit-and-run searching. A student might simply need to do no more than look around for information. Other reasons were related to time constraints imposed by the teacher or by the number of workstations available.

During a hit-and-run search, the student generally printed the found article, taking no notes and making no use of the copy/paste features of the encyclopedia. Generally, students identified important information on the printout with a highlighter, often in lieu of note taking. This type of searching may be a function of students' analysis process since they seemed to need to have information in hard copy, or their searching skills may not have been fine-tuned enough to take notes online.

As students gained experience they moved toward an analytical search strategy, which enabled them to look for connections or patterns within their topic. They began to distinguish between the Boolean operators, using them to narrow or broaden their search. Identifying search terms became one of the most challenging steps in the students' search process. The index or word list in the browse mode of the electronic encyclopedia was found to be helpful. For the search to be successful, it was important for the students to understand that their word-search process had to be developed and revised several times.

Peer teaching and collaboration were effective in achieving a searchable subject. In a group setting, one student often emerged as a leader and became the main searcher. At this level of searching there was a great deal of frustration and reworking of terms to fine tune the search. Boolean logic was often used to narrow the search.

Once a student became a comfortable user of the electronic encyclopedia, she was willing to show other students. In peer teaching it was often observed that the student/teacher did not always use the method of searching outlined by the library media specialist.

We observed that students still missed the on-screen prompts of the electronic encyclopedia. These miscues could be attributed to lack of attention, a problem in the software, or the student simply being overwhelmed with the amount of information available.

Most of the students failed to use any information filtering strategies. This suggests that students need to develop criteria for filtering information found in the electronic encyclopedia since the search will typically identify more information than the student can use. (Filtering criteria might include the date of information or general versus specific details.) Students should be encouraged to use their filtering criteria with information as it appears on the screen, perhaps highlighting specific sections and pasting them into the notepad feature of the encyclopedia. The notepad typically has a simple word processing program so students can add their own notes along with the quotes from the encyclopedia. The students should also include notes for their bibliographic citations.

Summary

Our observations provided much useful information about the way students, teachers, and library media specialists use electronic encyclopedias. The students were highly motivated by the encyclopedias and were not afraid to explore. They often taught themselves to use the encyclopedia. In spite of students' affinity for the electronic resources, librarians should not assume students have the needed knowledge and skills for searches. Left on their own, most students remained at the browse level and failed to proceed to a more analytical search process. Librarians should also offer training to teachers before the teachers' students work with the electronic encyclopedia.

We found the observations to be helpful and continue to observe students working with electronic resources. We encourage library media specialists to initiate their own observations.

•

Basic Skills Still Needed In Electronic Searches

In the Fall 1993 issue of *School Library Media Quarterly*, Shu-Hsien Chen of Clark Atlanta University in Atlanta, Georgia, reported on her observations of 35 eleventh graders new to an online catalog. She undertook the study to pinpoint problems the school librarian should address in information-skills instruction. Although many of her subjects were able to use the catalog successfully after instruction in online searching, she found basic problems in library and language skills accounted for some of their difficulties. The former school librarian believes that any program to teach online searching skills must also include academic skills, such as spelling, reading, interpreting, and knowledge of library classification systems. She concludes that research is needed among different age groups to provide "a basis for designing effective online skill development programs for younger users."

Bugs and Frogs and Trees and Doggy Friends

SEARCHING IN THE ELEMENTARY REFERENCE WORLD

by Joyce Valenza

The world of electronic reference for elementary schools is populated by some unusual creatures: space frogs, knowledge bugs, dog detectives, tiny video kids and animated trees. It is a world where children are encouraged to play as they explore, solve problems and learn searching skills.

Concise But Thorough Information Is Key

Use of electronic reference materials by young students, however, presents some unique problems. How is a broad (encyclopedic) amount of material to be covered in interesting, digestible units? Young children may not be preparing research reports, but their natural curiosity drives them to seek information and answers. Products for this age group need to present concise but thorough summaries of topics. A few of the products we examined were, in fact, specialized encyclopedias limiting their scope to specific thematic concepts.

Another important issue is how information is presented to pre-readers and nonreaders. In our evaluation of various products for these children, we found three basic categories, ranging from a "no text/just narration" approach to concise interactive cards to traditional full-text articles. Some of the reference sources serve to concisely answer the questions of the curious. Others provide lengthy printed output.

Information Must Be Easy to Find

Information-seeking strategies for pre- and nonreaders must be simple. Younger children may have difficulty posing questions and identifying keywords. They may have trouble categorizing to fit a concept within a larger context. Many of the vendors have responded with attractive, logical, graphical arrangements that also offer strong audio support. In most cases, the products offer picture menus so younger users need only click to select and may hear their choice read aloud. Some products provide more advanced searching options for older users. Hypertext links are presented in much the same way as in the higher level products. Vendors have also included notebooks for collecting text and adding comments.

Animation, Sound, and Graphics Are Important

Instead of the traditional help icons, most of the products introduce "video kids" (one product calls them Video Kids) and animated, friendly guides who speak directly to kids' questions. These guides also function as cheerleaders during kids' attempts at games and activities.

In many ways comparing primary reference products is an apples and oranges dilemma. *First Connections Golden Book Encyclopedia* (Hartley) and Heinemann's *Children's Multimedia Encyclopedia* are similar in format—they offer traditional search formats and text-based information interspersed with an assortment of related graphics, sound and video. Of the two, *Golden Book*, despite its younger looking interface, offers more text and a more comprehensive scope. *Children's Multimedia Encyclopedia* offers more search flexibility and a format that would appeal to a wider age group. Both products would give students a good start for a first report and would be useful in

Continued on page 28

A Product with Text, Games, Bells and Whistles

Aimed at an older audience (ages seven through 12), *Random House Kid's Encyclopedia* offers a hip, surrealistic search environment in a town peopled with helpful Video Kids. The product is a result of a new co-publishing arrangement between Knowledge Adventure and Random House.

The encyclopedia comes packaged as two disks—Games CD-ROM and Reference CD-ROM. From the Reference disk, users go directly to the futuristic "Fact-ory" environment, where they can examine any of the narrated entries. There is a searchable time line, globe, A–Z search, random tours with a Video Kid guide or a category approach. The A–Z search is clearly the most effective way to locate information. Within each letter is a list of the topics covered. Unfortunately, there is no word search function to get directly to a topic. The globe function does not provide articles specifically about countries, cities or states. Clicking on Brazil brought up the article on anteaters. The time line was also a bit disappointing. It is not clear why certain selections were made to represent a particular year.

On the Games disk, users may choose to visit the Arcade or visit the Movie Theater for 120 videos and animations. All games are based on knowledge contained within the encyclopedia and are provided for reinforcement.

Text or images may be magnified to full screen. Most articles are about one page long and offer adequate concise information. Text is printable; the graphics are not particularly useful. The article on horses contains a video of horses and three fairly irrelevant pictures—cars, camels, and a donkey.

A bibliography function lists sources and suggested further reading for each article. Though the student testers quickly learned how to navigate, they became a bit frustrated by the number of moves it took to enter a room or activity as they traveled through a series of halls to get to a door.

Report Card

– Does the product foster discovery learning? - A

– Does it answer curricular questions? - A

– Teach research skills? - C

– Is it easy to use? - B

– Is it fun to use? - A

A = Excellent	D = Fair
B = Good	F = Poor
C = Average	

	Children's Multimedia Encyclopedia (1995)	First Connections Golden Book Encyclopedia (1992)	Explorapedia: World of People (1995)	Explorapedia: World of Nature (1994)	Kid's Encyclopedia (1994)	My First Encyclopedia (1994)	Junior Field Trips: Farm (1995)	Junior Field Trips: Airport (1995)
Publisher	Heinemann Interactive/Reed Interactive Online Computer Systems 20251 Century Blvd. Germantown, MD 20874-1196 (800) 922-9204	Hartley 3451 Dunckel Rd. Suite 200 Lansing, MI 48911-4216 (800) 247-1380	Microsoft One Microsoft Way Redmond, WA 98052-6399 (800) 228-6270	Microsoft One Microsoft Way Redmond, WA 98052-6399 (800) 228-6270	Knowledge Adventure, Inc. 4502 Dyer Street La Crescenta, CA 91214 (800) 573-5223	Knowledge Adventure, Inc. 4502 Dyer Street La Crescenta, CA 91214 (800) 573-5223	Humongous Entertainment 13110 N.E. 177th Pl. Woodinville, WA 98072 (206) 485-1212	Humongous Entertainment 13110 N.E. 177th Pl. Woodinville, WA 98072 (206) 485-1212
Ages	6 to 12	K–3 (Also special needs)	6 to 10	6 to 10	7 to 12	3 to 6	3 to 8	3 to 8
Price	$69.95	$149.95	$34.95	$34.95	Single user: $47.95 Lab pack: 5 for $179.95	Single user: $42.95 Lab pack: 5 for $119.95	$29.95	$29.95
Platform	Windows, Mac	Windows, Mac	Windows	Windows	Windows, Mac	Windows	Windows, Mac	Windows, Mac
Scope	General: 11 volumes of Heinemann Children's – Earth & Beyond, Famous Men & Women, Plants, Arts & Entertainment, People, Technology at Work, Animals, Countries & Homes, Sports & Leisure, Travel, & Communication	Comprehensive	Archeology, airplanes, books, cities, clocks, dogs, electricity, farm animals, human body, magic, opera, photography, pollution, puppets, religions, rocket, sailing, soccer, trains, trucks	Environments: Rain forests, grasslands, mountains, lakes, savannas, polar regions, deserts, deciduous forests, coral reefs, seashores, oceans, country, rivers, evergreen, forests, wetlands, the universe	Subjects include: science, culture, geography, history, and nature	10 areas of learning space: geography; the body; buildings and cities; food; transportation; arts & culture; earth & nature; careers; sports & famous people; animals	Farm environment	Airport environment: places, aircrafts, jobs and machines defined and explained
Information format	Most articles are about a page	Articles range in length Robot narration (optional)	Information is presented on interactive "cards" (optional narration by kids)	Information is presented on interactive "cards" (optional narration by kids)	Separate enlargeable text & media screens (optional narration)	Narration	Narration Concise articles	Narration Concise articles
Strengths	Traditional research format Easy to search Excellent search features	Traditional research format Thorough user's guide and teacher's guide Notetaking feature Detailed articles Optional narration	Entertaining interactivities Animations Narrations Attractive presentation	Entertaining interactivities Animations Narrations Attractive presentation	New "Homework Helper" feature connects to Internet resources Clever games Attractive interface Great video	Appropriate for nonreaders Engaging multimedia Effective tree format Excellent user's guide	Windows 95 ready Educational games Cute animated scenes to manipulate Narrations	Windows 95 ready Educational games Cute animated scenes to manipulate Narrations
For the update	Increase length of articles Enlarge scope Hypertext links need to be checked	Pictures do not print Awkward text to sound No "word find" feature	Limited amount of information for reports Takes a while to learn to use	Limited amount of information for reports Takes a while to learn to use	Make globe functions clearer Add more dates to time line Add a "word find"	No printed information Add "find" or "contents" search feature	Add a "word find" feature for spellers	Add a "word find" feature for spellers

elementary classrooms and libraries.

Needed—Keyword Search Capabilities

We wished that many of the products offered a keyword search approach. Getting to a specific piece of information was tedious for many of our users. Younger children might likely be in situations where, with some spelling help, they might want to get directly to their destination without exploring.

The products we reviewed clearly tested the memory capacities of our six-month-old 486 machine. Schools will have trouble keeping their hardware up to the standards required for new intensively multimedia software. If there is any good news about this, it is that updates for these products are infrequent. Your investment is protected a bit longer than with the products for older students.

Pre-readers will enjoy the *Junior Field Trips* (Humongous), *My First Encyclopedia* (Knowledge Adventure), and the *Microsoft Explorapedia* products. Though they may need a bit of help getting started (especially with *Explorapedia*), students can use these products independently—learning while listening and viewing. The narration is friendly and clear; the activities are engaging.

Our kid testers were completely taken by the cool, colorful *Knowledge Adventure*. They loved the activities and played for hours on the games disk of *Random House Kid's Encyclopedia*. They enjoyed clicking around exploring the Humongous *Airport* and *Farm*, though Buzzy the Bug loses a bit of appeal for kids beyond second grade. Are the games important? The kids clearly thought they were.

My testers were not driven by strong research needs—probably because learning among younger children often occurs at home in a less formal setting. The multisensory appeal is important. Games, colors, sights and sounds keep kids' attention while appealing to a variety of learning styles. **TC**

Joyce Valenza is the Media Specialist at Wissahickon High School, Ambler, Pennsylvania.

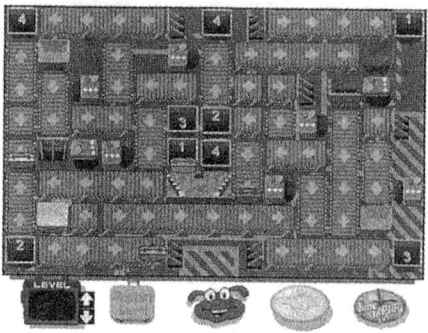

Products Featuring a Thematic Approach

Microsoft Explorapedia: World of People, World of Nature is based on the print *Random House Encyclopedia for Children*. Our guide for both programs is friendly frogonaut Thaddeus (Tad) pole. On Tad's space ship, users click on the controls to navigate the product. The main menu is represented by pictorial maps located in the center of Tad's ship. Clicking on the map brings users to the 16 scenes in *Nature* (representing the biomes of the world) or the 13 scenes in *People*. Word search is the quickest way to get around for the more sophisticated user. All text is narrated by kids—an option which may be turned off.

Clicking on the Wisecracker Bird causes her to lay a "quegg" or question egg designed to inspire exploration through a scavenger hunt. The Wise Visor lists creative projects. Games (or interactivities) are interspersed throughout the scenes. Generous hypertext links—"leap words"—are scattered throughout.

However, those looking to walk away with a few printed pages of information will be disappointed. Information is presented in the form of illustrated cards. These cards would make excellent teacher transparencies. Most pictures contain star-like twinkles. Click on the twinkle and more information about a topic or picture pops up. Pre- and non-readers will enjoy clicking and exploring the animated scenes. Teacher Guides offer activities and extenders and scavenger hunt exercises. Words and pictures may be printed or copied to the clipboard.

Report Card
- Does the product foster discovery learning? - A
- Does it answer curricular questions? - B
- Teach research skills? - B
- Is it easy to use? - C
- Is it fun to use? - A

Like the Microsoft products above, *Farm* and *Airport* of the *Junior Field Trips* series (formerly *Farm Junior Encyclopedia*) from Humongous have a specific scope. Menus are graphical and begin from a bird's eye view of the farm or the airport. Your guide around these environments is Buzzy, the Knowledge Bug. Young users click to find displayed words and audio explanations in a variety of scenes, controlling where they want to go and how much information they receive. In *Airport*, users may choose to visit the cockpit of the Concorde, the baggage area or even the magazine stand. Around the *Farm*, students can explore the chicken coop, the silo or a beaver dam. Scattered throughout the scenes are amusing animated objects. An A–Z feature allows searching of all topics by scrolling through the alphabet. All text is narrated. Articles are appropriately concise. Each disk contains a coloring book and four games. Here, too, a keyword find feature would be helpful for slightly advanced users. These products would be excellent additions to preschool through first grade classroom units.

Report Card
- Does the product foster discovery learning? - A
- Does it answer curricular questions? - B
- Teach research skills? - C
- Is it easy to use? - B
- Is it fun to use? - A

Traditional Text-Based References

From the opening screen of *First Connections Golden Book Encyclopedia*, users have four choices: "World of Words" (where they can choose from graphically represented categories: city, zoo, playground, arts center, history center, or farm); "Seek and Find" (a topic tree approach where users choose from lists of questions on presidents, weather, United States, space, sports, human body, food, famous places, dinosaurs); "Sights and Sounds" (random assortment of the pictures, sounds, movies, maps and speeches); or "ABCs" (choose a letter and examine the words within that letter). Unfortunately, there is no "word find" feature for older users to type in a search term and go directly to an article.

A handy tracking feature allows retracing steps. Bookmark and notebook features are available. Graphics are not printable. Earphones appear when narrated help is available and for sound clips. Highlighting text and clicking on the robot will activate a robotic voice to read the text selected.

The User's Guide and Teacher's Guide are thorough and outstanding. The classroom set also includes idea cards, activity guides, a hand puppet and a poster.

Students would need some reading skills before they can use this product. Even after choosing a graphic, reading skills are needed to sort through and recognize items among alphabetical lists of words.

The articles have more depth than those in any of the other products. The closest comparison is with *Heinemann's*, the only other fully text-based product. The article on World War II contains two maps, an audio clip of Roosevelt's "Day of Infamy Speech," photos of airplane bombings, Normandy, and concentration camps accompanied by five pages of comprehensive text. Articles on the states are detailed.

Because the text has some depth, and because it is easy to read, this product may have more flexible use. There were, however, a few notable omissions. Only 17 of our presidents have individual profiles. The general article, "Presidents of the United States," has a paragraph on each president with no links to the longer articles on the 17 fully treated presidents.

Report Card
– Does the product foster discovery learning? - C
– Does it answer curricular questions? - A
– Teach research skills? - B
– Is it easy to use? - B
– Is it fun to use? - C

Heinemann's Children's Multimedia Encyclopedia offers a format similar to many of the products aimed at older children. The intended audience is ages six through 12. Users may search by a broad content list or type a word or phrase. Advanced search features allow use of the ability to annotate, add bookmarks and see search history. A reference section contains tables, such as the Richter Scale. There are multimedia lists of pictures, movies or sounds that lead to articles.

Though designed appropriately for beginning readers and perhaps the easiest of the group to search, there are some serious content issues. Young users may appreciate the brevity of the articles that range from a few sentences to a page in length. Some researchers may be disappointed. The original print set is based on a British product, possibly accounting for the omission of articles that might be heavily used by students in the United States. For example, articles on the states are noticeably absent. Our testers happened upon an article on Barbara Hepworth (1903–75), one of the leading English sculptors of her time, and wondered why she was included when "Pennsylvania" was not. The article on Europe is six sentences. The article on World War II is suspiciously simplistic, with the first sentence blaming Hitler for the entire war. There is no mention of the Holocaust, or any of the generals or battles. There are some problems with the links. The article on Europe has no links to individual countries. The article titled "Dogs and Cats" has no link to the article on pets.

Report Card
– Does the product foster discovery learning? - C
– Does it answer curricular questions? - C
– Teach research skills? - A
– Is it easy to use? - B
– Is it fun to use? - C

Of the bunch, *My First Encyclopedia* is the only one directed specifically at early and pre-readers. It is also engaging to older users. Users navigate by selecting items from a metaphorical "tree of knowledge." Children may choose to click on any of the many items on the tree or enter any of 10 "learning rooms" dealing with particular interest areas: food, transportation, arts and culture, jobs and sports, geography, space, jobs and recreation, buildings and towns, anatomy and medicine, geology, animals. Each room has a "question and answer" section hosted by a "video kid." These real kids offer conversational narration of words and concepts. There are 575 narrated entries in addition to video animations and music. The Real Kids guides (videotaped and layered on top of the animated environment) vary in ethnic background, dialect and approach. Our testers enjoyed the over 50 games and activities modules, some of which were a bit challenging. They include a variety of matching activities, sliding puzzles and identity games. The kitchen had a recipe file with actual recipes to be printed and used with a parent. The product also offers five subject-based coloring books and a full paint program. An "Adventurers" section includes home videos, artwork and writings submitted by kids from all over the world. The User's Guide describes the activities in each room and provides suggestions for using the product effectively with young children.

Though browsing the tree menu works well for curious younger children, it is a bit slow. Older users should be able to choose information from an A–Z menu or a keyword approach. There are no printouts here. Students cannot walk away with their information, but that may not be important for this audience. This product is a lot of fun because it allows young pre-literate students to work independently. It would be a wonderful addition to the kindergarten classroom and an enjoyable tool for parents and children to use together at home.

Report Card
– Does the product foster discovery learning? - A
– Does it answer curricular questions? - C
– Teach research skills? - D
– Is it easy to use? - B
– Is it fun to use? - B

More on Electronic Encyclopedias

This page contains information in chart form on the electronic encyclopedias we discussed in the October 1995 issue of TECHNOLOGY CONNECTION (page 29). We thought it would complement this article on elementary reference works, as well as provide a quick overview of the electronic products.

	Compton's Interactive	Encarta '96 Encyclopedia	Grolier Multimedia	World Book Multimedia	Encyclopedia Americana	Britannica 2.0
Features they couldn't improve...	• Engaging use of media • Ability to copy pictures, sound, and video • Interface switching • Tour and explanations with Patrick Stewart • Editing room for multimedia • Kids loved moving pics with "handles" • Recent events slideshow • Can enter year or event timeline	• Engaging use of media • "Fly out" menus • Terrific atlas (greatest number of maps) • Great city maps with links • Attractive annotated further reading lists • Interactivities • Can adjust text size • Links to contributors' credentials and related articles • Yearbook Builder–monthly online updates (see original chart) • Print citations on maps and media	• Clearest Boolean search screen (in "more choices") • Easy to use • Great maps (including cities of the world) • Interactive animations • Thematic timelines with event list • Historic documents (96) • Year in review (96)	• Printing options are the clearest • Articles aimed at curriculum • Outlines • Factboxes • Citations print on everything • Uncluttered screen • Questions follow articles • Diagrams • Quality maps • Dictionary features • Nice preference options for printing and multimedia	• Hybrid disk runs on both platforms • Search options for sophisticated users • Depth and size of database • Scope of articles • Can adjust text size	• Search engine • Flexible search options • Depth and size of database (largest) • Nations of the World and Book of the Year • First paragraph display • Next version will access Internet resources
Adjustments to consider for the update	• Add Boolean search • Improve the atlas • Enlarge menu bar • Create icons for fact boxes • Simplify partial printing • Enlarge movie screens • Equalize Mac and Windows versions • Make it networkable	• Clarify printing command. • Make outlines printable • Include fact boxes for more than 40 countries • Adjust "Pinpointer" so filters are automatically removed after a set time.	• Clarify on the command menu that partial printing is enabled • Print citations on maps	• Note the Boolean options on the screen • Maybe a bit more "kid appeal" on opening screen? • Timeline does not allow searching by year	• Create an option to print or view entire article • Make icon functions clearer • Allow a permanent spot for the table of contents on the Mac	• Requires much hard disk space • Price may be prohibitive

Electronic Encyclopedias: Stacking Them by Numbers

Product	Database	Phone	Article	Words	Still images	Videos animation	Fact boxes	Maps	Hypertext links
World Book Multimedia	World Book	(800) 621-8202	17,000	10,000,000	5,000	38	Countries, states, presidents	260	60,000
Encarta '96 Encyclopedia	Funk & Wagnall's	(800) 426-9400	26,500	9,000,000	8,000+	118	For 40 countries and states	950+ (48 detailed city maps)	300,000
Grolier "95	Acadamic American	(800) 285-4534	33,000	10,000,000	8,017	118	Countries, states, presidents	638 (11 are animated)	120,000
Compton's Interactive	Compton's	(800) 862-2206	35,000	9,000,000	7,000	90	Countries, states (follow articles)	136	112,500
Encyclopedia Americana	Americana	(800) 285-4534	45,000	25,000,000	1,200	None	Countries, states, presidents (700)	No	19,000
Britannica CD 2.0	Britannica	(800) 323-1229	65,000	44,000,000	3,400+	None	Nations of the World	300+	700,000

Product	Sound clips	Boolean search	Timeline	Platform	Network	Standalone price	Text export	Media export
World Book Multimedia	76	Yes	Yes	Mac, Windows, DOS (text only)	$1295 site license	$99	Yes	Images
Encarta '96 Encyclopedia	2,000 (9 1/2 hours)	Yes	Yes	Mac, Windows, online through Microsoft Network	$49 for each additional workstation	$54.95	Yes	Images, audio, video frame
Grolier '95	507 (6 hours)	Yes	Yes	Mac, Windows, DOS	Lab pack 5 for $299.75, 10 for $599.50	$59.95	Yes	Images
Compton's Interactive	(15 hours)	Natural language	Yes	Mac, Windows	No network version	$70-$90	Yes	Images, video, sound
Encyclopedia Americana	No	Yes	No	Mac, Windows, DOS	$1295 (2-8 users), $2995 (9-50 users)	$595	Yes	Images
Britannica CD 2.0	No	Yes	No	Mac, Windows, Net	$1295	$995	Yes	Images & net stuff

BONING UP ON BOOLEAN SEARCHING

By Linda Turrell

Too often, students who've been assigned research projects enter the library, switch on the computers, and ask "Now what?" Computer neophytes are usually clueless about how to construct search strategies and evaluate their search results. It's essential that all students learn to perform a few types of Boolean searches, along with simple keyword searches. It's equally important that they understand the logic behind these searches so they can choose the type of search that best suits their purposes.

They need to understand, for example, that a Boolean search using the keywords "ecology" AND "soil pollution" will retrieve information on soil pollution and how it impacts ecology. A Boolean search using "ecology" OR "soil pollution" will yield results about one or the other, or both. A Boolean search using the keywords "ecology" AND NOT "soil pollution" will yield information about ecology with no references to soil pollution. To successfully access information about ecology and soil pollution outside the United States, the Boolean connectors need to be changed.

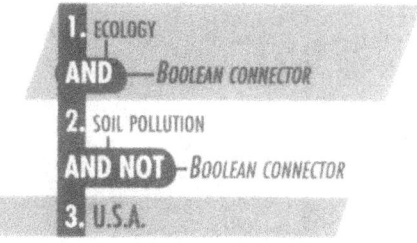

It's helpful to give students sample Boolean search circles. Creating sample worksheets that require students to think through their research questions also helps, as does requiring them to analyze research questions to see if they fit in a simple search or Boolean format.

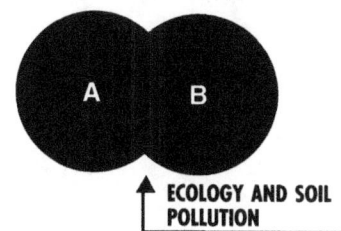

ECOLOGY AND SOIL POLLUTION

Such questions will guide students as they analyze the value of their own research questions. They need practice, practice, and more practice in the higher-level thinking skills required to create these questions and to select appropriate keywords. The simple commands required to conduct the searches are easily taught. **TC**

Linda Turrell is the national winner of the 1995 Texty Award for Academic and Instructional Materials, and an Educational Media Specialist at Raritan High School in Hazlet, New Jersey.

SAMPLE STUDENT WORKSHEET

Think about each of the following research questions and decide whether you would do a subject search or Boolean search. Explain your choice.

- What information is available about the giant turtle?
- Find general information about turtles and list the places where they are endangered.
- How much information can you find about Amelia Earhart?
- How does crime affect U.S. teenagers?
- How is use of chemicals in the rainforest related to soil and water pollution?

Notes

A Manual for CD-ROMs

By Jacqueline Sewald

A year ago when students returned to school, they found nine computers on our network with a tower of seven CD-ROMs. Altogether, we now have 46 programs and keep the most often used ones in the tower.

Single-use discs are installed on one stand-alone computer, which still ties into the network for printing purposes. At the present time, *WilsonDisc Readers' Guide* remains in the stand-alone work station, although it may be included in a new tower. It is our most widely used research resource.

On the network, students make great use of the SIRS discs and *DISCovering Authors* (Gale), all of which are user-friendly. But not all discs are user friendly. Some are difficult to access or do not offer on-screen directions. Others provide instructions in manuals that are not generally accessible to the student-user.

To help students I went through every program with the purpose of uncovering problems that might arise for novice users. I combined my original instructions, if no others were available or did not cover the problem, with instructions from the producers' manuals to create a booklet for our students. In some cases I took information from the producers' manuals that are not available to the student user.

I expect to continue to update and improve the booklet (8½ × 11 sheets) as questions arise. I have found that students do use the booklet and make fewer demands on the staff.

Jacqueline Sewald is the Media Specialist at Red Bank Regional High School in Little Silver, New Jersey. She is also a published writer of gothic mysteries, a young adult novel, and poetry.

Notes

Lesson Plans Shared In New PGS Book

Media specialist-written manuals and worksheets are much in evidence in the new book from Linworth Publishing, *Teaching Information Literacy Using Electronic Resources for Grades 6-12*. Not only are there basic explanations for using an online catalog but also detailed lesson plans for searching a variety of CD-ROMs, commerical databases, and the Internet.

One lesson plan from the new book is reproduced below.

Other plans cover such diverse activities as
- a travelogue created with *HyperCard* from videodiscs and print materials. (Students use a scanner to digitize pictures.)
- how to introduce Internet searching to groups of students.
- multimedia projects using the Personal Education Authoring Kit (PEAK) from Digital Imaging Associates.
- a multipage set of worksheets and instructions for using the high school's public access catalog (Follett's *Catalog Plus*).
- suggested activities or questions for adult learners, which can be used in inservice training or in demonstrations for parents.
- and many more, including the plan reproduced below:

Lesson Plan
Comparing Electronic and Print Indexes
By Joyce Valenza, Wissahickon High School, Ambler, Pennsylvania

Skills Category
Searching print and electronic media

Grade levels
Ninth through adult

Time required
Ten to fifteen minutes

Overview
An introduction to searching

Objectives
Students will be able to compare the results of a manual search to a similar CD-ROM search; students will be able to list advantages of print and electronic indexes and will appreciate the speed and efficiency of CD-ROM searching.

Prerequisites
A basic understanding of database searching and use of print indexes.

Materials needed
New York Times Index for 1992 (or similar print index)
Work station with *New York Times Index* (UMI) loaded
New York Times on microfilm
Microfilm reader/printer

Procedure
(1.) Lead a discussion about how research has changed in recent years; how we have moved from print to electronic indexes.
(2.) Tell students; today we are going to have a race. Two groups are going to compete to see who can find information faster. An obituary can be a wonderful source of biographical information. Obituaries in the *New York Times* are especially thorough and well-respected. The prolific author Isaac Asimov died in 1992. Each of our groups will attempt to find his obituary.
(3.) Assign two groups of three students to be the racers. One from each group might be the spokesperson to describe problems as the search progresses.
(4.) Supervise groups of searches and solicit helpful ideas from onlookers. Students searching the print index under "Asimov" will be led to "see references" under "Books and Literature," and they will then have to decide which citation will be the obituary and interpret the citation to determine which microfilm reel they will need and in which part of the paper their article is located.
(5.) Students searching the electronic index will need to make certain decisions: Should Asimov be searched as a keyword, or is the name in the subject index? How can I isolate the obituary (browse through all articles on Asimov or search "Asimov and death")? In any case, it should take significantly less time to perform the search electronically and retrieve the full text.
(6.) Gather the racers with the rest of the group following the demonstration to discuss results. What was the time difference? Are the print users eager to return to the print index? What searching problems occurred in both groups? Although the electronic index was probably much faster, are there any reasons it might be better to use the manual index?

Evaluation
The librarian evaluates the group based on their participation during the "race" and participation during discussion.

Comments
This lesson has worked well for me with parents and board members. The adults got easily frustrated with the print index and thought CD-ROM a justifiable purchase. The activity may be adjusted to include more students by proposing additional searches. Have other groups compare SIRS electronic index to the indexes in the print notebooks or both versions of *Facts on File*. Others might compare *Readers' Guide* to TOM, *ResourceOne*, or *Magazine Article Summaries*. Comparisons of these resources would be most effective with problems involving combination of two concepts (e.g., cooking in China). In your conclusion try to emphasize there may be some valid reasons to choose a print index first. For example, *Readers' Guide* allows you to focus on a one-year period and provides archival indexing not yet available electronically.

Notes

Tips and Other Bright Ideas

Make Keyboarding Cool at Your School

To motivate students to improve their keyboarding skills, have a contest every couple of months and award prizes to those who type the fastest with the fewest mistakes. -*Tim Vermillion Marshall Middle School, Wexford, Pennsylvania*

Self-tutorials for Make-up Work

For students who need to "make up" library research work, prepare detailed, self-tutorial instruction sheets for each CD-ROM database. Ask some students to proof the sheets to ensure that directions are easy to read and that no steps have been omitted. Print sheets for each database on a different colored paper; then laminate the sheets. Store the color-coded sheets in labeled stacking trays near the computers, and encourage students to use the computers independently. Following these guides should reduce the need for staff assistance. -*Jeanne Minetree, Dinwiddie (Virginia) High School*

Coming Prepared

During the first few months after our computer catalog was installed, the question most asked was "How do you spell...?" Invariably the question had to be answered more than once as the student laboriously wrote down the spelling. (Yes, the computer would get close to the selection if the word was misspelled, but it wasn't close enough for some youngsters.) Now, during our computer catalog instruction, we emphasize that the youngsters should come prepared with the subjects, authors, or titles that they wish to look up, written on a piece of paper. Even the youngest students have more success with their searches. -*Sharron L. McElmeel, Harrison Elementary, Cedar Rapids, Iowa*

Bibliography Cards for CD-ROMS

Using the citations form required by teachers, I have printed bibliography cards for every CD-ROM program available to students. The cards are displayed on a bulletin board located near the computers. When students are using a program, they can easily copy the bibliographic information in one sitting.-*Robyn L. Matthews, Thomas E. Harrington Middle School, Mt. Laurel, New Jersey*

Create a Nifty Database

I set up a database in Microsoft Works for different Internet sites that includes the site, address, curriculum area, and any special notes such as login commands. I have it open when I am on the Internet (particularly when I am on LM_NET). This way, I can easily cut and paste any interesting sites mentioned into the database. I am getting quite a collection that I can easily sort for reference and share with staff. -*Rosemary Knapp, Camas (Washington) High School*

CD-ROM Instructions on Jewel Box

We have many CD-ROMs being checked out at the circulation desk for use on a particular computer. We have attached an instruction card to the jewel box that gives the computer number to be used and the specifics needed to enter the particular program.
Peggy La Porte, Marquette High School, Chesterfield, Missouri

Signs at Circulation Stations

On the walls near the computer stations I've placed signs with pictures to help children spell the subjects they're looking up. Example: Dinosaur would be printed out with a picture of a dinosaur on it. I used Print Shop (Broderbund) to make the signs. Children find the books they need quicker. This enables more students to use the stations. - *Louise Warren, Beaverbrook Elementary School, Griffin, Georgia*

How to Publish a Practically Painless Computer Manual

Stumped about how to put together all those computer how-to's into a manual? Here's how we did it at Appomattox County High School. We collected all the procedures and troubleshooting helps and organized them this way:

Managing the Network:

how-to's for taking down the file server in case of storm, bringing it back up, adding network or faculty users, assigning rights, and making backups.

Operating the Network Lab:

procedures for opening in the morning, closing at the end of the day, dating and installing ribbons in specific printers, formatting disks, and managing print functions.

Using the Automated Circulation System:

how to start the system and move from screen to screen, how to check in and check out

books, how to locate the daily backup disk, how to remove a find, how to shut down the system, and how to use the automated card catalog stations. More complex jobs like adding patrons, printing reports, and creating MARC records should be included also.

Using the Windows Environment:

procedures for checking and resetting the mouse control, resetting default printers for applications, accessing various applications, and moving through Windows using keystrokes in case a mouse dies.

Using CD-ROMs:

a troubleshooting guide, how to install updates, and how to add local titles or users. Write your guide using simple, step-by-step instructions, type it double-spaced and give a draft to each library/computer lab staff member. Ask for feedback from each person and urge them to use the wide margins and intervening spaces to make corrections and additions. Revise again and again until no discrepancies can be found. I put the manual in a binder that can also hold computer lab seating charts, equipment inventories, and problem (error message) logs. -*Nancy B. Williams Appomattox (Virginia) County High School*

Notes

Using the Internet for Research

The most exciting research tool at our disposal today is, without a doubt, the Internet. It is also a challenge to teach students how to find, evaluate, and utilize its resources efficiently and effectively.

For decades the research tools whose uses we teach have been fairly static. Colors of bindings changed, or a publication might be bought by a new publisher and issued with a slightly different arrangement or index. But once you instructed a class on how to use a particular book or CD-ROM, that item wouldn't change the next time a student picked it up.

Not so with the Internet! Three years ago I attended a workshop that stressed VERONICA and gopher files. I don't think I've heard those terms five times since. Searching and accessing the information on the Net are becoming increasingly user-friendly. Sites that were recommended in various (recent!) publications I rely on no longer exist, or have new URLs, when I sit down to access them with a student. The information that was in a site yesterday *could* be completely different today. And there is no guarantee that a site that held no potentially sensitive or objectionable material, or links to such material, on the day you discovered it, will remain pure.

In addition, the Internet is like a massive galley proof of a reference book without an index. Keyword and Boolean searching usually get you where you want to go. But there have been scary times when I've found what I wanted by misspelling (sometimes on purpose, sometimes accidentally) my search term.

The Internet is also like a bookstore where scholarly reference is intershelved with the wordless picture books, and the covers don't always indicate which item you've chosen. (I was about to compare it to a library rather than a bookstore, but a library implies more selection and evaluation, and more organization.) My seventh graders were thrilled to find a site that claimed to offer information on many varieties of whales, with all the characteristics and information they needed for their reports. When we got into it, we discovered that the site had been created by second graders, complete with charming illustrations. My class needed something with more authority. Now that I have more experience, I'd probably pick up this detail about the site's source right from the URL. But propaganda and downright misinformation abound on the Web in sites that look legitimate at first glance.

Add to all of this the sheer volume of information available on the Net-and students' propensity for printing *everything* and looking through it later, if at all. Many of my students want *every* picture of, say, a cheetah, that they can find on the three or four CD-ROM encyclopedias available to them; in addition, printing an entire article involves so much less brainwork (especially given limited time) than highlighting pertinent sections. What they find on the Internet simply overwhelms these youngsters.

Some of the initial articles I've included here are designed for staff development programs. They are here rather than in the chapter on staff development because they offer ideas and skills applicable to teaching students as well as teachers; the rubrics are interchangeable.

When we teach searching, we need to address *pre*-skills before our students ever sit down at the keyboard. We need to brainstorm keywords and their synonyms, review Boolean searching, and examine the similarities and differences among the search engines and directories available. Pre-searching and bookmarking useful sites keep students focused, but kids are kids. When I do this, there is always at least one student who has a question we can't answer in the sites I've selected. We can't pre-select the sites forever; at some point, we have to teach students how to do the searches themselves, as efficiently and effectively as possible. I would like to see a study done someday comparing the Internet search strategies and success rate of a library media specialist with that of someone who is proficient in the use of computers and the Net but not trained as we are in research skills. I think such a study would do our profession proud.

I enjoy visiting the home pages of libraries and schools. In many schools, the room that generates the home page is the library media center. Sometimes the library media specialist is the creator and curator; sometimes it's another faculty member. Students are often involved in choosing what will appear on their school's page, and how it will look. As in creating multimedia presentations, this activity offers a wonderful learning opportunity in research, creative writing, and design. New software is making the mastery of HTML less and less necessary, but familiarity with its codes remains useful.

The school's home page can also be a teaching tool. Some of the best I've seen include recommended reading lists, summaries of each teacher's assignments, brief tutorials on using research sources, samples of student work, and exciting educational links. We can instruct students on how to make a home page, but we can also instruct *through* a well-designed home page.

The potential of e-mail as an instructional tool was one of the first uses of the Internet recognized by elementary teachers. Youngsters can write to experts in fields of interest, to favorite authors, and to fellow students around the world. But, as some of the authors of these articles point out, we cannot simply turn young people loose in cyberspace and expect happy results. Few children have had the experience of writing *real* letters to a *real* person, although they may have composed dummy letters for a class unit. They may not be aware of what is or is not appropriate to say or ask in correspondence; they may not have had the experience of *human emotional response* to something they have written. In addition, e-mail assumes its own rules of "Netiquette," which students need to learn.

The Internet should make librarians feel good about themselves, in a backhanded-compliment sort of way. Much has been written about misinformation on the Web, about the public's blind acceptance of the truth of whatever they read or see on the Internet. I wonder if libraries are not inadvertently to blame for this gullibility! For years we have offered information services on computers: CD-ROMs, online catalogs, and the like. And we are as careful as possible to ensure that the information we give our public, through books, magazines, and controllable computer programs, is accurate. Then we offer the public the Internet, and the public assumes that this, too, should be as accurate as the library's other resources. We've long taught critical thinking skills-distinguishing fact from opinion, checking the credentials of an author for bias, considering the copyright date. With the Internet, these evaluative skills are more essential than ever. We need to teach a guarded cynicism.

The Internet is still in its infancy. It's an exciting tool that can become better. Teaching young people to use it, and to create on it, even as it evolves, is a challenge.

URL UPDATES

The World Wide Web in Three Lessons:
   The Akhnet Internet
   www.akhnet.freeserve.co.uk/

SCORE One for Students and Teachers:
   http://score.rims.k12.ca.us/

Search Engines Become Another Unit in Library Skills:
   Magellan
   http://magellan.excite.com/

   Lui, Jian.. "Understanding WWW Search Tools."
   www.indiana.edu/~librscol/search/

   Tyner, Ross. "Sink or Swim: Internet search tools & techniques."
   www.ouc.bc.ca/libr/connect96/search.htm

Creat Your Own Home Page: A Step-by-Step Guide:
   Web Power Index of Icons and Graphics
   http://www.webcom.com/html/icons.shtml

   http://www.lme.mankato.msus.edu/ded/ssv.html

   "A Beginner's Guide to HTML"
   www.wilsoninternet.com/packages/

Integrating E-mail into the Curriculum:
   JASON
   www.jasonproject.org/

Seduced and Abandoned on the Web:
   Kathy Schrock's excellent Educator's Guide site
   www.discoveryschool.co.com/schrockguide/

   Duke Univeristy's Guide
   www.lib.duke_edu/libguide/evaluating.htm

   The UCLA evaluation guidelines, required of students in certain courses...
   www.library.ucla.edu/libraries/college/instruct/web/critical.htm

   SITES THAT ARE "FALSE FOR USE IN DEMONSTRATIONS
   www./me.mankato.msus.edu/NewHartford/newhtfd.html

It Must Be True. I Found It on the Internet!:
   FDR Cartoon Collection
   www.wizvax.net/nisk_hs/fdr/index.html

   www.discoveryschool.com/schrockguide/eval.htm

   Kathy Schrock's Guide for Educators
   www.discoveryschool.com/schrockguide/

Producing Information Consumers: Critical Evaluation and Critical Thinking:
   Milton's Web
   <http://milton.mse.jhu.edu:8001/research/education/net.html>

   Evaluation tools for students....
   www.discoveryschool.com/schrockguide/eval.htm

Notes

INTERNET SKILL RUBRICS FOR TEACHERS

While needed skills for using the Internet seem to change almost daily, they can be used as a starting point for measuring staff competencies.

By Doug Johnson

THE INTERNET has blown onto the education scene like a tornado. Local, state, and national initiatives are howling for classrooms to be "wired" to this massive information resource. But like all tools, the Internet does little good unless it is used skillfully and purposely. Media specialists and classroom teachers need formal training in its use. The following rubrics will help staff development designers plan and measure educators' effective Internet use.

Not long ago, formal instruction about the Internet focused primarily on how to use a wide variety of specialized tools for locating and retrieving files. Tools like gophers, newsreaders, e-mail programs, telnet, and ftp were all dedicated to single tasks and each required extensive training in its use. Now most Internet resources can be easily accessed using a properly configured Internet browser like Netscape or Explorer. The specialized tools have become modules built into these powerful programs. For all but the most demanding Internet users, a web browser configured with some "helper applications" will be the only tool needed for Internet.

The interface to the Internet has changed dramatically as well. Only a few years ago the Internet was accessed almost exclusively through text-based interfaces running on large computers to which one's workstation only served as a "dumb terminal." This model of access has been largely replaced by workstation-based programs that use the workstation's processing power to provide point-and-click simplicity of use and to display information in colorful formats that include text styles and fonts, graphics, sounds, animations, and digital video. "Streaming" is quickly allowing Internet users to play music and hear discussions. Using the Internet as a telephone is becoming more common. "Push" technologies deliver up-to-the-minute news, weather, and business information to one's desktop, relieving the user of the responsibility of finding and retrieving it.

These changes in access and content have allowed Internet instructional time to be spent less on:

- How do I find files and data?
- How do I use specific Internet tools?
- How do I download the information to my computer?

And increasingly on:

- How can I focus my searches?
- How can I determine if the information is accurate?

Article continues on page 40 after Teacher Instructions for Internet Skill Rubrics

Teacher Instructions for Internet Skill Rubrics

Please judge your level of achievement in each of the following competencies. Circle the number that best reflects your current level of skill attainment. (Be honest, but be kind.) At the end of the training program, you will complete the same set of rubrics that will reflect your level of skill attainment at that time. (Level 3 is considered mastery.) This tool is to help measure the effectiveness of our training program, and to help you do a self-analysis to determine the areas in which you should continue to learn and practice. Keep a copy of these rubrics to refer to during the training.

This is an anonymous assessment. You do not need to sign the pre- or post-evaluation tool. Individual results will be aggregated to determine how effective the program has been for the group as a whole. You should, however, keep track of your own individual progress.

1. Internet basics

Level 1 - I do not understand how networks work, nor can I identify any personal or professional uses for networks, including the Internet. I do not have an account on any network nor would I know how to get one.

Level 2 - I can identify some personal or professional uses for networks, and understand they have a value to my students and me. I've read some articles about the Internet in the popular press. I can directly use network access to a library catalog or CD-ROM.

Level 3 - I can describe what a computer network does and how it can be useful personally and professionally. I can distinguish between a local area network, a wide area network, and the Internet and can describe educational uses for each. I can describe the history of the Internet, recognize its international character, and know, to a degree, the extent of its resources. I have personal access to the Internet that allows me to receive and send e-mail, download files, and access the World Wide Web. I know that I must protect my password, and should restrict access by others to my account.

Level 4 - I use networks on a daily basis to access and communicate information. I can serve as an active participant in a school or organizational planning group, giving advice and providing information about networks. I can recommend to others several ways of obtaining Internet access.

2. E-mail and electronic mailing lists

Level 1 - I do not use e-mail.

Level 2 - I understand the concept of e-mail and can explain some administrative and educational uses for it.

Level 3 - I use e-mail regularly and can:
- read and delete messages
- send, forward and reply to messages
- create nicknames, mailing lists, and a signature file
- send and receive attachments
- use electronic mailing lists and understand the professional uses of them
- read and contribute to a professional electronic mailing list

Level 4 - I can send group mailings and feel confident that I could administer an electronic mailing list. I use activities that require e-mail in my teaching. I can locate lists of subject-oriented mailing lists.

3. The World Wide Web

Level 1 - I do not use the World Wide Web.

Level 2 - I am aware that the World Wide Web is a means of sharing information on the Internet. I can browse the Web for recreational purposes.

Level 3 - I can use a Web browser like Explorer or Netscape to find information on the World Wide Web and can list some of the Web's unique features. I can explain the terms: hypertext, URL, http, and html. I can write URLs to share information locations with others. I can use Web search engines to locate subject specific information and can create bookmarks to Web sites of educational value.

Level 4 - I can configure my web browser with a variety of helper applications. I understand what "cookies" do and whether to keep them enabled. I can speak to the security issues of on-line commerce and data privacy.

4. Search tools

Level 1 - I cannot locate any information on the Internet.

Level 2 - I can occasionally locate useful information on the Internet by browsing or through remembered sources.

Level 3 - I can conduct an efficient search of Internet resources using directories like Yahoo or search engines like Excite, Lycos, or Infoseek. I can use advanced search commands to specify and limit the number of hits I get. I can state some guidelines for evaluating the information I find on the Internet and can write a bibliographic citation for information found.

Level 4 - I can identify some specialized search tools for finding software and e-mail addresses. I can speculate on future developments in on-line information searching including know-bots and other kinds of intelligent search agents.

5. Newsgroups, gophers and telnet

Level 1 - I have no knowledge of newsgroups, gophers, or telnet functions.

Level 2 - I know that there are resources in a variety of formats available on the Internet, but cannot confidently access them.

Level 3 - I read the newsgroups that interest me on a regular basis, and I can contribute to newsgroups.

I understand the use of gophers and can locate several that help me. I can write directions to locating a gopher so that others can find it as well. I can access a remote computer through the telnet command, including remote library catalogs. I can find the help screens when emulating remote computers and can log off properly.

Level 4 - I know how to find, configure, and use the specialized tools for newsgroups, gophers, and telnet access. I use the resources found in these areas with my students.

6. Obtaining, decompressing, and using files

Level 1 - I cannot retrieve files from remote computers.

Level 2 - I know that documents and computer programs that are useful to my students and me are stored on computers throughout the world. I cannot retrieve these files.

Level 3 - I understand the concept and netiquette of "anonymous FTP" sites. I can transfer files and programs from remote locations to my computer, and can use programs or plug-ins that help me do this. I can extract compressed files, and know some utilities that help me view graphics and play sounds and movies. I understand the nature and danger of computer viruses, and know how to minimize my risk of contracting a computer virus.

Level 4 - I use information I have retrieved as a resource for and with my students. I understand the concept of a network server, and the functions it can serve in an organization. I can use an ftp client to upload files to a server.

7. Real-time and push technologies

Level 1 - I use only static documents and files I retrieve from the Internet.

Level 2 - I have some information sent to me on a regular basis through e-mail and I check some sites on a regular basis for information.

Level 3 - I use chat-rooms and customized news and information feeds. I can listen to audio streamed from the web. I know the hardware and software requirements for web-based videoconferencing.

Level 4 - I can use real-time applications to design a "virtual" classroom or interactive learning experience. My students use videoconferencing for communication with experts and project collaboration with other students.

8. Web page construction

Level 1 - I cannot create a page which can be viewed with a web browser.

Level 2 - I can save text I've created as an html file with a command in my word processor. I know a few, simple html commands.

Level 3 - Using hand-coded html or a web page authoring tool, I can:
- view Web pages as source documents
- create a formatted web page that uses background color, font styles and alignment, graphics, and tables
- include links to other parts of my document or other Internet sites in my page
- know basic guidelines for good web page construction and the district's web policies

Level 4 - I can use the web as an interface to databases. When appropriate, I can register my pages with search engine sites. I can help write web creation policies for design, content, and use.

9. Learning opportunities using the Internet

Level 1 - I am not aware of any ways the Internet can be used with students in my classroom.

Level 2 - I occasionally allow my students to use the Internet to find information.

Level 3 - I know a variety of projects and activities that effectively use the Internet to instruct and involve students. I know a source for collaborative projects, can direct students to on-line tutorials and learning resources, and encourage a variety of key-pal activities.

Level 4 - I can design and implement an Internet project or maintain an educational Internet site.

10. Netiquette, On-line Ethics, and Current Issues Surrounding Internet Use in K-12 Schools

Level 1 - I am not aware of any ethics or proprieties regarding the Internet, nor am I aware of any issues dealing with Internet use in a school setting.

Level 2 - I understand a few rules that my students and I should follow when using the Internet. I understand that the Internet is sometimes a controversial resource which many educators and parents do not understand.

Level 3 - I have read a guideline for Internet use such as Rinaldi's "The Net: User Guidelines and Netiquette" or other source, and follow the rules outlined. I know and read the FAQ files associated with sources on the Internet. I am aware that electronic communication is a new communications medium that may require new sensitivities. I can identify print and on-line resources that speak to current Internet issues like:
- censorship/site blocking software
- copyright
- legal and illegal uses
- data privacy
- security

I can list some of the critical components of a good Acceptable Use Policy and know and use our district's.

Level 4 - I can use my knowledge of the Internet to write good school policies and activities that help students develop good judgment and good information skills.

- How do I interpret and take meaning from the information?
- How do I use and communicate the information within an educational setting?
- How do I prepare my information so it can be displayed on the Internet?
- How do I construct meaningful activities for students using Internet resources?

The older skills, while at times frustrating to teach, were easier to master! Over the past six years, I have used variations of these rubrics working with teachers and media specialists. While the needed skills for using the Internet seem to change almost daily, they can be used as a starting point for measuring staff competencies. The Internet rubrics, along with support materials including class outcomes, portfolio suggestions, training tips, and other resources, can be found in my book, *The Indispensable Teacher's Guide to Computer Skills*, Linworth, 1998. The book also contains ten basic computer literacy rubrics and ten advanced computer use rubrics, all with support materials.

Each of the Internet rubrics has four levels:

Level 1: Pre-awareness
Level 2: Awareness
Level 3: Mastery
Level 4: Advanced

Prior to training, we assume most teachers are at level 1 or 2, and our district's training efforts are designed with that assumption. By the end of the training, we anticipate teachers will be at level 3 or 4 in most skill areas, and have gone up at least one level in all areas. At minimum, 30 hours of direct instruction are needed for the mastery of all ten competency areas. These rubrics, then, serve two purposes:

- By asking teachers to complete an anonymous self-assessment using the rubrics before training and again after training, we can judge the effectiveness of our staff development efforts. Simple graphs showing the percentage of training participants at each level pre- and post-training are constructed. These results can be shared with staff development committees and the administration.
- The rubrics also provide a "road map" for teachers wanting to improve their Internet skills. By examining the specific skills described, teachers know in what areas they need to practice or continue to take classes.

Please feel free to use and modify the rubrics for your district's specific needs and as technology changes. BR

Doug Johnson is the Director of Media and Technology at the Mankato (Minnesota) Area Public Schools and can be reached at johnsd9@mail.mankato.msus.edu

Notes

Internet Staff Development: A Continuum

By Mary Alice Anderson

In the beginning, classes were titled "What's the Internet?" "Let's Go Gophering," "Introduction to Browsers," "Using a Modem and SLIP Connection," and "What's E-mail?"

Since 1993 teacher needs and our staff development offerings have evolved and matured along the Internet. More recent offerings have focused on curriculum integration and issues, Web page design, and advanced technical skills needed to keep up with today's students as well as with the Internet.

Graduation standards present in many states and the new informantion literacy guidelines as described in Information Power II give added relevance to this second tier of classes.

The Internet's rapid change means that media/technology program staff at Winona (Minnesota) Middle School constantly strive to keep encouraging staff growth and awareness. We try to meet current needs, introduce staff to skills they didn't know they needed, and help them see that the Internet is just another resource but one with unique potential. The overall goal is always to prepare teachers to better provide relevant learning opportunities for their students, the first generation to grow up in an age of digital information.

With the Internet available throughout classrooms and labs, on 45 workstations in the media center, and in many homes, good skills are critical. Now that most staff have achieved the basics, emphasis is on the information and curricular aspects of the Internet.

We hope a synopsis of some of our popular classes will be useful as you plan your classes this school year. These classes are designed for beginning to advanced learners:

Technology Connection

Title: What's the Internet?

Audience: All staff, including paraprofessionals who have no experience using the Internet

Participant outcomes:
- Gain a general awareness of the Internet
- Learn how the school is connected to the Internet
- Learn basic Internet terminology
- Have a successful information-seeking experience

Teaching tips and reflections: Make sure everything works; anyone who is a skeptic will become more so if something fails. Provide a good vocabulary lesson and examples of how the Internet can be used in education. "What's the Internet?" works well as a combination demonstration and hands-on class. With the prevalence of the Internet in today's education, all educators should have at least this exposure. The class can help displace any misconceptions and create excitement in those who are reluctant to use technology. Even technophobes can have success. Encourage people to search for things they are interested in. One elementary teacher who is a true technophobe excitedly found information about Irish pubs and antiques. Another who was convinced the Internet was inappropriate for elementary children found information about a disease a colleague's child had, and yet another found a picture of her sister who was on a North Pole expedition. People will enjoy sharing what they've discovered.

Title: Navigating the Net Using Browsers

Audience: Staff who have surfed and want to learn how to get around

Participant outcomes:
- Learn how to use the items listed on the menu bar
- Learn how to move forward, back, set bookmarks
- Learn how to save and print files
- Learn how to search in a directed way

Teaching tips and reflections: If facilities allow, do the demonstration in a space away from the computer so eager searchers don't distract you and others. If this is not possible, respectfully ask them not to use the keyboard and mouse while you are demonstrating and talking. (I always tell staff that if they were students I'd ask them to sit on their hands.) Provide handouts that have screen shots and vocabulary words. If your audience has a large number of people with limited computer experience, be sure to have an assistant to help with basic computer skills such as using the mouse, moving among windows, and saving files. This is a fun class to teach because everyone can be successful and "newbies" get excited. The most excited and difficult group to control will be a group of teachers who haven't seen each other for a long time. Be patient.

The Internet's rapid change means that media/technology program staff constantly strive to keep encouraging staff growth and awareness.

Title: Advanced Browsers

Audience: People who have used browsers and are comfortable with the computer

Participant outcomes:
- Become comfortable with setting and organizing bookmark files
- Learn how to set personal browser preferences
- Learn how to copy and save graphics and text
- Become familiar with search capabilities
- Become aware of pitfalls of using the Internet and develop ideas for curriculum integration

Teaching tips and reflections: Encourage people to come with a search plan in mind, so they move beyond the exploration stage. Provide time for sharing and an opportunity to develop integrated activities. Provide disks and printer access.

Title: Introduction to E-mail

Audience: Everyone who has an e-mail connection on a regular basis should take this class. Others who have access should be encouraged

Participant outcomes:
- Learn the purpose of e-mail and how it works
- Learn how to configure personal settings and preferences
- Become comfortable with sending and receiving messages

Teaching tips and reflections: Surprisingly, a number of us have found that e-mail is not always easy to teach. There is often confusion between user names and passwords and protocols that disregard some of the rules of capitalization and punctuation we've always known. Remind people to come to the class knowing their password and user name, but don't be surprised if some forget. Set up a few generic (e.g., teacher1, teacher2) accounts to be used during class. Typical questions are "How can I find another person's e-mail address?" and "Where does my mail go?" Take time to answer these questions and explain technical aspects in a nontechnical way. Make sure everyone in the class has a successful experience receiving and sending messages. Encourage people to frequently interact with colleagues. If possible, take a field trip to show people the mail server and other Internet equipment; after people see the equipment, the level of understanding increases. Send follow-up messages to thank everyone for attending.

Notes

Title: Advanced E-mail

Audience: People who are comfortable sending and receiving e-mail

Participant outcomes:
- Learn to send, receive, and open attachments
- Learn to set up an address book entry to send a message to multiple recipients
- Learn to access e-mail from multiple computers
- Copy and paste between e-mail messages and between e-mail and another application
- Explore listservs and their use in education

Teaching tips and reflections: Sooner or later, every e-mail user will move beyond the basics, but only those thoroughly comfortable with sending and receiving are ready for advanced e-mail. Provide plenty of time for practice and to answer questions once participants have some experience. Set up practice files; these could include address files and graphic and text attachments.

FULL SPEED AHEAD ON THE INTERNET

Harnessing Internet Resources for the Student Researcher

by Carol Simpson

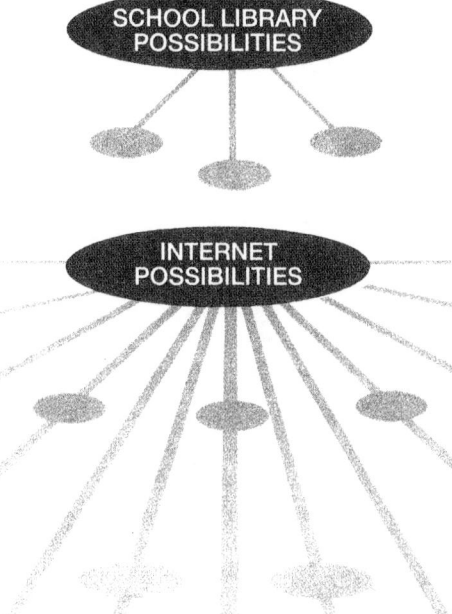

What the Internet entails and that it is an instructional resource, not a subject in itself, are two main concepts to understand before attempting to integrate the Net into a school's curriculum. New users sometimes have difficulty fathoming the expanse of the Internet's holdings. The school library may have one or two resources on a given topic. By contrast, the Internet may produce such a flood of information that the researcher is overwhelmed. And, if the researcher chooses to venture into the morass of data, the problem then becomes one of evaluating its quality and authenticity.

Compare the Internet to a large library. One wouldn't expect to be able to locate and retrieve all types of information at once. Learning to use the Internet is similar to learning to use a library; and, Internet skills, like library skills, are best taught in conjunction with real assignments. For example, for a lesson in maps one might look for atlases. For a lesson on weather, one might look for accurate and current Internet sites that provide constantly changing weather maps, radar data or temperatures. The actual resource, and even the type of resource, can be selected based on the lesson objectives, ages and maturity levels of the students, and the type of Internet connection available.

Selecting Services

Many users assume that using the Internet means using graphical browsers such as *Mosaic* or *Netscape*. These programs and their kin are powerful tools, but there are also other facets of the Internet that are appropriate for classroom use. Teachers should consider classroom organization before selecting tools. Will this be a cooperative and collaborative activity? Could there be work involving groups in different locations? E-mail, telephone, video or chat software might be appropriate for students in remote locations across town, across the country, or around the world who are working on joint projects.

Other projects might require more individual research. Especially in the middle grades, students are often permitted to select their own topics. Frequently students select topics for which the library has few, if any, resources. With the wealth of information on the Internet, especially on current topics, using one of the powerful Internet "search engines," software programs such as *AltaVista*, *Web Crawler*, *Lycos* or *Yahoo* will produce usable resources. All these "engines" are also available through nongraphical browsers such as *Lynx,* if your network connection does not support the heavy demands of graphics.

The age of the student is important when teaching Internet resources. Electronic mail lends itself well to interdisciplinary projects because writing, grammar and spelling skills come into play along with math, science or social studies content. Almost as soon as students begin to write, they can compose simple e-mail messages. Typing the message provides keyboarding practice, and sending it involves little risk of exposing students to inappropriate materials on the Internet, especially if the teacher establishes the correspondence between classes or locates and assigns keypals.

Other Internet tools such as gophers and Veronica permit students to locate information while training them in logical thinking and organization as they follow the sequence of menus. Intermediate students can navigate "nested" menus if they know there is a gem buried within. (Nested menus lead to other menus.)

Here are a few questions to ask before choosing the type of Internet service to introduce:

- What is the age of the student? Older students may be able to choose and use Internet services more accurately than younger ones.
- What is the goal of the lesson? Does this type of information support this goal?
- Can the Internet work effectively with the classroom organization pattern? Do students work alone? In groups?
- How will the lesson be evaluated? Student paper handed in? Group presentation? Project format? Can the information retrieved be used successfully to support the final product?
- Will students require graphics for their final product?

Evaluating Sources

The Internet is not always the best source of information for every topic. Research can still be successfully conducted in a traditional print library. The idea is to offer the Internet as another source, just as one would search *Readers' Guide*, the card catalog or the vertical file. The student then must evaluate the information and select the most appropriate information to support the thesis of the paper or project.

Students can use one of several models to evaluate an Internet site to determine its accuracy and authority. Teachers must also evaluate sites for appropriateness, content and presentation. Here are some questions to ask when selecting an Internet resource for a specific assignment:

- Does this site have all the necessary information for this assignment? If not, what will the student use to fill in the gaps?
- Is the reading level of the site appropriate for the students? Many sites are put up by and for university students who may use sophisticated vocabulary.
- Does the site offer links to games, chat rooms, or popular culture not associated with the assignment? Will students be lured from their task?
- Is the site reliable? Can you count on it to be up and active during your class time?
- Is the site heavily graphic? Some schools may find that accessing the graphic-intensive sites can be slow. Consider turning off graphics, using a text-only browser, or sticking with text-based resources such as gopher.
- Does this site have a search engine? How can a student locate additional information buried under several layers of pages? An index or search capability makes it simpler for students (especially young students) to be successful searchers.
- If you have a student who is not permitted to use the Internet, what resources will be available for him to use to complete the assignment?

Integrating the Internet into the curriculum is much like teaching library skills. The key is knowing what to teach, how to teach it, who is going to learn it, and why it is important. Thanks to new, comprehensive search engines, locating the resources will be simple. The hard part comes when students attempt to select the best information from the wealth that is available.

Carol Simpson is the Editor of TECHNOLOGY CONNECTION.

Notes

FULL SPEED AHEAD ON THE INTERNET

Guidelines for Using the Internet

by Mary Alice Anderson and Cathleen Wharton

A few basic tips can go a long way in making sure students and staff have a successful Internet experience. These guidelines are intended as a checklist and reminders of some of the things to consider before implementing a class project. They were developed by myself and Cathleen Wharton of U S WEST Advanced Technologies, Boulder, Colorado. These guidelines are appropriate to all research and a reminder that the Internet is an information resource to be used with an information objective in mind. Students will usually be more successful if the teacher or media specialist gives them good directions and instruction before beginning a search.

Mary Alice Anderson is a Media Specialist at Winona (Minnesota) Middle School.

The checklist can be downloaded from:

http://wms.luminet.net/training/maryalice/guidelines.html.

The training Web site (http://wms.luminet.net/training) also includes teacher and student activity guides and the slide show "Making Successful Internet Connections," which may be used for staff development.

Teachers, have you

☐ selected more than one relevant World Wide Web site?

☐ set bookmarks or Web pages on the computers or saved a bookmark file to disk?

☐ designed "thinking" questions for the students?

☐ instructed the students in the mechanics of using the Internet (explained menus, taught them how to save, and download text and graphics)?

☐ provided instruction about search strategies?

☐ explained that all search engines do not provide the same results?

☐ instructed the students in how to save/export bookmarks, download files and print only what is necessary?

☐ scheduled the use of the computer labs or computers?

☐ scheduled the use of projection devices?

☐ made sure the necessary helper applications (such as graphic converters and other tools to help) are installed on the computers?

☐ arranged for team-teaching with the media or technology specialists or others who can assist you?

☐ talked with the students about Netiquette, including guidelines for downloading, saving, and printing?

☐ developed "Plan B," for students who cannot use the Internet or in case there are technical problems?

☐ included Internet-specific directions to your students such as...

  ☐ Did you pay careful attention to the instructions?

  ☐ Did you look at all of the resources your teacher has pointed you to?

  ☐ Did you record or bookmark URLs and any information you might want to use later?

  ☐ Have you recorded information you will cite in your bibliography?

  ☐ Did you answer all of the questions using your own words?

  ☐ Did you investigate only project-related sites?

SEARCHING

How to Teach the 'Net

By Lesley S.J. Farmer

Internet has been described as a room full of books scattered all over the floor, with someone saying, "Go ahead and dig around—there are some great treasures." No wonder librarians are inclined to look with horror at the relative chaos of the Internet world!

How do we teach access to this ephemerous cloud of data? As with other reference tools, we must first learn to navigate it ourselves. Instruction methods include courses, conferences, collegial help, manuals, and—last but not least—cyberspace surfing.

Learn with a Collaborator

When teaching others, the key is hands-on, regardless of group size. For a large class, you can prepare simulated Internet sessions for the group to follow if phone access is a problem.

As you begin training, remember that those working closest with you can bounce back ideas most easily, and help you polish your delivery. In fact, for novice Internet-navigating librarians, collaborative exploratory sessions with a staff member or strong student aide techie are often the best method of instruction through learning.

There are two viewpoints about how to teach the Internet. One view holds that the Internet is a tool and access to it should be taught the same way that we might teach the characteristics of a dictionary. The other view is that application should drive the instruction, just as curiosity about a current event leads to instruction on how to use a magazine index.

Show the Entire Process

In the tool model, the learner tends to browse the Internet for interesting "stuff." In the latter, a subject approach is used in instruction. In either case, learners need to see the entire process: log-on, search strategy, database/file location, document retrieval and downloading, and log-off. They also need to see the breadth of sources: from weather forecasts to movie reviews, from Spanish-language news to Project Gutenberg, from educator chat sessions to federal health reform documents, from ephemeral memos to Steven King's latest book online.

To assure good results in front of your audience, it's a good idea to store successful searches ahead of time, using bookmarks or personal folders. You can also save searches using file or screen dumps and later print out those search sessions to use as examples for your learners.

Learners also need to see the structure of the library's Internet gateway or "access road" and what applications are provided: e-mail, electronic bulletin boards, conferences, remote sites, online databases, and file transfer protocol (FTP). In fact, most telecommunications services include far more than Internet access. How are applications linked? Does front-end software enable the user to develop a search offline? These questions need to be answered when instructing users.

Include Theory and Practice

Instruction should strike a balance between theory and practice. Each concept should be introduced, explained, and tested out. A basic glossary is also a must. Other training aids include "cheat sheets" of commands, sample searches, lists of recommended Internet sources, and simulation tutorial disks. Overhead transparencies of Internet sessions are valuable backups when phone busy signals or equipment failures hinder instruction. Training sessions can also be videotaped and used again later.

The other major component of instruction should be to design lessons that complement the curriculum. The most satisfying approach is to work with an enthusiastic teacher to plan a model Internet session based on up-

Continued on page 4

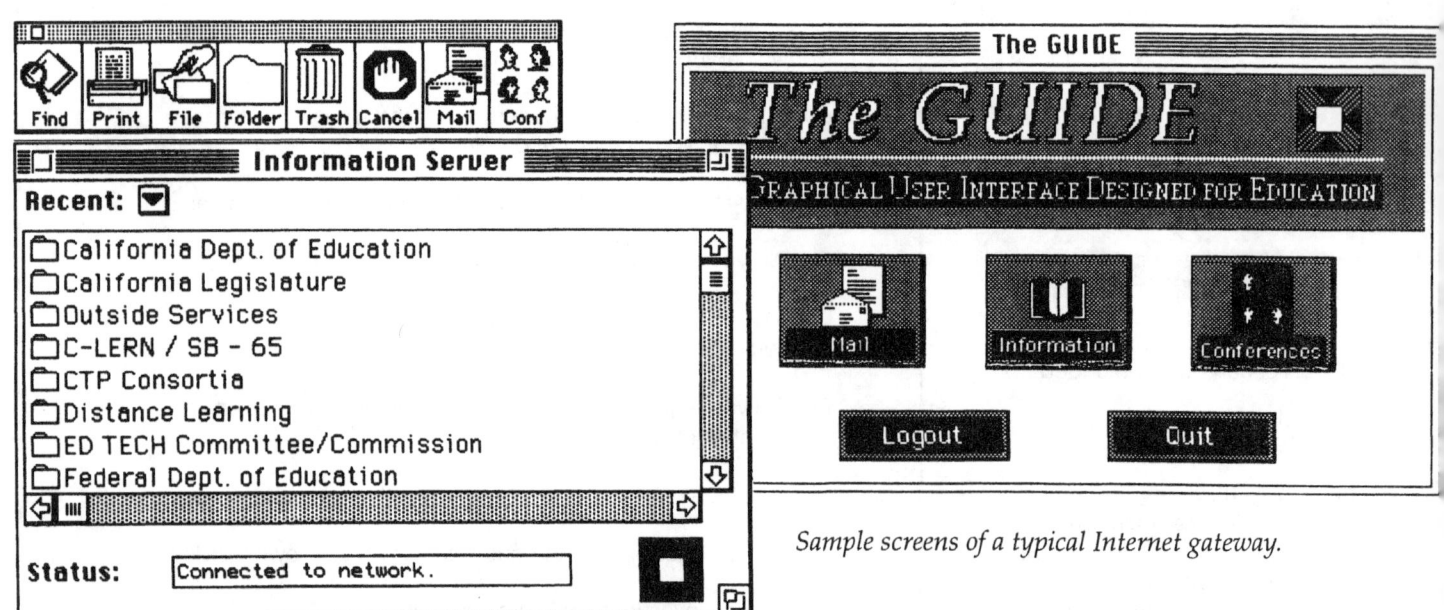

Sample screens of a typical Internet gateway.

Reprinted with permission of The California State University GINA™ project.

Continued from page 3

coming coursework, i.e., a unit on dinosaurs for which you can search the Internet for relevant sources. Current digs may be documenting their findings on the Internet (which is actually a common practice among those enthusiasts, perhaps because of "Jurassic Park.")

You can document and download those sessions to share with the teacher to illustrate Internet navigation methods. Even if the teacher is reluctant to personally use the Internet, you can suggest that he appoint a few students to act as Internet navigators for the class. If research is done in small cooperative groups, one student in each group can act as the Internet expert.

Build a Team of Student Navigators

Now let's look at making the best use of library instruction time. After a general discussion about searching for information, gather the student Internet navigators and show them how the system operates. Pull out saved searches with high-quality Internet "hits," and show them what information is available to them. Then let students loose, guiding them on their searches. As the searching progresses, have students describe what they are doing so everyone can see how search strategies evolve. Have them share what is happening as databases and files are located.

To save connect time charges, have students download what they've found to read later. After finishing the online session, students can copy the downloaded files onto personal diskettes to be further evaluated at personal computer workstations.

One benefit of this instructional approach is that a cadre of student Internet navigators is built naturally, and their expertise can be transferred to other coursework. They can also train their peers in Internet operations, thus freeing up valuable librarian instructional time. These same students are often the best instructors for their own classroom teachers. An Internet navigator card serves as a simple document to allow responsible students access to direct Internet connectability—and accountability.

Be Playful, Take Risks

Perhaps the most important factor in Internet instruction is risk-taking, by learners and librarians. We must take time to "play" in the Internet world, to make mistakes, and to cheerfully risk teaching others about this unruly and exciting tool. TC

Lesley S.J. Farmer is the Library Director of Redwood High School in Larkspur, California. She is the author of Creative Partnerships: Librarians and Teachers Working Together, *published by Linworth Publishing, Inc.*

Notes

Partnering With Teachers For Internet Incorporation

By Lesley S. J. Farmer

Librarians need to carve out time to explore the Net and create Internet-rich products, such as interactive presentations on information literacy skills.

THE INTERNET IS NEW enough that some teachers still have misconceptions about its usefulness in education. While some view it as a panacea that contains all the information students need, others worry that students will merely download required assignments and will not develop critical thinking skills. And some teachers are even more skeptical about the Internet, believing either that it contains mostly rubbish or that it is more difficult to search than library shelves.

While these perspectives have validity, they are overreaching in their generality. Librarians who have worked with the Internet, and especially those who have helped students navigate the ether waves, have both blessed and cursed the Net and know that its viability depends on several factors:

- the information desired
- the ability of the user
- the access in terms of time and speed
- the teacher—through the content objectives, direct instruction (method and time), incorporation of the Internet into class activities, and the teacher's own ability to use the Internet.

At this point, all teachers should be comfortable with the Internet, but they may not have a full grasp of all the fine points. Teachers act similarly with the library's print collection. They tend to specialize in their own field of knowledge and typically do not know the entire DDC system or see the variety of incoming periodical articles. Savvy teachers plan with the librarian because they realize the librarian can make important connections with sources to broaden opportunities for student learning. Compare the limited number of access tools and strategies available to a print collection with the vast array of search engines and other access methods for Internet sources. Theoretically, teachers should be even more apt to work with Internet-experienced librarians in order to maximize student learning. Sadly, this is not always the case.

Since nothing succeeds like success, librarians who want to insure the incorporation of technology need to offer concrete ways for teachers to use media effectively. By building bridges for technology-based partnerships, librarians can provide better service and attain a higher professional reputation. Students will learn more.

Access to the Internet

Beginning Internet users can waste lots of time trying to find good information. Given enough time, most students can develop a sense of what is valuable on the Net, but in a one-hour class, especially where students have to share computer access, such time-intensive browsing doesn't result in immediate returns, and a student's grades may suffer in the short term. Particularly for students without home access to the Internet, every minute counts when the teacher schedules library Internet time. What's a student or teacher to do?

If the content objective is to glean information about a certain topic, then bookmarking good Web sites is a logical step. Of course, that means the teacher must let the librarian know ahead of time about the assignment, so the librarian has time to uncover good sites to be bookmarked. Obviously, the more detail the teacher can give the librarian, the closer the fit of the Web sites. Are pictures needed? Are primary sources preferred? Would sound bites be useful? Is a narrative or short-fact approach preferable? The more closely aligned sites are with the assignment, the easier it is for students to extract the information and see what constitutes as a good site.

Ideally, bookmarks can be stored on a disk and imported to all of the Internet-accessible computer systems. However, if labs are located away from the library, the librarian either has to give the disk to the teacher or aide or find a way to put the information on the local area network. As a quick fix, the librarian can print a Web site poster to be posted in each appropriate room. She also can develop and distribute a Webliography, listing both print and non-print sources along with Web sites. In these cases, the students must type in the addresses. While they may make mistakes, the kinesthetic process can help reinforce these valuable Internet addresses.

If the library has its own Web page, then lists of bookmarks and Webliographies can be easily imported onto the Net. With today's word processing programs, such as Word 97, simple documents can be saved as HTML files for easy Web inclusion. As an added benefit, such HTML documents can be read on either Macintosh or PC platforms. I also have put handouts and Webliographies in "common" folders for network access; however, the typical user didn't know how to convert the information into readable form.

Too busy to hunt for Web sites? CD-ROMs are now linking their content to the Net. Britannica's Encyclopedia, Grolier's Americana, and Microsoft Encarta are examples of offline encyclopedias that link to online information. Britannica also provides thousands of pre-selected Web sites through its Web site.

Pro-active Internet Use

If the librarian waits for the teacher to take the first step, then the library will be seen as a reactive place, rather than a vanguard of technology integration. Just as librarians should always be on the lookout for a good book, they should also keep a constant eye out for appropriate Web sites. An easy method is to keep Rolodex cards handy at all times; copy the URL onto the card and test it when the Net is accessible. Good sites then can be indexed by subject and inserted alphabetically into the Rolodex file. You also can create a binder by printing the first page of valuable Web sites.

If the library has a Web page, the entire list of Web sites can be posted. A good practice is to focus on noting and annotating sites that are well-reviewed lists of indexed or searchable Web sites. It is better to provide 100 excellent sites than 1,000 mixed-value URLs. Furthermore, you can easily update the list as new sites are found.

Finding good sites is another way to partner with teachers and students. Sending teachers a note or quick e-mail about good sites makes the library more technologically reputable. Librarians also should encourage teachers and students to share their Net treasures. Keep a stack of blank cards beside the Web rolodex for users to add to the virtual collection. However, it is a good idea to review these sites until you are certain the contributor is a critical reviewer. Greater participation in this effort results in greater ownership of the process and greater student learning.

What's Good about the Internet?

The most frequent curricular use of the Internet is as a source of information. Students could well be creating traditional five-page written reports with information found on the Internet. On the other hand, non-curricular student uses range from chat rooms to gambling, from Sailor Moon fan clubs to car buying, from last night's pro game results to video game cheats. In any case, the information needs to be examined for accuracy and authenticity.

The traditional library took care of that issue because each book and periodical was reviewed, evaluated, and selected by the librarian. On the Net, anything goes, and monitoring is not consistent. If librarians and teachers were to select all the sites and deny student access to other addresses, they would not have time to do other tasks. More important, students would not learn how to examine and evaluate Internet sources critically.

Unfortunately, some teachers say there is not enough time to teach students how to evaluate sites, and students have to "pick it up" on their own. It may take several assignments where students wander aimlessly around the Net or pick false sites for teachers to realize the need for instruction in Internet evaluation. Again, the librarian can facilitate this process by diplomatically sharing observations with the teacher. The librarian is likely to note if students are off-task by recognizing frozen screens or interactive game sounds. And the librarian is likely to hear student dialogue, such as "I don't get how to do this," "Where do I

> While the librarian often spends much time coaching individual students through research issues, student questions could be raised to a higher critical level if classes were given basic instruction on searching techniques.

begin?" or "How do I know if this is any good?"

While the librarian often spends much time coaching individual students through research issues, student questions could be raised to a higher critical level if classes were given basic instruction on searching techniques. Several methods may be used:

- Show factual and opinionated Web sites on the same topic side by side, and have students determine the critical differences.
- Demonstrate successful searches by using Net harvester programs to download procedures and results.
- Use PowerPoint presentations to show how to navigate the Net and find good resources.
- Have students search the same topic using different search engines and compare the results.
- Develop guide sheets on Internet navigation and interpretation.

Another option is to have students complete online tutorials on Internet searching. However, such self-paced instruction may go awry for students who are easily distracted or do not sense any kind of accountability. It is usually a better idea to walk through these tutorials with the class before letting students explore for themselves.

Making Active Use of the Internet

Another strength of the Internet is its interactivity. The most obvious example is real time "conversation" over the Net. Students can access user groups and chat rooms via the Internet. They can hold video conferencing sessions with experts worldwide. Global Schoolhouse is especially known for this practice. They can respond to mass media programs or events by accessing the accompanying Web site. In effect, students are witnessing information being created and are helping to create it.

This sense of original work empowers students in a meaningful way. Simple presentation programs, such as the newest versions of ClarisWorks and PowerPoint, enable students to incorporate Web sites into their work. For example, a student could present a background about Bosnia's troubles and then link to a present-day dialogue with a Bosnian student or a recent video clip of terrorist action in the country. Just the simple importing of images from the Net can enliven a paper or presentation.

Hypermedia programs, such as HyperStudio, HyperCard, and Digital Chisel, allow students to create sophisticated branching programs that meld text, imagery, and sound. And with the live links, the storage space needed to run these interactive files is relatively manageable. Each of these experiences enriches student learning, but each also involves additional skill in the accompanying software. Again, the librarian and teacher should work together to insure maximum learning with the least frustration. A number of issues must be addressed:

- Who will teach the authoring tools—the librarian, classroom teacher, or computer specialist?
- How will those skills be taught—as part of the content class, as a unit in a computer literacy course, or to a subset of the class as extra credit?
- How structured should the product be? Developing a template for students speeds their time, but requires more front-end work for the educator.
- How will classes be scheduled in terms of facilities—for computer labs, library research, Internet access (including video contact time), and formal instruction?
- How much does the teacher have to know about these technologies? Who else can help students in the process?

Who's Doing the Learning?

The incorporation of technology first requires educators to be comfortable with technology. Librarians need to carve out time to explore the Net and create Internet-rich products, such as interactive presentations on information literacy skills. But librarians also need to encourage teacher training through inservice workshops, online tutorials, local continuing education offerings, in-house mentoring, videotape courses, and user-friendly manuals. A binder of good Internet lessons can stimulate

teacher ideas. Photocopying a particularly successful project description in the teacher's field of expertise can offer a model to replicate. Being a tech buddy is another effective way for two educators to help each other gain technological expertise. Once a successful application of the Net is made, the gateway is established to further Internet exploration and incorporation into the curriculum.

Lesley S. J. Farmer is the Library Media Specialist at Redwood High School Library in Larkspur, California

Notes

The World Wide Web in Three Lessons

By Claudia Vandermade

When the long-awaited pulses began flowing through the miles of computer cables winding above the ceiling tiles of our high school, my feeling was analogous to the arrival of boxes in the mail from a book distributor or publisher. I'm not at peace until the books are in students' hands, and I couldn't wait to begin exploring this newest wonder—the World Wide Web (WWW)—with an eager audience of eighth graders (approximately 160 of them in our eighth through twelfth grade population). My goals for the lesson were not only to introduce the procedural skills needed to navigate the Web, but also to offer students ways to critically evaluate the sites they find in terms of accuracy, timeliness, and quality. I began the lessons with this grade because our new state testing program includes a technology component for eighth graders, and I also felt that the younger students would enjoy "ruling the school," at least for a little while, when it comes to the World Wide Web.

Eighth graders had been coming to the library from their English classes for various lessons once every two weeks since the beginning of the school year, so by the time I taught this lesson in the Spring I had already established a teaching pattern with these students. The Web lessons were taught on the same schedule, which gave me two-week intervals to work with students on their homework assignments. During the earlier sessions in the library, I had introduced the students to basic computer resources, including the electronic catalog, navigating the desktop, and specific CD-ROMs, as well as Boolean searching techniques.

At an early stage in technology planning the school system decided to initially favor individual classroom computers over lab settings. Therefore, the library has only four computers with Internet access (though students can also ask individual teachers to work on classroom machines). As a result, I had no place where I could put every student at a machine and teach a hands-on lesson. Our computer applications teacher was unfailingly generous in loaning me the school's sole multimedia projector, which I used with the classes to introduce concepts and demonstrate basic operations. Students then had two weeks to schedule machine time and complete hands-on homework assignments.

There are usually two ways of teaching new skills to students in a high school library setting: One is to bring students in from class and spend one or more days concentrating on a specific lesson; the other is to teach the skill in the context of existing assignments that require students to come to the library. In my eleven years as a high school librarian, I have flipped and flopped from one method to the other. I feel that better learning takes place with the second method, but the drawback is that you will miss those students who are not enrolled in the particular class that has come to the library for an assignment. For this project, I decided that I wanted all eighth graders to have a basic understanding of the World Wide Web with the faith that reinforcement would occur frequently as they visited from other classes. The lesson described here was taught to all but a very small developmental group of eighth grade students (who had a separate lesson that I could deliver hands-on). Our students are a heterogeneous group ranging in degree of Web experience from advanced to developmental, but with small changes in the pace of the lessons and the amount of homework, each student received the same basic training.

The lesson involved three class sessions, two homework assignments, and one written project that students also presented in an oral presentation to their class. Lessons were held in the library and accompanied by the multimedia projector.

Technology Connection

Lesson One

Goal

Students will:

- learn basic Web terms and definitions
- learn techniques for maneuvering through Web resources
- begin to understand the scope of the Web, get an idea of what types of information they can find, and begin to think about evaluating the quality of information they do find.

Procedure

- Begin by asking students what they know about the World Wide Web, and get an idea of their levels of experience (for us, this varied greatly).

- Next, have students take notes from the screen that gives key terms and definitions (World Wide Web, Internet, hyperlink, URL, HTML, etc.).

- With the projector, demonstrate how to access the Internet from the Windows desktop. Then show how to type in an address from the Web browser screen—I chose the Washington Post site, <www.washingtonpost.com>, but people in other parts of the country might want to choose a closer big newspaper site. From this site demonstrate selected toolbar and menu bar icons that appear on the window, and show how to scroll. Introduce hyperlinks, and show how to move around in a site.

- Type in the address for the Internet Public Library, <www.ipl.org>, and tell students about virtual libraries in general. Demonstrate how to maneuver in the site—go to the Reference section (and then to the "Reference" part of the illustrated room), and under Geography go to the site, *The 50 States of the United States*. Students were eager to find information on the state bird, flower, etc., of their favorite states. Also show students the Teen section of the site, and then demonstrate how the *Newspapers* link leads to domestic as well as international news sites. Students used this part of the site all year long for reports on foreign countries and for their language classes.

- Finish the lesson with a site on roaches, <www.yucky.com/roaches/>, basically for fun, but also to reinforce maneuvering skills.

Homework Assignment #1

The homework, which was in the form of worksheets, took 20-30 minutes to complete, depending on the student's basic skills with a keyboard. I hadn't initially anticipated the number of students who would need a member of the library staff to be next to them for the entire homework assignment, but with the two-week span between lessons, the library aide and I were able to individually work with those who required more help. This is where some great learning took place, as we were able to personally assure students that they could be successful.

For the homework, students were required to visit three sites by typing in the addresses, and then working with the site content. The sites students visited were designed to be quality sties that would continue to help them gain an understanding on the variety of information available on the Web.

- Students went to the Library of Congress site, *THOMAS*, <thomas.loc.gov/home/thomas2.html> and answered specific questions about our local representatives.

- Next they visited the site of our local newspaper and were asked to find information from the teen page.

- The third site was *Virtual Antarctica*, <www.terraquest.com/antarctica/index.html>, and students were asked to identify bibliographic components of the site as well as find a map of Antarctica.

Two books that I found helpful as I developed this lesson are:

Ackermann, Ernest and Karen Hartman, *Searching & Researching on the Internet & the World Wide Web*, Franklin, Beedle & Associates, 1997.

Miller, Elizabeth B., *The Internet Resource Directory for K-12 Teachers and Librarians, 1997/98 edition*, Libraries Unlimited, 1998.

Goal

Students will:

- further understand the motivations of people/organizations who post information on the Web
- learn how to use Web search tools
- distinguish between the different types of tools: search engines, directories, meta-tools
- discover that no one tool can solve all searches.

Procedure

- At the beginning of class, we discussed what motivates people or organizations to create Web pages and how those motivations affect content.

- Students take notes on search machines, defining search engine, directory, and meta-tool. Discuss the differences between the three and the advantages/disadvantages of each.

- Given the amount of interest generated by the movie *Titanic*, I decided to use Molly Brown as the subject of my search demonstrations. Using the search engine HotBot, <www.hotbot.com>, demonstrate how students should enter the search using quotation marks: "Molly Brown." Review the results, and notice that too many sites are not on target. Then refine the search by using Boolean operators, and enter the search as "Molly Brown" AND "Titanic." Students are able to see that the revised search results in more relevant sites. Examine a number of sites, point out quality features as well as clearly inaccurate information (we found a good example in a site that claimed that Molly Brown rowed her lifeboat to shore).

- Repeat the search using the meta-tool MetaCrawler, <www.metacrawler.com>. Discuss the different nature of this tool and the way results are displayed.

- I also wanted students to see the directory, Yahoo!, <www.yahoo.com>, but by this point, they were saturated with Molly Brown. Because the Winter Olympics were going on at this time, I switched to a search on the Olympic snowboarding team to show the features of this search tool. Though the Olympics will be over by the time I teach this lesson again, I'll find no shortage of popular sports searches that students will enjoy.

Homework Assignment #2

Students went to the meta-tool Dogpile, <www.dogpile.com>, and answered questions about this search tool by looking at the "Help with Syntax" part of the site. Then they looked up "monarch butterflies" and were asked to find two sites: one with good scientific information about butterflies and another concerning commercial uses of butterflies (there were several sites for each category). Students answered questions about the sites (these questions asked students to locate bibliographic elements of the sites in order to prepare them for doing MLA-style citations).

Next, students went to HotBot and looked up "hope diamond." They answered a couple questions about sites they found. Then they revised the search by applying Boolean logic: "hope diamond" AND curse. Students answered basic questions about a site they found.

A note on MLA citations:

"Correct" MLA citations for Web resources seem to be a moving targets at the moment, and I hesitate to burden our students, particularly eighth graders, with all the opinions that have been posted on the topic. At the time of the lesson, I devised a simplified format for students to use, but this will probably need to be revised as a more standard form emerges. For more information, see the MLA site <www.mla.org/main_stl.htm>.

Lesson Three

Goal

Students will:
- understand and recognize the features of a good quality Web site
- understand the benefits as well as the possible hazards of using information found on the Web
- be able to produce an accurate MLA citation for a Web site
- understand what is expected in their final project

Procedure

- In a class discussion, we talked about features of a quality site:
  — person/organization responsible is identified
  — site has date or indication of currency
  — information is accurate
  — site has been constructed carefully with no grammatical/spelling errors.
- In a class discussion, talk about the strengths and weaknesses of the Web.
- Put up a sample WWW MLA citation on the projector. We gave students our library handout on electronic MLA citations at this point. *The Akhet Internet* <wkweb4.cableinet.co.uk.iwhawkins/>, which features ancient Egyptian topics, is a good site for showing students how to pick out the parts of a citation. Students enjoy "The Clickable Mummy" link where they can find out how various parts of the body were preserved by clicking on different sections of the mummy.
- Introduce final project.

Final Project

For the final project, students searched a topic on the Web. They could work individually or in groups of no more than three. I gave students a list of possible topics, or allowed them to come up with one of their own, but I discouraged topics that involved individual celebrities or popular music, games, etc. Students submitted project proposals to me before they began, so that we could fine-tune their approach or offer ideas about how to expand, if necessary. Though I cringed at the number of "Titanic" variations they were able to generate, the results were surprisingly good.

For the final paper students were required to:
- List five to 10 (depending on the level of the class) quality sites on their topic. For each site the students gave:
  — the title/URL
  — the person/organization responsible
  — the date of the site or update information
  — a summary of the site's contents
  — a rating for the site (1-5) and an explanation for the rating.
- Complete an accurate MLA citation for two of the sites
- List three to five (depending on the level of the class) search tools used. For each tool, the student gave:
  — the name of the tool
  — an explanation of what type of tool it was (engine, virtual library, etc.)
  — a discussion of the way they structured the search and any revisions they needed to make as the search progressed
  — a rating for the search tool (1-5) and an explanation for the rating.

Students had one month to complete the project, and our four library machines were reserved nearly every possible moment for that month.

Oral Report

Having students present their findings to the class was a great way to synthesize many of the things they learned over the past several weeks. Students used the multimedia projector to display one or two of the best sites they found in the course of the project, and they discussed their experiences using the Web. To save time, we required students to come in before their presentations and save their sample sites on the computer we use with the projector.

I was pleased with the learning that students accomplished during this introductory session. These students have been coming in steadily since the lesson for science projects and history papers, and are able to confidently approach the offerings of the Web. I'm sure that other librarians have found that once students use the Web, it can become difficult to convince them that other information sources have value, too. In further lessons, I will continue to work with these students on how to assess information value and relevancy given the vast resources available. ∎

Claudia Vandermade is a Librarian at the James Monroe High School in Fredericksburg, Virginia.

CONNECT YOUR STUDENTS ELECTRONICALLY TO LEARNING

feature

Rather than allowing students to "surf and drown" in the uncharted seas of the Internet, SCORE provides a safe lagoon which students can explore.

SCORE ONE FOR STUDENTS AND TEACHERS

By Bob Benoit and Peter Milbury

Rather than allowing students to "surf and drown" in the uncharted seas of the Internet, Schools of California On-line Resources in Education (SCORE) provides a safe lagoon which students can explore. SCORE was funded by the California County Superintendents Educational Services Association (CCSESA) in the spring of 1996.

Educators from the Butte and San Bernardino County offices direct this online project, which includes a Web page with indexed history-social science sites in alignment with the California History-Social Science Framework. These sites were evaluated by 14 expert teachers, who submitted 2,000 student-oriented sites.

For example, a high school U.S. history teacher will direct students studying World War II to the SCORE page to access grade 11, and see each unit from the framework. A click on the World War II button produces an annotated and rated set of links to other sites. In addition, there will be an opportunity to search by theme or topic, such as "immigration." Of course, students can leave the lagoon and

> *The grade-level lessons stress information literacy and focus on use of the Internet.*

> *Teachers find that students know more about some topics than the teacher because of the wealth of information available and opportunity for students to individualize research apart from the textbook.*

explore the great uncharted (and unedited) Internet. Other buttons lead to the SCORE listserv, model lessons, and information about resource-based and problem-based learning. A final button takes the explorer to similar sites in mathematics, science, and language arts.

The grade-level lessons stress information literacy and focus on use of the Internet. One lesson, for example, has students investigate similarities among ancient structures. Students must decide if great Mesopotamian, Egyptian, Mayan and Aztec structures were the result of space invaders, copycats, or independent inventors.

Other lessons have students research 19th-century historical figures, pick a geographical site for a future Olympics, or seek to balance trade on the Pacific Rim. Each lesson culminates with a project or performance which requires extensive research. These lessons ask students to identify a problem, select information to solve the problem, and to access, evaluate, and synthesize information.

With such an approach, students take more responsibility for the work, and the teacher becomes the facilitator of learning. Teachers find that students know more about some topics than the teacher because of the wealth of information available and opportunity for students to individualize research apart from the textbook. **Tc**

Bob Benoit is Curriculum Coordinator for the Butte County (California) Office of Education. He has directed numerous NEH summer institutes and International Studies institutes, and is a member of the 1997 California Framework Conference planning team and director of Icarus, a problem-based learning network. Here he describes SCORE, a project he co-directs with Peg Hill of the San Bernardino County Schools office. You can visit the site at http://www.rims.k12.ca.us/SCORE/. You also can phone Bob Benoit at 1-916-538-7847 or e-mail him at bbenoit@bcoe.butte.k12.ca.us.

Peter Milbury is the Librarian at Chico (California) Senior High School and an Editorial Consultant for TECHNOLOGY CONNECTION.

Search Engines Become Another Unit in Library Skills

By Dixie Talbot

Teach yourself how to use search engines and your students at the same time with this unit.

WHILE AT A CONFERENCE this summer, it became apparent to me that of the 50 librarians, I was the only one who had taught students how to use search engines on the World Wide Web. All were trying to add this instruction to already jam-packed schedules.

My advice is not to *add* instruction in the use of the searching software but to incorporate actual search engine use into already existing units. After all, you can find information in every subject area on the Net.

I put by theory into practice while working with a group of eight graders in a computer literacy class, and accomplished two goals at the same time. First, I taught myself through teaching the students. I personally knew little about search engines and had used them sparingly. Up to that time I had found sites because I had the URL, or Web address. Second, I trained a group of excited learners who are ready to teach others.

The first step was to introduce the three types of search engines—directory, keyword, and meta (engines that search other engines). I spent more time on *Yahoo!* at this point, tracking the correct use of it as a directory and never keyboarding in any words. Since we are in Kansas and I am a Kansas Jayhawk basketball fan, I framed a search starting with "recreation" and ending several points-and-clicks later with the Kansas Jayhawk basketball page. I emphasized that the correct use of a directory search engine will cut down the number of hits and bring only the most relevant to you.

> **My advice is not to add instruction in the use of the searching software but to incorporate actual search engine use into already existing units.**

I then divided the class into seven small groups (cooperative learning) and assigned each of these groups a different search engine. (I used *AltaVista, Excite, Magellan, Yahoo!, Webcrawler, Infoseek,* and *Lycos.*) The number seven was not divinely determined but just the logical number for that class. Each group researched its assigned search engine for its history (when was it formed, who owns it, awards, and so forth) and, more importantly, its search parameters. Students were specifically told to determine if their engine uses Boolean searching, required words, case sensitivity, phrase searching, or truncation. Sources for the research included the Web site of the search engine, other Web sites I had found that explained search engines, and magazine articles.

Each group was given seven phrases to search on their engine, first as individual words without parameters and then as a phrase. This was a particularly important step because it reinforced the difference between phrase searching and individual word searches.

From this research, the class made a chart for our computer lab. The chart lists the Web addresses of the seven search engines and their search features. Each group also made a chart and the best one was reproduced and given to every student in the school. The charts were also placed by Internet access stations in the building.

This approach could easily be incorporated into any research unit. Simply assign different search engines to groups in the class. It may take longer to complete the unit, but the result will be student experts on several different search engines. And you will be miles ahead in your own quest to be the search engine expert in your school.

Search Engine Races

My work with the eighth graders culminated with a search engine race. The "race" began with each group explaining its search engine's parameters or handing out any information they may have printed. Then the groups were given time to practice on their search engine so each member got a feel for the parameters.

I wrote a phrase on the chalkboard (junk mail, Cherokee Indians, Chicago Bulls, Kansas and basketball)

Notes

and gave the students the parameters for the search (Boolean, phrase, truncation). The competition was to see if the group's search engine produced more hits than the other groups' engines.

You should do the searches yourself before the race so you will know the correct number of hits. It is important to keep abreast of changes in search engines. For example, one engine that only allowed keyword searches when the groups did their initial research had added a directory component by the time of the race.

Hints

Several Internet workstations are necessary for the search engine races. The research can be done with just one station; it will just take more time. Each group needed about an hour to research its search engine. The group was required to print out the search tips and hints from the Web pages of the search engines and turn those printouts in with their final product. (This meant that I didn't have to go back to the pages to find these tips.)

This unit quickly taught students that they needed to be accurate in their keyboarding. Most of the students who say they can find nothing on the Web have simply keyboarded some part of the search incorrectly.

Since doing this project originally, I have added the search engine *HotBot* to the research. Since it is really a point-and-click engine with only the topic being keyboarded, I like to end the unit with it. The students seem to love being able to just point and click whether they are

> *Most of the students who say they can find nothing on the Web have simply keyboarded some part of the search incorrectly.*

want to search by a phrase, Boolean operators, or an image.

Some experienced Web users advise others to find the search engine they like best and then use it until they need more information. But most users agree that no one engine fills all needs. This unit helps the students get a feel for several different engines but then allows them to choose the one they like best.

I piloted the unit with an eighth-grade class but plan to use it with all English classes (grades 7-12) this year. Eventually I should be able to limit the search engine units to the incoming seventh graders each year.

Dixie Talbot is the Library Media Specialist at Valley Heights Junior-Senior High School in Blue Rapids, Kansas.

Search Engine Home Pages

The home pages of the eight search engines used in this project are:

AltaVista
http://www.altavista.digital.com

Excite
http://www.excite.com

HotBot
http://www.hotbot.com

Infoseek
http:\\www.infoseek.com

Lycos
http://www.lycos.com

Magellan
http://www.mckinley.com

Webcrawler
http://www.webcrawler.com

Yahoo!
http://www.yahoo.com

For More Information

Liu, Jian. "Understanding WWW Search Tools."
http://www.indiana.edu/librcad/search/

"Search Engines: Indexes, directories and libraries."
http://www.netstrider.com/search/

Tyner, Ross. "Sink or Swim: Internet search tools & techniques (version 2.1)"
http://oksw01.okanagan.bc.ca/libr/Connect96/search.htm (July 3, 1997).

NETWORKING

Create Your Own Home Page
A Step-By-Step Guide

by Don Descy

Third graders can do it and so can you if you follow the step-by-step instructions here. Join the growing list of schools that publish on the World Wide Web.

World Wide Web home pages are so easy to make that even my dog has one! <URL:http://www.lme.mankato.msus.edu/ded/bedlington.html>.

Okay, I admit my help was needed—but I know third graders who have created them unassisted. To view the world's first school Web page, point your browser to the one created by Hillside Elementary School in Cottage Grove, Minnesota: <URL:http://hillside.coled.umn.edu>. A complete list of school Web pages can be accessed through <URL:http://web66.coled.umn.edu/schools.html>

SOME WEB WORDS YOU SHOULD KNOW

Most World Wide Web pages are written in HyperText Markup Language, HTML for short. HTML is easy to learn. A markup language is a collection of tags placed around words or groups of words in a text document. These tags tell the browser software used to access the Web when to start a new paragraph, add a graphic, italicize a word, or add a link to another Web page. There are many browsers. Popular ones include *Netscape, Cello, Lynx, MacWeb, Web Explorer,* and *InternetWork*s. However, not all browsers read and format an HTML tag in the same way and not all Web browsers understand all HTML tags. When designing and viewing your Web page, remember that people using other browsers may not see your page formatted the same way. A word to the wise: if possible, view your page through several browsers and modify it if necessary.

HTML markup tags are delimited by angle brackets: <markup tag>. (The letters within the brackets are not case-sensitive. <title>, <TITLE>, <Title>, and <tItLe> are interpreted the same way by a browser.) Some tags occur singularly such as the <p> tag that indicates a paragraph break in the text. Other tags must be used in pairs (container tags): one tag (<tag>) instructs the browser software to start a specific format and a second tag (</tag>) instructs the browser to end a specific format. It's possible to use several container tags at one time. For example, <i>Descy</i> tells the browser to present the text in bold italics: **Descy**.

A third set of tags is placed in the HTML document to keep it organized for the person writing the document. <html> and </html>, <head> and </head>, and <body> and </body>, are examples of these tags.

HOW TO CREATE A WEB PAGE

To make a World Wide Web page, you need a word processing program that can save your document as a text (or ASCII) file. *ClarisWorks, Microsoft Works, Microsoft Word,* and most other word processing applications can do this. HTML documents are saved as ASCII files because this file format can be read and edited on any computer platform. Text or ASCII files can also be transported over any network.

Open your word processing program, turn off the "smart quotes" feature and use the following as your guide. Using this format, type in your own favorite lists and sites in place of mine.

<html>

<head>

<title>Welcome to My First Web Page</title>

</head>

<body>

<h1> Welcome to my Web home page! </h1>

<hr>

<p><h2>These are Web Sites that I like to visit often:</h2>

<p>I love to start my day at the <a href=http://cool.infi.net/> Cool Site</a> of the Day!

<p>The <a href=http://ericir.syr.edu/>AskERIC</a> home page contains links to great information for teachers including <ahref=gopher://ericir.syr.edu/11/Lesson>lesson plans</a>, searching AskERIC, and links to ERIC collections.

<p>A great <a href=http://www.ucalgary.ca/~dkbrown/index.html>Children's Literature</a> WWW resource page.

<p>The <a href=http://www.infomall.org/Showcase/Linworth/>Linworth Publishing</a> has information about their products.

```
<p> A nice list of <a href=http://
hanksville.phast.umass.edu/misc/
NAresources.html >Native
American</a> Internet resources.
<p>Don's guide to <a href=http://
www.lme.mankato.msus.edu/sites.
html>teacher resources</a>.
<p>Don has a Web site for his stu-
dents that contains <a href=http://
www.lme.mankato.msus.edu/ded
/int.html>helper applications and
information</a> to help produce
WWW pages.
<p>
<a href=http://www.lme.
mankato.msus.edu/ded/don.html
>Don Descy</a> wrote the article
that helped me write my first Web
page.
<hr>
<p>Updated: Month, Year<br>
Type your name here<br>
The location of page should go here
</body>
</html>
```

Save this as an ASCII or text file on a floppy disk. Label it first.html if you have a Macintosh or first.htm if you are using DOS or Windows (most DOS file extensions can have only three letters). Congratulations! You have written your first Web page. Now let's take a look at it. As long as you have a browser on your computer, you're all set. You don't even need an Internet connection.

If you're using *Netscape*, open up the browser and open the file (first.html or first.htm) by going through "Open File" in the File menu. If you're using *NCSA Mosaic*, open the browser and open the file (first.html or first.htm) by going through the "Open Local…" under the File menu. If your computer is connected to the Internet, you may want to click on your hypertext links.

How to Import Graphics to Your Web Page

One way to add graphics to your page is to import them from other Web pages. Archives containing thousands of graphics can be accessed through the World Wide Web Power Index of Icons and Graphics <URL:http://www.webcom.com/power/icons.html>. You may practice by importing graphics from my Web page. You will need a newer version of *Netscape*—version 1.1 or above: try <URL:ftp://ftp.mcom.com/netscape/> or <URL:http://home.mcom.com/comprod/mirror/index.html>. You will also need an Internet connection.

One way to add graphics to your page is to import them from other Web pages. Archives containing thousands of graphics can be accessed through the World Wide Web Power Index of Icons and Graphics.

First, use your word processor to reopen first.html. Next, open *Netscape*. Now, press the "open" button on the top bar or under the file menu, choose "open location," and type http://www.lme.mankato.msus.edu/ded/int.html in the window that will appear. Click on "open" and wait for my Internet links page to appear. You will retrieve the graphics for your page from this page. Go to the bottom of this page. You should see a rainbow colored line, a smiley face, and green ball icons. You will copy these three images to your disk.

Now, use your mouse to place the arrow curser on a green ball icon. If you are using a Macintosh, hold down the mouse button for a second or two. If you are using Windows, click the right mouse button. In either case, a dialog box or menu will appear. Click on or choose "Save this image as…" and save it onto the same disk that contains first.html. (Notice that the green ball icon is called greendot.gif.) That is all you have to do to capture graphics using *Netscape*. (Caution: Many images on the Web are copyrighted. So don't copy whatever you see. The images on my Web pages are not copyrighted. You may copy images from any of my Web pages.) Now use the same technique to capture the smiley face (smile.gif) and the rainbow colored line (hline.gif).

You should now have four files on your floppy disk: first.html (your original HTML document), greendot.gif (the green ball), smile.gif (the smiley face), and hline.gif (the rainbow line). To add these or any graphics to your page, all you have to do is put a markup tag in your HTML document in the place where you want the graphic to appear. These tags tell the browser where to find the graphic and where to place it on the page.

How to Link the Graphics to Your Page

We will add three tags to first.html. The generic image tag is <IMG SRC=image location ALT="text browser display">. Another way to explain this is: <IMaGe SouRCe (location)=location of image ALT(what will be displayed if someone is using a text-only browser)="word displayed on text-only browser">. Notice that HTML uses the term *image* for graphic. Since your images are in the same location (folder, directory, disk) as the

When you design and view your Web page, remember that people using other browsers may not see your page formatted the same way. A word to the wise: if possible, view your page through several browsers and modify it if necessary.

HTML document, all you have to do is tell the browser the name of the image. The three graphics tags that you will add to your page are:

```
<IMG SRC=hline.gifALT="++++++
+++++++++">
<IMG SRC=greendot.gif ALT="*">
<IMG SRC=smile.gif ALT=":-)">
```

Now, place the image tag in the HTML document where you want the image to appear on your Web page. Replace the top <hr> (horizontal rule) tag with the tag for the rainbow line, put a green ball icon tag in front of each of your links, and place a smiley face tag in front of your name at the bottom of the page.

This is a test: (1) Try to add these images before you check the HTML sidebar, and (2) add a link to your Web page that will access Arlene Rinaldi's "The Net: User Guidelines and Netiquette". This document can be found at: <URL:http://www.fau.edu/rinaldi/netiquette.html>.

Save this new page as a text or ASCII file labeling it firstpix.html or firstpix.htm. Notice that I changed the name. You now have two Web pages! View your new page as I described above.

Now that you've learned how easy it is to make a World Wide Web home page, you will probably want to download "A Beginner's Guide to HTML" from <URL:http://www.ncsa.uiuc.edu/General/Internet/WWW/HTMLPrimer.html>. This is a wonderful guide to help you further explore HTML. As you continue your work you may also want to look at a list of Web page design criteria found at <URL:http://www.garlic.com/rfwilson/smalbus/12design.html>. **TC**

Don Descy is Associate Professor of Library Media Education at Mankato (Minnesota) State University. His e-mail address is descy@vax1.mankato.msus.edu and his Web page is <URL:http://www.lme.mankato.msus.edu/ded/don.html>.

Editor's Note: CompuServe, America Online, and Prodigy—all with direct links to the WWW and the rest of the Internet—provide step-by-step directions on creating home pages, along with simple page-making software programs you can download. For more information on their Web page services and capabilities, go to WebCentral on CompuServe and select Home Pages; go to Personal Publisher on America Online; on Prodigy, go to Personal Web Pages.

What HTML Tags Tell the Browser Software

<html>	This tag tells the browser a document is written in HyperText Markup Language.
<head>	This tells us the words will appear in the header of the browser you are using. (NOT on the WWW page itself.)

(Remember, there are three types of tags—two are necessary and one is not. The ones that are not required are helpful to the Web page developer. <html> and <head> are helpful, but not absolutely necessary.)

<title>	The following text will appear in the header of the browser you are using.
</title>	This signifies the end of the title.
</head>	This signifies the end of the header. Not required.
<body>	This is the beginning of the information that will actually appear on the Web page. Not required.
<h1>	Display this text as a level one heading—largest letters available. (Note: There are six levels of headings, <h1> to <h6>, with <h1> the largest and <h6> the smallest.)
<center>	This centers the text—This is a *Netscape* extension. *Netscape* and several other browsers can read it. Many browsers cannot.
</center>	Stop centering text.
</h1>	Stop the level one size header.
<hr>	This places a horizontal line across the page — nice!!
<p>	Insert blank line and start a new paragraph.
<a href=http://cool.infi.net/>	This is the power of HTML. The <a > tag signifies an "anchor." Whatever is typed between the anchor tags (<a > and </a>) becomes a hypertext link to another document, picture, or sound. The words between the anchors <a> and </a> usually appear underlined and in color on the browser. This line tells the browser that this is an anchor or link (<a) to a Hypertext REFerence (HREF) or location found (=) at (http://cool.infi.net/).
</a>	This is the end of the hypertext link.
<p>	Add a blank line and start a new paragraph.
<a >	Another hypertext anchor (link) location.
</a>	End of second hypertext anchor.
""	Several repeats of the above.**
<hr>	Place a horizontal line across the page.
<p>	Add a blank line and start a new paragraph.
 	Break this line but do not add a blank line.
</body>	End of information that will appear on the Web page. Not required.
</html>	End of HTML document. Not required.

How to Create Your Own Graphics

One way to make your own graphics is with a paint or draw application such as the one in *ClarisWorks*. Another way to add graphics to your page is to use a scanner to scan the graphic onto your disk. You must remember to save the graphics as either a GIF file or a JPEG file. Applications that can change graphic formats to GIF format can be downloaded from <URL:http://web66.coled.umn.edu/Cookbook/Pictures/Pictures.html> for Macintosh or

Create a Home Page with Netscape

by Peter Butts

Last year everyone wanted to know your e-mail address. This year, they want the URL to your home page. If you're already using Netscape to tour others' home pages, now's the time to think about creating one of your own. Don't be intimidated—it's easy to do.

In fact, while you've been surfing and adding bookmarks to all those cool sites, Netscape has been building a page just for you. When I opened up Netscape for staff and students last fall, I wanted to have at least a locally accessible home page on my hard drive that I could use to "manage" the sites used at our school. Here's how I did it just two months after downloading Netscape.

Step 1.

Make sure you've got a few favorite sites bookmarked.

Step 2.

Open the Bookmark file using the "Open File..." command under the "File" Menu. Look in the System Folder for the Preferences Folder where the installer placed a Netscape Folder, then open "bookmarks.html."

Step 3.

To customize this page you will need to save a copy of the HTML (HyperText Markup Language) file. First pull down "View" to "Document Source." What you see next is the raw HTML in Teach Text or Simple Text.

Step 4.

Unless you prefer to read from the screen, this is a good time to print. While the printer is chugging away, "Save As..." something catchy like "My.Home.html" in the folder that has your Netscape application.

Step 5.

If you printed the file, use a highlighter to highlight anything embedded between the brackets < > (e.g. <TITLE>, </TITLE>, <p>, <H1>, </H1>, etc.). These are the tags used to format text, create lines, and activate links to graphics, sounds, and other Web pages. In nearly all cases there's a beginning tag <TITLE> and an ending tag </TITLE>. The best way to learn the tags is by copying and mimicking the formatting of existing pages. Anytime you come upon an interesting page layout, go to "Document Source" to view the raw HTML.

Step 6.

Now it's time to customize. First you'll notice a Comment line found between the brackets <! and ->. This is a hidden reminder for programmers, you can either replace the DOCTYPE NETSCAPE...information with your own name and the date of the file's creation, or delete everything up to the <TITLE>. Second, you'll want to change the title, found between the tags <TITLE> and </TITLE>. This is the text that appears on the window's title bar. Third, change the text between the <H1> and </H1> tags: this is the main heading of the page. "Cool Places I've Been" or "HMS Home Page" are typical headings.

Step 7.

Time to save your changes and go back to Netscape to see how it looks. Again go to "Open File..." This time the window should show your new title and heading.

Now it's time to look at the list with the eyes of a new user: how could this be made more user friendly? If your list is long, some reorganization and subject headings might be handy. An introductory paragraph with instructions or general information might help. Also, those nifty lines might give your page a more finished look.

Step 8.

Ready to do some serious HTML? First, let's add some information at the beginning. Place your cursor on the line under that <H1> Subject Heading </H1>, and add <BR> to create a line break. Next add <p> to tag a paragraph of text, type in the information, and then close with the </p> tag. To finish off this first part of the page with a line, add the tag <HR>.

Second, go back to your highlighted printout to see how each of the individual bookmarks is tagged. At the top you'll see the tag <DL> for a "definition list" and each bookmark begins with <DT> for "definition term." The heart of the link is the tag <AHREF=.....> with the title or phrase that appears on the page, then the closing tag</A>. To rearrange the bookmarks using the Cut and Paste commands be sure to begin your selection with the <DT> and end with the </A>. (Just so you know, the URL for each site must be in quotation marks. Also, Netscape's bookmark system includes the information identifying copies of the sites saved in the Cache Folder (also found in that Netscape Folder in Preferences). These are the ADD_DATE=, LAST_VISIT=, and LAST_MODIFIED= statements. You may leave them intact or delete them if you choose. Just be sure that the <A HREF=...>tag contains the complete URL in quotation marks with the closing bracket.)

Third, to add sub-headings to identify categories within your list, begin by placing the cursor before the first

BUTTS—

<DT> in the category. Next add <H2> for a second level heading (slightly smaller than the one at the top of your page), type the sub-heading as it should appear, closing with the </H2> tag. If you'd like, you can add some space with a break <BR> tag before and/or after the sub-heading. Repeat for each group of bookmarks. Don't forget to save the file and test it in Netscape by opening or reloading the file.

Step 9.

To make this your default home page when you open Netscape, select and copy the location information from Netscape's location window (e.g. file:///HD/Netscape/my.page.html), then open "General Preferences" from the "Options" Menu. Look for "Appearance: Browser starts with Home Page Location." This window should contain the URL for Netscape's own home page. You can highlight this and replace it with the URL you just copied for your own page.

Step 10.

After I created a customized local home page, I asked the Webmaster at our local Freenet if we could post it. If this is an option for you, don't hesitate. Use the popular file transfer program Fetch to upload your pages. It's easy!

Voila! You have created a functional, if spartan, launchpad for your Web journeys. If you've gotten the bug for authoring Web pages, there are many options. Just searching a Web index such as Yahoo for HTML authoring programs and information, you'll turn up dozens of hits. You can also consult a book. Most Netscape overviews will provide the information you need to add in line graphics and sounds. There are also dozens of HTML cookbooks on bookstore shelves. If typing in HTML tags isn't your idea of a good time, you can download one of the shareware HTML editing programs or order a commercial program like Adobe's PageMill. **TC**

Peter Butts is a Media Specialist at East Middle School in Holland, Michigan.

Editor's Note: CompuServe, America Online, and Prodigy—all with direct links to the WWW and the rest of the Internet—provide step-by-step directions on creating home pages, along with simple page-making software programs you can download. For more information on their Web page services and capabilities, go to Web Central on CompuServe and select Home Pages; go to Personal Publisher on America Online; on Prodigy, go to Personal Web Pages.

Notes

NETWORKING

Library Home Pages: A New Knowledge Environment

Creating a Web home page boldly says that the library is the center of information access. It places the library in the forefront of educational technology. What kinds of information and services can such a home page provide? How can you make it work for you, especially in your role as instructional leader?

The opening home page serves as a four-second first impression of the library. The library's name should appear exciting and distinctive—and welcoming. To accomplish this, explore options in font style, size, and color. A sharp-looking graphic would complement the title. Note that variations in World Wide Web appearance can alter the graphic; so be sure that the visual isn't too big or wide. The next line should give a 25-word "sound bite" about the library's role. Make sure that the description sounds flashy and impressive because you have very little time to hook a potential library user.

The main body of the home page should show the variety of library services and resources. The easiest approach is to develop a short list of linked options. That way you can point to a number of important pieces of information without making your users plow through details that don't interest them. These links may refer to embedded "pages" or to external files. This menu approach also insures that the page will be interactive; the user is in control of the knowledge environment. Here are some topics to consider:

- Library resources, rules and regulations, statistics
- A floor map
- Staff and volunteers (get permission if you include photos)
- The newsletter
- New print and nonprint resources, services, or staff members
- Announcements of upcoming events
- Book reviews and booktalks
- Book or CD-ROM of the week
- URL (Uniform Resource Locator) of the week
- Trivia contest
- Reader's advisory booklists
- In-house databases (hotlines or community contacts)
- Pathways>>>>WebQuests (see below)
- Links to other school pages

Remember to give users a way to contact the library, by phone, U.S. mail, or an e-mail connection. One effective approach is to encourage students to ask the librarian questions via e-mail. It can be as easy as this: "Can't find what you need? Ask the librarian by clicking on this address: accountname@ domain.address." The account is an active link so the student can type in a specific request. Of course, this feature requires the staff to answer in a timely manner. Otherwise, the benefit is lost. The student must also have an e-mail address to receive his answer. For students who do not have an address, you can provide a generic student account with one name/address, such as student@school.edu. This single account works like an electronic bulletin board; all messages are public to anyone who knows the account name. Students can check their messages at any time from any site. Before attempting this option, though, you will need to know your constituents and security systems well, in order to avoid communication abuse.

A Study in Detail

Pathway guides are used by many librarians and teachers to help students locate resources on a topic. (See sample below.) Now you can use the guides in a new way: transform them into Web pages and expand the library's role in information literacy instruction. Such online guides can direct students to print resources and other holdings as well as remote sites. With some creative thinking, you can make sure the Web pages do not just duplicate the paper version; color, clip art, and linked information make the new format more attractive and useful.

Selecting and evaluating the useful Web sites requires skill. If other library staff or aides work on this task, make sure you check their results. A simple method is to examine their search history, which will be indicated in most Web browsers. In some cases, you may want to show end users the line of strategy, such as going from a general directory to a more refined topical set of files. In designing the pathways page, begin with an overview of a broad subject, such as "Science" or "Renaissance," and list

INFORMATION LITERACY SKILLS: GRADES 7-12, 3RD EDITION   142

resources that give a general treatment. Then you can subdivide the topic yourself, or use an index such as Yahoo to list more specialized references.

What Does It Look Like?

The difference between a traditional paper document and a Web page is the interconnectivity. The electronic form provides a more complex set of links than a print document would typically offer, even with a good index. Because it is so easy to go from link to link, it is important that you keep those connections straight. One way to maintain an overall perspective is to draw a flowchart of the various pages, so you and your users won't get lost in the information web.

The appearance of the page is as important as the quality of the content. A dull-looking screen will be an instant turn-off. The goal is to make your Web page "zing" without looking chaotic. Basically, visual elements should help users find information, not distract them. Here are a few principles:

Keep the type face simple. Use only a couple of font or typeface styles, and make sure they are easily read. Stick to commonly used fonts so remote machines will be more likely to translate the text. Use only a couple of font sizes, and be consistent in their use. That way, they can act as a visual cue to the importance of the content. Thus, headlines would have a larger size than the main body of the text. Use boldface and underlines sparingly, since these features don't always transfer well to other systems. A good practice is to develop a style sheet. In that way, library aides can enter information in a consistent manner.

Use color and texture for emphasis. Keep color variations to a minimum; some colors may change when picked up by other systems. Textured backgrounds can lend atmosphere to a page. Make sure, though, that any background is light and subtle so the viewer can decipher the text through it. Be sure to check the resolution and color range of graphic images so they are easily read by other systems. One trick is to test the appearance of the Web page by calling it up on another, unlike system.

Watch edges and columns. Because monitor size varies, try to have all elements arranged so the user doesn't have to scroll across the screen. This is another case where it helps to test the Web page on different systems. Because columns can also be unpredictable, it is safer to list menu items in a single column or with center justification.

Go for the uncluttered look. The ideal is a home page with one page of introduction and one page of menu links. That way people don't get lost. (The backup button is much easier to use for navigating than long scrolling fields.) The number of menu choices should be limited to eight or fewer so users can remember their options.

Use graphical organizers. Most HTML languages permit horizontal bars to separate text blocks. Newer mark-up programs include frames to group related text together. Remember, though, that older systems might not be able to read these frames. Also, background color and texture may not carry over to all systems.

Explain yourself. Links should either be self-explanatory, such as "Library Map," or they should include a brief annotation to explain them. For instance, the option "What's New?" might be followed by "Get lists of latest books and CD-ROMs that have arrived in the library." Images should also be self-evident or captioned. Note: make sure you have permission to use a graphical element, and cite that permission if it is required.

Maintenance tasks rise to a new level of timeliness on a Web page. Users' expectations for current information and novelty rise dramatically. As new materials come into the library, announce them immediately. Pathway files can also reflect new holdings as they go into circulation. Be sure to review links to resources at least monthly to make sure the resources haven't disappeared or moved. And, new URLs need to be added as well. If e-mail is offered on the library home page, examine messages daily.

As users become accustomed to pathways for research, the demand for more such guides will increase. If teachers notice that students use the guides and improve their research skills, they may ask for more.

Sample Pathway

1) For general background information, use an *encyclopedia*: [title of encyclopedia]
2) Generate a set of *keywords or terms:* [suggest terms]
3) For specific facts, use *specialized reference books, such as:* _____. Some *CD-ROM reference titles* in this field include: _____.
4) For current information, consult *periodicals* by using a magazine index, such as _____.
5) Some specific periodicals in this field include: _____, _____.
6) For current information, check the *Internet*. Remember to evaluate what you find because quality varies greatly. Some good sites include: http://_____ gopher://_____.
7) For in-depth information, examine *books*. Use your keywords to locate books through the library's catalog. Some Dewey Decimal Classification call numbers in this field include: _____, _____.

Networking

Obviously, updating and expanding the library home page will have an impact on staff hours and efforts. Some maintenance tasks can be handled by student aides and volunteers. If given the information, they can enter it into the computer. Students may find helpful URLs and pass them along to the librarian for future inclusion on the home page. Such suggestions confirm user interest and involvement. Students may even try their hand at developing research guides. (If you include students' work, be sure to give credit to them.)

Professional time is needed to develop high quality Web pages. The impact of such effort is great because it is potentially accessible to a broad spectrum of users both on and off campus. If anything, producing Web pages demonstrates the critical and highly developed skills that librarianship offers. And it offers a unique service to the school community. **T𝐂**

Lesley S.J. Farmer is the Library Director of Redwood High School in Larkspur, California. She is the author of the forthcoming book Training Library Student Staff *to be published by Linworth Publishing, Inc.*

Notes

THE INTERNET: CONNECTING WITH THE CURRICULUM

feature

Integrating E-Mail into the Curriculum

By Debbie Abilock

> Just as teachers and librarians can participate in discussions of educational issues with colleagues and experts, children can communicate with keypals related to their curriculum. In these e-mail exchanges, students learned the value of networking, how to ask pertinent and thoughtful questions and to advocate eloquently online for their beliefs and values.

Just as teachers and librarians can participate in Internet discussions of educational issues with colleagues and experts, children can communicate with keypals related to their curriculum. For example, the Intercultural E-Mail Classroom Connections (http://www.stolaf.edu/network/iecc/) is intended for teachers seeking partner classrooms for international and cross-cultural electronic mail exchanges. Teachers can request help with specific classroom projects, and both teachers and students can post requests for assistance on projects, surveys, and questionnaires.

The third and fourth graders at The Nueva School in Hillsborough, California, have become keypals with other students in the JASON VII Aquatic Field Study, an online project sponsored by the National Aeronautics and Space Administration (NASA). They are exploring conditions for life in the coastal marine habitats of Southern Florida as part of our school's year-long interdisciplinary curriculum called Adaptation: Choice and Chance. Students, who called themselves "mudfellows," brainstormed the kinds of data they needed to request in order to compare types of wetlands.

Besides writing to other students, they asked Jonathan Howland, an on-site specialist with the JASON Project, about the pros and cons of his job. His responses went beyond the information available locally, providing students with a sense of adventure and the cooperative nature of scientific investigations:

> I get to do things that most people only dream of, and I get paid to do it. For example, next month I'll be flying to Florida and work on a coral reef using a nuclear submarine. Several months later, I'll be flying to Barbados, and sailing for the mid-Atlantic to work on hydrothermal vents. I work with very bright and motivated people, and we all have to depend on each other...I also like the tremendous sense of accomplishment that we often get when we finish a difficult job.

JASON keypals can be reached through: http://seawifs.gsfc.nasa.gov/scripts/JASON.html.

The results of the Nueva students' research can be seen at: http://www.nueva.pvt.k12.ca.us/~essci/.

Interviewing is less predictable than finding information in a book because the process is more emotionally engaging than a literature search. Students are challenged to make sense of fuzzy or irrelevant answers, intrigued by assuming the role of investigative reporters and flattered by the seriousness with which adults treat their questions. For example, some third and fourth graders are interviewing Vietnamese-American boat people to understand the response of immigrants to a new culture and environment. This is the human side of adaptation. The interviews have been powerful, emotional experiences for young children, as they read accounts of family dislocation and personal courage. A 19-year-old girl, located through the Berkeley Vietnamese-American Students' Home Page, writes of fleeing Vietnam without her parents at the age of 10:

> It was a small cargo boat that barely fit 48 of us. We did not have room to move. Lemon and sugar were our food. We [had] a limited amount of water also...I was lonely and homesick. I cried a lot and I wanted to go home to see my mom and dad. Of course that was not possible but I did

not understand at that time till after three months knowing that my tears could not change anything, I just turned numb.

Some sixth-grade students are corresponding online with women who use mathematics in their jobs at Hewlett-Packard. They were curious about what attracted these women to technical careers. One respondent, who acknowledged the influence of a female algebra teacher and a computer programming teacher, wrote:

> However, the person that gave me the monumental shove into engineering was my guidance counselor in high school. I had no idea what I wanted to do when I "grew up." She talked me into going to college, and she also suggested that I try engineering since I liked my math and science classes. This sounded better than staying at my waitressing job...so, I took her advice. Thank goodness! I'm a pretty good engineer, but I was a lousy waitress!

Hoping to create a gender-equitable school climate, our staff takes part in seminars based on the Wellesley College model known as Seeking Educational Equity and Diversity (S.E.E.D.) Project. Online interviews with female mathematicians provide role models that may influence our sixth-grade girls in their own career decisions.

For older students, learning through interviews prompts both activism and service. In a school project called Wounded Knee: Past and Present, eighth graders examine the history of the United States in relation to its Indian population. Native American correspondents located through Internet discussion groups such as NATCHAT, TRABALLAW, and NATIVE-L were generous with their time. In addition to suggesting books to read and Web pages to visit, they networked students to other Native American experts. For example, one student was probing how successfully the movie industry has answered long-time concerns about cultural authenticity and historical accuracy in portraying Native Americans. He corresponded with David Yohn and Diane Way whose organization, ABLEZA, a Native American arts and film institute, is committed to correcting the mistaken notion that Native American artists only produce things that "look Indian." In turn, this couple offered to connect our student with Native American actors from Hollywood films or people who had done the voice-overs for Disney's Pocahontas. After the students had completed their research, this couple and other Native Americans visited the school at an evening presentation to discuss the students' findings.

Another student was assessing Leonard Peltier, an American Indian Movement (AIM) activist currently incarcerated, who has been characterized as a "prisoner of war" by his supporters. Upon reading online of a Leonard Peltier rally in San Francisco, the student sent an e-mail "persuasive essay" to his teachers arguing that the school should sponsor a field trip to the demonstration. "I think that it would be a

---

Interview Workshop

Name: _____

Which of these questions or techniques were used? Which were used effectively?

Kinds of Information

Factual -- who, what, when...?

Personal point of view -- what do you think about...? why?

Emotional Response -- how do you feel about... what was that like for you...?

Techniques

Follow-up -- what do you mean, list, detail...?

Clarification -- I'm not clear on that... could you restate that for me...?

Drawing Conclusions -- summarize... are you saying... does that mean...?

Open-Ended & Fishing -- What are some of the... so what did I leave out...?

How Nueva Connects Students and Teachers to the Internet

The Nueva School provides e-mail accounts to current students, parents, staff, alumni and staff and students of partner public schools. Each individual requesting an account receives a copy of the acceptable use policy and a consent-and-waiver form. A parent or guardian must read the policy and sign the form together with the student applying for the account.

The library teaching assistant enters new accounts and changes passwords once or twice a week, averaging five minutes for each account. We are developing a guideline for how to create a password that is easy to remember and maintains as much security as possible. The students' accounts, as well as the others, are private accounts. Teachers sometimes have requested that messages sent to others involved in students' projects be copied to them. Nueva uses the Pine e-mail program.

Our systems administrator regularly monitors all accounts to ensure that our acceptable use policy is being followed.

— *Kathryn Tsushima, Teaching Assistant, The Nueva School*

---

very empowering experience ...after reading *Lakota Woman* I feel very strongly about this cause."

Questioning whether classroom learning about Native Americans had any effect on biases, another student located teachers through LM_NET who were willing to have their class surveyed before and after studying Indians. The student composed the survey that was sent over the Internet as well as to local schools, testing his assumptions.

In these e-mail exchanges, students learned the value of networking, how to ask pertinent and thoughtful questions and to advocate eloquently online for their beliefs and values. Unlike the known-answer questions that are often modeled in schools, students asked authentic questions—questions they did not know the answer to and about which they were genuinely interested.

Effective questioning requires metacognitive thinking and practice, time for reflection, and modification. With the help of a middle school teacher, seventh graders are treated as apprentice journalists. They are taught to tailor questions to a desired outcome, to develop probing follow-up questions, to ask for verification or supportive evidence, and to request a considered judgment from the person being interviewed. (See "Interview Workshop" form.)

In a different use of e-mail, a group of Nueva's fifth graders and a group of sixth graders from Borel Middle School have been reading the unpublished manuscripts of two children's authors located through the listserv CHILDLIT. Students are "dialoging" on the typed manuscript and responding to the text via e-mail messages to the authors. Correspondence online has varied from literary analysis to editing, from unbridled enthusiasm to analytical commentary. Writes one critic, "I don't think that you should keep adding characters so quickly." Another corrects, "In kickball you don't come up to bat; you really kick the ball." Both authors responded promptly to their mail and were thick-skinned about the blunt comments. To their delight, one author flew from Bloomington, Illinois, to visit with her student editors.

Each of these projects can be managed with one telephone line and a computer, in a classroom or the library. They illustrate the flexibility and versatility of using e-mail to generate authentic reading and writing experiences. **TC**

Debbie Abilock is a Librarian at The Nueva School in Hillsborough, California. The school won the AT&T/Time Educational Program Online Contest with its year-long curriculum called "The Forties: An Intergenerational Program Teaching Point of View."

Notes

Telementoring
Providing Authentic Learning Opportunities for Students

By Helen Adams

DURING THE 1997-98 school year, five students from Rosholt (Wisconsin) High School participated in the Hewlett Packard E-Mail Mentoring Program. They were matched one-on-one with company employees worldwide for telementoring, defined by HP as "a mentoring relationship via some medium of telecommunications, such as e-mail." Eleven hundred other fifth through twelfth graders in the United States, Canada, Australia, and France also participated in the program.

The Rosholt students were enrolled in the local FLITE (Future Leaders in TEchnology) program and received credit for serving as high school computer lab assistants. Their main responsibilities were to assist other students and staff with software and hardware questions and to help maintain lab computers. The HP program provided the students, from a small, rural district, with authentic learning opportunities through interaction with employees in a global technology company. According to the HP E-Mail Mentor Web site, one of the objectives of the program is to help students "begin a paradigm shift to perceive school as a resource for them to pursue their unique interests rather than something that just happens to them."

The e-mail mentoring program began in 1995 when David Neils, an HP software engineer based in Fort Collins, Colorado, created an Internet class for a local school. Neils found the students eager to learn about topics of personal interest related to technology, so he recruited other technology professionals to interact with the students via e-mail. Both HP and the school district encouraged him to expand the program. Describing the program in an HP brochure, Neils says, "The primary emphasis is to encourage students to excel in math and science. But we also help develop the skills to pursue primary passions that will lead to a satisfying career. We need more students graduating from high school who not only understand their passions about life, but also have the skills to pursue those passions."

The HP E-Mail Mentor Program has four components: teacher contacts (media specialists, technology staff, and classroom teachers), student participants, HP employee mentors, and HP itself, which devotes significant resources to its involvement with students and teachers. All

> The HP E-mail Mentoring Program is project based and intended to be part of the regular school math, science, or other curriculum.

teacher contacts who enroll in the mentoring program must supervise students in grades 5-12 who are dependent on them for a subject grade. There is no limit to the number of teacher contacts a school may enroll in the program. Each teacher may enroll up to 10 students.

Making the Connection

Teachers may begin applying in April for the following school year. The process has four steps:

- reading information about the program on the HP E-Mail Mentor Web site (http://mentor.external.hp.com)
- submitting initial lesson plans for the October through December instruction period
- completing an online contact-teacher application
- participating in a telephone interview with an HP E-Mentor Program staff member

Contact teachers are responsible for developing lesson plans for student participants on a regular basis throughout the year. HP believes formal written lessons plans with clear objectives, beginning and ending dates, a description of what students will accomplish, clearly defined roles of the teacher and mentor, and an evaluation component are critical to the success of the program. Sample lessons, suggested links to online projects, and a lesson plan template are available at the HP Web site.

Student participants must have personal e-mail accounts and computer access opportunities to enable them to communicate with their mentors at least two to three times per week.

One Participant's Story

As a library media specialist in a small, rural district, I wanted our high school student computer lab assistants to have regular communication with persons who develop and use various forms of technology in business. After hearing about the HP E-Mail Mentoring program at a national conference, I applied in September 1997. The online application was not difficult; using the teacher resources at the HP Web site, I prepared and submitted lesson plans for two months. My application as a contact teacher was approved within one week.

As a contact teacher, I was responsible for knowing the program's objectives, selecting student participants and encouraging them to apply, creating and sending lesson plans, monitoring and evaluating all student/mentor projects, and maintaining regular communication with the students' mentors. HP provided such resources as the monthly *HP Telementoring News*, with inspirational stories from teachers and mentors, technology news, and recommended links for possible use in projects. To allow contact teachers to exchange ideas, the company initiated an online discussion group.

Once my contact-teacher application was approved, I could recruit students. Students at all levels, from at-risk to gifted and talented, are eligible. In recruiting students, I had to carefully describe the requirements and level of commitment needed to participate in the program: putting forth one's best efforts in all messages to mentors, completing assignments made by the contact teacher, taking advantage of experience and information sources available from mentors, and submitting a short online monthly evaluation that reports the level of satisfaction with mentor/student communication and progress on the current project's schedule (i.e., on time, ahead of time). To encourage the continuing assessments, HP holds drawings for prizes for students and mentors who submit two online evaluations per month. A Rosholt student was thrilled to receive a dictionary/calculator as a reward for his regular submissions.

To become part of the program, a student, under supervision of the contact teacher, completes an online application and is matched with an HP mentor. The cutoff date for stu-

dent applications is October 31, though HP attempts to complete the matching process by mid-October. When matches are made, the contact teacher and student are notified. While awaiting the assignment of a mentor, each student prepares a personal biography including family information, favorite subjects, extracurricular activities, and career interests. The student shares the biography with his or her mentor.

The HP E-mail Mentoring Program is project based and intended to be part of the regular school math, science, or other curriculum. Rosholt students in the FLITE program researched and worked on a wide variety of projects. Since the district's telecommunications access had increased dramatically during the summer, from only two school Internet/e-mail accounts to over 50 stations on a dedicated data line, initial student activities centered on receiving personal e-mail accounts, learning a new e-mail program, and becoming familiar with the district's newly created Library Resources Home Page. Another early lesson involved learning Microsoft PowerPoint presentation software. (Two Rosholt students were gratified to learn that their mentors were also learning PowerPoint.) In the lesson related to investigating computer-related careers, our students learned the educational and career paths their mentors had taken. Mentors spoke seriously of their careers, training, and travel commitments; one shared how her job had evolved and said she was interviewing for a senior consultant position. From there, students went on to learn and communicate with their mentors on topics ranging from computer intranets and internal security to programming languages to "cookies." Karen Menard, a first-year mentor, commented that the students' lessons "reached beyond 'surfing the net' to ... lessons in history, marketing, communications, and ethics (along with basic computer skills)."

Rosholt students found participating in the telementoring experience worthwhile. In a final evaluation one student wrote, "I enjoyed corresponding with my mentor. He told me what it is like to work at HP and what he does. After this, I am even surer that I want to go into a computer related field." Another enjoyed "experienced help on computer topics and the story my mentor sent me about Microsoft Smart House."

Mentors of Rosholt students also expressed very positive comments regarding their experiences:

I very much enjoyed being involved in the HP mentoring program. I had been schooled in the suburbs of Boston (K-9) and rural Wisconsin (10-12). Based on my own observations and memories, many rural students don't see beyond their own backyards and need opportunities, like the HP mentoring program, to help broaden their horizons.
— Karen Menard

This was my first mentorship. A lot of the ideas and questions not only came from my student, but I found myself asking just as many questions to him.
— Michael Ybarra

He came up with things to talk about, challenged my responses, and presented original ideas in our conversations. Because I showed interest in and had a lot in common with things he liked (Playstation games, martial arts, basketball), I was able to remove the boundaries sometimes put up between child and adult or student and teacher, which allowed him to communicate openly without fear.
—Kevin Kawahara

As for benefits for myself, I am rewarded by seeing a child's self-esteem grow.
—Karen Rains

The Hewlett Packard E-Mail Mentoring Program met the Rosholt students' needs for ongoing contact with persons working in a technology-related career. For a district with a primarily agricultural base, students working with HP mentors formed the perfect business and school partnership. Via telementoring, the Rosholt students learned valuable lessons in a classroom without walls. As a contact teacher, I appreciated the positive, caring attitude shown by the mentors.

Based on the personal growth witnessed in Rosholt's telementored students, I encourage you to consider incorporating a telementoring program into your school's curriculum. Teacher applications are accepted annually April through September.

Helen Adams is a High School Library Media Specialist and Technology Coordinator for the Rosholt (Wisconsin) School District. Questions and comments may be directed to her e-mail address, hadams@coredcs.com.

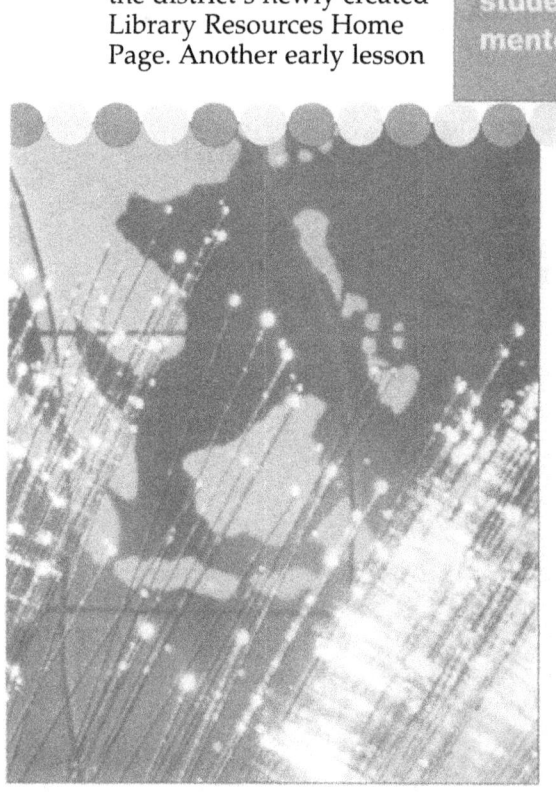

> As a contact teacher, I was responsible for knowing the program's objectives, selecting student participants and encouraging them to apply, creating and sending lesson plans, monitoring and evaluating all student/mentor projects, and maintaining regular communication with the students' mentors.

SEARCHING

Adventures In E-Mail Land

When It Comes To Developing Interpersonal Skills, E-Mail Speaks Volumes

I've been surfing the Internet for about four months and have traveled to telnet sites all over the world. But there's no place like home—my favorite spot to visit is my own mailbox.

My Listserv

On LM_NET, I have found a community of friends who help me with all my professional problems. I am the only librarian in my building, and the only high school librarian in my district. But—thanks to my listserv—I am not at all isolated.

My online colleagues have offered advice on how to load software, provided grammar tips, and argued good-naturedly about whether it's better to start as a school or public librarian. I've gotten the low-down on what to read, what to buy, and how to get along with teachers. I've gotten the scoop on everything from locating great sources for government documents to finding German-speaking "keypals." There have also been some wonderful ideas on what to do with those old card catalogs. My mission for this year is to get many other teachers matched happily with the right listservs.

Keypals

I have gathered around me a group of diverse students—some considered popular, some whom others consider "nerds," and some with a variety of disabilities. All have discovered that e-mail is blind. This anonymity has been refreshing. Even students who "hate to write" love to write e-mail.

However, there is a trick to motivating high school keypals. It really helps to match older students with the opposite sex. A bit of flirting may help to break the ice online.

This is exemplified by an incident with our Tasmanian friends. A number of the boys asked for metric conversion tables. Thrilled with their new interest in exploring math, I dug up tables and formulas. Can you guess the reason for this interest in things metric? The Australian girls had been sending their measurements! We discouraged further activity of this nature.

Another of our students, upon realizing that he was brighter and more affluent than a counterpart in North Carolina, wrote a letter expressing a "superior air." His keypal's response expressed hurt feelings. Our student was shocked that his short note had such an impact on another person. No lesson from me was needed there.

To avert these types of situations, I now monitor all e-mail and my students know it! I'm proud that other, perhaps more relevant, cultural exchanges have taken place—we've learned a lot about the climate in Australia, cultural differences, Tasmanian devils, and slang expressions.

We're now embarking upon a new creative writing project with our keypals from North Carolina. After linking students by interests, communicated via a database, those involved have exchanged friendly letters to get to know each other. They are now collaborating on writing suspense stories online. To round out our keypal program, we are planning e-mail relationships with high school students from Japan. This will be particularly exciting because of a new Japanese language program in our district.

Other interesting e-mail happenings:

1. Debate students are sharing tips on the national topic of immigration with students from other states.
2. Exchange students are communicating with their families and friends abroad.
3. Students are practicing foreign language skills with native speakers or others studying the same language.
4. Students and teachers are communicating with children and friends away at college.
5. Students are tracking concert schedules of their favorite groups through e-mail addresses they've discovered inlibrary directories.
6. I make embarrassing apologies the cowardly way—through e-mail—and avoid face-to-face contact.
7. I can now easily contact my colleagues to change or verify dates for committee meetings.
8. We are now exploring mentorship arrangements with local businesses and established e-mail "experts."

by Joyce Kasman Valenza

E-mail has built our students' self-esteem and opened a world of new friends beyond our library. It's little wonder that they have learned to love e-mail as much as I do! TC

Joyce Valenza is the media specialist at Wissahickon High School Library, Ambler, Pennsylvania.

TELECOMMUNICATIONS AND  DISTANCE LEARNING

Making the Most of E-Mail

HOW TO BE CONCISE, COURTEOUS, AND CORRECT ONLINE

by Leticia Ekhaml

Electronic mail has become a popular and indispensable method of communication. However, it has a few disadvantages. It can sometimes cause misunderstandings because, like letters, it offers no clue about the sender's facial expressions, body language, or tone of voice. A second problem is that you cannot send a message without knowing the receiver's e-mail address. Finally, you need to check your e-mail frequently, since the quantity can quickly overwhelm you.

Readers hesitate to read unusually long messages. Don't be a blatherer.

When you type a message on a text editor of the e-mail system and send the message, the program tells you, the sender, that the message has been sent. The message goes to the mailbox of the receiver on the same central computer. After the receiver reads the message, he or she can choose to reply to the sender, forward the message to someone else, delete the message, print it, file it, or simply quit.

Avoid These Mistakes

- Inaccurately typing the receiver's address. "Addressee unknown" or "undelivered mail" messages specify this problem.
  Remedy: Always check the person's address before mailing.

- Failing to give an appropriate subject line to the message. A subject line helps the receiver identify the summary or importance of the message. Examples of inappropriate subject lines are:
  Subject: Your June 6th response
  Subject: Your reply yesterday
  Subject: Urgent message
  Remedy: Summarize your message in a phrase on the subject line or use key words in your subject line. Some authors recommend that you tell the receiver what to do instead of what your message is about. For example: Subject: Send copy of the July 26th Minutes.

- Using conventional greetings such as Dear Sirs, Dear Madam, Dear Jane.
  Remedy: If you know the person well, address the person by the first name without the "Dear." If you know the group of persons you are writing to, write "Greetings." If you are writing to someone you don't know, use Mr. ___ or Ms. ___.

- Using long paragraphs or long messages that occupy more than one screenful. Readers hesitate to read unusually long messages. Don't be a blatherer.
  Remedies: Break a long paragraph into several short paragraphs to increase readability. Limit your message to one or two screens. Make use of journalists' *inverted pyramid* style—that is, put the who,

Misspelled words can be annoying or confusing and give the impression that you are sloppy, incompetent, or careless.

what, why, when, where, and how in the first paragraph. Use subject headings and double line spacing before and after a heading. Use double line spacing between paragraphs and do not indent paragraphs. Use bulleted or numbered lists. Include an *executive summary*, a short, beginning paragraph that summarizes the key points of the message. You can also break up your long message into several short messages.

- Using space bar spaces to align numbered lists or bulleted lists and to separate them from the text. This can cause problems in displaying the message on the receiver's screen.
  Remedy: Use tabs.

- Misspelling words. Misspelled words can be annoying or confusing and give the impression that you are sloppy, incompetent, or careless.
  Remedy: Check your spelling with the help of your spelling checker (if your e-mail system has this feature) or use your dictionary.

- Using all capital letters in the message. This can cause readability problems.
  Remedy: Use both capital and

lowercase letters when writing.
- Using font features such as boldface or italics. Some receivers' computers and e-mail systems cannot reproduce these effects.
Remedy: Use an asterisk on each side of a word or phrase, indicating that it is italicized or boldfaced. If you need to emphasize important ideas, use boxes consisting of hyphens or asterisks or pipe characters. (Example shown below.)

```
*************************************
*                                   *
*  Send Minutes as soon as          *
*  possible for approval!           *
*                                   *
*************************************
```

- Failing to delete unwanted messages immediately which can take up disk storage space.
Remedy: Delete all unwanted messages.
- Using conventional methods of closing. "Sincerely yours," "Yours," "Yours truly," "If you have further questions, contact me" are not used.
Remedy: Close with "Thanks" or "Regards," plus your signature or initial. It is recommended that you put one or more hyphens before your name to separate this line from the body of the message. For someone who does not know you well, include your title/position, the name of your organization, and your e-mail address. Some people even include the number of their voice mail. Avoid elaborate graphics in your signature.
- Not answering e-mail messages promptly.
Remedy: If you need more time, send a quick message to let the sender know that you have read the message and that you will soon reply.
- Sending a file when an e-mail message is sufficient. Some receivers' e-mail systems may not handle this. Sending a file also requires extra work on the part of the receiver since the receiver will need to decompress and download the file, then start an application and open the file.
Remedy: If you have to send a file, compress the file and let the receiver know that the file is compressed. Make sure the receiver has the same compression program to decompress the file.
- Using jargon or technical words to impress the reader.
Remedy: Write simply. If you need to use jargon, make sure the reader understands it. If you need to explain the jargon, explain it in simple, layman's language.

Be a professional and competent communicator! Avoid these mistakes. Get to know more about e-mail rules and conventions. Happy e-mailing! **TC**

Leticia Ekhaml is Professor of Media Education at West Georgia College in Carrollton, Georgia.

Notes

SEARCHING

Can the Internet Be Used with K–5 Students?

The Answer is Elementary!

by Madeline Buchanan

Electronic mail projects are not merely sending e-mail messages.

Many people agree that the Internet offers outstanding resources for high school and college students. However, because they lack keyboarding skills and don't yet engage in research, its value for elementary students is questioned. Is there anything for young children on this vast electronic resource? There is at Barrett Elementary School in Birmingham, Alabama, the first public elementary school in the area to provide Internet to its students. Since Gopher, Telnet, and FTP were beyond the abilities of the kindergarten through fifth grade students attending the school, they were introduced to telecommunications through e-mail.

Before You Begin

Typing can be tedious to impossible for elementary school students; those without any keyboarding skills may take an hour to compose even one paragraph. Older students who can type or adult volunteers will speed up the process.

Typing directly on many Internet screens is beyond the reach of elementary students who need to compose their thoughts beforehand. On the other hand, uploading to the Internet from many word processing programs is a trial-and-error procedure, so do a trial upload beforehand to make sure it's possible.

Direct Internet access provides mail programs in which mail can be composed offline on a screen similar to that of a word processor, as well as a more user-friendly way to access Gopher and FTP files. The World Wide Web, accessed through *Mosaic* or *Netscape*, offers pictures and sound as well as text.

Letter-Writing Activities Improve Grammar, Spelling

There are two types of electronic mail projects: individual messages sent by one student to another student and whole-class or group projects than can be linked to almost every elementary school subject.

One of the better known discussion groups is Intercultural E-mail Classrooms Connections. This group addresses educators wishing to find partner classrooms for their students. The e-mail address for subscribing to this list is iecc-request@stolaf.edu. The educational area of Usenet provides penpal lists, projects, and even a section where students can request penpals themselves.

Letter-writing skills, along with correct capitalization, punctuation, spelling, and grammar, are the most obvious links from computer to classroom. Even if the students can't key in their own correspondence, they must put their thoughts down on paper in such a way that a typist can interpret them. If a group of students is able to compose a message using a word processor, they can view and correct mistakes on screen that might be harder to identify on a piece of notebook paper. (It's important that students use standard English, since regional dialects might not be understood by a recipient halfway around the world whose native language is not English.)

Social Studies Projects Spark Curiosity

Another important student e-mail link is in social studies. Students learn about other cultures and different ways of life. One fourth grade student was surprised to learn why it took her pen pal in Israel so long to respond—it was news to her that the Israeli students did not speak English as a native language and had to translate letters before sending them by computer. Birmingham elementary students were also very interested in how Australian children celebrated Christmas, since the holiday occurs in the middle of their summer. E-mail correspondence inspired students to carry out research in the media center to learn more about the places their new friends lived.

Electronic mail also increased students' knowledge in science and mathematics. For example, Birmingham children learned to convert temperatures from Fahrenheit to Celsius in order to compare weather statistics. Gasoline sold by the liter seems to be a lot more expensive than by the gallon. Students learned how to convert monetary values to find the cost of things in different countries.

Students enjoy electronic mail because it provides another way of learning. For instance, a first grade class participated in a project that required them to describe a monster's hair. Other classes from around the country described different parts of the monster's body. These young students learned how to write a description and to use the description to actually construct the entire monster. Several of the teachers sent pictures of their monsters to everyone who participated.

E-Mail Leads to 'Snail Mail'

As a result of their e-mail correspondence, a Barrett fourth grade class exchanged videos with a fourth grade class in Saskatoon, Saskatchewan, Canada. This video exchange allowed them to see their penpals, hear the different accents, and see what their penpals' school is like. It's expensive to convert videos to the system used in Europe and Australia, but students can exchange souvenirs, photographs, and postcards with partner classes. Some students continue their relationships by "snail mail" during the summer. **TC**

Madeline Buchanan is a Library Media Specialist at Barrett Elementary School in Birmingham, Alabama.

Notes

Where on the World Wide Web is the Library?

Seduced and Abandoned on the Web

(or How Users Are Seduced by the Internet and Then Abandon Their Critical Faculties)

By Mark Williams

Why is it that information obtained from the Net seems to seduce the student into blind acceptance?

"BUT MR. WILLIAMS...it has to be true. I got it from the Internet!" The sound you now hear is a frustrated librarian banging his head on a nearby wall. This student and I had been working for weeks on a major paper, and he had proudly asked me to give it one final look before he turned it in. In the first three paragraphs, there were three serious factual errors that rendered the paper worthless.

I have become increasingly concerned about the abuse of the Internet as an information source for classroom assignments. Why do students who would normally do at least some minimal checking of sources for accuracy and relevancy abandon such behavior when dealing with information from the Internet? This phenomenon is not limited to students; more than a few adults, including faculty, also are guilty.

Of course, we should apply the same standards to information regardless of its source, but why does information obtained from the Net seems to seduce students into blind acceptance? I think it is partly because of the seductive nature of computers. Kids love them and often prefer them to print materials. Partly it is the ease with which young people learn to work with electronic equipment, and partly it is because the media have portrayed computers as a kind of magic bullet that will cure all problems and answer all questions. And, of course, it involves the fact that when they

are working at their best, computers are undeniably good at retrieving bits of information from a welter of material.

One of our most important jobs as librarians is to teach both students and staff to evaluate the sources of their information. Nowhere is this more important than when dealing with information from the Internet. Our students and adult patrons have come to expect that when they walk into a library they will find accurate, balanced information because someone professionally trained has selected the materials for accuracy, currency, and relevancy. We have no such assurance on the Internet.

Anyone with a few dollars, a computer and a bit of experience can launch a professional-looking web site and fill it with whatever (mis)information he wants. The advent of web page authoring software obviates the need for extensive knowledge of HTML encoding. You cannot judge by appearance alone. Both good, solid information and trash can, and often do, come across the computer screen looking equally professional. We are accustomed to instructing students in methods of evaluating print resources. I suggest that we must be equally vigilant in doing so with electronic resources, especially with web sites.

But the interactive nature of the medium adds another dimension. Although accuracy must be our top concern, the way information is presented in a web site can make that information either easy to find and use or difficult in the extreme. So other considerations enter into our evaluation. I have found it helpful to break evaluation rubrics into four broad areas: content, source, access, and structure.

CONTENT

This important criterion strikes at the heart of any evaluation. What information is contained in the site and how comprehensive is it? Does the site present an overview of the topic or does it go into detail? Is the level of detail consistent, or are some areas covered well and others poorly? How current is the site? Is the most recent revision date clearly stated? How complete and accurate are links to other sites? (Of course, this will involve taking the time to pursue those links and applying the same criteria to them that were applied to the original site.) Are the URLs for the links still valid, or do you get the dreaded "404 Error" message when you attempt to go to the site? How does the site compare to print sources? Does the site present information that is not readily available in other formats? Are the multimedia elements relevant?

SOURCE

Equally important is the source of the information presented. Librarians naturally tend to look at this criterion before others.

Is the author of the site clearly stated? Do you have some indication of this person's or organization's credentials and level of expertise? Is the site sponsored or co-sponsored by a reputable organization? Are documents quoted directly or paraphrased? Are quotations fully credited? Are pictures, graphs, and charts clearly labeled as to source and date? Is there any evident bias, either in the information itself or in the sources selected for presentation? Are links clearly identified as to authorship? Again, all the criteria used for evaluating the original site's sources should be applied to any links.

ACCESS

This criterion is based on the assumption that the even best sites are worthless if they cannot be found easily or used by the typical user.

Is the site indexed on major search engines or only on the more esoteric ones that access only a limited number of sites or index a narrow range of topics? Is there a text-only option to speed loading of the site? This is especially useful where the Internet connection is slow, where there are a limited number of stations available for patron use, or when a site is heavily laden with multimedia goodies that do not relate directly to the information presented.

Has the author used standard HTML formatting and codes, or are proprietary extensions used? This can cause some parts of the site to display in ways greatly different than the author intended or not at all. Is downloading time reasonable? This is often a function of the service provider, but it also relates to the placement of multimedia elements in the site itself. A large graphic at the beginning of a site may slow the loading of any useful information below it.

Is the site stable? Is the URL consistent, or does it move from server to server? Note that service providers do go out of business, and site owners may be forced into changing the URL for their pages. But a site that seems to have a new address each time you access it may indicate questionable authorship.

STRUCTURE

As a visual person, I pay close attention to the way a source looks. Students tend to rank this area highest because it grabs their attention. In reality, the way the information is presented on a page does not affect the accuracy of the source or the value of the information. But if the page is unreadable because of a poor choice of background color or typeface, or if it is so poorly organized that it is frustrating to use, then the site is not helpful regardless of how it ranks on the other criteria. Pages that are "busy" with graphics or animations may impede effective use of the site.

Is the site clearly organized? Are descriptions of what the user can find located near the top of the site? Are directions for navigating the site clear and concise? Are there easy ways to move from one place to another, or must the user scroll endlessly to get from one part of the site to another? Can a novice navigate the site without the need for constant help? Can an expert user quickly retrieve information from various parts of the site and develop a trail of information from link to link? Are help dialogs or screens readily available for novice users?

Are the graphics and multimedia elements functional or merely decorative? While decorative isn't necessarily bad, it shouldn't be overdone because graphics take time to download. What elements of creativity are evident? Does the site do anything better than print sources. Of course, a primary reason for web sites is the ability to bring together sight, sound, and movement in a compelling presentation of factual information. Are background patterns and colors suitable? Do such background patterns or colors interfere with the reading of material? Can sounds be turned off? Is the typeface and size appropriate? Are key elements readily discernible? Are links clearly indicated with some form of contrasting typeface color or size or a graphic? Is the "look" of the page exciting and involving?

So what is the best way to get students and faculty to apply these critical criteria to web sites? One approach is for faculty and the librarian, either at the site or district level, to develop a rubric for the evaluation of Internet resources. This is an excellent chance for the school librarian to build influence on campus by demonstrating some of the principles that Gary Hartzell discusses in his book, *Building Influence for the School Librarian* (Linworth, 1994), particularly those of shaping perceptions at the site and district level. Although this does reinvent the wheel somewhat since there are numerous Internet sites that display ratings sheets and rubrics for evaluation, there is great value in local groups creating their own rubrics. Groups that develop their own rubrics are much more likely to apply them than if they simply are handed a canned set of criteria.

A useful tactic is to have the group meet and discuss some potential problems that would arise from the blind acceptance of material from the Internet. I like to illustrate this with a site that purported to show that the dictator Pol Pot had asked for and received political asylum in Sweden. Although professionally done, the entire site with photographs and video clips to accompany the "news release," is a fabrication. A more complete discussion of this site can be found by accessing Andy Carvin's posting of July 7, 1997 in the LM_NET listserv archives with the subject heading "Getting the truth online: Pol Pot in Sweden."

After reviewing the four broad criteria—content, source, access, and structure—the group is broken into four sub-groups, and over a 20-minute time block, the goal is to develop specific criteria within their category. The sub-groups present their lists to the whole group as individuals record them on a worksheet. Suggestions and comments are encouraged. At the end of this process, each group member has a completed worksheet that is, in essence, a rubric for evaluating web sites.

Ideally, the group will then immediately move to a lab setting and apply the newly-created rubric to several pre-selected sites. Discussion and further refining of the rubric may follow, and in the remaining time, they can surf the Net and apply the refined rubric to sites they find.

Another aspect of this process is the need to educate parents and the public about the need for critical viewing of Web-based resources. We all have heard the horror stories of students accessing inappropriate sites and the school being taken to task for allowing such incidents to happen. One way to fend off some of the criticism is to take a proactive stance and inform the public about the need for care when using web sites. This can be done through parent workshops conducted in conjunction with PTA meetings, newsletters, and flyers. Letting the public know that we are teaching students to critically evaluate the information they retrieve from the Internet can help foster a view of schools and school libraries as responsible users of technology.

Local cable access programs sometimes can be used for such training. Service organizations often are looking for short programs for lunch or evening meetings. Presenting a brief version of a workshop detail-

---

SITES THAT HAVE EVALUATION GUIDES:

Kathy Schrock's excellent Educator's Guide site...
www.capecod.net/schrockguide/eval.htm

Ohio State's guide for site evaluation...
www.mansfield.ohio-state.edu/writecnt/webeval.htm

Duke University's guide...
www.duke.edu/~del/evaluate.html

The UCLA evaluation guidelines, required of students in certain courses...
www.library.ucla.edu/libraries/college/instruct/critical.htm

SITES THAT ARE "FALSE" FOR USE IN DEMONSTRATIONS

www.tass.net (Note: this site has NOTHING to do with the ITAR-Tass news agency in Russia)

134.29.12.207/NewHartford/tour.html (Note: someone went to a LOT of trouble with this site..it is filled with all sorts of nice stuff......there IS no New Hartford, MN....a tip off is that none of the businesses profiled have phone numbers, and the map uses county highways that don't exist.)

SITES THAT SHOW EXAMPLES OF POORLY DESIGNED WEB SITES:

www.webpagesthatsuck.com/index3/html
www.worstoftheweb.com/

Seduced and Abandoned on the Web

ing the rubric your site or district has developed not only can provide them with useful information but also can garner some positive publicity for your school. Communities want to feel good about the schools their children attend, and such outreach can help develop those feelings. It also lets people know that school librarians do more than stamp dates in books.

Instructing students to use a rubric to evaluate sites is more difficult. Sometimes it is simply overkill to give students a complicated rubric to use with each site they access. I conduct a short lesson with classes using my current faked site to demonstrate the perils of swallowing unquestioned what they find on the Net. I give the students a handout that details selected questions listed under the content and sources sections of the larger rubric, and we discuss these as a group. Students then are better equipped to evaluate what they find.

Teachers are encouraged to incorporate the serious evaluation of web sites when they discuss the evaluation of other sources in preparing their students for research projects or assignments. If this is done through the library, I always stress that all information should be subjected to the same critical appraisal.

It took us years to get library users to routinely evaluate the sources of information they access. We need to continue that effort with the wealth of information available to them on the Internet.

Mark Williams is a Librarian at Colton (California) High School.

THE INTERNET: CONNECTING WITH THE CURRICULUM

feature

It Must Be True. I Found It on the Internet!

By Kathleen Schrock

"Look at the copyright date."

"Is the author an authority on the topic?"

"Is a bibliography included?"

These questions are familiar to library media specialists. We use a set of criteria to evaluate a print item for purchase and know how to instruct students in critiquing an item for use in research projects. However, another set of standards is needed for evaluating information taken from the World Wide Web. Users need to learn to evaluate the technical aspects and subject content of a World Wide Web page to determine whether it meets their needs.

Training students to evaluate this new medium means blending media literacy skills with library reference skills. The bottom line is that before accepting information they find on the Internet, students need to verify it with a second source. If the primary source material is found only on the Internet, like the FDR Cartoon Collection (http://www.wizvax.net/nisk_hs/departments/social/fdr_html/FDRmain.html), students must decide whether an item has been altered from its original state.

I have designed a set of evaluation instruments for use at the elementary, middle, and high school levels. These instruments may be found at http://www.capecod. net/Wixon/eval.htm, along with two essays dealing with the topic of assessing a Web page. The two essays will help readers determine which elements of a Web page should be evaluated.

Lesson Preparation

I recently conducted a four-lesson Internet unit with six fourth-grade classes and incorporated the critical evaluation of a Web page as the third lesson. The lesson plan and a copy of the evaluation tool for the elementary grade level are included here. In the future, I will post the entire four-lesson unit on my home page, Kathy Schrock's Guide for Educators, at http://www.capecod.net/Wixon/wixon.htm.

To replicate this lesson, you need some HTML-writing knowledge and a standalone HTML editor or word processing program, a graphical Internet account (PPP or SLIP), and a copy of *WebWhacker*, software that allows you to "grab" a Web page address (URL) while surfing online and then "whack" (download) the entire page, graphics included, to your own hard drive.

Later, you can simply open your graphical browser and view the whacked page as a static HTML document. In this way, you can simulate the Internet experience even if you don't have a connection in your classroom. All you need is a computer with a Web browser. You can download a 30-day trial copy of *WebWhacker* at http://www.ffg.com.

[Editor's Note: There is considerable controversy over the copyright implications of copying Web pages. At the time of this writing, the U.S. Congress is holding hearings on modifications to copyright law and practice to protect Internet documents.]

To design a lesson on the critical evaluation of a Web page, I used a topic that most fourth-grade students know a little about and are interested in—dinosaurs!

I first went to the UC-Berkeley Museum of Paleontology site and used *WebWhacker* to download the entire page about *Tyrannosaurus rex*. I then opened my HTML editor (*HTML Assistant Pro* by Brooklyn North Software) and proceeded to edit and create six different versions of the page: one version was the original page; one version had a lot of spelling errors; one version had completely erroneous information (*T. rex* was a plant eater that weighed 50 tons); the other three versions were unsigned, with no updates and no author information.

I printed out one color copy of each of the six different pages and laminated them. So that each student could have a copy, I photocopied four copies of each page. I also made a copy of the critical evaluation form for each student.

Remember to obtain permission from the Webmaster of the page you want to use and will be "whacking." A short note explaining what you are teaching and how you are going to edit the pages will usually result in permission to use the material. If not, try another page and another Webmaster!

Conclusion

With the advent of new technologies, there is always a new set of skills to be learned. Anyone can publish and distribute information on the Internet and the World Wide Web. It is imperative that library media specialists provide students with the skills needed to evaluate the accuracy, authenticity, and applicability of information found on the Net. TC

Kathleen Schrock is a Library Media Specialist at Nathaniel H. Wixon Middle School in South Dennis, Massachusetts.

> *Users need to learn to evaluate the technical aspects and subject content of a World Wide Web page to determine whether it meets their needs.*

The Lesson Plan

Brush Up on the Internet Week 3: Critical Evaluation of a Web Page

Purpose: To have students realize that Web pages need to be looked at critically and evaluated for content accuracy and authenticity.

Materials: Six laminated Web pages; a set of four photocopies of each laminated page; 24 copies of the critical evaluation checklist; one overhead transparency of each laminated page; Internet connection or *WebWhacked* Web page that meets all of the criteria for a good Web page; large screen projection device for class viewing

Procedure:

1. The library media specialist will poll the students to see if they know some of the methods for critically evaluating a print source (copyright date, bibliography included, information about the author included, and so on). The library media specialist will remind students that the Internet is a huge repository of information, but students need to be able to verify whether the information presented is accurate and useful for their purpose.

2. The library media specialist will project on the large screen an exemplary Web page that includes all criteria. These include, but are not limited to, a descriptive title, a photograph or drawing, a date of last update, a signed page, information about the author, sources used to prepare the page, and links to other related sites. Using the checklist, the library media specialist will model aloud how to critically evaluate the Web page.

3. The library media specialist will present students with the scenario that they are doing a report on dinosaurs and will need to evaluate information on that topic found on a Web page.

4. Working in six small groups, students will evaluate the copy of the page at their table by filling out the checklist. Encourage students to use traditional print sources to verify questionable information. Each group will then present its results to the class using the overhead copy of its particular page. (Some of the questions on the evaluation checklist, such as those on sound or loading, will not be applicable for this static Web page lesson.)

Summary: Using *The Important Book* by Margaret Wise Brown (Harper, 1949) as a model, ask students to fill out the following summary sheet. (This picture book identifies the key characteristics of common objects.) Students will give the main concept in the first and last statements and three supporting details in the middle. For example,

The important thing about Web pages is you need to check the information.

They **should be signed.**

They **should be current.**

They **should contain a good title.**

But the important thing about Web pages is **you need to check the information.**

Producing Information Consumers: Critical Evaluation and Critical Thinking

By Kathleen Schrock

IT IS WIDELY ACCEPTED that, at the end of the 20th century, we have become an information society. It is more important than ever, therefore, for educators to provide students with the awareness and skills required to critically evaluate the tide of information that floods our culture. This is especially true of the information that can be found on the Internet, because so much of it does not undergo any type of review process. Students must be able to evaluate the quality of such information, which means that they must be able to think critically.

In their online essay, *"Tactics that encourage active learning"* (Center for Critical Thinking, <www.sonoma.edu/CThink/K12/>, September 22, 1996) Paul Richard and Linda Elder suggest that "critical thinking involves learning to realize how one thinks and forming opinions and perceptions based on this process. Students need to be presented with lessons which actively engage them in thinking and evaluating the content of a particular topic. They should be able to relate this content to their own knowledge, make connections between related concepts, summarize what an author or teacher has said, and give examples to clarify what they, themselves, have stated."

Elizabeth Kirk in her online essay, *"Evaluation information found on the Internet"* (Milton's Web, <milton.mse.jhu.edu:8001/research/education/net.html>, September 22, 1996), states: "Establishing and learning criteria to filter information on the Internet is a good beginning for becoming a critical consumer of information in all forms."

If students look at the layout and content of an information source, and then ascertain whether the information is appropriate and useful through a guided evaluation process, they should acquire the skills to become these "information consumers" and have the knowledge to critically evaluate information of all types.

In the case of the Internet, the evaluation of content and appropriateness is a bit different than the same process with the printed word. Books and journals are usually evaluated first by editorial boards and then by review sources, before they are purchased by librarians for a reference or subject collection.

Commercial databases are often created and evaluated by subject matter specialists and indexers. Producers of these databases are careful to check the authority of the author and the authenticity of the content before an addition to the database is made.

Given the global, distributed nature of the Internet, material found on the Net is not likely to have gone through any such review process before being published. Anyone may publish on the Internet, so some addition-

Notes

al criteria need to be considered by students when evaluating Internet pages. Because of the proliferation of World Wide Web pages, the focus will remain on evaluation of the type of information found on the Web.

Before starting any research project, students and teachers need to recognize the current limitations of information found on the Internet. Book and magazine publishers are not likely to have full-text copies of their information available freely on the Net. There may be portions or supplementary material available, but students must realize that printed materials will still be their primary source of information.

Most information on the Internet is recent. There have been some compilations of historical data put on the Net, but the majority of statistical and empirical data presented is still post-1993.

Due to the varying limitations of bandwidth on the Internet, most of the useful information is in text or photograph form. If a student wishes to view a video of the Hindenburg airship disaster, a CD-ROM, videotape, or videodisk would be the most appropriate place to begin.

Once students recognize the type of information that will be found on the Internet, they should formulate a search strategy by identifying the information that is necessary to complete the project at hand. Teachers can facilitate this process by providing a simplified reference interview to allow students to recognize what information is being sought.

Once a search has been conducted and a site has been identified, each level of student (elementary, middle, and secondary) should evaluate the site using the same set of criteria. The evaluation questions may be phrased differently for each level, but the concepts will still be the same—evaluation of author authority, content, and presentation.

Authority of Author

The author should be recognized as an expert in the field. Some items to consider include:

- Has this author been cited by others?
- Can the students find the author's name attached to print resources?
- Does the author list his or her qualifications?
- Is an e-mail address given so the author may be contacted for further information?

Content, Bias, and the Authenticity of Information

Because the content is the most important aspect of the site for students collecting information, these questions should be taken into consideration:

- Does the author state a purpose for the site?
- Does the author describe the audience that the site is intended for?
- If the content is controversial or biased, does the author give an explanation for this?
- Can the content be verified in a print source?
- If currency is important, is the information current?
- Is the page dated with the date of last update?
- Is a lot of information presented or just an overview?
- Is a bibliography included for verification of information or further research?

Presentation

Due to the varying speeds of Internet access, types of browsers, and ages of students, the presentation of a site on the Web is also important.

- Is the page easy to use?
- Is the information on the page well organized?
- Is the page pleasing to look at?
- Is the page free of spelling, grammatical, and HTML errors?
- Do included graphics enhance the presentation or supplement the content?

Evaluation tools for students at the elementary, middle, and secondary school levels may be found at <www.capecod.net/schrockguide/eval.htm>.

After students have evaluated the author, content, and presentation of a site using these evaluation instruments, they should be able to judge whether the information is applicable to their purpose. Using some higher-level thinking questions, students are asked to justify the use of the site for their project. Have students compare the information they outlined as important in the beginning reference interview with the sites they have critically evaluated, and come up with a rationale for using or not using the site in their project.

By training, and modeling for, our students how to become critical evaluators of information that we find, we shall be producing the well-educated "information consumers" of tomorrow. Given the massive amount of information and information sources available, this is truly an important skill for the 21st century!

A great Internet site that has links to many pages of critical evaluation of Web page research is *Teaching Students to Think Critically About Internet Resources* <weber.u.washington.edu/~libr560/NETEVAL/index.html>.

Kathleen Schrock is a Technology Coordinator at Dennis-Yarmouth Regional School District in South Yarmouth, Massachusetts, and can be reached at kschrock@capecod.net

Notes

Evaluating Web Resources

By Ruth V. Small & Marilyn P. Arnone

Evaluation is an important critical-thinking skill. Information literacy includes skills for evaluating information and information resources. Even our youngest students are exploring the World Wide Web for reasons ranging from seeking information to help with homework assignments to browsing just for fun, and we must teach them the skills to assess the quality of the Web sites they find. In this article we describe a tool developed to provide very young children with hands-on experience in evaluating the strengths and weaknesses of Web sites. It also includes some ideas for incorporating Web evaluation into your instruction.

Ruth V. Small (left), Ph.D. is associate professor and coordinator of the school media program in the School of Information Studies at Syracuse University. Her research and teaching focus on the instructional and motivational aspects of information presentation and use.

Marilyn P. Arnone, Ph.D. is President for Research & Development at Creative Media Solutions in Syracuse, New York. She is adjunct professor at the School of Information Studies at Syracuse University. Her research centers on curiosity motivation and learning.

Web Evaluation Criteria

When evaluating Web sites, three general criteria may be considered: functionality, content, and motivational quality. Functionality focuses on whether the various features at the Web site (e.g., navigation buttons, response time, hot links) work the way they should. Features that add value to a Web site's information (e.g., relevance of the information, organization for easy access, appropriate amount of information) comprise the content criterion of Web evaluation.

Motivation of Web sites may be defined in terms of expectancy-value theory (V. H. Vroom, *Work and Motivation*, 1964, Wiley), which proposes that people's motivations to engage in an activity relies on both a perception that there is something of value in the activity and the expectation that they will be successful in accomplishing that activity. Adapting this theory to the Web environment, a Web site that is stimulating, engaging, useful, and credible may be considered a valuable Web site; a Web site that is organized for ease of use and is satisfying and effective promotes a positive expectation for success. The degree to which these qualities are present comprises the motivational quality of that Web site.

While there are many instruments for evaluating Web sites that focus on the effectiveness of the functional and/or content aspects, few target the motivational quality of Web sites. Furthermore, most Web site evaluation instruments are designed for use by adults; few are created for independent use by young children or as a tool for teaching children a structured method for evaluating Web sites.

WebMAC Junior

WebMAC Junior, a Web evaluation tool for students in grades one through four was designed to help young children diagnose, analyze, and assess Web sites from a child's perspective. It was adapted from the Website Motivational Analysis Checklist (WebMAC), the original (adult) version of the instrument designed by the authors. Both instruments emphasize the motivational quality of Web sites and include functionality and content-related items, but they frame these factors in terms of their effect on motivation.

WebMAC Junior may be used by an individual child or an entire class. The instrument allows children to rate the motivational quality of various aspects of a Web site and plot the scores on a grid, allowing quick visual assessment of the strengths and weaknesses of that site. The reasonable length of the instrument permits students to easily pinpoint specific areas in need of improvement. WebMAC Junior's administration guidelines include definitions of several common Web site terms (e.g., home page, button, link), a brief overview of its theoretical foundation, ideas for curriculum-related activities, and step-by-step directions for completing and scoring the instrument.

Children are given about 15 minutes to explore a Web site before evaluating it in order to get a sense of its content and structure. They may then complete the items independently, or, with very young children or children with lower reading abilities, the administrator may want to read each item aloud.

WebMAC Junior contains 24 items in a Likert-type scale with 12 items corresponding to each of the expectancy-value components. The instrument is presented in a pleasant, easy-to-read format. Children are instructed to fill out each item as if they are "judges" where there are no right and wrong answers. In response to each item, the children must circle one of the four faces that most appropriately describes their feelings in response to that item. Each face has a rating score from "0" (poor) to "3" (excellent). Some examples of Value items are:

with Young Children

"When you first arrived at this Web site, did it look like this would be an interesting or fun Web site to explore?"

"Were there pictures, movies, or sounds that captured your attention?"

"Were there enough choices for things you wanted to do?"

Some examples of Expectation for Success Items are:

"Did the designers of this Web site make it easy to find the information you needed?"

"When you wanted to do something, were the buttons easy to find and understand?"

"Did this Web site have connections (links) to other Web sites where you could find more information?"

The final page of the instrument includes qualitative items asking children to describe the best aspect of the Web site and ideas for improving it.

Once all items have been rated, children transfer their scores for each item into one of two columns on a tally sheet. Each column is then totaled and the two total column scores are plotted along the "How Interesting" and "How Well It Works" axes (representing Value and Expectation for Success, respectively) of a grid. Children then draw the intersection point of the two scores; this point represents an overall motivational rating for that Web site. When the intersection point falls in the upper right section of the upper right-hand quadrant of the grid, it is considered an "Awesome Web Site!" An example of a completed grid appears below.

A second tally sheet allows the administrator to use WebMAC Junior with an entire class. All class members' scores may be tallied, summed, averaged, and plotted on the grid for a visual representation of a total class rating for a particular Web site.

WebMAC Junior and Information Literacy

Evaluating Web sites offers a meaningful and enjoyable activity for children to develop an important critical-thinking skill. Instruments such as WebMAC Junior provide an exciting opportunity for library media specialists and teachers to work together to plan and teach curriculum-integrated lessons that promote information literacy. Here are some ideas for incorporating Web site evaluation into your lessons.

- When assigning students projects for which they have to gather

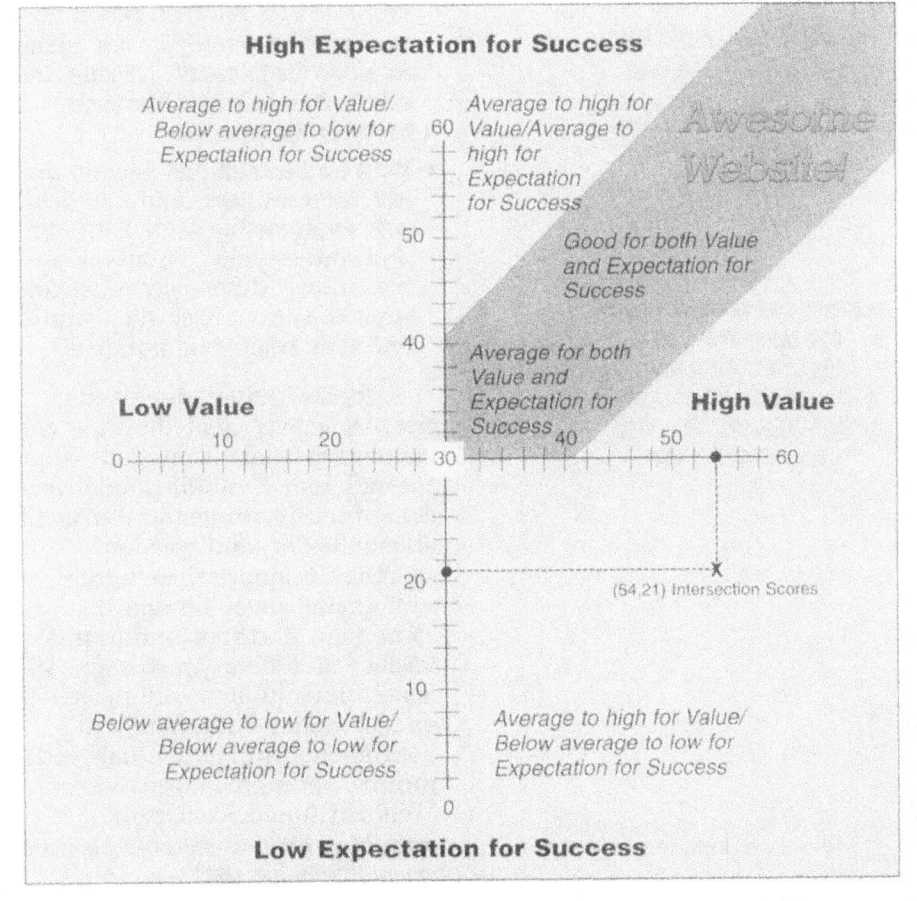

information from a variety of information resources (including one or more Web sites), require them to evaluate one or more of the Web sites and include written summaries of their evaluations with their projects.

- Have students write an assessment of your school's (or library's or classroom's) Web site for a class or school newspaper, including constructive ideas for improvement. This could be continued throughout the school year, providing ongoing Web site evaluation information by students for students.

- Introduce Web site evaluation as part of a broader information skills lesson on evaluating information.

- Sponsor an activity in which students act as "Siskel and Ebert" for Web sites, debating evaluations of the same Web site and/or describing their choices for the "best" and "worst" Web sites on a particular topic. Perhaps videotape some of these debates to show to parents at a PTO meeting or on Parents' Night.

- Have a class discussion on the differences between evaluating networked electronic resources and other types of resources such as books or videos. With the class, create a list of the "Top 10 Features" to address when evaluating all resources.

- Integrate Web site evaluation into curriculum-related assignments, such as: a math lesson on graphing, writing a Web site evaluation summary as part of a language arts project, or comparing two Web sites that present the same scientific concept.

- Compare and discuss Web site evaluations by different classes within the school or compare and discuss evaluations of different Web sites by the same class.

- Evaluate several class or school Web sites to help guide students as they design their own Web site(s).

- Have students evaluate a specific Web site and ask their parent to evaluate the same Web site (using an adult instrument). Discuss the similarities in and differences between the results.

- With an international keypal project, have students and their keypals evaluate the same Web site and share results. Discuss possible cultural differences in perceptions of various Web site features and their relative importance.

WebMAC Junior, described in this article, was created for use with elementary students in grades one through four. A middle school version of this instrument is also available while the adult version WebMAC is appropriate for use with grades seven through 12. More than 50 current and future teachers and library media specialists throughout the world have tested and validated the WebMAC instruments with individuals and groups. For more information on WebMAC Junior, contact the authors at *drruth@ worldnet.att.net* or *arnone1@ibm.net*.

Webliographies

Much More Than Just a Bibliography

Creating a webliography can give students the experience of evaluating sources of information as well as learning technology skills.

Nancy Robinson Marino

YOU ARE LOOKING for information on the Internet. Even if you go to a search engine, such as *Webcrawler, AltaVista* or *Lycos,* you find yourself with hundreds, thousands, or even a million sites. Finding a useful, reliable source on a particular topic can be frustrating even for the most experienced searcher. Any experienced searcher knows there's a lot of garbage out there. So, how can you help students find relevant and useful sources on the World Wide Web? One method is to create webliographies.

Webliographies are a collection of Internet sites on a particular subject. They can be printed on paper, placed on a home page, or entered into a computer-accessible file so that students can automatically link to relevant Web sites. The similarities to a bibliography cannot be overlooked and the learning advantages are similar. By examining and evaluating sources, students improve critical thinking skills.

One way to start a webliography project is to begin a lesson on how to evaluate information. Students naturally make decisions regarding the validity and relevancy of information in their daily lives. Make students aware of their evaluative abilities by playing the "Who Would You Believe Game." Students are given a question or problem to solve and a choice of two possible sources of reliable information. Have the students decide which source they would believe and why. Here is an example of questions and information choices:

WHO WOULD YOU BELIEVE?

Questions	Sources of Information
Why are dinosaurs extinct?	Your little sister or a scientist
What you are having for dinner?	Your parents or a scientist
What are the coolest fashions?	A 1985 book or this month's fashion magazine
Will the United States will ever pass a federal law regarding the Internet?	The President of the United States or the Mayor of your town
Will a traffic light be placed at an intersection near the school?	The President or the Mayor

This exercise can be used to begin a discussion on why some information sources are more valid than others. It can also point out that no one is an authority on everything. While the scientist may be the expert on dinosaurs,

> *The similarities to a bibliography cannot be overlooked and the learning advantages are similar.*

mom (or dad) is probably the expert on what's for dinner. By explaining why they would believe their source, students begin to develop a criteria for evaluating information. This criteria should include organization of information, currency of information, and authority of the source.

When students decide on a criteria, review some Web sites together. Unlike books and magazines, which are generally the product of professional writers and editors and often the subject of review, the World Wide Web is a vehicle for anyone who has something to say. Web pages can be created by anyone who has a little knowledge of computers. Therefore, students must be careful when evaluating their use and relevancy. To illustrate this point the Reference Department at the B. Davis Schwartz Memorial Library, C.W. Post Campus, Long Island University, uses the example of two "whitehouse" Web pages. http://www.whitehouse.gov is the official White House page. http://www.whitehouse.org is a spoof of the official White House Web page. These web pages look very similar and have very similar addresses, but are quite different in purpose and usefulness.

One way to help decide if a Web site will be useful is to look at the domain name. The domain name shows the purpose of the organization where the Web page originated. Using the White House examples above, the domain name "gov" shows that one page comes from a government agency. The name "org" shows that the page comes from an organization.

Other examples of domain names are .edu (educational organization) and .com (commercial organization).

Several new domain names may be introduced in the near future:

.firm (for companies or firms)

.store (for companies selling goods)

.web (for organizations involved in Web-related activities)

.arts (for organizations involved in arts and cultural activities)

.rec (for organizations involved in recreation and entertainment)

.info (for those providing information services)

.nom (for individuals)

Before beginning the actual webliography project, have students spend a class session comparing and contrasting two Web sites on a particular subject. Students can choose their own subject, perhaps one they have a special interest in, and evaluate each site. The students could create a table with the criteria for evaluating the pages listed on the side and the names of the Web sites as a heading.

Another way of organizing this information is by creating a Venn diagram. Each circle represents a Web site with their common elements in the overlapping area.

When you're ready to start the webliography project, students will begin to search the Web. In addition to search engines such as *Lycos* (www.lycos.com) or *AltaVista* (www.altavista.com), students can use *Yahooligans* (www.yahooligans.com), a search engine for children. Don't overlook print sources. Directories, such as *The Yellow Pages for Kids and Families* by Jean Polly (McGraw Hill, 1997) and *Internet for Kids* by Deneen Frazier (Sybex Inc., 1995), offer lists of kid-friendly Internet sites. Another excellent source is the *Internet Resource Directory for K-12 Teachers and Librarians* by Elizabeth Miller (Libraries Unlimited, 1997). Miller's book is designed for adults, but the easy-to-use format makes it an excellent source for children.

Using print sources in the webliography project helps to reinforce the fact that information comes in many forms. The children may discover that they need to integrate print and Internet information to find some of the best lists of Web sites. Also, by examining print sources, students learn about the elusiveness of Web sites. What was on the World Wide Web yesterday, may not be there today.

During the search part of the project, students can work in collaborative

Continued on page 19

HOW TO SET UP A WEBLIOGRAPHY WEB PAGE

After opening up the Notepad program, type the following:

<HTML>

<HEAD><TITLE>Title of Your Project</HEAD></TITLE>

<BODY BGCOLOR="#FFFFFF" TEXT="#OOOOOO" LINK="#8BOOOO"

ALINK="#6B8E23"

VLINK="#96FB98">

<CENTER><FONT SIZE=5><B>Title of your class

project</B></CENTER></FONT>

<FONT SIZE=4>

<UL>

<H3>Subheading for your webliography</H3>

<LI><a href="http://www.firstwebsite.xxx">Name of first web site</a>

Type a description of your first web site. This can be as long as you want. When you are done with the description, type

<LI><a href="http:secondwebsite.xxx">Name of second Web site </a>

Type description of your second Web site.

<H3>Second subheading for your webliography</H3>

<LI><a href="http://www.firstwebsite.xxx">Name of first Web site </a>

Type description of your second web site.

</UL>

</BODY></HTML>

Tips and Other Bright Ideas

Set Your Sites on Research

A fellow librarian came up with a great idea: to thoroughly research Internet sites on a topic before classes come into the library to work on research projects. First meet with teachers to discuss the parameters of the subject. Then print out a list of authoritative and reviewed sites that are relevant to students' projects. This narrows the students' searches and eliminates extraneous searches. *LaDuska Adriance for Ruth Milin, Washington Irving Middle School, Springfield, Virginia*

Bookmarks Help Newbies Navigate

Before our elementary students begin to use Netscape to navigate the Internet/World Wide Web connection at our school, we presearch the system and mark appropriate locations with bookmarks. After the students have learned to navigate those locations, we show them how to move to other locations suggested on bookmarked home pages. Later, we teach students individually or in small groups, how to conduct searches to locate their own URLs and how to bookmark them for their classmates. *-Sharron L. McElmeel, Harrison Elementary School, Cedar Rapids, Iowa*

Domain Alerts

When you are teaching kids how to be selective and evaluate information from the Internet, tell them how to check URL addresses for the identity of the sources. If the domain ends in .gov or .edu it is probably reliable information from a government agency or an educational institution. If it ends in .com, warn the students that the source is probably a business or special interest group. If any other domain appears in the address, students should look at the information closely. *Shelley Glantz, Arlington (Massachusetts) High School*

Search Engines vs. Directories

Search engines and directories are different! A search engine index, such as Alta Vista, Webcrawler, Lycos, and HotBot, is created by a computer program (called a robot or spider) that goes out onto the Internet and indexes information found on servers according to a set of criteria set up by the programmer. The information in the index is then searchable by keywords. A directory, such as Yahoo and Magellan, is created by human beings adding sites to a database. The compilers may use a search engine, but someone still made a conscious decision to add a site to a directory. I have created a slide show about this topic. There is also an article titled "The Spider's Apprentice" (http://www.monash.com/spidap.html) that explains how the major search engines index the information that they find. - *Kathleen Schrock, Nathaniel H. Wixon Middle School, South Dennis, Massachusetts*

Search Engine Rules

For optimum search accuracy, always check the "help files" of each search engine for specific search rules that apply. I have printed each set of search rules and used tab dividers for quick reference in finding rules for each search engine. This allows the students to prepare searches offline without tying up the terminal while they try to figure out how to construct an efficient search. There are too many individual quirks to keep them all straight.- *Alice Trussell, Manhattan, Kansas*

Each One Teach One

To help all intermediate students learn how to compose mail offline for "flash" sessions, we used Scholastic Network's Bookwoman Literature Game as a vehicle. Each day the students have to e-mail their answer to Bookwoman. As library media specialist, I taught one child in each participating class how to compose their class's e-mail message with the answer. Then on following days that student shows others how to compose the e-mail message to Bookwoman, and eventually those students begin to "pass it on." Takes a minimal amount of time on my part, but now most of our intermediate students can compose e-mail messages. *Sharron L. McElmeel Harrison Elementary School Cedar Rapids, Iowa*

Multimedia Presentation Programs

With amazing rapidity, presentation programs have moved out of the boardroom and into the classroom. Their capacity to incorporate text, graphics, photographs, color, motion, and sound opens up worlds of creative alternatives to the traditional term paper. These exciting programs also offer the library media specialist (presumably the faculty member with the greatest comfort level with technology) opportunities to become involved as never before in the end products of research. We're usually the people teachers turn to for help in locating and choosing appropriate research tools and useful information.

The subject area teacher, however, has traditionally been the person to give students the format for the final paper. Some teachers feel that we are infringing on their territory when we discuss the organization and presentation of information and ideas with their students. But our familiarity with such programs as KidPix, PowerPoint, and HyperStudio, and with recording and input devices like digital cameras and camcorders, allows us to infringe with impunity. We can get involved in all phases of a research project, from brainstorming, through information gathering and note-taking, to interpreting and organizing data and choosing the most appropriate format to communicate it.

Many of us have learned the basics of PowerPoint through a workshop or two and some hands-on experience. But because of the courses most of us had to take to become library media specialists, we have skills that can be applied to this new situation as we teach others to use yet another tool. I remember storyboarding a slide show (the camera type; this was way before PowerPoint), then shooting "live" slides and creating titles and credits using a variety of photographic techniques. How many of us painstakingly applied press-on letters, paying careful attention to font, height, spacing, margins and white spaces, to design our own transparencies-sometimes including overlays? And most of us quickly learned, and taught to our students, the value of having a clear idea of what you're filming *before* turning on the camcorder.

We are also critical viewers-and often reviewers-of various media: film, television, multimedia CD-ROMs, audiotapes. We know what works and what doesn't, and we can articulate *why*.
With this rich background, we can give our students much more than the mechanics of how to create a new slide, change backgrounds and colors, and incorporate motion. We can teach them storyboarding techniques, some elements of graphic design, and dramatic use of sound and movement. And, because a technically perfect show is worthless if it does not communicate a worthwhile message effectively and accurately, we can remind our students to look critically at *what* they are saying as well as *how* they are saying it.

Technology may still change several times over before our teenagers enter the business world. PowerPoint may seem as primitive as hieroglyphics compared to the presentation programs they will use in five or 10 years. But the basics of creating an effective presentation in *any* format, print or nonprint, are standard, and will remain valid and applicable long after our present generation of IMacs and PCs have turned to dust.

❏ URL UPDATES

PowerPointing the Way:
   http://discoveryschool.com/schrockguide/

The Writing-Technology Connection:
   Global Show-n-Tell
   www.telenaut.com/gst/

   KidPub
   www.kidpub.org/kidpub/

Primary Sources: Second to None on the Web: American Memory at the Library of Congress
http://rs6.loc.gov/amhome.html

The American Memory Site
<http://rs6.loc.amhome.html>

MULTIMEDIA—MORE OF EVERYTHING FOR LEARNING

Why Students Should Use MULTIMEDIA

Not every report or research paper is best prepared with the glitz of multimedia. Like other information mediums, it has its appropriate and inappropriate uses.

By Katherine Bucher

What are the benefits for teachers and librarians?

Multimedia presentation software can be used to produce attention-getting, dramatic, audio and visual lessons and reports. Using solid instructional design principles (objective, content outline, materials list, storyboard, and so forth), a teacher or SLMS can produce a variety of multimedia instructional materials that should keep the interest of most students. Librarians can produce library orientation, reference guides, and skills instruction programs that students and teachers can use at any time.

Why should students use this software?

Let's go back in time several centuries to the year 1560. Gutenberg's invention of moveable type has been in existence for over 100 years. Yet, in a small room in a monastery, an apprentice scribe bends low and laboriously copies a book by hand. Hearing the master scribe enter the room, the weary apprentice asks why the monastery does not use the technique discovered by Gutenberg. Then, many more books could be produced and learning would spread. The master replies that Gutenberg's idea is just a passing fancy and will never really catch on. Its product just cannot compare to a handwritten text, and, besides, copying by hand is a good exercise for the mind.

Now move back to the end of the twentieth century. Think about some of the reasons you may have heard against allowing students to produce multimedia presentations instead of written reports. Do you see any of the master scribe's logic in them? After all, how many "term papers" does the average person write once he or she completes school? Compare that to the number of presentations to clubs, church groups, civic organizations, and government agencies (city council, school board) that the person will probably give. Don't the presentations outweigh the research reports?

Contrary to some opinions, allowing students on all levels to create multimedia presentations to replace or supplement written reports does not mean the death of books and learning. In researching the information needed to prepare a multimedia presentation, students use the same print and electronic sources that they use to create a written report. In

INFORMATION LITERACY SKILLS: GRADES 7-12, 3RD EDITION 173

BUCHER—
Continued from page 19

addition, students are able to combine traditional library/information skills (i.e., selecting and narrowing a topic, preparing an outline) with the higher level thinking skills (i.e., critical thinking, problem solving, and decision making) when they are actively engaged in authoring their own multimedia presentations. If they work in groups, they are developing cooperative learning skills.

Giving students this opportunity also takes advantage of the students' various learning styles. Often, we forget that many high school students are tactile-kinesthetic and learn best by actually doing things.

To see how school librarians have worked with their teachers to help students make multimedia presentations as part of their assignments, watch school librarians Connie Scott and Star Wolven at Hampton High School in Hampton, Virginia, as they work with an English class that is studying American poets. These dynamic librarians are fortunate that a Macintosh computer lab is located off the library and that Connie has become quite proficient in using *HyperCard*.

- In the classroom, the teacher has assigned groups of students to report on specific poets.
- Using the library's reference collection (print and CD-ROM), Star guides the students as they gather information.
- Since most of the members of this class had used *HyperCard* in their social studies class in the fall, Connie meets the groups in the Mac lab, reviews the basics of presentation planning, and helps the groups organize the information that they found through their research into a computer multimedia presentation.
- Students work on their presentations in the lab with their teacher (and sometimes Connie or Star) during their class periods and during other times when the lab is available.
- The scanner is used as one group decides to use a portrait of the poet in its presentation while another wants to incorporate some artwork that the students think illustrates the mood their poet tried to convey in some major works.
- Another group wants to incorporate a brief audio selection into its presentation.
- Finally the presentations are ready and are used as the groups present their reports to the class.

While both librarians agree that a project like this takes time, they also say that it is worth it. It's exciting to watch students become involved in their work and teach each other how to use the computers, software, and references. Everyone seems to be learning. Students who often are the first out the library door, now return after school to polish their presentation or to try to find one more piece of information that they need. In fact, students who have been allowed to use the computers to create a multimedia presentation in one class help convince other teachers to try it.

What can students do?

With a little help from teachers and the SLMS, students in elementary, middle, and high school can use multimedia presentation programs. Although some teachers may be reluctant to allow students to create multimedia presentations because they are not familiar with the software or are not sure how to evaluate the product, with a few suggestions, most are willing to give multimedia a try.

While presentations can be created on almost any subject, here are some suggestions for various curricular areas.

Social studies:
- Research local history. Supplement the text with illustrations that are scanned in from postcards.
- Present a person in history, including a picture, the reading of a famous quotation, a brief part of an important speech or, for recent figures, a film clip.
- Select a time period and present an overview of it. Include music (audio) and art (visual) as well as information about important historical events.
- Prepare a brief economic report on a major U.S. corporation that is listed on the New York Stock Exchange. Include graphs and charts as well as illustrations of its products.

English:
- Select a favorite poet. Provide biographical information and a visual interpretation of one of his poems.
- Select one novel and have different characters tell their side of the story.
- Develop a multimedia book report that will encourage others to read the book.
- Write a short story that includes options for the reader. (Think of this as a computerized "choose your own adventure.")

Science and math:
- Prepare a short tutorial that other students can use. Include an information section, an activity, and a short quiz.
- Create a tutorial to help others learn basic science terminology.
- Illustrate a mathematical concept or formula.
- Using Mammals as a guide, prepare a report on an insect, bird, or fish. Use the results as the beginning of a class science encyclopedia.

Foreign language:
- Instead of a written report on a foreign city, create a visual one. Any narration should be in the foreign language.
- Prepare a tutorial stack that shows items or actions and then describes them in the foreign language. Then try the reverse by making a statement in the foreign language and letting the user click on a button to see what it represents and hear the English translation.

Art:
- Prepare a biography of an artist and include samples of his or her major works.
- Select one of the basic artistic elements (form, line, shape) define it, and show how several artists used it. **TC**

Katherine T. Bucher is an Associate Professor at Old Dominion University, Norfolk, Virginia.

Reprinted from *Computers & Technology in School Library Media Centers*, published by Linworth Publishing, Inc.

Integrating Multimedia into the Curriculum

By Nancy Lou LeCrone

Can students create multimedia products in your media center? If you give the students the tools, they can. With the help of other district librarians, our teachers and staff changed our traditional library into a flexibly scheduled, integrated library program. Our students became producers of multimedia products. Travel brochures using *ClarisWorks* (Claris) were produced by our sixth graders during their unit on Egypt. *KidPix* (Broderbund) slide shows complete with text, voices and other sounds came from our fourth grade Indian unit, researched and produced in the library. How did this happen? Add a technology mini-grant from our district to a staff and student population eager to try new technology and you get a winning multimedia library program.

The Premise

The faculty's vision of technology use by students was of paramount importance in this effort. We wanted products from each classroom unit to incorporate multimedia in some way. We did not want the technology to take over but to help present the information students were gathering. As we planned the units, I, as the building librarian, suggested technology-based student products for the teachers to choose from. I had to come up with ideas that would tap into the students' knowledge of software and computers. The steps used to plan the units are from J'Lynn Anderson, a librarian in our district, and Donna Miller's book, *Developing an Integrated Library Program* (Linworth, 1996).

Our integrated library program uses grade-level planning for thematic units. We made library-skills task cards for the students to follow. These step-by-step instructions were placed on construction paper and laminated.

The Payoff

Use of technology cannot exist only in the library. Even though extended classroom units allow more time to absorb and understand information, synthesis seems only to occur when the students carry the information into other areas of study. The students begin to see products instead of assignments. Each activity is another opportunity for them to use what they learned in the library.

MAJOR BODIES OF WATER

Using the *U.S. Atlas* CD-ROM, determine the major bodies of water in your region. (Examples: lakes, rivers, streams.)

Double click on the U.S. icon.

Go to the menu bar across the top of the screen and point and click on Map.

Drag the mouse pointer down to highlight Topo Maps. A pop-up box with a list of the regions will appear.

Select your region by clicking twice on it in the list. This will make your region appear on the screen with the major bodies of water labeled.

On your map, label the major bodies of water (lakes, rivers, streams).

When finished labeling your map move the mouse pointer to File and drag down to Quit.

You are a pro at using the CD-ROM!!! Way to go!!!

Instead of writing a book report or completing a worksheet, they want to know if they can make a slide show in *KidPix*. Sixth graders who made brochures for their Egypt unit now can make a slide presentation in *ClarisWorks* as well. The key is to let them try, and be around to help when they need it.

How to Do It

When using a multimedia program for the first time with students, make sure the staff member is already comfortable with its use. Give a demonstration to the class and prepare a handout that clearly explains each step of the process. Don't give "beta" versions to students. Have the teachers test each task card as it is being developed. No matter how many times I reread the procedure, I would still miss a step that someone unfamiliar with the program would find.

I chose *My First Incredible, Amazing Dictionary* CD (Dorling Kindersley) for the second graders to use in their unit. It's simple enough for even limited readers. In planning the activities, I asked teachers in the lower grades to tell me if the demands of the task were appropriate for these students. It turned out the students used regular dictionaries off the shelf but also used the computer dictionary for comparison of answers. The students had become adept at using the mouse and following the onscreen directions. These skills will grow as students use them in other multimedia projects in succeeding years.

The fourth-grade students used the information they gathered about Indians to make simple *KidPix* slide presentations. Drawing, painting and stamping in *KidPix* is a lot of fun and really brings out students' creativity. We had the students create a simple storyboard of ideas on paper before going to the computer. Group work skills were imperative because we had only eight computers in the library.

The sixth-grade students researched a unit on Egypt complete with cartouches and pyramids. To end the unit, each group made a travel brochure for Egypt using *ClarisWorks*. Other groups worked on a newspaper, writing stories about new pyramid construction or the recent death of a pharaoh.

Help your students make friends with multimedia tools and watch for successful results.

Here are some ideas to keep in mind when using multimedia for student products:

- List the products you usually make during the course of a unit. Use this list to brainstorm which products could be made just as easily using available software.

- Become so familiar with the software programs that you can feel comfortable in explaining them to others.

- Demonstrate the programs to the whole class. Use a video converter or projection panel to demonstrate the software to large groups.

- Make sure your handouts explain exactly what to do and in what order.

- Have the teachers test all task cards for errors or steps that were left out.

- Offer assistance to the small group or individuals as they begin work on their product.

- Write down what works well and what doesn't. Adjust or change what doesn't work.

- Have fun and don't let the media ruin the message. Remember it's just a tool.

- Remember your goal is to set the students and teachers up for success. **TC**

Nancy Lou LeCrone is a librarian at Wilkinson Middle School in the Mesquite (Texas) Independent School District.

LAND FORMS

Using the *U.S. Atlas* CD-ROM determine the land forms of your region.
Double click on the U.S. icon.

Go to the menu bar across the top of the screen and point and click on Map.

Drag the mouse pointer down to highlight Topo Maps. A pop-up box with a list of the regions will appear.

Select your region by clicking twice on it in the list. This will make your region appear on the screen with the land forms labeled.

On your map, label the types of land forms found (valleys, plateaus, mountains, basins, ranges, plains). Please *note* that not every type of land form will always be labeled.

When finished labeling your map, move the mouse pointer to File and drag down to Quit.

You have completed this task card!!! Good Job!!!

WHY MULTIMEDIA?

feature

Guidelines for Effective Multimedia Design

By Elizabeth Downs and Kenneth Clark

The affordability of multimedia presentation programs has led schools to purchase programs such as *PowerPoint* (Microsoft), *Astound* (Gold Disk), and *HyperStudio* (Wagner). The media specialist often is called upon to help faculty and students in the design and production of programs. The following guidelines are designed to be used by media specialists in helping others use these programs effectively. The central themes of the guidelines are simplicity and appropriateness. Novice users tend to go overboard when they discover the many color, text, graphics, and special effects options available. You must help them understand these effects are not an end in and of themselves but tools to help them to get their message across.

Color

Use color with care. Color should be used to create a realistic effect or to focus attention. Most computers are capable of generating millions of colors. As a result, the designer can quickly overpower the viewer with confusing hues and values.

Text

Again, the user is confronted with many options, including font, size, color, placement, justification, case, spacing and style. Designers should consider the content being delivered when deciding on the screen text format.

Graphics

Graphics should be used only when they support the topic being covered. Keep in mind that developmental level influences the viewer's ability to understand the graphics. Consider the type of graphic with respect to its message. Do you need a pie chart or a photograph? A major consideration is the degree of realism of the graphic representation. For example, graphic representations can be simple black-line drawings or complex full-color images of a real person, object or event. If one of the latter is your subject, then use the most realistic representation available.

Special Effects

Special effects such as transitions and "builds" should be minimized. Transitions are the time variables and screen designs selected to move from one screen to the next. The screen designs include wipes, dissolves, split screens and checkerboard effects. These can prove to be distracting. Consider the audience's attention span when choosing transition speed. If the designer chooses slow transitions, the audience may lose interest. Builds are special effects used to bring text onto the screen. Builds for text can include "flying" text, dissolves and checkerboard text. These can help direct the learner's attention to the relevant material if the builds are not distracting. When using transitions and builds, be consistent throughout the program, and only to enhance the content.

DESIGN PRINCIPLES

Simplicity is the best model to apply when adding elements to a single screen. At the same time, creativity is important, and the designer should be encouraged to try a variety of techniques. By incorporating some basic design principles, you can provide suggestions for faculty and students to consider as they create a multimedia program. Try offering these guidelines:

COLOR

Limit the selection to two colors per screen for everything other than graphics.
Use a text color that will contrast with background color.
Use solid color background for screens; avoid textured or designed backgrounds.
Be consistent throughout the program in use of colors for text and background.
Use color to direct the user's attention.

TEXT

Use simple block fonts that do not contain endstrokes.
Select a text size that is 18 points or larger.
Limit text to six or seven lines per screen.
Present a single concept or topic per screen.
Choose a text color that will contrast with the background.
Left-justify text.
Use headings and subheadings to provide hierarchy of the content.
Use a combination of upper and lower case letters; avoid using all upper case.
Use a minimum of 1½ spaces between lines.

GRAPHICS

Choose a graphic that is directly related to the content of the text on the screen.
Consider the developmental level of the viewer when selecting the complexity of the graphic.
Use realistic graphics when content is dependent on visual detail.
Limit the number of graphics per screen to one for most topics, two if showing a contrast or comparison.

SPECIAL EFFECTS

Use special effects sparingly.
Be consistent in use of builds and transitions throughout a program.
Avoid builds that use overpowering effects such as flying or walking text.
Avoid effects that are slow transitions from one screen to another.
Avoid transitions that change the viewer's focus of attention such as checkerboard dissolves or diagonal wipes. **TC**

Elizabeth Downs is Assistant Professor and Kenneth Clark is Associate Professor in the Department of Educational Leadership, Technology, and Research at Georgia Southern University in Statesboro, Georgia.

The SLAPPS Model
Guiding Students through the

Process of Multimedia Presentations

By Tim Gavin

As a media specialist, I guide sixth-grade students through the process of planning, creating, and delivering multimedia presentations for their social studies classes. To ensure that students understand the entire process, I teach them the steps of the process, using the SLAPPS Model as the framework.

To teach the model, create a multimedia presentation and then ask the class for their criticism. The students evaluate my multimedia project in the following areas: clear controlling idea (thesis statement), relevant details, appropriate media, validity of primary and secondary sources, depth of knowledge, and presentation skills. The instruction is geared to model what works and what doesn't work when presenting a multimedia project. I ask the students the following questions to help them evaluate my presentation:

- What was my controlling idea?
- What sources did I use?
- How did the media support my controlling idea?
- Did the media help or hinder my controlling idea?
- How were my presentation skills?
- Did I address the audience?
- Did I rely on my note cards too much?
- Did I ask the audience questions?

All of the answers to these questions help the students formulate what a good multimedia presentation should be. At this point, I introduce the SLAPPS Model.

The SLAPPS. Model is student-centered, not teacher-centered. The question I ask when developing a lesson plan is not, "What am I going to do?" but "What are the students going to do?" Since the SLAPPS Model is process-oriented, teachers and media specialists find

> *The SLAPPS Model allows teachers and media specialists to collaborate on content, research strategies, presentation skills, and student evaluations.*

it easy to provide a safety net for the students to make sure they complete all the necessary steps to produce a successful end product.

When the students receive their research assignment, they break the assignment into smaller steps, creating a priority of tasks, by following the model. They feel the model is a useful guide and use it as a checklist of what they have completed and what they need to do. Even though the teacher and media specialist are closely involved in the students' progress, each set of questions also helps the students monitor their own progress.

The model fits into other learning models, such as Eisenberg and Berkowitz's Big Six Skills and Bloom's Taxonomy, and is not intended to displace these models. However, the intellectual skills emphasized in the SLAPPS Model are geared to enhance information-seeking skills, information-processing skills, and presentation skills. Also, the SLAPPS Model requires students to inform the teacher and the media specialist of their progress. Therefore, the teaching-learning process becomes a continuous loop through constant evaluation of the steps that students take

When the students follow the SLAPPS Model, they deliver unified, well-supported, and coherent multi-media presentations, which are entertaining and informative for their classmates.

Meet the SLAPPS Model

Select Topic - What is my assignment? What is my topic? What do I know about the topic? How can I learn more about the topic? How much information is available on this topic? Who can help me? (These questions help students realize how much research is required. When students have completed this step, they should inform the teacher of the selected topic.)

Locate Resources - Where is the information? How can the information be gathered? Does the information include primary and secondary sources? Are the resources in a variety of media? Is there enough time to learn about the topic to create a multimedia presentation by the due date? (Students are required to meet with the media specialist to discuss research strategies. After meeting with the media specialist, students should discuss their progress with the teacher.)

Analyze Resources - Have I read, viewed, and listened to my resources? Have I gathered as much knowledge as possible? Do I need more information? Am I ready to narrow the focus of my research? Can I move toward creating the controlling idea of the multimedia presentation? Have I taken enough notes, selected relevant media, or determined if I need to create new media? Have I written my opening statement? Have I organized a working outline? Should I meet with my teacher for feedback? Should I meet with the media specialist for further suggestions?

Personalize the Research - Have I integrated my notes with my own opinions? Have I created a controlling idea for my multimedia presentation? Does the focus of my work unify and support my controlling idea? Have I created a final outline of my multimedia presentation and determined if the outline is coherent? Does all my information and media fit into the final outline? Does the outline create a unified, well-supported, and coherent multimedia presentation? Do I need to meet with the media specialist for final touches on media selection and media production? Do I need to meet with the teacher for final feedback and instruction?

Practice - Have I reserved my equipment needs? Do I know how to operate the equipment? Have I practiced delivering the multimedia presentation? Have I asked my classmates for assistance to operate equipment and lights, to hand out print information, and to help with setting up the room for the multimedia presentation?

Showing - Presentation day. Am I relaxed? I will remember that the audience wants a good show, and the audience is on my side. I will remember that the controlling idea is important. I will involve the audience. I will make eye contact. I will ask questions. I will meet with my teacher for a final evaluation. I will help other students with their multimedia presentations.

to create a multimedia presentation.

When students follow the model, they deliver unified, well-supported, and coherent multimedia presentations, which are entertaining and informative for their classmates. Furthermore, the model allows teachers and media specialists to collaborate on content, research strategies, presentation skills, and student evaluations. Interestingly, the library media specialist is brought into the classroom and the educational process as much as students are brought into the library. The teaching-learning team includes the subject teacher, the library media specialist, and the student. Ultimately, students consult with two experts to guide them through the world of multimedia research and presentation. **TC**

Tim Gavin is Director of Media Services at The Episcopal Academy in Merion, Pennsylvania.

Notes

– Showcasing Technology –

Tokyo Students Create Hypertext Books

By Vicky Downs

Andrew Hoover's eighth-grade social studies students at The American School in Japan, in Tokyo, weren't at all hyper about using technology to create books in hypertext. Working in groups, students chose a part of the city in which they were particularly interested, then researched its history, culture, economy, religion, and values. Each student then wrote a short research paper about the city, a script featuring a creative work of some kind, and contributed to a hypertext book about Tokyo with area "chapters" on the hard drives of five multimedia machines.

Within each group, a producer managed the group's work, a technical coordinator scanned pictures and did other computer work, a researcher researched and wrote about the group's overview of their area in Tokyo, and a Japanese speaker translated during student interviews and helped the group with words as they wrote.

The groups began by brainstorming what they already knew about Tokyo, with Hoover encouraging them to bring out the "story behind the topic." For example, he suggested one student in the group focusing on Harajuku write about the area's Meiji Shrine and the Shinto religion. Another student writing about the National Stadium near the shrine was reminded to include information about the Japanese attitude toward sports.

For their research, students relied heavily on a library cart filled with reserve books on Tokyo. They also found information on our Elite Magazine Article Summary (EMAS) which contains many full-text articles,

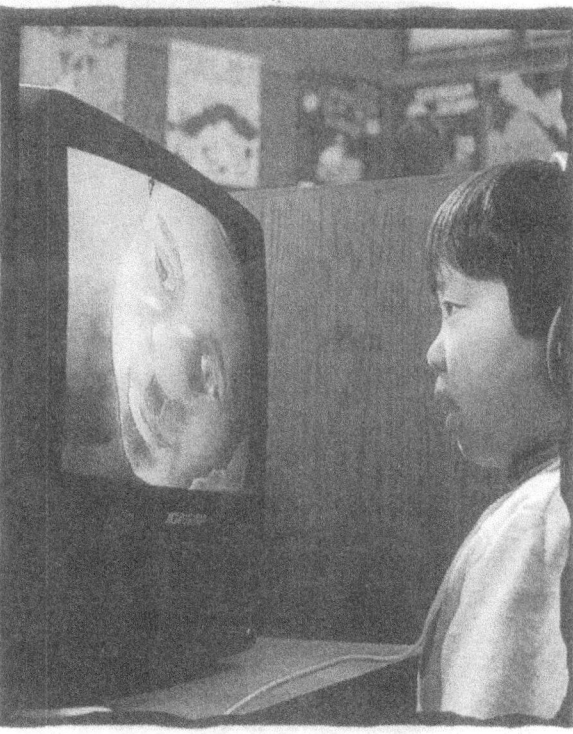

and our Nikkei Database, a local, English-language database from the *Japan Economics Newspaper*. Many conducted keyword searches to locate articles on their topic from local newspapers. Finally, they checked local English-language magazines with subject indexes made in our own library.

Each group used a disposable camera supplied by their teacher to photograph scenes from their area of study to use in their final hypertext chapter. Several students used tape recorders to capture sound effects and record interviews. When students finished writing their research papers, they created scripts based on their papers that featured photos, pictures, sound, and creative works such as poems or dialogue. Scripts were worked out on large index cards, with information on one card for each page of hypertext. Many students attached a photo and surrounded it with explanatory text. Groups then used their cards to plot their chapters.

Librarian Polly Casmar taught the technical coordinators how to use *ToolBook 3.0* to import text, visuals and sound. Technical assistant Lynn Nichols taught them how to use the H.P. Scanjet to scan pictures and drawings onto diskettes. Then Casmar and library assistant Lyn Patrick helped group members build their chapters. The final products were definitely group affairs. Although each group's technical coordinator had final responsibility, each student was deeply involved in how his or her own script appeared in the final product. Music, dialogue, and other sounds were added to the chapters, and some students even figured out how to import digital video clips.

When all chapters of "Hyper Tokyo" were complete, five multimedia machines were set up in the commons to share the project. Students of all ages enjoyed clicking buttons on the home pages which took them to their selection where they could read and appreciate student-written, -designed and -researched information about our city.

We were all impressed by the quality of the final product. Students were generous in their praise of outstanding work by the translators, photographers, technicians, and others who contributed to "Hyper Tokyo."

Because *Toolbook* is a DOS product and our Internet node is currently only available on Apple machines, we can't put "Hyper Tokyo" on our school's WWW Home Page just yet. However, Hoover and his students are selecting research papers which will be put on the Internet to make them accessible to students world wide. Our school's address on the WWW is:

http://WWW.asij.ac.jp

Please click on the M.S. home page and find out which papers were selected! TC

Vicky Downs is the Head Librarian at The American School in Japan, located in Tokyo.

For their research, students relied heavily on a library cart filled with reserve books on Tokyo. They also found information on our Elite Magazine Article Summary (EMAS) which contains many full-text articles, and our Nikkei Database, a local, English-language database from the *Japan Economics Newspaper*. Many conducted keyword searches to locate articles on their topic from local newspapers. Finally, they checked local English-language magazines with subject indexes made in our own library.

The Romance and the Reality of Developing Hypermedia Modules

By Lesley S.J. Farmer

As more and more school libraries are wired for information retrieval, there are challenging implications for library skills instruction. This author is now working on a HyperCard program to teach library skills.

YOU'VE HEARD THE HOOPLA ABOUT computer-assisted instruction (CAI): How it provides self-paced, interactive learning. How it holds students' interest and offers immediate and accurate feedback. How it could enable you to custom-design a library instruction unit that could be used by students when they need it, and as many times as they need it.

And you've seen how students will stand in line to use the CD-ROM *World Book's Information Finder* rather than go to the shelves for a newer print version of an encyclopedia. Computers attract students, who believe that the computer is always more current, more accurate, and faster than books. They prefer to "push the button and get the answer." At-risk students often connect better with computers than with books, and feel more successful doing it.

Then you see students using HyperCard in the library to create reports and games. Looks easy. Looks like fun and it's interactive. HyperCard comes with the new

---

Lesley S.J. Farmer is the Library Director of Redwood High School, Larkspur, California. She is the author of a number of articles and books on librarianship and computer applications, including Creative Partnerships: Librarians and Teachers Working Together *(Linworth Publishing, 1993) and* I Speak HyperCard *(Libraries Unlimited, 1992).*

Macintoshes so cost is not a problem. There are books and classes available for the over-30s (and under-30s) to learn HyperCard techniques, and students are always willing to be your coach if you get into programming trouble. So why not take advantage of that natural affinity between students and computers to teach students how to use the library?

Finally, after you've explained how to use *Readers' Guide* for the seventeenth time to the same student, you are thoroughly convinced that computer-aided library instruction is for you. Ideally, you'll find a colleague who is also interested in computer instruction and a $1,000 grant to "take the summer and design a HyperCard program that students can use come September." You figure you can use the money to pay for babysitters while you script stacks to your heart's content. Such thinking is the romance of creating hypermedia for library instruction.

Beginning my fourth year of instructional designing, I have experienced both the romance and the reality of such work. While designing computer-assisted instruction is rewarding (CAI does appeal to students), the process can be trickier than it seems at first blush.

My CAI work has been done in connection with the Computer-Based Library Instruction Project (CLIP), a consortium of librarians in California who are creating HyperCard library instruction units for school, academic, and public libraries. Started in 1990, CLIP has gone through several phases and turnovers in membership, but the main goal—a collaborative effort to create bibliographic instruction by computer—remains.

The romance of collaborative development is the belief that a group of motivated librarians can create bibliographic instruction modules with a consistent look yet reflecting personal style. In such a scheme, benchmark deadlines will ensure timely progress and a steering committee will coordinate the efforts. A couple of librarians should serve as technical consultants to get other librarians through the tough spots. Less computer-experienced librarians will serve as evaluators of content and design and test the modules with their clientele.

The reality of collaborative development is that a group is more likely to design a camel than bibliographic units. Try to imagine ten librarians agreeing on a design for a menu bar within ten hours! In reality, consensus on the menu design took almost a year. Other matters of design protocol took almost as long. We became mired in details. As a result, a more traditional organizational structure evolved, with one person having the final say on design.

As for deadlines, reality set in when staff cutbacks in the participating librarians' institutions created greater workloads for these librarians. Some had to do the work of two or three people in their own libraries. Since blocks of uninterrupted time were needed to concentrate on developing the HyperCard stacks, the demands of their regular jobs constrained the librarian-developers. Fortunately, the participating institutions gave released time to the principal developers, who wrote grants to get the funds to pay for that time allocation. We also found that the principal developers should live nearby so they could easily follow through on their work. Consequently some of the developers, who lived some distance from the others, became evaluators of their colleagues' work.

We developers also found that our knowledge of HyperCard was not sophisticated enough to enable us to produce high-quality stacks. Few of us could write scripts; even the technical experts were learning on the job. While I have programmed in several computer languages and enjoy working with HyperCard because it easily combines text and graphics, the first sessions in creating stacks were frustrating. In fact, another librarian and I wrote a manual on designing stacks to save other librarians from some of the learning difficulties we experienced (*I Speak HyperCard*, Libraries Unlimited, 1992). E-mail was a corollary skill that we needed to learn in order to speed up development.

One quickly dispelled fantasy was that graduate students could do the detail work in stack development, either in terms of instructional design, graphics or computer programming. The fact was that finding competent people was difficult, and supervising them was even harder. After seeing the students' work, we realized that graduate students who were considered skilled by their instructors lacked the broad expertise needed to help with our stacks. Graduate students usually had one skill rather than a repertoire; the challenge was to find that skill and give specific directions for its use in the stacks.

Because of program upgrades and the experience of the writers in the industry, today's HyperCard stacks are much more sophisticated than they were in 1990 when we began our project. However, our stacks must be able to compare favorably with commercial products if the instruction is to be accepted by students. As we librarian-developers worked on our stacks and looked at others' stacks, we learned better programming and content skills. The downside of higher expectations and expertise was the temptation to go back and revise what we had already done. We did numerous revisions, each of which took valuable time. After a while I felt as if I was promoting vaporware (industry jargon for software that has been announced but not produced). A balance has to be struck between the romance of developing the perfect CAI product and the reality of getting out a program in a timely fashion.

If you too are intrigued by the idea of developing computer-based library instruction modules, be assured that it is possible, and will be a valuable learning experience for you as well as your students. By the time you finish, you will know your subject inside and out. Here are some pointers to help you design the nearly perfect CAI-BI (Computer-Assisted Instruction—Bibliographic Instruction).

• Start with a good bibliographic instruction product, in print or non-print format. Study other librarians' instructional strategies and adapt them for your own use (giving credit as appropriate).

• Remember there are several ways to develop stacks. You can work with a rough draft that begins with content and adds graphics. Or, you might begin with a menu and fill in the content. (I alternate between approaches.)

• Get an overview of the stacks by flowcharting or storyboarding the unit. Take advantage of the medium by using nonlinear links. Nothing is more boring, or a greater waste of the technology, than to translate a print text into a sequential series of hypermedia cards.

• Systemize the content so that one idea and one graphic appear per card.

• Develop one module or stack per instructional unit. For example, one module on indexes and another on encyclopedias. If you plan to create a series of modules, be consistent in their structure so students can navigate them easily and independently.

• Maximize CAI capabilities by incorporating the unique features of hypermedia— animation, maps, set-ups for reviews and tests, and simulations.

• Follow basic principles of graphics layout, such as left-to-right or top-to-bottom flow of text and graphics, legible type faces, and balance between visual and written material.

• Include hypermedia "goodies" (icons, pop-ups, card transition effects) but don't overuse them to the point that they distract from the information.

• Make it easy for the user to navigate through the stack by using menus and navigation bars.

• Document the stacks with script remarks, notes for applications, and ways to use and modify stacks.

If you go in with a clear picture of what you want to accomplish, if you're willing to commit the time to learn and develop as you go, and if you maintain high standards while keeping a realistic view about doable projects, you can create exciting hypermedia programs for your students.

Overcoming School Barriers To Technology in the Library

Kieth Wright, a professor of library science at the University of North Carolina at Greensboro, has written an analysis of the impact of the computer on the school library for the AASL series Focus on Trends and Issues. *The Challenge of Technology: Action Strategies for the School Library Media Specialist* reviews many of the issues surrounding computer-related technology in the schools before the author gives librarians some practical points to overcoming barriers. Among them,

• Work with the school administration. Needed changes such as flexible scheduling and networking of libraries cannot happen without support from the top administrative staff.

• Find out how others feel about their work situations, equipment, and resources. Involve teachers and others in evaluating library services and facilities.

• Evaluate how you spend your time. (Wright offers a time-priority chart.) If you find that you are spending too much time on low-priority administrative functions, ask if there is a computer-related technology that will make the job go faster.

• Read widely—education journals, computer magazines, and state education agencies' reports on school-related technology. Get on the mailing lists for free computer-related publications.

• Ask questions about computer compatibility and connectivity throughout the school system. Wright notes that rapid changes in hardware and software are causing problems in all types of organizations not just in school systems. "One school system—one brand" is a difficult rule to follow, but it would ease many of the problems, Wright says.

The Challenge of Technology is available from the American Library Association, 50 East Huron Street, Chicao, Illinois 60611. 122pp., 1993, 0-8389-0604-4, $22 pbk.

WHY MULTIMEDIA?

feature

PowerPointing the Way

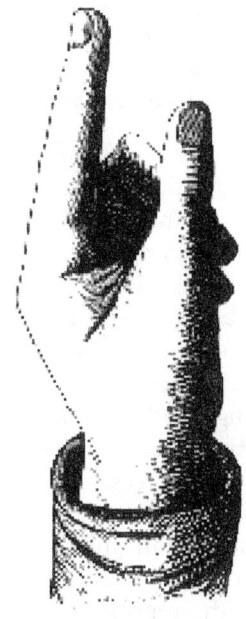

By Deborah J. Stafford

Recently the school district planned a week-long summer workshop for educators. We were to stress curriculum uses for "presentations" software programs and part of my assignment was to teach *Microsoft PowerPoint*. Although my experience with the program so far was in making transparencies for small group presentations, I wanted to make myself familiar with the program and tell my fellow teachers how to use the program in their classrooms and subject areas.

My first thought was to ask LM_NET subscribers for examples of curriculum uses for *PowerPoint*. I also posted a message on K12ADMIN, another listserv I follow. Within three days I had more than two dozen replies from all grade levels and subject areas. I combined them into workshop ideas, and three broad categories emerged: open house-type presentations, tutorials, and student-produced projects. The participants in our workshop discovered the same three uses once they began using *PowerPoint*.

During our first session, participants prepared a three-slide presentation to give information for the first day of school—name, course, class rules, for example. With a simple presentation we covered the basics of preparing a slide and using the outline feature to prepare a whole presentation. All participants then began to embell-

> *...Three broad categories emerged [for using presentation software]: open house-type presentations, tutorials, and student-produced projects.*

ish their projects. They liked the idea of a presentation they could show as often as necessary. A fellow media specialist worked on a media center introduction. By the end of the week her final product covered the media center program, used color and clip art, and could be set to run continuously for teacher orientation and open house.

In Paula Galland's school at St. Simons Island, Georgia, teachers use a digital camera to take pictures during a school day, then incorporate them into a *PowerPoint* project with information about their classrooms. This is shown during PTA open house. They run the show non-stop, avoid repeating information for each group, and dazzle parents.

During the workshops *PowerPoint* demonstrated different kinds of presentations and delivered some of the instruction. As we included graphics, a high school science teacher at my school began to work on a subject-oriented project for his classroom. His product became a tutorial outlining the Scientific Method and giving examples. He planned to make it available as part of a teaching center as well as for direct instruction. Students could replay it if they missed the initial presentation or if they needed reinforcement to digest the material. He plans to make more tutorials of this kind.

Kraig D. Pritts of Moravia, New York, uses *PowerPoint* for music history discussions for his sixth-grade general music classes. His presentations loosely follow the textbook, which is kept for reference. He plans to incorporate multimedia with icons that allow him to play music by the composer being discussed. Students give him positive responses. He reports, "All classes now receive the same information. Using *PowerPoint* insures that I cover the same material with each class. If kids miss a class, they can catch up outside of class time by going through the slides on their own at my computer. Using [a computerized presentation] allows me to add a wide range of colors and changes to the presentation in its design. This also maintains student interest."

A high school health and science teacher at my school plans to bring her students in for lessons on *PowerPoint*. Then she will assign a topic, have students collaborate on research, and design a presentation to show to her classes. She feels the program has great potential for student collaboration and synthesis of information.

> Jean Townes, a media specialist at Waverly Elementary School, worked with second and third graders to prepare a report on Japan. Students chose the topics. They scanned pictures to go with the text, although pictures can also come from a digital camera or clip art files. Townes found it a great way to make reports on any classroom research project.

By the end of the week the workshop participants had made several projects and were excited about the possibilities for classroom use. Projects can be produced for viewing on single computers, showing to groups via fancy projection devices, or printing overhead transparencies. Participants could see ways to incorporate the technology in the classroom. I plan to help teachers and students with the technology and with the research they need to complete these projects.

> Kathy Schrock from South Dennis, Massachusetts, turns *PowerPoint* presentations into GIF files to use on her Web page slide shows <http://www.capecod.net/Wixon/wixon.html>.

PowerPoint projects can be printed out in several formats: individual slide, handout sheets with 1, 2, 3 or 6 slides per page, outline view, and notes (sheets with one slide on top and room to add speaker notes at the bottom). The handout and notes sheets make great handouts for the class. Students have the information from the slides and room to take notes during the session. The handout and notes master can be used to customize these sheets.

Because we started with simple uses and modeled *PowerPoint* as a teaching tool, participants gained a good understanding of the program's potential. **TC**

Deborah J. Stafford is a media specialist at General H.H. Arnold High School in Wiesbaden, Germany.

Projects can be produced for viewing on single computers, showing to groups via fancy projection devices, or printing overhead transparencies. Participants could see ways to incorporate the technology in the classroom.

How we introduced MS PowerPoint

We began *PowerPoint* sessions by showing the group a short presentation that outlined some of the main Windows features, especially the buttons for different views.

Then each participant began a new presentation, starting with a title slide. We switched to the outline view. From it they could see the text they had entered. They completed two more slides in outline view before we showed them slideview. The projects were kept simple. Because we were also demonstrating *Microsoft Word* and *Microsoft Excel* in other sessions, we did not dwell on some functions common to the other programs.

For the second session we prepared a *PowerPoint* tutorial showing how to add objects to a slide. The tutorial showed how to add an eclipse, autoshape (a group of predrawn shapes from which you can select—arrow, for example), free form and clip art. The participants worked in teams of two, one person pulled up the tutorial and ran the presentation while the second person followed the directions in adding objects to a new presentation. Working together, they learned to add objects. We planned for them to switch roles but most didn't feel it necessary.

In the third session we introduced builds (when individual items on a slide appear in order) and transitions (changes between slides). Much experimentation went on at this stage. Some projects grew to 10 slides. Finally, we showed them the templates (pre-prepared backgrounds) and Wizards (presentation formats already prepared and needing only the data typed in). While these are good for final projects, or a quick presentation, we felt that by showing these last, participants first learned to make their projects fit their needs.

CONNECTING WITH  THE CURRICULUM

The Writing–Technology Connection

By J. Miguel Guhlin

Technology has brought sweeping changes to how we write and publish. Just a few months ago, an article of mine was published in a journal without my ever going to the post office. Nor did I have to send my unsolicited writing to an editor. Rather, the editor came to me. All was done electronically through the Internet. My tools were a computer, a word processor, and a modem. These same tools are available for our student writers.

I remember my first attempt at word processing when I was 13 years old (in 1983). I used my brand-new Apple IIe to make print statements in a BASIC program. Each print statement would print a sentence I had written. My high school English teacher wondered out loud why my sentences came in paragraphs. Things have changed. This past summer, at the Kids Summer Computer Camp sponsored by the Mt. Pleasant Independent School District, students used Macintosh computers to copy and paste graphics into their computer journals. They used e-mail to "converse" with students in San Antonio, Texas.

Research over the past few years also suggests that children tend to enjoy writing more when writing on a computer. Children think writing on a computer is easier and more fun than using pencil and paper because it eliminates recopying compositions. In *Writing and Computers* (Addison-Wesley, 1985), C. Daiute reports that children usually write more and stay with the writing task for longer periods of time when they are using computers. Other studies have found that children continued to write on pieces produced on previous days, did more conferencing with their teacher about writing, included more detail in their writing, revised more, and seemed to be more involved in the writing process.

The introduction of multimedia software has made a significant impact on the writing process. When first-grade students in Suzi Thomas's class, at E.C. Brice Elementary in Mt. Pleasant, Texas, wrote their story about "The Fuzzy Worm," they did so using Broderbund's *Kid Pix 2*. Each child contributed a line and illustration to the story. After entering the children's sentences and illustrations

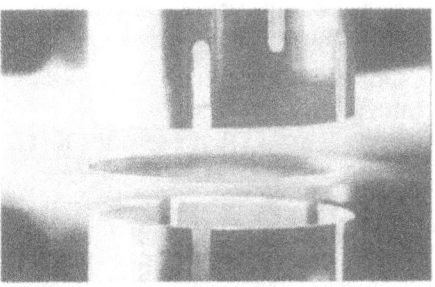

into this collaborative writing project, the teacher recorded each child's reading of his sentence using the microphone built into the Macintosh computer. According to the classroom teacher, one child would not have spoken if it had not been for the computer. Thomas later shared this multimedia slide show with the school board. Have no doubts about how well the school board received this work.

At the same school, third-grade teacher Tina Baker also used multimedia software, Roger Wagner's *HyperStudio*, to raise the level of excitement for students in publishing their "My Most Important Book." Students created a *HyperStudio* stack that incorporated what they had learned about the solar system, written as short journal entries with illustrations. Students also recorded themselves reading their writing. These two multimedia documents, one a slide show and the other a hypermedia document, were published along with other student work on the Kids' Web Project found on the World Wide Web managed by Ken Task (e-mail: ktask@tenet.edu). Work from bilingual children (K–grade 3) is also featured on the Kids' Web Project.

After having taught writing in grades 3–6, I believe the key to writing success is something referred to as postwriting. Postwriting, according to Larry Nicholls, includes all the activities that teachers and students can do with a finished piece of writing. Nicholls writes:

A writer's message needs to be shared aloud, sent to a pen pal, entered in a writing fair, stuck in a bottle and tossed out to sea. Yes, in some fashion, it must be published, in the root sense of the word: made known to other people. (Nicholls, Larry. "Postwriting: A classroom newspaper," in *From Literacy to Literature*, University of California, 1989, pp 143–162.)

Through the use of technology, especially computers and telecommunications, publishing student work is a phone call away. Students can publish their writing through online magazines, which have few guidelines. One such online children's writing publisher is ISN

KidNews (e-mail: powens@umassd.edu). It is located at the University of Massachusetts, Dartmouth. According to its managers, "ISN KidNews is a news service for students and teachers around the world. Anyone may use stories from the service, and anyone may submit stories. We also invite comments about news gathering, teaching, and computer-related issues in the discussion sections for students and teachers."

Publishing guidelines are a bit different from what many of us have come to expect as writing teachers. Here's an excerpt from ISN KidNews's guidelines:

- *When submitting a story, please include your name, your grade, your e-mail address, your school, and a headline (optional).*
- *Please try to be aware of readers from around the world and edit your submissions so that people who don't know you or your school can make sense of your story.*

With Internet access, children can exchange e-mail messages with other children around the globe. They can also publish their writings online and participate in online discussion groups with other same-age writers. The power of technology can bring the power of postwriting into the hands of young writers.

I can still hear the "Wow!" that echoed in my bilingual third-grade class when I told them their *HyperStudio* stack had been published on the Internet on the Kids' Web Project. That "Wow!" carried with it the pride of being published, of knowing that millions of people could see their work. The Kids' Web Project, ISN KidNews, and the use of e-mail to share student writing across the globe are only some of the ways technology can be used for postwriting. **TC**

J. Miguel Guhlin is the Instructional Technology Specialist for the Mt. Pleasant (Texas) Independent School District.

ONLINE PUBLISHING OPPORTUNITIES

Here are four online student publishers, all of which are accessible on the World Wide Web. The information was taken directly from their home pages.

Global Show-n-Tell
Home page: http://www.manymedia.com/show-n-tell/

Global Show-n-Tell is a virtual exhibition that makes it possible for children to share their favorite projects, possessions, accomplishments, and collections with people around the world. It consists of links to children's artwork in the form of multimedia pages residing in World Wide Web or FTP services. There is no charge to participate. Send e-mail to show-n-tell@manymedia.com. Include the following information: In the subject line, include the URL (or the FTP site and filename) of the page where the text or graphics reside. In the body of the message, provide a sentence or two that can be pasted into the exhibit page. This should contain the child's name (first names only are acceptable), age, hometown (or region), and medium in which the item was created.

ISN KidNews

ISN KidNews is a news service for students and teachers around the world. Anyone may use stories from the service, and anyone may submit stories. Comments about news gathering, teaching, and computer-related issues in "Discussion sections for students and teachers" are invited. Send e-mail directly to powens@umassd.edu or webmaster@umassd.edu.

KidPub
Home page: http://en-garde.com/kidpub/intro.html

KidPub is a corner of the World Wide Web where children are encouraged to publish their stories and news about their schools and towns. To publish a story, children should e-mail it to KidPub@en-garde.com. With the story, they can publish a brief note introducing themselves, including such things as their favorite food, hobbies, and pets.

MidLink Magazine
Home page: http://longwood.cs.ucf.edu/~Midlink/

MidLink Magazine is an electronic magazine for kids in the middle grades—ages 10 to 15—and includes art and writing from all over the world. It is intended to be published bimonthly and each issue will have a different theme. To participate: send e-mail to Caroline McCullen at caroline_mccullen@ncsu.edu or log on to the home page directly.

SCHNABEL—
Continued from page 11

AIDS/HIV information on the Internet. We may put on a short example of the videotape, as well.

We've recovered from our initial journey and are already planning our next big trip on the Internet. This one should be a doozie. We're going to research the national debt. **TC**

Jerry Schnabel is Media Director at Fillmore Central High School in Harmony, Minnesota. His e-mail address is 0228hsh@InforMNs.k12.mn.us.

Questions to Ask Before Starting Your 'Journey'

1. **What do you want to do?**
   Every well-designed project begins with an objective in mind. Once it's defined, choose resources that best meet the objective. These resources may or may not include the Internet.

2. **What use will you make of the Internet resource?** *Primary, secondary, or not appropriate? Contrary to popular myth, not everything is on the Internet.*

3. **Who will use the Internet?**
   One student, teams, the whole class, or teachers?

4. **How much time do you have?**
   Unlimited direct connect or limited dial-up access?

5. **What search strategies and software will you use?**
   Simple boolean searching or more advanced? Veronica, WebCrawler, Lycos or other WWW search engines?

6. **What is the Internet experience level of students and teachers?**
   Beginner, experienced user, or somewhere in between?

7. **What will your final product be?**
   Paper, oral report, multimedia presentation, videotape, WWW page, gopher, or other format?

8. **Who is your audience?** *Using the Internet implies that you will present your findings to others. Who will you present it to? Classmates? The teacher? The world?*

Special Education Students Become Authors As They

BY SUSAN MONAHAN AND DEE SUSONG

Two special education teachers wanted their students to feel good about themselves as writers, to learn more about literature, and to work cooperatively. Voila! The Author Slide Show Project!

Our Mac lab is a writing lab, and to create the "write" atmosphere we named each of our computers after a popular children's author. This was a good start, but we wanted our students to know more about the authors who lent their names to the computers. Our after-school computer club, composed of learning disabled, at-risk, and hearing impaired students, was given the job of creating a slide show for each namesake computer in the lab. We used *Kid Pix* Slide Show and created our text in *ClarisWorks:* Drawing.

The students worked in groups of two or three. Each group chose an author and read several books by her or him. Then, based on biographical information they found in their research, they wrote a short life story of the author. To guide the students in their research, we created a form that asked specific questions; for example, "Where was your author born and is the person still living?" or "What advice does your author give to young writers?"

The students wrote both to the authors and to their publishers. We spent time generating questions that could be asked and then guiding the students in composing and typing their letters and in researching addresses. To gather more information about authors' lives, students read reference books such as *About the Author* and short bios on book jackets and in children's magazines. Monthly book club catalogs such as *Trumpet* and *Scholastic* often print short author features along with great photographs of the authors. We had been collecting these over the years and found them to be a valuable resource. Publishers sent us a variety of information—brochures, photographs of the authors, colorful posters. Some authors were especially friendly and personal. Donald Crews and Jan Brett addressed their letters directly to the students and gave details about their lives and their motivation for writing.

In a few cases we were able to meet the authors in person at book signings at our local bookstore, Toad Hall. We went to the signings armed with questions and requested permission to videotape and take photos. The authors were gracious and chatted with the students about their projects.

We teachers were eager to include content areas other than language arts, so we required that each slide show include at least one map slide showing where the author was born or lives presently, or both. Black-and-white maps were very effective visually when the *Kid Pix* Paint Bucket was used to highlight the states where an author had lived.

The biography of the author made up half the author slide show. The second part involved a review of the book the students chose. We asked them to include the elements of story grammar—characters, settings and problem—but not to give away the ending! We encouraged them to do most of the illustrating of the slide shows themselves. Only minimal use of *Kid Pix* Stamps was allowed, and we included scanned photos, video stills and sound from our face-to-face visits. We had access only to a black-and-white scanner, but we scanned photos from brochures and book jackets and the students dressed them up with colorful borders and embellishments. Our Video Spigot allowed us to capture stills from the videotapes we took at the bookstore and provided a quick way to get color stills of our student authors for the credits slide at the end of each show.

> **Organization, both on and off the computer, is extremely important in creating a *Kid Pix* slide show.**

Notes

MONAHAN—

Word processing in *Kid Pix* does not allow easy editing or enough variety in fonts. We taught our students to type their text in *ClarisWorks*: Graphics. In *ClarisWorks*, the students could revise and edit and make font and color choices, then cut and paste their finished text onto their *Kid Pix* slides. We saved the text, too, to be printed out as a "script" for recording later.

We didn't have the students record sound on every slide, but we felt that using the students' voices on some slides was an effective way to personalize the show. We used a short song on the Don and Audrey Wood Slide Show that the authors sang at Toad Hall. (We played the videotape back and picked up the sound with our LCII microphone.) One student created his own train sound effects for his book review of *At Big Mama's*, by Donald Crews. Another student simulated a great smacking kiss for *Beauty and the Beast* by Jan Brett.

We learned that organization, both on and off the computer, is extremely important in creating a *Kid Pix* slide show. Each author had a folder on our file server, and we taught the students to be very specific when labeling their documents so that arranging them in the show later would be easier. We also encouraged them to be careful about saving their work in the appropriate folder.

Students had opportunities to "publish" their work. They impressed an audience of a hundred at the Texas Computers in Education Convention in Austin when they presented their author slide shows. We also invited teachers and parents to a special Author Slide Show Open House in our writing lab. Completed slide shows are permanently housed on our file server and can be accessed by any user by clicking on the Meet The Author! button on our At Ease screen. TC

Susan Monahan is an Itinerant Teacher for the Auditorily Impaired at the Regional Day School for the Deaf in Austin, Texas, and Dee Susong is a Special Education Teacher at Brentwood Elementary School in Austin, Texas.

CONNECTING WITH  THE CURRICULUM

Authors! Authors!

By Lisa James Delgado

"This looks like a real storybook!" exclaimed one of our young authors as she pulled her completed pages from the laser printer. Her pride and pleasure were obvious but not unique. Over the past two years, I have heard similar expressions of satisfaction from other fledgling writers using our technology-based publishing center, which we set up with a grant from the Innovation Program at the Georgia State Department of Education. As students prepare their work for publication, they improve their reading and writing skills as they proofread, revise, and complete what they begin. Their teachers note that the program gives students ownership of their writing and engages them in authentic and challenging tasks.

THE PUBLISHING CENTER IS HOUSED IN THE LIBRARY

Imagine a room humming with activity as students create their own books. One fifth grader uses a word processor to complete his latest mystery while another uses a paint program to draw a whale for her ocean story. A kindergartner listens to the computer as it reads what he has typed. An adult volunteer helps a second grader scan a photo of her dog. Over by the printer, a third grader waits for several copies of her story. One is for her mother's birthday, the second will go into her writing portfolio, a third will be placed in the media center, and the last copy is for herself.

The publishing center is located in a small room within the media center, and I'm able to answer questions and troubleshoot problems without leaving the library. The center is equipped with seven Macintosh computers—two of them on wheeled carts that can be moved to classrooms for use by teachers creating class books. We purchased software, a scanner, and a digital camera to help students add illustrations or photographs to their books; however, we found that many younger students preferred to

> They may also choose to donate copies of their completed books to the media center. Those who do enjoy looking up their names in the online catalog.

draw directly onto their laser printed pages. Because our laser printers produce only black-and-white printouts, the children's own colorful drawings are my favorite illustrations.

DIFFERENT WORD PROCESSING PROGRAMS MEET DIFFERENT NEEDS

Students who word process their books choose between *The Writing*

Publishing Center Procedures

The walls of our publishing center are covered with directions for each program, examples of a variety of fonts, font sizes, illustration methods, and layouts, along with samples of students' writing. The enlarged step-by-step directions aren't intended to include all possible options, but rather to illustrate one approach. Volunteers receive letter-size copies of these directions during training.

Originally, students saved their stories on a class disk. This quickly became a problem when more than one student from the same class needed to use the disk. Now each student has his or her own disk, which is used until the student completes fifth grade. Not only did this solve the class disk dilemma, it also provides an archive of each student's published writing! Fifth graders' disks are reformatted at the end of the school year and are used for incoming kindergarten students, unless students wish to keep the disks and give us new ones to replace them.

Another concern has been how to handle the issue of composing on the computer. We know this is the best way to optimize the capabilities of computers, but we don't have enough computers in our classrooms to teach students to write this way all the time. As a compromise, we do allow fourth and fifth grade students the opportunity to compose on the computers in our publishing center, but ask younger students to bring us their stories completed and ready to be published.

Center by The Learning Company and *Kid Works 2* by Davidson. Most students use *The Writing Center* (and I would choose this one if I could buy only one). However, *Kid Works 2* has an excellent paint program and also allows students to hear what they've typed. Kindergartners and first graders who come in with one sentence "stories" are usually encouraged to use *Kid Works 2*. We use *The Writing Center* for stories one page or longer so we can take advantage of the spell check and page break features not available in *Kid Works 2*. Many students enjoy searching for illustrations for their stories in *The Writing Center's* graphics library.

We also bought *MacPaint* by Claris for older students who wanted to use software to illustrate stories they had already written. Our original version of *Kid Works 2* wouldn't allow illustrations to be exported into stories written with other word processors. We've now updated *Kid Works 2* to a version that permits this, but *MacPaint's* black-and-white screen still gives our students a better idea of what their finished products will look like with our black-and-white printers.

The most recent program we bought was *Kid Desk* by Edmark, a desktop management system that we use to make volunteer training easier and to limit the number of files accidentally deleted. We also hoped *Kid Desk* would help us prevent people from saving stories on the hard drives, but the "Open/Save Limited To: Floppy Disk" feature could not be used if we wanted access to the graphics files in *The Writing Center*. I hope Edmark will revise the program so we can take advantage of this feature.

Binding and (Sometimes) Shelving Student Books

After they have written and illustrated their books, our young authors choose how to bind them. We have a comb binding machine (the most popular), a sewing machine, and selection of wallpapered cardboard covers. Poster board, brads, and rings along with heavy duty and long arm staplers are available for binding oversized class books. A labeling machine is used to put neatly printed titles and authors' names on the covers. Students may also choose to complete all or part of their books by hand.

They may also choose to donate copies of their completed books to the media center. Those who do enjoy looking up their names in the online catalog. We provide these students with a checklist of requirements that must be met for the book to be shelved. The checklist includes the standard parts of a book, a brief summary (for the online catalog), and the teacher's signature assuring us the piece has been edited.

A recent conversation I had with a fifth grader typifies our students' enthusiasm for the publishing center. When I commended him for his dedication in publishing his lengthy story, he told me he was working on two more at home. **TC**

Lisa James Delgado is a Media Specialist at South Jackson Elementary School in Athens, Georgia.

Staffing the Center

Our biggest challenge has been finding enough volunteers to staff the center. (We require a trained volunteer or teacher to be present while students publish.) Many of our parents work or have to care for young children at home. We are constantly requesting help through school newsletters and at school functions. We ask volunteers to put in as little as two hours a week; in exchange, we offer them computer training and a wonderful opportunity to become involved in the learning process at our school. One grandparent volunteer completed a story of her own while working in our publishing center and has mailed her manuscript to several publishers. To help solve this shortage of volunteers, we've trained several fifth graders to work in the publishing center each morning before school.

LOGGING ON—
Continued from page 7

those used in textbook adoptions. In California, this idea is being discussed. Knowing that in four years the site would have technology funds to upgrade, purchase, or continue leasing equipment would make it easier to budget limited and dwindling school funds.

If technology funding becomes a reality, educators won't need to look to business to provide them with obsolete machines that some organizations refurbish. Refurbished machines will not run the software programs on the market today. They will suffice as word processors or keyboarding machines, but to try and use them to teach the skills of integrated software will not work. The use of donated equipment has become an issue in some states as organizations hoping to increase the student-to-computer ratio have become misguided. The organization leadership feels that a computer of any sort is better than none at all. In focusing on the student-to-computer ratio, the question they forget to ask is "what are the overall curricular goals and objectives?" Refurbished machines suffice as keyboarding machines, but are not capable of allowing students to access, analyze, and communicate information. These outdated machines cannot provide the higher end processing skills needed by students to create multimedia products, portfolios, or projects needed in the real work world.

As school media and technology specialists, we experience these realities every day. We need to continue to provide accurate information and to help plan for hardware and software changes to prevent the technology gap from widening into a chasm of obsolescence.

Catie Somers is the Library Media Specialist at DePortola Middle School in San Diego, California.

Of Letters, Diaries, and Laserdiscs: The Primary Source

By Augie E. Beasley and Carolyn G. Palmer

Many research assignments in the secondary English and social studies curriculum require that students consult some primary sources in their search for information. While working with our students, we discovered that many of them did not have a clear understanding of the concept of primary source material; consequently, they were having difficulty distinguishing between primary and secondary sources.

Anxious to help solve this problem, we decided to design a lesson that we could use to introduce primary sources to our students. First, we consulted with our teachers to learn more about the students' research assignments and to receive opinions about the lesson which we were planning. The teachers and the library staff agreed that the lesson should be presented a day or two before the students' research actually began.

In designing the lesson, we wanted to help reinforce the students' higher-level skills such as critical thinking. We hoped that students would
- learn to distinguish primary and secondary material;
- learn to use sources other than books for their research;
- learn to draw conclusions from the facts they uncover; and
- develop their critical thinking skills.

To grab students' attention, we distribute two short, unsigned letters. After reading the letters, the students are asked to place the letters in a particular time period and location. We also ask them what conclusions they can draw from the letters concerning the identity and state of mind of the writer and the situation being described. Here are two samples:

My Brother John,

It is with a joyous heart that I write to you this crisp April morning. We have struck a blow for freedom on this glorious day.

Our brave lads met the soldiers of the oppressor in the square and fought them to a draw.

Many of our brave lads were killed, but they felled many of the soldiers before they died.

My Dear Emma,

It is with heavy heart that I must write to you about the recent troubles. A group of ruffians and ne'er-do-wells attacked a group of soldiers, and they in defending themselves killed many of these ruffians.

May God help us when it is unsafe to walk the streets. These are evil times. What are we to do?

Short entries from a diary are equally effective.

The letters have never failed to create a lively discussion. Student ideas concerning the letters are always interesting. For example, some students have felt that the writer of the "My Dear Emma" letter had to be a man since a woman would not address another woman by "My Dear." Another group of students immediately reminded them that they were applying contemporary values to a situation that had occurred in the past. Several students have felt that the letters were written by an educated person since the average person could not read and write.

We explain that letters, diaries and documents are important sources of primary information about the early periods in our history and that the letters they have just read actually describe the Boston Massacre. To demonstrate a secondary account of the same situation, we show them an article describing the Boston Massacre in an encyclopedia. We also point out that in the "Dear John" letter it states that both sides had casualties; however, the account of the Boston Massacre in the encyclopedia indicates that only colonists were killed. This shows the students that even primary sources such as letters, diaries, journals, and interviews must be checked for accuracy. We hope that they will see that they must decide whether the material is fact or opinion, or whether there is any bias present.

A display of other primary sources—photographs, legal documents such as birth and marriage certificates, journals, newspapers (We also display the *New York Times Greats* programs, on microfiche, which hold original articles from *The New York Times* and are available from UMI, 300 North Zeeb Road, Ann Arbor, MI 48106.), statutes, and real objects—is set up in the teaching area to generate interest. At this point, we talk about some of the sources included in the display.

Many of our students do an "I-Search" paper, which relies heavily on the personal interview. In and "I-Search" paper, the students research topics related to something they want to know (how to prepare for a particular job) or possess (a certain type of car). The final paper includes a description of the students' previous knowledge of the topic, the reasons for their interest in the topic, the story of their search for the information, and the knowledge they gained or failed to gain. Interviewing experts on the topic is one of the requirements for this type of paper; therefore, we give the personal interview coverage during the lesson. Allowing students to listen to a portion of an audio-taped interview is a good way to demonstrate this source. If a community resource file is kept in the media center, make sure students are aware of it (Incorporate the community resource file into the card catalog. A different colored catalog card—such as bright pink—can be used for these listings, and parent volunteers can be in charge of updating it.)

We close by introducing the students to a new format for primary source material—*The Video Encyclopedia of the 20th Century* on laserdisc. *The Video Encyclopedia* provides 79 hours of primary source material recorded by film and television news cameras without any added commentary, music, or sound effects. Students are fascinated with this resource, and it serves as an excellent way to motivate their upcoming research and study. To demonstrate the difference in primary and secondary sources once more, we show the class a laserdisc of the Vietnam War (we use *Vietnam: The Ten Thousand Day War* by Peter Arnett, Embassy Home Entertainment, 1901 Avenue of the Stars, Los Angeles, CA 90067). We explain that commentary has been added to the original film clips, making the program a secondary source.

We certainly would not argue that the lesson settles all students' questions about primary and secondary sources; however, students who participate in the lesson appear to be more aware of primary sources. They also seem more comfortable using sources other than books for their research. Our teachers have been pleased with their students' active participation in the lesson, and we think that it is definitely worth the effort.

For librarians interested in designing their own lesson or learning center on primary sources, we suggest taking a look at *How to Use Primary Sources* by Helen H. Carey and Judith E. Greenberg (Watts, 1983). Information on *The Video Encyclopedia of the 20th Century* on laserdisc may be obtained by contacting CEL Educational Resources (515 Madison Ave., Suite 700, New York, NY 10022). *The Video Encyclopedia*, including a Pioneer Laserdisc player, is approximately $10,800. Since this price is out of the range of most school library budgets, a school district could purchase one for use by all its schools. A demonstration tape and 12-page brochure are available from CEL (Call toll-free, 1-800-235-3339).

Augie E. Beasley and Carolyn G. Palmer are Media Specialists at East Mecklenburg High School in Charlotte, North Carolina. Their most recent article in THE BOOK REPORT, on public relations, appeared in the May/June issue.

Notes

HEAD FOR THE EDGE

The Changing Face of Student Research

By Doug Johnson

Consider these research assignments:
- High school students trace the history of buildings on their town's main street.
- A middle school class researches and recommends a location for the new city landfill.
- Elementary students use e-mail and the Internet to collect holiday customs celebrated by students from around the world.

These projects are not unusual. The first comes from Minnesota's new performance assessment package for inquiry; the second is from California Media and Library Educators Association's book *From Library Skills to Information Literacy: A Handbook for the 21st Century* (Hi Willow, 1994); and the last is a typical project coordinated through the Internet's Global School House http://www.gsn.org/. Do you notice any similarities? I can think of three attributes that make the projects both powerful and potentially frustrating. They are qualities that invite media specialists (again!) to rethink their roles as information specialists.

1. Increasingly, research focuses on topics of local significance. Whether researching a building, person, ethnic group or custom, the emphasis is on things in the students' immediate geographic area, if not in their own households. Even when the topic is of national or international scope, such as pollution, the global economy, the Gulf War, technology, or health issues, teachers are asking students to assess the impact of policies and events on their own families and communities.

2. As a result, researchers are being asked to use primary rather than secondary resources. Local history is scanty in most school media centers. When it does exist, as in back issues of the local newspaper, often it's not indexed. Primary information sources such as the county courthouse, a local university, original surveys, government statistics (published on the Internet), and the memories of local "experts" are being used more and more.

3. Each of the examples above is purposely designed to be meaningful to the student researcher. The issues of recycling and pollution become relevant (and exciting) when the new landfill might be located next door to one's own house or favorite recreation area. The genuine voices of another culture's students speak louder than any text or reference book.

So, is there still a place for the school media specialist as research becomes primary-source based? When the school's collection is not adequate or relevant to the task at hand, what does the "information specialist" contribute?

Quite a bit, actually. The tasks involved in the inquiry process, regardless of the source of the information, remain pretty much the same. Students still need to formulate good questions and identify what information is needed. They will continue to gather, record, organize, and analyze the data, whether with paper and pencil, video camera, database or e-mail. More than with secondary information sources, the primary data should be critically evaluated. For example, a student felt she had hit the jackpot when she found a woman on the Internet who was willing to share her adventures as a fighter pilot in Vietnam. Later, the student discovered through other research that there were no female fighter pilots involved in that conflict.

As performance-based assessment becomes a standard means of evaluating student work, communicating the research results becomes increasingly important. Students need guidance to decide the best medium to display their findings, whether they compose thoughtfully crafted charts and graphs, a multi-media presentation, computerized slide shows, or even web pages.

Many teachers were probably not asked to do primary source research until they were in graduate school, if then. The use of orig-

Notes

Head for the Edge

inal research and the use of primary sources may be as new to them as it is to their students. Our job as information specialists may well involve as much teaching of good information literacy skills to the teachers as to the students.

So, will the reference books sit dusty on the shelves? Will the library catalog monitor burn out and not be reported for months? Will our carefully made lessons on using the CD-ROM periodical guide mold in a drawer? No more state reports or posters of African animal facts or "social problem" term papers? I hope not. As excited as I am about constructivist, hands-on, experiential teaching and learning, I also firmly believe real education demands that students learn both process *and* content. And information technology (and technologists) will help with both. TC

Doug Johnson is the District Media Supervisor for the Mankato (Minnesota) Public Schools, and can be reached by e-mail at djohns1@west.isd77.k12.mn.us (or) palsdaj@vax1.mankato.msus.edu.

PRIMARY SOURCES

By Peter Milbury

Second to None on the Web

Do the words "primary sources" conjure up images of a book about politics by an "anonymous" author? Or vague thoughts of political drama, intrigue, or misadventure? Maybe a voter handbook on an upcoming election? Tattletale first graders?

For educators who are using the Web for instruction, a primary source is none of these. A primary source is in fact, a very useful type of teaching resource, one that is becoming increasingly available online. A primary historical source is an eyewitness account of an event, a firsthand view or experience of it. Events or facts may have been recorded via a speech, film, letter, photo, document, or other medium. On the Web, this ends up being a digital or facsimile version of whatever the actual primary source format was. Another useful type of primary source, though not necessarily considered "historical," is a statistic or set of data.

A secondary source, by comparison, is something that interprets or makes an edited representation of a primary source. For example, an acceptance speech by a Nobel laureate is a primary source, but a newspaper report about that speech is a secondary source. However a journalist's eyewitness account of the speech being given may be used as a primary source for a particular purpose, such as examining bias in the press.

Although it may seem like splitting hairs, a proper study of history or analysis of events does become a matter of perspective. Actually, perspective becomes a dynamic force, a tool that educators may use to challenge and motivate learners. Primary sources are some of the most rich, vivid, and powerful teaching tools at our disposal. They are particularly welcome to those who have become concerned about the commercial nature of the Web, and its accompanying biases and underlying motivation.

UNDERSTANDING AND USING PRIMARY SOURCES

One of the pleasant surprises about primary sources on the Web is that some of the organizations that make them available online provide various introductory materials or

helping tools for us. These organizations also tend to create displays, exhibits, or essays that assist us in the use of primary sources. This is especially true of two institutions, the National Archives and the Library of Congress, both of which contributed to my motivation to use and spread the word about primary sources.

By now, you are probably saying to yourself that primary sources are not new to education, nor are they new to the Internet. That is quite true, but they are traditionally under utilized. Although I had long been aware of primary sources on the Internet, it took two different experiences to really get me hooked and "on board."

One of the first and most effective uses of primary sources which caught my attention was an exhibition, *When Nixon Met Elvis*. This is a highly interesting and perhaps even amusing look at how two types of primary source media may be combined. The exhibit, which is still available at the National Archives Online Exhibit Hall (<www.nara.gov/exhall/exhibits.html>), makes striking use of written communications between President Nixon and Elvis Presley. Letters and memoranda between Presley and Nixon are supplemented with photographs taken when Presley visited the White House.

Another big impression was made on me while I was attending a summer institute at the Library of Congress. The participants were treated to a virtual tour of the American Memory collections of the National Digital Library. [*Editor's note*: For more information about the American

Search Guides

Memory project, see "Cool Stuff on the Web" in this issue.] Our guide made highly effective use of the Walt Whitman and Matthew Brady collections. Our guide, who was also a student of literature, recalled that Whitman had served as a medic during the Civil War. This gave him the idea of exploring the two collections to see if there was a way to connect them. As we watched, he moved back and forth between Whitman's notations from a day of the particularly bloody battle of Antietam to the Brady Collection's images from the devastation of that battle. He then used the vivid sense of history that he created with the notes and images to underscore Whitman's poem "O Captain, My Captain," the poet's elegy to his beloved, fallen president, Abraham Lincoln.

Being able to see those documents side by side, and in a meaningful sequence, was deeply moving and powerful. Most impressive was how the guide, by arrangement and commentary, added insight, meaning, and value to seemingly unrelated materials. In this case it was especially powerful, because those documents were all highly believable primary sources: photographs, images from a notebook, and a poem.

Letters, diaries, and photographs can all be interesting in and of their own right. When combined with other primary sources offering different perspectives on events and ideas, or when combined into an exhibit, the synergy creates new meaning and interest.

With a little practice, you too can make primary sources come alive for your students. It is your background knowledge, along with your understanding of your school's curriculum that become important factors which bridge the gap. That is why it is important to get to know some of the best, most useful collections of primary sources available on the Web. If the goal of educators is to move students from being passive recipients of information to active, thoughtful producers of meaningful knowledge, then primary sources on the Web will serve them well.

PRIMARY VIEWS: EXCELLENCE IN PRIMARY SOURCE WEB SITES

If you look carefully around the Web, you will find that there is something for just about any interest or curriculum area. Listed below are some superb Web sites, covering a variety of subject areas.

San Francisco Fine Arts Museums
<www.thinker.org/index.shtml>

The De Young Museum in Golden Gate Park and the The Legion of Honor in Lincoln Park comprise the Fine Arts Museums of San Francisco. These two museums house a comprehensive, high quality art collection. More than 70,000 images are available in their Imagebase collection, including paintings, drawings, etchings, porcelains, sculpture, silver, glass, furniture, textiles, and other media.

ATHLETICS:
International Amateur Athletic Federation

The official Web Site of the International Amateur Athletic Federation (IAAF) includes world records, landmarks, images of current and past personalities, results and statistics, competition lists, descriptions of the sports and events, and other information on worldwide amateur sports and athletes.

AGRICULTURE:
Livestock Breeds
<www.ansi.okstate.edu/breeds/>

From the Department of Animal Science at Oklahoma State University comes an excellent collection of background and links to information on a wide variety of livestock breeds: cattle, horses, goats, sheep, swine, poultry, and other breeds. The site has a well-written introduction, and many photographs, plus bibliographic references and links for additional research papers, as well as other information and materials.

ENGLISH AND LANGUAGE ARTS:
William Shakespeare, Complete
<www.tech.mit.edu/Shakespeare/works.html>

This is an online version of the complete works of William Shakespeare, from the Massachusetts Institute of Technology. The site's sophisticated search engine permits you to specify or isolate individual works to be searched. Results are displayed in brief context and organized by their dramatic work. The site also includes the Shakespeare quotes from *Bartlett's Familiar Quotations* and links to other Internet information resources related to Shakespeare's life and times.

FOREIGN LANGUAGES AND LITERATURE:
Internet Public Library Reading Room: Newspapers
<www.ipl.org/reading/news/>

This site features links to hundreds of newspapers, magazines, and media throughout the U.S. and the world that allow students to read newspapers in their native languages. The links are grouped alphabetically according to country, state, and city. A search engine pulls up links to newspapers according to your keywords. (Does not search the contents of the newspapers.)

GEOGRAPHY:
INCORE Country Guides
<www.incore.ulst.ac.uk/cds/countries/index.html>

INCORE is a current list of links to information about countries and regions of the world which are at war, have the threat of war, or need peacekeeping forces to prevent warfare. This phenomenal site features maps and links to "prime" sources related to the many countries of the world involved in conflicts.

HEALTH:
Environmental Factsheets and Pamphlets
<www.niehs.nih.gov/oc/factsheets/fsmenu.htm>

This National Institutes of Health site lists resources that cover a number of basic environmental health topics. These are primary documents in the sense that their information and data are supported by or represent the statistics, research, and recommendations of an official U.S. government agency.

HISTORY:
American Memory at the Library of Congress

This is the premier Web site for primary historical sources. It features a growing set of more than 40 separate collections, as well as a multitude of supportive curriculum materials. It includes multimedia sources that are mostly free of copyright restrictions, in the following formats: photos and prints, documents, motion pictures, maps, and sound recordings. [Editor's Note: For more information see Cool Stuff on the Web in this issue.]

NUTRITION:
Fast Food Facts—Interactive Food Finder
<www.olen.com/food/>

Use the interactive form on this page to calculate the nutrition of fast foods served at the most common fast food restaurants in the U.S. The site includes data for more than 1,000 fast food items in the major fast food chain restaurants. The information is based on the book *Fast Food Facts*, by the Minnesota Attorney General's Office.

MATHEMATICS:
Measure 4 Measure: Sites That Do the Work for You
<www.wolinskyweb.com/measure.htm>

This site is a collection of links to other Web sites that allow you to calculate a large variety of things, from area conversions, astronomical, and body surface to precious metals and wallboard—it even includes a window-door estimator. This fascinating resource makes mathematics approachable.

MUSIC:
Robert Altman, Photographer
<www.cea.edu/robert/Catalog.1.html>

Rock stars and music groups, as well as selected historic events of the Sixties and later, are shown in the photos of professional photographer Robert Altman (not the film director of the same name). Many of these photos are "classics," easily recognizable from the media. The images include not only singers, musicians, and bands, but also related cultural personalities of the era's various sociopolitical "movements." This collection provides hard-to-find images and contributes to the understanding of the decade as a historical period.

NEWS AND MEDIA:
The Online News Hour
<www1.pbs.org/newshour/>

This site is the online home of *The NewsHour with Jim Lehrer*, the highly respected news program from public television. It offers current program transcripts and voluminous archives of past programs. It includes images of the famous, influential, and authoritative program guests, within the context of the transcripts in which they originally appeared. Many important issues are covered, with the full text of the programs (plus actual audio) available online. For an impartial, unbiased view of the issues, this is one of the best places to go.

SCIENCE:
The Nine Planets
<www.seds.org/billa/tnp/>

This site is a "multimedia tour of the solar system with text, pictures, sounds, and an occasional movie." Each of the planets and major moons in our solar system is briefly described and illustrated. With a few clicks, you can see pictures and images provided by NASA's and other scientific organizations' telescopes—images that just a few decades ago could only be dreamed about. Also included are a number of informative essays by astronomical scientists.

SOCIAL SCIENCE:
Economic Statistics Briefing Room
<www.whitehouse.gov/fsbr/esbr.html>
Social Statistics Briefing Room
<www.whitehouse.gov/fsbr/ssbr.html>

These sites provide easy access to current federal economic and social statistics indicators as produced, maintained, and updated by the statistical units of government agencies. The sites are well illustrated through the use of appropriate and understandable charts and graphs. Also included are links to the information's originating agencies, where additional data is available. Typical data topics are crime, demographics, education, and health.

PRIMARY SUPPORT: TEACHING TOOLS FOR TEACHERS

High quality curriculum materials about primary sources and use for them in teaching are readily available to educators. The National Archives and American Memory Web sites each have a variety of materials, activities, and informational resources that are designed expressly for use in K-12 schools. The American Memory site (<memory.loc.gov/>) offers by far the most resources in this area. The Library of Congress has held a series of American Memory Fellow summer institutes in which collaborating teams of teachers and librarians from around the U.S. develop lessons, activities, and curriculum units using the American Memory collections. These materials were used in the participants' schools during the following year and are currently available in the American Memory Learning Pages section. The Library of Congress also used subject experts to prepare a number of materials related to the use of primary sources, including games and activities such as The Historical Detective. This game introduces students to problem-solving skills in order to answer intriguing questions such as, "Was Billy the Kid really killed by Pat Garrett at Fort Sumner, New Mexico?"

Other curriculum materials include:

The Big Picture, 12 sets of jigsaw puzzles made from American Memory photographs. Students solve the puzzles to discover the theme of each set of puzzles.

Using Oral History, a lesson that uses the words of ordinary Americans interviewed during the Great Depression to teach social history.

Framework for Using Primary Sources with Students, a teachers' guide addressing the rationale for using primary sources, the source selection process, instructional organization, and activities for the instructional cycle.

Using Primary Sources offers suggestions for using primary sources to enhance the social studies curriculum using authentic artifacts, documents, photographs, and manuscripts from the Library of Congress Historical Collections and other sources.

Projects Using Primary Sources from the Library of Congress, a list of proven tips for using primary sources to teach critical thinking, creative writing, historical research, and local history.

The National Archives (<www.nara.gov/>), which offers two areas that educators will find very interesting and helpful as they make use of primary sources: The Online Exhibit Hall and The Digital Classroom.

The Online Exhibit Hall is a collection of exhibits featuring various documents in the National Archives. They serve to heighten interest, model possible uses of the sources, and provide background on the subjects covered. Current exhibits include *When Nixon Met Elvis*; the *Powers of Persuasion*, propaganda posters from World War II; and *Portrait of Black Chicago*, Pulitzer Prize-winning photographer John H. White's collection of images of 1970s Chicago.

The Digital Classroom at the National Archives site offers information about programs, publications, lessons, and activities for teachers and students. Primary Sources and Activities offers reproducible primary documents, lesson plans, and cross-curricular connections. A number of the activities are correlated to the National History Standards and have been taken from *Teaching With Documents*, an NARA print publication, which may be purchased. All online materials are free. Some of the activities that caught my attention are:

Glidden's Patent Application for Barbed Wire. These documents and teaching activities have students explore the impact of invention of barbed wire on the development of the West.

The U.S. Recognition of the State of Israel. The 50th anniversary of the establishment of Israel is observed with teaching activities related to a key press release and telegram.

Constitutional Issues: Watergate and the Constitution. A 1974 memorandum from the Watergate Special Prosecution Force related to the seeking of an indictment against President Nixon after he resigned.

A Date Which Will Live in Infamy. Students analyze the first typed draft of Franklin D. Roosevelt's War Address in this lesson.

Women Suffrage and the 19th Amendment. Historical documents, teaching activities, and a script used as teaching tools for this important topic.

You can now see that there is a growing abundance of high quality primary sources available on the Web. They cover important and also seemingly trivial subjects and topics in culture, history, and the human experience. But that is not all. There are also many accompanying curriculum materials which help you make use of these sources. They are there on the Web just waiting for you to use them in your teaching, with your colleagues, and with your students—please make frequent and good use of them.

Peter Milbury is a Library Media Teacher at Chico High School (California) where he is the Webmaster for the library's home page at <dewey.chs.chico.k12.ca.us>.

Laser Discs, Barcodes, and Books...
A GREAT COMBINATION

By Erica Peto

Are your laser discs collecting more dust than accolades? If so, you may want to make them more accessible by using barcodes to link them with books. Here's what I did:

I have the entire set of Optical Data's *Windows on Science* laser disc series on earth science, life science, and primary science. However, because teachers found the laser disc player remote control bulky, slow and difficult to manage, the discs were seldom used.

Getting the Bugs Out

I solved the problem by buying a nonfiction paperback book on bugs. I then searched the laser disc directory for all the still images and short movies of bugs. I used Optical Data's *Lessonmaker* program to make the barcodes which would display these images, printed them out on a laser printer, and taped them into the bug book. I taught a lesson on bugs using the information in the book; during my presentation I used the barcode reader to display related laser disc images on the TV screen. (A barcode reader is a handheld device that can be used as a remote control; it's also used to scan barcodes that access the laser disc.)

I flicked the barcode reader over the barcode and pulled up the still images and short movies on several bugs. Afterwards, I taught students how to use the barcode reader themselves. The lesson was a resounding success. I followed up by having each student research a bug, draw a picture of it, and then make a barcode to affix to the picture. As a finale, students read their information and used the barcode reader to "wand" their barcode and show an image of their bug on the TV screen.

Planting the Seeds of Creativity

Another project combined fairy tales with laser disc images of plants. I showed second graders nine laser disc movies (each about 30 seconds long) on plant-related topics. Some of the plants were shown, in time-lapse video, growing from a seed or toward a light. Other movies described how maple syrup was collected and how cocoa beans become chocolate. Students each chose a plant movie and wove it into a letter to a fairy tale character, using the book *The Jolly Postman* as a model. Each child's assignment was to describe his or her plant's special characteristics and convince a fairy tale character to buy it. These letters were typed into the computer, along with creative addresses, and were placed in handmade envelopes. We taped a barcode for each movie onto each envelope, then taped each envelope onto a page in a class book. Students then decorated the pages and shared their letters with classmates; they took turns using the barcode reader to display their plant movies on the screen.

Showing Space to Students

Another time, I was asked to show some space-related laser disc images at an all-school assembly promoting a space-themed reading week. Making the barcodes assured me that the presentation would go without a hitch. I printed the barcodes in the order I would show them—starting with a space shuttle liftoff, showing several planets, and ending with the same space shuttle liftoff. I printed descriptions of what was on the screen along with brief notes of what I would say during each scene. I zipped down the list with my barcode reader and produced a professional-looking presentation—completely avoiding the deadly lulls that can happen when fumbling with a laser disc remote control.

Our Laser Discs No Longer Gather Dust

Since my initial barcode project with bugs, I've made 15 more books on subjects such as the rain forest, recycling, plants, reptiles, space, farm animals, the skeleton, the brain, the digestive system, ocean animals, and dinosaurs. I am currently planning a new one on weather and storms.

Students use these books daily during recess time in the library to read and show laser disc images. They also use them for research. When students have a book in front of them along with the laser disc, they can get information from the theme-related book as well as from the laser disc images. Students waiting their turns for the barcode reader or pausing between barcodes can read and look at additional pictures in the barcoded books. Teachers now can check out a book and the corresponding laser disc to use for lessons or research projects. Teachers enjoy using the laser discs with the barcoded books and, together, they're the perfect tools for making laser disc technology accessible to students.

Tips on Making Laser Disc Books

- **When making the barcode, type in the description of the image and indicate whether it is a still image or a movie.** If it's a movie, type in the running length.
- **Use transparent tape.** The bar code will work even better through any kind of transparent tape because the barcode reader will slide easier. Place the tape completely over the barcode so that no edges are sticking out. This results in fewer tears of the barcode. Also, don't overlap two pieces of tape on the actual barcode. This makes it harder to read.
- **If your barcoded books will get lots of use (mine do!), you might want to purchase prebound books from a dealer such as Permabound, Bound-to-Stay-Bound, or Econoclad.** They will hold up much longer than paperbacks.
- **Write the title, volume number, and side (if appropriate) of the corresponding laser disc on the inside cover of the book.** When the books get mixed up, you can easily tell where it goes and whether it will work for a particular disc.
- **Use barcodes from only one laser disc for each book.** This way, you won't have to switch discs in the middle of a lesson and you won't confuse students using the books independently. If you have barcodes from the same subject on two different discs, buy two books on the same subject.
- **Organize the books and laser discs so that the books to be used with a particular laser disc are in the same compartment.** For example, I have five books on different topics that correspond to one laser disc. I keep them all together in the same compartment of a desk organizer for papers. That way, several students can take all five of the books and use them at the same time by passing the barcode reader around, regardless of the subject.

How to Get a Barcode Reader to Bring Up Laser Disc Images

- **Turn on the power, insert your laser disc, and push PLAY.**
- **Make sure the barcode reader is inserted correctly** in the front of the laser disc player. Remember: while the barcode reader is inserted, the keypad will not work, but the buttons on the machine will.
- **Hold the barcode reader as you would a large pencil.**
- **Press the blue button down with your forefinger.** The red light at the end of the reader should come on. If not, check the batteries.
- **With the blue button still pressed down, slide the reader gently across the barcode.** Slide it back and forth across the barcode until you hear the beep. You must read the entire barcode at one time so it might be helpful to wand PAST the barcode on both ends to make sure you are reading the entire barcode. Don't worry, it won't read anything but the barcode. Don't press too hard—you can rip the

HOW TO MAKE BARCODES

It's easy to make barcodes! It involves little more than typing in the frame number of the laser disc image you want. For movies, type in the starting frame number and the ending frame number; the barcode will start and end the movie for you. Then you can type in a description of the laser disc image. The barcode program will print out the barcode, the frame number(s), and the description—all in a long strip. You then cut the strips and tape them into the book on appropriate pages. Wanding the barcode with the reader will cause the player to search for the frame number you've programmed and will either stop on that frame number (for a still picture) or begin playing the movie. You can also rearrange the barcodes and print them out in any order. This is perfect for making individualized lesson plans or presentations.

I used Optical Data's *Lessonmaker* program to make the barcodes. There are other programs—each has its own strengths and weaknesses. *Report Generator* by Laser Learning Technologies allows you to make laser disc barcodes for times on a laser disc as well as for frame numbers, making it possible to use CLV discs (accessible only by time) as well as CAV discs (accessible by frame number). It is more complicated but has more features than *Lessonmaker*. *MediaMAX*, a Videodiscovery program, is the most expensive and is tailored to be paired with the company's laser discs. All of these programs will work for the project described here and can also be used to run the laser disc player from the computer instead of with the barcode reader. *Lessonmaker* and *Report Generator* are available only for the Macintosh. *MediaMAX* is available for both the Macintosh and PC.

PETO—

barcode. (Regular transparent tape over a barcode can help with wear and tear and makes sliding the reader easier.)

- **The beep tells you that the barcode has been read** and the laser disc player will search for the frame number associated with that barcode. If it's a still picture, it will show the picture in freeze-frame mode. If it's a movie, it will begin playing the movie and will stop at the last frame of the movie. Some commercially made barcodes for movies take you only to the first frame of the movie and you must use your barcode reader to scan the barcode command PLAY (or push PLAY on the machine). Most laser disc players have command sheets with them that can be kept near the laser disc player for ease of use. (This is also handy for changing the AUDIO in a hurry if you have forgotten to do so.)
- **To use the barcode reader as a remote (without plugging it into the machine), aim the flat part of the reader at the player after you hear the beep and press the SEND button.** This involves two steps for each bar-code but can be handy if you want to stand farther away from the player or move around the room.
- **To REPEAT the movie you have just shown (as long as you didn't have to additionally push PLAY to show it), press the red button on the barcode reader.**
- **Press the STOP OPEN/CLOSE button twice when you are done and take out the laser disc.** Press the same button again to retract the disc table and turn off the power. TC

Erica Peto is a Media Specialist at Daniel Elementary School in the Kent (Washington) School District.

WHO SELLS BARCODE READERS?

Lessonmaker
Optical Data
30 Technology Drive
Warren, NJ 07059
(800) 524-2481
List Price: $75
Available only for Macintosh.

Report Generator
Laser Learning Technologies
120 Lakeside Avenue, Suite 240
Seattle, WA 98122-6552
(800) 722-3505
e-mail: llt@seanet.com
List Price: $69.95
CLV/CAV version: $89.95
5-computer lab pack: $139.95
10-computer lab pack: $199.95
Available only for Macintosh.

MediaMAX
Videodiscovery
3333 Elston Avenue
Chicago, IL 60618-5898
(800) 621-8086
List Price: $199
Available for Macintosh or PC.

Notes

Notes

Chapter 7

Collaboration

How are real-life school library media specialists collaborating with teachers to develop projects that teach both content and information literacy and research skills? What kinds of innovative assignments are they creating? While many of the articles in this volume describe hands-on projects, often dealing with discrete skills, this chapter offers assignments that combine skills and involve critical choices and decisions.

In the fifth grade library skills curriculum I developed some years ago, the final class meeting was a test. Students received a page of questions. Naming the resource they thought would contain the answer was as important as locating and recording the answer. In a real-life problem-solving situation or research assignment, youngsters are faced with a confusing array of potential tools. While they may have mastered individual resources in preparatory assignments, they now need to demonstrate the full extent of their knowledge and know which tool to use when. In this Internet age, I need to remind even adults that sometimes what they need and want is not a Web site, but the local telephone directory! These are the kinds of decisions researchers make in the real world; they are the kinds of decisions that should be reflected in the best hands-on projects making use of information skills.

As in other chapters in this volume, while most of the selected articles deal with middle or high schools, some elementary school projects are described as well. They offer ideas that can be adapted for older students, or they are applicable as is for classes with minimal research background or special developmental needs.

Perhaps the most challenging and exciting idea lies in "The Senior Exit Project," about a school in which graduating seniors *must* choose a topic, thoroughly research it, and make a presentation before a panel of evaluators. Once, only those of us who chose to pursue honors with our university theses found ourselves under that kind of pressure!

The true test of information literacy skills is not a single successful research assignment, however massive and complex. It lies in the application of learned skills in other areas of life, in the future. Our students will practice these skills years after we watch them process down the aisle at graduation, perhaps in ways we cannot imagine.

But the collaborative projects we put together with subject area teachers, carefully designed, come as close as anything can to the real-life experiences we are preparing our students to encounter and surmount.

URL UPDATES

Technology Adds Immediacy, Excitement, and Controversy to Research Projects:
> Major Views projects
> www.fcps.k12.va.us/mtvernonhs/index.html

A Research Project Filled with Real World Technology:
> www.gazetteonline.com/special/neighbor/harrison/index.htm

Teacher-Librarian Collaboration in Practice... Global Warming:
> http://nueva.pvt.k12.ca.us/~debbie/library/cur/globalwarm.html

> The Building Blocks of Reasearch
> ww.neuva.pvt.k12.ca.us/flibrary.html

> http://nueva.pvt.k12.ca.us/~debbie/library/cur/science/globalviews.html

http://nuevapvt.k12.ca.us/~debbie/library/cur/globconf.html

MULTIMEDIA

TECHNOLOGY ADDS IMMEDIACY, EXCITEMENT, AND CONTROVERSY TO RESEARCH PROJECTS

by Terry McConnell, Bernie Glaze, Harry Sprouse, Betty Lindholm, Rob Sanders, Kelley Durham, Jan Mosher, and Toni Mason

How many educators does it take to initiate a new project to teach students to use technology to do library research? In this case it took eight of us—a reading teacher, a social studies teacher, an English teacher, a business teacher, two librarians, an assistant principal, and a technology specialist.

> Our high school has block scheduling so most class periods are 100 minutes long, which gives the students time to finish research and begin typing out a rough draft in one class period.

What makes our project special—besides the fact that so many of us collaborated—is that the project, called Major Views, goes beyond teaching research skills. It also teaches students to develop points of view about their subjects, and to use technology to communicate their views to classmates through cable TV and to the world on a home page of the Internet. Major Views creates discussion and debate on issues and a level of excitement in the classroom that stimulates more student research projects.

First, Students Define Their Theses

This process begins in the classroom where the teacher encourages the students to think about topics of interest. One technique for this is student journaling. The teachers ask "What interests you most about our current subject?" and the students begin writing. That journal entry is the beginning of an "I Search" about a topic each student will begin researching in the library.

To help them stay on track, each student relies on a graphic organizer. Before the search for facts begins, the student writes his or her thesis statement on the graphic organizer. An example of an effective thesis statement would be "the arms embargo of Bosnia should be dropped."

Orientation and Research Come Next

After students have written their theses, they come to the library in groups of four to six for library orientation. The groups are placed at various stations around the library, with one educator or parent volunteer assigned to show each group how to operate the computer card catalog, CD-ROM stations, and the Internet/Dialog station. Students learn how to print out only the information they need; the adults also help each student determine what facts would be relevant to his or her thesis. For example, if a student's thesis is that the U.S. should intervene militarily in Bosnia, the number of Bosnian Muslims killed might be a relevant fact. This small group approach to library orientation ensures that each student will be able to find the information needed.

Next Stop: Library Word Processing Center

Once a student has found her facts, she walks over to the word processing center in the library to begin hammering out her rough draft. Our high school has block scheduling so most class periods are 100 minutes long, which gives the students time to finish research and begin typing out a rough draft in one class period. Armed with his graphic organizer, the student has an excellent outline on which to base his paper. The printouts from information on CD-ROMs come in handy when students need specific information and direct quotes. We encourage the students to use markers to highlight the most important information they printed out. Students who need more time can either finish typing after school or take the disk home if a compatible machine is available.

Scripts Are Prepared for In-School Cable TV

After students rewrite and polish their rough drafts, they choose which topics should be transformed into video scripts. At this point, students become highly motivated. Now they are not just writing for themselves and the teacher. They have a more important purpose—to communicate their projects over our in-school cable TV system. In deciding which student-researched topic will be viewed via cable, they take into account which topics have good visual footage available from *CNN Newsroom*. CNN allows teachers to edit in *CNN Newsroom* footage in a student-produced video shown within a school.

Once the topic has been selected, students formulate survey questions to find out their fellow students' opinions. For example, Major Views students found that 51 percent of their classmates favored the U.S. intervention in Haiti in September, 1994. Results of these types of surveys, along with student interviews, and research information, are incorporated into a TV script. The script is shorter than the paper and uses simple and direct language.

> Information is now important and newsworthy because our students are using it to make a point about a topic they care about.

Some students write the script while other teams or individuals are learning how to operate the camera, do video editing or find relevant visual material to edit into the show. The camera team should include two students who hold cue cards on 8-1/2" by 11" sheets of paper held vertically right above the camera lens. This is the poor man's teleprompter.

This is the first video production experience for most youngsters. Our students have found the Panasonic cameras and editor VCRs, like the AG-1970, are easy to use. This equipment uses the S-VHS format which guards against loss of quality when tapes are edited and duplicated. We shoot the anchorperson's comments first and then edit in student interviews. Next we video insert (add new picture while keeping old sound) the visual footage from *CNN Newsroom*.

Once the video is completed, the student body sees it on the in-school cable system. This is the heart of Major Views. Information is now important and newsworthy because our students are using it to make a point about a topic they care about. For example, one student wasn't interested in Haiti until he found out in the Major Views video that his best friend thought "our troops should get the heck out of there." This airing of views encourages more library research projects.

Project Summaries Are Published on the Internet

Some students write summaries of their Major Views projects, including their survey results. These summaries are conveyed to the world on our school's home page (http://pen.k12.va.us/Anthology/Div/Fairfax/Schools/MtVernon-HS/mtvernon.html). For an up-to-date description of current Major Views projects, select "Technology and Internet" on our home page. (For information on how to create a home page, go through the Internet on *Netscape* to Yahoo (http://www.yahoo.com), click on the word "Search," type in "hypertext markup language," then click on the "Search" button. Contact us on the Internet at jmcconn@aol.com for more information.)

'Major Views' Gives Everyone a Chance to Shine

Major Views creates student excitement. In each phase of the process, a different student has a chance to excel. Angie writes a lucid script. Randy's camera work is well composed. Tonya shows a flair for video editing. The eight educators share in their excitement. **TC**

Terry McConnell, Bernie Glaze, Harry Sprouse, Betty Lindholm, Rob Sanders, Kelley Durham, Jan Mosher, and Toni Mason are educators at Mt. Vernon High School, Alexandria, Virginia.

Students Give High Marks to These High-Tech Resources

Students truly enjoy using high-tech information sources to get the information they need. An event in Bosnia that happened two months ago can easily be found using a reference tool like *Proquest Full Text USA Today* on CD-ROM ((800) 521-0600). What makes this so great is that the computer can access and print out the needed article in a minute and the language of *USA Today* is simple enough for most high school students to follow. What about an event that happened yesterday regarding illegal aliens in Sacramento, California? Go online to Dialog ((800) 334-2564) and pull up the local newspaper, the *Sacramento Bee*, to get it!

Netscape software, has made it easy to browse the Internet. For interviews with Holocaust survivors, hop on the Net at Yahoo (http://www.yahoo.com) and go to the Cybrary at the Holocaust Museum in Washington, D.C. The online DRA/Inlex ((800) 444-6539) computer card catalog tells what books on the Vietnam War are available in our library and other local libraries.

Is a magazine needed to get a specific point of view on welfare reform? Full-text *Proquest* for magazines on CD-ROM ((800) 521-0600) with its offering of 100 magazines will render a current article with either a liberal or conservative slant. Students who did their research on U.S. intervention in Haiti found SIRS *Researcher* on CD-ROM ((800) 232-SIRS) provided great background information from various magazines and newspapers throughout the world. These high-tech sources make the Major Views project exciting to students because the information needed can be obtained quickly and easily.

For more information about using *CNN Newsroom* footage, call (800) 344-6219.

Teachers and Librarians; Ideas To Bring the Relationship To Life

Change is something we can do to our own roles; we don't have to wait for it to happen. This author has some ideas for making the librarian's role in the curriculum more visible.

Alan Haskvitz

IDEALLY THERE SHOULD BE NO closer professional relationships than those of elementary school librarians and teachers. Together these two occupations serve almost the same clientele and enjoy the same literacy and learning objectives. And yet, despite this symbiotic relationship, there are few ongoing programs that foster and enhance this relationship. In fact, in the ten school districts where I have worked, I can't remember an inservice program that was designed to bring teachers and librarians together for planning and sharing needs and goals.

In many schools, librarians are seldom consulted or informed about curriculum changes that could impact their resources. This hinders our efficiency in ordering books and other materials to support change.

Clearly there is a need for cooperation. To this end I have designed some short projects to encourage collaboration. These projects are also designed to help librarians and teachers meet the changes in standardized tests. It is common knowledge that new assessment tools will require students to display critical-thinking and problem-solving skills. Because the results of these tests sometimes reflect on the stature of the school and even community property values, there is an even greater need for librarians and teachers to work together.

The key point is for the librarian and the teacher to get together over this article and explore ways these projects can be implemented, expanded or altered. Perhaps the projects could become the starting place for developing a relationship or continuing an existing collaboration.

1. All encyclopedias are not the same

The first project is designed for elementary school age children and involves the students' ability to use encyclopedias—the basic reference work for this age group. It is also designed to help the student develop critical thinking skills and to promote writing.

First, the teacher gives this assignment: From your history or social studies book, select one person, one event and one place. Write these down on three pieces of paper.

The student is given these instructions: Using the index of three different encyclopedias, write down the volume number and page number of all the citations that refer to each of the three subjects (person, event, and place). Also write the copyright date of the encyclopedia. Next, read the material on each subject and take notes on it. (For example, the student would have information on the Atlantic Ocean from three different encyclopedias.) Then, write one paragraph explaining which encyclopedia did the best job of explaining the subject to you. List any examples of conflicting facts; that is, is the size of the ocean the same in each encyclopedia?

Elementary school students often believe that all encyclopedias and reference books are the same. This assignment demonstrates that they are not. It also gives the librarian some insights into which encyclopedias best serve the children. Finally, the critical thinking involved matches that of the newly developed standardized tests.

2. Using travel books for fictional settings

The second lesson involves helping English teachers with creative writing. This project is designed for grade 3 and up. Most teachers find that students' creative writing has its setting in their home or school. This lesson can help the teacher integrate the English, geography and social studies curriculum, and give students a broader choice of settings. The lesson can also familiarize students with the travel and foreign country sections of the library.

The lesson starts when the teacher cuts up an old world map and writes a student's name behind each section. Then the teacher hands the sections out to the students who must assemble the map after they have written down the names of the countries on their part of the map. (If an old map is not available, the teacher simply writes longitude and latitude numbers on a paper and the student must locate the country from this data.)

Once the countries are identified, the student reads a book about his assigned country. The setting of the next creative writing assignment must feature the place names and geographical features of the country. The story could even include multicultural events such as holidays and rites of passage. Thus, the student is using more sections of the library and becoming more knowledgeable about other cultures; the teacher is getting more interesting work.

3. A Résumé that teaches the reference section

The third assignment helps the students learn about the reference section as well as teaches them how to write a résumé.

The teacher gives students this assignment: You are going to write a résumé for a presidential candidate. In order to do this you are going to use several books in the library. First, find books in the library that give meanings of first names. Find a name you like, write its meaning, and give your candidate this name and your last name.

To give the candidate a city and state of residence, the teacher gives students a page number from the national atlas. Each student will select a city and state from this page. From postal code books, the student will find the zip code for the candidate's city. Similarly, the student will find area codes for the candidate's city from the telephone directory.

The students use the guides to universities and colleges to select three institutions for their candidates' résumés. The students must also list a major and minor and both undergraduate and graduate degrees. The pupils are going to spend a great deal of time asking questions during this segment of the assignment, but what wonderful questions they are going to be as they discover that there are professions other than medicine and law.

Next, the students list three jobs that their candidates have held. They can use the guide to occupations for this assignment.

When the occupations are done, the student goes to the business section of the library and there, using such reference materials as the *Fortune 500*, selects four companies the candidate has worked for. The student must write the name of the company, its location, and the phone number of its president.

For the final part of the résumé, the student selects four articles in the *Readers' Guide to Periodical Literature* that the candidate, as a leader, might have written. Each of the three articles must have been written in different years and they must be on different topics related to current happenings in the country such as economics, government and unemployment.

After this information is listed under publications, the next assignment is to find personal references. This is done by using the *Current Biography* books. The entries include not only the stories of important individuals but their addresses as well. The students should be reminded to select individuals who would have interests in common with the candidate, not popular entertainment figures.

With the listing of references, the résumé assignment is complete.

During the course of this assignment, students have worked in several sections of the library they may not have used before. They are also learning how to write a résumé. In addition, they are starting to see the qualities that are expected of leaders. This can tie in with both English and social studies.

The résumé assignment can be changed to reflect the reference section and materials available in the school library. Hobbies, foreign countries visited, material from almanacs and other such tidbits can be added to force the students to learn more about the library, leadership, and how to write a résumé.

> *"The key point is for the librarian and the teacher to get together over this article and explore ways these projects can be implemented, expanded or altered. Perhaps the projects could become the starting place for developing a relationship or continuing an existing collaboration."*

Each of these projects can be a great sharing experience for teachers and librarians. They were designed to make the bond between these two occupations stronger while helping students develop new patterns of work and learning.

At the end of these three assignments the student is going to have a working knowledge of much of the library as well as a better, more critical understanding of reference books.

Obviously, these ideas require extra work. To partially offset this you may be able to tap into a new program that is becoming mandatory in some school districts: community service. This program gives students class credit for work with community groups and organizations. A manpower-short librarian would be calling the local high schools right now asking to be considered for the program or asking how one could be started.

Sharing year-round

A final element of importance to the relationship between librarian and teacher is communication throughout the year about upcoming research projects. This would enable the librarian to place appropriate books on display or perhaps on reserve. The librarian and teachers might also place exemplary research work on display in the library. What better place to view finished work that shows what students can do and the importance of the library to the development of reading and writing skills.

Alan Haskvitz has worked 22 years as a librarian and teacher. He has won over 25 local, regional and national awards for his programs and has been frequently featured on radio and television. Most recently he was given the Hero in Education Award by Reader's Digest. *Haskvitz has published over 30 articles and he speaks nationwide on education. Canadian educated, he has worked in both Newfoundland and Ontario.*

Notes

TECHNOLOGY: IT'S ELEMENTARY FOR YOUNG LEARNERS AND THEIR TEACHERS TOO

A Research Project Filled With Real World Technology

By Sharron L. McElmeel

When our elementary school was about to create a World Wide Web site, we considered whether to define our efforts as a technology initiative or as a research experience for our students. With the focus on technology, it is very tempting to define such projects as technology. However, in collaboration with the fourth- and fifth-grade students who worked on the project, it naturally evolved into a primary research project. The students compiled information from original sources and then shared it with the world via an Internet site. Classroom teachers, library media specialists, and resource specialists assisted students in researching information that met their objectives. In the process, they used a variety of technology and related skills.

Setting a Task and Staying with It

Defining a project goal gives the research a focus. With a goal, researchers can recognize when they have found enough information and whether it is appropriate. The students generated several lists of topics and categorized them into groups that provided an outline for the Web pages. They established a hierarchy of pages and formed research groups to work on specific topics. As some were working on the text, others were creating graphics and finding photographs that would complement the text.

Challenging Students to Think and Research

For many elementary students who have been involved in library skills lessons, the answer to every quest for information is in a book. The way to locate any book is to look in the library media center's catalog. Never mind that the topic might be so obscure that few if any authors will devote an entire book to the subject. For example, one student tried to locate the name of the newly elected mayor of Cedar Rapids, Iowa. The mayor had been elected in November and took office in early January; the date of the "research" was January 15. The library media center did not have back issues of local newspapers. Even if it had, few newspapers are indexed extensively enough for an effective search. The student tried to use the keywords "Mayor" and "Cedar Rapids" on the computer catalog, an inappropriate resource for the topic. In a research conference, the student was asked to think about other places to find the answer. He thought that the newspaper would have the mayor's name, or since the mayor had taken office, perhaps he could call the mayor's office and ask the secretary for the name and correct spelling. He did, and he got his answer. That is primary research. Technically, the strategy for locating that piece of information did not require library skills. Critical thinking and research skills were important.

Another group of fourth/fifth-grade students was beginning to gather information for the planned Web site on literacy. Their topic was "newly literate people," and they wanted to interview a few people who were newly literate and share some of their thoughts on the Web site. So the first question was "Where will we find people who have just learned to read and write?" They looked under "literate" on the computer catalog even though they didn't know what they were looking for. They had been given keyword instruction often enough that they used the topic, rather than the question, as their guide. It did not occur to the students that even if they found a book on literacy, it would not contain the information they needed: names, addresses, or telephone numbers of local people who were newly literate and willing to be interviewed.

The library media specialist helped the students back up and rethink the process. Where would an adult acquire the skills to read and write? With a little thinking time, the students decided to find local programs that might have taught some adults to read, and they called the public library. The response lead the researchers to a local community college where they made contact, by telephone, with a program director who put them in contact with two individuals who were pleased to tell their story. Once the researchers had arranged an interview time, they prepared questions for the interview. The material they needed came from the interviews, and the students added information about the program itself from a brochure. It was the primary research, the interview with the newly literate adults, that was one of the keys to a successful and meaningful research experience.

The Research

The students researched the information to be put on the Web site, they wrote the copy and designed the pages, and then worked with a web designer to compose and construct the pages. Their research took them to public libraries, to a bookstore established in 1893, through old newspapers on microfiche, into historical books and documents, and on interviews with real people. They read, conducted telephone interviews, wrote letters, and gathered information. Their findings were shared with the world on their Web sites. They learned about primary and secondary sources and about sifting information to find what is needed. These students used technology in the real world. They learned to scan pictures, create graphics, save the pictures and graphics in a specified format, write with word processors, spell check their narratives, and e-mail messages. The students and the educators found that technology means much more than using the Internet and that research skills transcend the basic library skills. The final products that were generated from the students' research and their use of technology can be seen on the World Wide Web at http://www.cedar-rapids.k12.ia.us/Harrison/harrison.html and at http://www.aea10.k12.ia.us/literacy.

The following is a summary of selected pages the students researched with a notation about the technology they used during their research.

For many elementary students who have been involved in library skills lessons, the answer to every quest for information is in a book. The way to locate any book is to look in the library media center's catalog. Never mind that the topic might be so obscure that few if any authors will devote an entire book to the subject.

Research Topic:
History of Harrison School
Search tasks:
- Locate archival newspaper articles about the school and its origin.
- Interview former students of Harrison.
- Interview former staff members to obtain pictures of the school and other artifacts related to Harrison School.

Technology skills used:
- Reading microfiche of archival newspaper articles.
- Telephoning to contact potential interviewees and arrange for interviews.
- Audio recording to tape interviews for verifying written notes.
- Scanning to digitalize photographs.
- Word processing to compose permission form for quoting from interviews and using photographs on-line.

Research Topic: Iowa's Schools of the Past as Compared to Today's Schools
Search tasks:
- Locate and research information about an old or "oldest" school in Iowa.
- Locate and interview former students of one-room school houses.
- Learn about the educational testing services that are based in Iowa.

Technology skills used:
- Using electronic periodical index to locate articles about one-room schools and older schools in the area.
- Telephoning to arrange for interviews and to contact the caretaker of the oldest school in the county.
- Using camera to photograph the site of the school and the former students.
- Scanning photographs.
- E-mailing to communicate with the spokesperson for the American College of Testing organization.

Research Topic:
Books (and connections to Iowa)
Search tasks:
- Locate mayors in major cities and ascertain their favorite childhood books.
- Locate and investigate a relatively new public library in our state.
- Locate and investigate an early bookstore in Iowa.
- Locate books (particularly children's books) that are set in Iowa.
- Identify children's novels or nonfiction titles to be recommended as read-aloud titles.
- Identify children's picture books for sharing.

Technology skills used:
- General computer catalog skills to identify books that fit the structure of the book recommendation pages.
- Boolean searches in the computer catalog to locate and identify books with an Iowa setting.
- Modem connection to search the local public library's online catalog to identify specific titles.
- Word processing to write a letter to the mayor requesting the title of her favorite childhood book and to compose a survey.
- Reading microfiche indexes to

In addition to acquainting students with the resources in their local media center, library media specialists should discuss other resources such as telephone access, area libraries, people, and the Internet.

locate articles about historical bookstores.
• Using local newspaper electronic indexes to locate articles about construction of new libraries.
• Telephone skills to contact a donor to a new public library and arrange for a presentation and interview and to contact the current owner of a book store.
• Speaker phone skills to conduct a group interview with a bookstore owner.
• Calculator skills to tabulate the results and figure percentages of the responses to the survey taken about school days in Iowa.

Research Topic: Authors/Books/ Children and Links in Iowa
Search tasks:
• Identifying and learning about nationally known authors with an Iowa link.
• Identifying and annotating books that describe pieces of Iowa's literary past.
• Profiling themselves as Web makers.
• Identifying and selecting Internet sites that provide information about Iowa.

Technology skills used:
• General computer catalog skills to identify books that fit the structure of the book recommendation pages.
• Internet search techniques to identify Web sites about Iowa.
• Using electronic post office or telephone book sites to locate authors identified through books and newspaper articles.
• Word processing to request permission to interview authors and to follow-up the interview with a letter and to compile their own collective profile and to compose a list of Internet sites.
• Audio cassette recording to tape interviews to verify notes. **TC**

Sharron L. McElmeel often writes about literature- and technology-related issues. Her recently released Research Strategies for Moving Beyond Reporting *(Linworth, 1996) shares strategies for developing research activities that provide real world applications. McElmeel is a library media specialist in the Cedar Rapids (Iowa) Community Schools.*

Editor's Note: The Web site described in this article is linked to Linworth Publishing's site at http://linworth. com. There you will find other links to sites that can serve as resources to readers of TECHNOLOGY CONNECTION.

Notes

Curriculum Integration In Practice

The theory of integration is put into practice by these writers.

A SECOND GRADE UNIT ON AFRICA

Renee Troselius

In our K-grade 5 school each grade level is assigned a continent to study for the year. Each grade determines what topics will be studied within the context of a continent study. It becomes my job to integrate library resources with the different continent studies and different grade level activities.

Second-grade students study Africa. One of their activities is to research famous black Americans, locating birth and death dates and several facts about the accomplishments of these men and women. This activity lends itself to teaching encyclopedia use, the advantages of print and nonprint encyclopedias, and citing references.

The lesson begins in the computer lab adjacent to the media center with copies of both a print encyclopedia and a CD-ROM encyclopedia. The children and I discuss the advantages and disadvantages of both formats. The students immediately cite the ease of searching a CD-ROM, as well as the "fun" of using this format. Even in second grade they recognize that the disc is likely to have sound and video, while the print version will have only text and pictures. I always make it a point to tell them that a print encyclopedia set will allow more students to use it at one time because most have at least 20 volumes as opposed to one disc on one computer.

The next instruction involves the process of accessing the information needed. Using an electronic encyclopedia, I teach the children to search the title list, which names all of the articles on the disc and serves as a searching tool. Since students were researching people, the title list was the easiest access point. I allowed them to try putting in a person's name in any order they chose. When they couldn't find any information, I'd explain that the last name must be entered first. In this way students can begin to see the importance of trying different search terms when the first choice doesn't yield answers.

Some students may need help reading the encyclopedia entry, but they should be able to pick out one or two facts that made a person famous. In this particular activity, students were also asked to find some information about the African heritage of the person they were researching. The electronic encyclopedia we used did not provide this information. This illustrated a good lesson in learning that it may be necessary to check more than one source. It also demonstrated that all encyclopedias are not identical nor do they have all the information a student might need to know.

Once students have found their facts, it becomes important to explain to them the importance of citing the reference. It's never too early to begin that lesson!

Our students have good computer skills and were able to complete the assignment in one 40-minute period. Since students finish the assignment at different times, I was prepared with the names of other famous Black Americans they could research.

Renee Troselius is a Media Specialist at Minnehaha Academy in Minneapolis, Minnesota. She is a reviewer for The Book Report *and* Technology Connection.

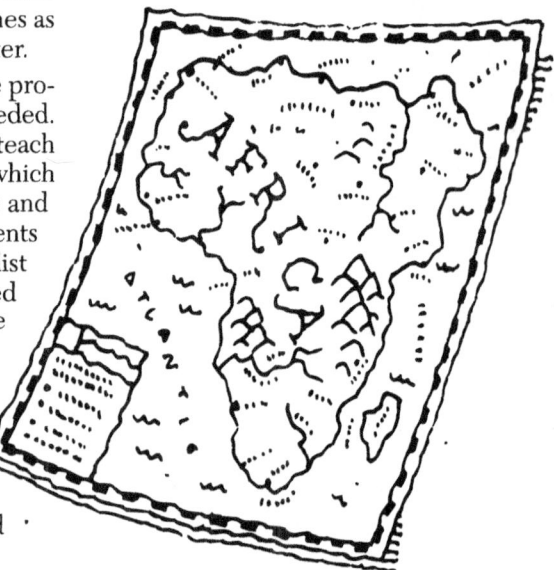

WORLD TRAVELERS IN A SCHOOL LIBRARY

Betty Dawn Hamilton

"Hey, I'm going to have to travel 11,560 miles one way! How long will that take?" Our sixth-grade reading students are becoming world travelers. Even though they physically remain in the library, in their imaginations they travel to the "remote corners of the earth."

In their classroom assignments, the students read books about other countries. Some read fiction set in a different country. Some read travel books, and others read history books about other places. The requirement was that each student had to select a location outside the United States, read a book about it, and then plan a trip there.

To incorporate higher-order thinking skills, the teacher and I devised a list of related information that they would have to locate, either in their books or in reference sources. For example, students had to learn something about the climate and things to do (so they would know what kind of clothes to pack); about food, culture, and customs (so they would be

considerate travelers); about the economy, currency, and manufacturing specialties (to know how much money to take for travel and for souvenirs).

The reading teacher gave instructions and handouts, and I gave instructions on how and where to find the information in the library. Like many good lessons, the idea grew. The teacher and I decided that students would need passports if they were to travel outside the United States.

To provide the experience of applying for a passport, we acquired a passport application from the local district clerk's office and had copies made for each student. The school counselor provided photocopied pictures (black and white) from student files so they could be attached to the passport form. I showed and explained my real passport to the students. (Another learning experience would be to find out if visas were required for a student's country.)

After the students read their books, they plotted their routes and wrote itineraries. Probably one of the most beneficial parts of the lesson was finding out how to get to their destinations from the land-locked, small town of Brownfield, Texas (no international airport and no passenger trains here).

One student who wanted to fly on the Concorde discovered that it can't land at all airports. He was forced to do even more research. Another student became so interested in the project that she brought an article on travel insurance to share with the class.

By studying maps and globes and *World Almanac* mileage charts, students decided whether they would have to embark from the East or West Coasts. Frequently, students found that they could not fly directly into a chosen destination, so they had to locate the nearest major international airport and then estimate the ground miles they would travel by using map legends.

Of the many units that require library use, this one seems to have been particularly productive. Even though the sixth graders did not write a formal research paper, they certainly experienced true "research" — locating, evaluating, and using information to fulfill a need.

Betty Dawn Hamilton is the Media Specialist at Brownfield Middle School in Brownfield, Texas.

Notes

Notes

TECHNOLOGY AND THE CURRICULUM: SOCIAL STUDIES

THE EVOLUTION OF A UNIT:
From Dusty Books to Paperless Projects

By Mary Alice Anderson

It's 4:30 p.m. on a sunny spring day, and the media center is filled with seventh graders finishing their multimedia geography projects. The Western European booklets, which students were making when I was hired in 1985, have evolved into paperless slide show projects and information presented using a variety of word processing, graphing, and graphics tools.

Back then, I was asked to introduce technology into a traditional media program. We introduced students and teachers to *Print Shop* (Broderbund), and suddenly a bit of technology was introduced to the booklet in a painless way. 1986 brought a lab and geography databases. 1987 meant an online catalog, and 1988 added a CD-ROM encyclopedia. Now there was a recognized need to teach students information skills. At the same time we began to teach teachers how to use technologies applicable to their projects.

Major progress occurred during a staff development day in the early '90s. A special education teacher with an interest in technology helped a geography teacher reorganize the booklet. She helped define specific student tasks, establish task management steps and write step-by-step directions, and she offered suggestions for integrating technology into the unit. For example, *MacGlobe* was introduced as a tool for students to gather information about a Western European country.

Technology options for the booklet now include making a time line of the country's history and drawing a flag using *ClarisWorks*. Students display comparative data with *ClarisWorks*' spreadsheets and graphs. Word processing interpretations accompany time lines and graphs. Students gather information from the Internet as well as from books and CD-ROMS, such as *The World Book Multimedia Encyclopedia* on our school's network.

> "Technology is an interesting tool both for teaching and for learning. It dresses up teacher instruction and is a hands-on vehicle for students to do their work."

Through the years the unit has evolved to include more diverse technology and increased student expectations. The factors that contribute to the unit's success include: clear expectations, directions, and

- deadlines for each part of the project,
- teachers' use of task management checklists,
- a variety of print and electronic resources that require different levels of expertise, and
- ample time to work in the media center.

Students are less overwhelmed because they have time to work, reflect, and improve as they go along. An overview of the 1995 version of this unit can be found in *Teaching Information Literacy with Electronic Resources: Grades 6-12*, published by Linworth in 1996.

Another major leap forward came with the decision not to purchase textbooks for each student. Instead we buy classroom sets of textbooks, and teachers are strongly encouraged to do more resource-based teaching. For the geography teachers, this meant shifting their teaching styles as they learned to use the videodisc players, disks, and computers we purchased with textbook money. The technology has helped them move beyond the textbook and become more comfortable with all forms of technology.

The Internet and multimedia presentation tools have brought about the most rapid change in how students access and communicate information. Two teachers have students complete paperless projects using the Internet and *ClarisWorks* or *Hyperstudio* (Wagner).

The booklet now fits on a disk in one teacher's classroom. Students gather information from the Internet and present it with a *ClarisWorks* slide show. In the past two years, student teachers have helped design and implement the project. To get the students off to a solid searching start, we updated our Western Europe curriculum Web site (http://wms.luminet.net/curricsites/socstudies.html) and provided *Alta Vista* searching help sheets. We provided copies of help sheets for making slide shows and working with graphics. The steps

of the assignment are:
- Choose a Western European country to study;
- Develop three questions related to the country;
- Describe the plan for data collection and organization (time lines, outlines, categories);
- Get approval from the teacher;
- Begin data gathering by focusing on specific topics relating to the question and explain why you chose the topics;
- Develop a research proposal that is the foundation for the Internet project and get approval;
- Gather data and visuals, and save them to disk; and
- Present the information in a multimedia slide show.

Slide show grading criteria include the presence of title, map, flag, research questions and answers, and bibliography. Students are also graded on their work ethic. Students evaluated the project and their work, and overall, they loved it. Most of the work was completed in a computer lab, and several students wished they had more class time in the media center and its lab because "the computers are faster and there are also books as well as the Internet."

Student comments also showed perceptions about their own abilities. Many regretted not making backup disks, writing down their sources, or taking advantage of the extended media center hours. They also realized they were learning from their mistakes and think this is a good way to learn. As for improvement, they would like more developmental instruction, especially in working with different graphic formats and "packets with answers to help kids out." Negative comments pertained to the need to "fight for a computer" in the media center after school and slow computers in the other lab. (The media center has 40 Macintosh LC580s and a variety of Power Mac models.)

Dedicated teachers provide these forward-thinking learning opportunities for more than 350 seventh-grade students each year, and each makes this happen in his own unique way. Greg, the teacher who first made changes in the booklet, still travels with his box of colored pencils, pens, rulers, atlases and almanacs. Technology is integrated slowly, but carefully and soundly.

Bob is a former football coach and physical education teacher who jumped into the process a few years after the other two teachers had begun using technology. With his open mind and positive attitude, he has learned quickly and adapted superbly to teaching something quite different from what he taught for more than 20 years. He takes almost every appropriate staff development class and is always ready for new ideas.

Harold is a well-traveled person who brings academic and technological skills to the classroom. He carefully researches Web sites and provides students with wonderful lists for Internet searching. He also develops handouts to help the students use technology. This past year his students completed five projects involving technology. Last spring we both observed how well behaved the students were as they worked in the media center on the projects. We agreed they would not have been so involved on a nice spring day a few years ago.

Harold's approach will move us forward into the next step. We recently discussed the need to move the students beyond finding facts and pictures on the Internet. The result was an assignment based on "thinking questions" related to Hong Kong. For example, instead of gathering facts and pictures of flags students researched the questions:
- How has Hong Kong changed during the time it has been under British control?
- What might the future hold for Hong Kong?

We noticed students were on-task and involved in their work. The thinking was something new for them, and they appeared intent on finding the answers. The finished project is a word-processed document, and students are required to turn in all phases of the project including printed notes, which include sources, handwritten notes, and draft.

Change is often hard to see when we are part of making it happen, but curriculum delivery, information access, and information presentations are radically different now than they were in 1985. Since the unit's evolution, student motivation is definitely improved, and teachers appear enthusiastic and rejuvenated. What was once revolutionary is now ordinary and expected. The media center has become a popular place for active, constructive learning. Our labs are booked solid, usually weeks in advance. As Harold noted, "Technology is an interesting tool both for teaching and for learning. It dresses up teacher instruction and is a hands-on vehicle for students to do their work." **TC**

Mary Alice Anderson is a Media Specialist at Winona (Minnesota) Middle School. She is an Editorial Consultant to TECHNOLOGY CONNECTION *and writes the technology column for* THE BOOK REPORT.

By Debbie Abilock and Molly Lusignan

TEACHER–LIBRARIAN COLLABORATION IN PRACTICE...

One hot summer evening in August 1997, in the midst of developing an energy curriculum for sixth graders, Molly heard President Clinton make a speech on setting national priorities about global warming, as a prelude to a conference to be held in December 1997. Nearly 170 countries of the world would meet in Japan to negotiate a binding agreement aimed at slowing the build-up of carbon dioxide in order to reduce global warming and the associated changes that it might produce. It was obvious to her that global warming would be a hot topic that fall, generating substantial debate because of economic interests, scientific differences and political implications. She called Debbie, who had been nagging her for some time about possible collaboration between science and library research classes, and proposed that this would be a natural project. They spent August coming up to speed on what was basically new to them both,[1] developing a web page www.nueva.pvt.k12.ca.us/~debbie/library/curriculum/globalwarm.html as an organizer for their thinking.

This wasn't the first phone call Debbie had ever gotten from Molly. For at least 20 years they have taught at Nueva, as the science specialist and librarian. During that time they have collaborated on everything from teaching notetaking from an encyclopedia to working with a team of teachers to design "Human Ascent, From Our Ancestors to Our Heirs," a cross-level, interdisciplinary curriculum on the creative "leaps" of humankind. Many conversations about science, library research, educational philosophy, and individual learners marked their interactions.

For the most part the science program at Nueva is "hands-on/minds-on/feet-in-the-mud," which means that it consists of a combination of experiments, simulations, and activities from which students construct an understanding of science concepts. It is also important to help students appreciate the relevance of science to their lives and, more broadly, to society. As students get older, more time is spent extending and generalizing the knowledge gained from the experiential learning. The choice of specific content topics, such as acid rain or plate tectonics, may vary from year to year, but science process skills are a constant. Since curriculum is designed yearly in a similar way throughout the school, the librarian always expects to integrate the information literacy skills[2] into the content as it develops. "The Building Blocks of Research" at www.nueva.pvt.k12.ca.us/~debbie/library/research/il/infolit1.html illustrates the information literacy skills framework developed for use at Nueva.

But more important than the right time and the right team is an agreement about the nature of the goals for students — the right "toolbox" to be teaching. In Science and Library Research, we realized that the disciplines had an analogous set of process skills — particularly between individual scientific investigations during science projects and information problem-solving during library research. This particular curriculum became an opportunity to flesh out the similarities and differences — a place for us to learn.

In problem-based learning, the student is confronted with an ill-structured problem that mirrors a real-world situation. We decided to develop "Global Warming" as a science-based simulation. With this topic we could integrate research, writing, speaking, science lab, and computer skills. The intense controversy among experts and their conflicting viewpoints about the nature and impact of global warming would allow students to experience the thinking within both our disciplines and to develop the skills necessary for problem solving. We planned that each student would develop a "character" who represented a particular viewpoint and would participate as that individual in the Nueva Conference on Climate Change (NCCC). We chose a November date to allow enough time for the students to understand the issues and finish their work in time to follow the actual events leading up to the Kyoto Conference. We also wanted students to have time enough to communicate their personal views to their elected representatives. Our plan was to develop basic background in energy and global warming during science periods (14 hours), while the library research and the development of the simulation (14 hours) would be team-taught.

ENGAGING

When Isidor Isaac Rabi, a nuclear physicist who won the Nobel Prize in 1944 for his work on atomic nuclei, was asked why he became a physicist rather than a doctor or a tailor like his father, Rabi explained that his mother unintentionally made him a scientist. He claimed that every other Jewish mother in Brooklyn would ask her child, "So, what did you learn in school today?" while his inquired, "Izzi, what good questions did you ask today?"

Students were asked to brainstorm "What do you know?" and "What do you want to know?" about global warming. Such queries engage student interest, activate and assess prior knowledge, and encourage students to share information. The Kyoto conference, which would take place in mid-December, was also discussed. During science periods, students accumulated basic knowledge through experiments, simulations, and some fundamental reading.

BROWSING AND BUILDING KNOWLEDGE

In problem-based learning, students must recognize that, just as in real-world problems, there are no simple right and wrong answers. However, that does not mean that the curriculum itself is "fuzzy." Well-designed curriculum demands that the teachers plan carefully to ensure appropriate and relevant learning goals. During late August and early September, we did hours of reading and online research to understand the issues better ourselves. From materials located, we created a Web page of references reflecting this controversy[3] www.nueva.pvt.k12.ca.us/~debbie/library/research/bib/globalviews.html. During science class students realized the ambiguity of scientific evidence as they tried to interpret graphs of real data on atmospheric carbon dioxide and global temperatures. To help them appreciate the array of opinions and predicted effects, we began to team-teach reading strategies lessons, using several *New York Times* news articles to prompt close reading, analysis, and discussion.

DEFINING AND FOCUSING

In early October, students browsed through the opinions expressed in our Web page resources. Looking for areas of personal interest, they were preparing for making their own choices. Organized by broad interest groups, these Web documents represented industry, environmental groups, a variety of geographical locations, and conflicting scientific opinions. From the students' choices, we created a cast of characters to represent various viewpoints at the Conference. The students gave themselves pseudonyms and began to develop their characters' interests and concerns about global warming. Knowing that they were "Director of Western Fuels Association," or "Executive Director of the National Resources Defense Council" sharpened the students' focus and investigations. This process of narrowing a topic, creating a focus question or hypothesis, and selecting a feasible chunk of a bigger problem is a common step in both science and library research projects.

DESIGNING AND PLANNING

During the design of a science project, coaching allowed students to visualize and plan the concrete steps for answering their hypothetical question. Students had to create a plan for conducting their scientific investigation, developing criteria for collecting data to test the hypothesis, devising a procedure to control

> *In problem-based learning it is important for students to recognize that, just as in real-world problems, there are no simple right and wrong answers.*

> *Narrowing a topic, creating a focus question or hypothesis, and selecting a feasible chunk of a bigger problem is a common step in both science and library research projects.*

variables, and developing a materials list and time line. Similarly, students had to identify likely sources of potential mentors, brainstorm synonyms as keywords, construct Boolean search strings, and create a to-do list and time line. In both cases, the students were eager to forge ahead with the experimentation or searching, while the teacher or librarian reined in the process to ensure clarity and rigor. Both processes involved some tinkering and preliminary experimentation, resulting in modified student project designs.

In a problem-based learning environment, students ideally set time lines and deadlines. There was a tight time line imposed by the Kyoto Conference date. When we assessed the students' initial understanding, and the ramifications of teaching such complex concepts, we created the research deadlines for students, provided them with library materials, and a Web page of links[4] — www.nueva.pvt.k12.ca.us/~debbie/library/research/bib/globalviews.html — rather than suggest that they surf the Internet for additional information.

We also grouped students into alliances based on common interests (e.g., health and environmental interests, corporate groups concerned with profitability, and representatives from low-elevation areas) so that they could help one another flesh out their positions. We had to monitor the social and emotional "temperatures" of these groups so they could remain productive. The more interested the students became in their roles for the conference, the less intervention and monitoring of the groups process was necessary.

GATHERING, ORGANIZING AND ANALYZING DATA

Students met weekly over a three-week period for two-hour blocks to examine, select, and highlight and to take notes from Web resources, current newspaper clippings and articles from the library's magazine database. In a science project, careful observation and accurate recording of the experimental results is followed by analysis and graphing of the data for each variable tested. In the information literacy model, a student selects and records data that may be useful, later analyzing and discarding less relevant information. In both processes there are often several rounds of data gathering as students develop additional questions, gain expertise, or anticipate opposition arguments or problems. During our Global Warming project, it was a challenge for students to understand the main ideas or arguments, locate the specific data they needed, recognize the relevance of information to their position, and evaluate the quality of their sources.

Teaming helped them teach with greater collective wisdom. As they coached individual students, Molly was able to ask Debbie for help with library research, while Debbie called on Molly's content understanding to help a student grasp a position. They also cheered each other through those dark moments when they truly believed they had bitten off more than they could chew.

DRAWING CONCLUSIONS, FORMING CONVICTIONS

In a science project, the conclusions and the discussion are written and defended orally before judges, parents, or peers. An original interpretation of evidence or, at the least, thoughtfully constructed conclusions should be part of any library information problem-solving. Teachers should not mistake a report (the restatement of information) for research (an analysis of information). Further, any culmination or "product" should add

> The more interested the students became in their roles for the conference, the less intervention and monitoring of the group process was necessary.

integrity to the process. Here, the product was a simulated conference with persuasive speeches, negotiated solutions, and on global policy, similar in purpose to the actual event.

On the evening of the Nueva Conference on Climate Change, students dressed in character as delegates and lobbyists assembled in front of their parents and cameras operated by four students representing the media. Following an Agenda www.nueva.pvt.k12.ca.us/~debbie/library/curriculum/globconf.html), they presented their positions in two-minute prepared speeches to the global assembly. Then they broke into working groups composed of two country representatives and a group of lobbyists. These committee meetings simulated the dilemmas that the real delegates would face. This "thinking on your feet" was the synthesis — an authentic assessment of the depth of each student's understanding. After hearing the proposals from each working committee, the entire assembly of students, parents and visitors voted to select a global treaty.

To reinforce their personal opinions and examine specific ways in which they could impact this problem, students sent e-mail to Congressional representatives, to President Clinton, and to Vice-President Gore. In science class students examined their own use of energy, followed the conference events, and discussed the political maneuvering leading up to the Kyoto Conference. During December they also watched videotapes of the events in Kyoto and listened to audiotapes of National Public Radio commentary.

EVALUATING THE PROCESS AND THE PRODUCT

Immediately after the NCCC, students organized all their research materials into a folder and summarized their characters' positions as part of the Web pages created for the project. This "publishing" helped coalesce their understanding. In written self-evaluations they assessed their research process as well as their effectiveness in collaborating with their allies, their oral presentations and their committee work during the simulation. Why were some sources better than others? How effective was my time line and organization? How well did I think on my feet when challenged? *During the course of the project and while writing narrative evaluations, Molly and Debbie spent hours discussing the students, the curriculum and what could be done differently. They began writing narrative evaluations just after the winter break, a process that took several hours for each child. Their deliberations were based on observations of the students during class and during the simulation, a review of the research materials students chose to use, examination of students' notes and culminating written work, and input elicited from their allies. Although both of them had taken notes on each presentation during the simulation, they reviewed the student-media's videotape of certain student speeches when their assessments varied. Evaluation of the process and product became a multidimensional learning experience for the students, the teacher and the librarian.*

POSING A NEW PROBLEM

We believe that throughout the curriculum our students should pose questions, construct meaning and acquire a toolbox of skills by performing authentic, complex tasks of increasing challenge. In exploring the parallel process skills involved in doing a science project and doing library research, we have developed collaboration and a congruent set of thinking skills. Recently, our school has begun a long-term investigation of the problems of environmental sustainability on our site. New building construction and play spaces for our growing student population must be balanced against protection of the natural habitats and the restoration of native vegetation. Ill-structured problems...substantive content...multidisciplinary perspectives...intrinsic interest to our students...here we go again!

Debbie Abilock is a library media specialist at The Nueva School, Hillsborough, CA, and editor of Knowledge Quest. *Molly Lusignan is science specialist at The Nueva School.*

NOTES

1. As an organizer for our own thinking, we created a Web page overview of the curriculum **http://nueva.pvt.k12.ca.us/~debbie/library/curriculum/globalwarm.html**

2. "The Building Blocks of Research" available online at **www.nueva.pvt.k12.ca.us/~debbie/library/research/il/infolit1.html**

3. "Global Warming: Resources for Viewpoints" available online at **www.nueva.pvt.k12.ca.us/~debbie/library/research/bib/globalviews.html.**

4. "Nueva Conference on Climate Change Agenda" available online at **www.nueva.pvt.k12.ca.us/~debbie/library/curriculum/globconf.html.**

Notes

Thumbs Up on Technology Used in Multicultural Research

By Jacqueline Seewald

"Multicultural" has of late become one of the popular buzz words in education. As an educational media specialist, I pride myself on maintaining a certain healthy skepticism regarding "in" notions. I'm always leary of jumping on bandwagons or paying lip service to current educational jargon. However, despite its political correctness, multiculturalism actually offered a tremendous benefit to my school.

The student body at Red Bank Regional High School in Little Silver, New Jersey, comes from ethnically and culturally diverse communities. One town's student population is mainly African-American and Hispanic. Another is predominantly white. A third is upper to middle class, while yet another community provides ethnically diverse students of working class background. Since our students are for the most part socially segregated until they enter high school, a multicultural project was a way of promoting understanding and tolerance.

POPULAR REFERENCES

Two years ago, a social studies teacher asked me to create a worksheet to help students prepare multicultural research projects for her Contemporary World Issues elective course. Students' research would focus on various cultures and their customs and holidays. I gathered for students such sources as Gale's: *The Folklore of World Holidays* and *Holidays, Festivals, and Celebrations of the World Dictionary*. Vertical file materials were also quite useful and abundantly available. However, the most popular tool besides general encyclopedias was *Readers' Guide to Periodical Literature* on WilsonDisc CD-ROM.

With only one workstation, students were required to take turns rapidly. Nevertheless, they quickly accessed valuable information. Generally, we pulled periodicals so that specific articles could be used for research, but sometimes the abstract alone provided sufficient information. Although our media center owns the print *Readers' Guide*, the CD-ROM version, which makes nearly ten years of subject searching available in seconds, was much preferred by students.

Our stand-alone IBM-compatible computer with CD-ROM provided access to *World Atlas*, a helpful geographical source that offers both maps and information concerning countries. We were also able to offer *World Factbook* and *Grolier's Multimedia Encyclopedia* on CD-ROM.

Some students went beyond the basics and asked me to help them prepare slides of pictures from books and periodicals for class presentation. These included various works of art, paintings, sculpture and architecture representative of different nationalities and ethnic groups. I told the students what kind of film to purchase, set up a 35 mm. camera on a copystand, and taught them to use it. I also loaned other students a camcorder so they could create their own documentary in the style of *48 Hours*.

Those who chose merely to read their written reports received a "Boring!" evaluation from their classmates. To prevent that happening the second year, I rewrote the worksheet to guide students to take notes in the media center while doing their research. I again pulled appropriate books and vertical file materials, but my emphasis was on helping each student plan something unique. No written report was required, but a detailed outline of the presentation was. The emphasis was on audiovisual presentations and explanations. A follow-up test was given to the students and test scores were very high. In this way, we determined that oral presentations combined with visual aids are extremely effective in teaching multiculturalism.

NEW CD-ROM NETWORK STIMULATED STUDENTS' RESEARCH

We found students much more involved and interested in the research process this year because of our new CD-ROM network. I could give eight students instruction at the same time on the use of a particular program while others used our WilsonDisc for searching periodicals or our stand-alone IBM-compatible computer for such single-user databases as *World Religions*. For the network, I had argued for the purchase of *SIRS Researcher*. The amount of use in a variety of disciplines has more than outweighed the cost. *SIRS Researcher* on CD-ROM proves to be much more valuable than *SIRS* in print form since the database is so user friendly. For the multicultural

Multicultural Research Worksheet

I. Choose an appropriate topic for research: country, region, ethnic group, holiday, custom.

II. Using the following list as a guide, write as much as possible about your topic. Think in terms of what you have discovered about your subject that is interesting and/or unusual. Be prepared to orally discuss and present your findings to the class.

III. A detailed written outline of your oral presentation is required.

1. Art
2. Celebrations
3. Clothing
4. Customs
5. Dance
6. Food
7. Geography (location, climate, etc.)
8. History
9. Language
10. Literature
11. Music
12. People
13. Religion
14. Other

project, *SIRS* offered many interesting and useful articles because of its global emphasis. Since our network does not have sound cards and therefore cannot offer full interactive or multimedia use, we have set up *Grolier's Multimedia Encyclopedia* on our Macintosh. This is proving to be very useful. For example, students researching music can listen to the actual music as they read about it. The final project presentations also reflected this higher degree of varied information.

EXPERIENCING DIVERSITY FIRSTHAND

Students also learned a lot from their ethnically diverse classmates. They got to taste Spanish soda and to discover that bagels originated in Poland. They tried their hands at origami, the art of Japanese paper folding, and knocked down Mexican pinatas.

We expect our third year of doing the multicultural project will be our best yet. We have access to the Internet via America Online, which is installed on our stand-alone IBM-compatible computer. We are also planning to hook into the New Jersey Link, another network which will vastly increase information availability and provide Internet access.

We were pleased to find that technology in our media center sparked students' enthusiasm for learning about different cultures. As Plutarch said: "The mind is a fire to be kindled, not (merely) a vessel to be filled." **TC**

Jacqueline Seewald is a Library Media Specialist at Red Bank Regional High School in Little Silver, New Jersey.

Making It Mine

Helping Students Use Information to Create an Original Report

By Ann van der Meulen

Many of my elementary school students find it difficult to grasp the concept of paraphrasing information to produce their own original reports. The following three group activities help them identify and practice that skill.

1. Recipe for Reporting

This activity begins with the question, "How is doing a report like creating your very own cookie recipe?" I direct the students to take time to think about what the question means. They briefly discuss their thoughts with partners, and then we record student responses on a group chart. Next, we brainstorm places in the library they might look to collect ideas about making up their own cookie recipes. That provides a tidy review of possible resources (e.g., cookbooks, encyclopedias, periodicals, computerized resources) and procedures (e.g., Dewey Decimal System, indexes, searching techniques).

I direct students to use these resources to create their own original cookie recipes. We discuss the need to look at several recipes to gather enough data to gain an understanding of the topic. Each recipe must be unique (not copied) but also within the realm of possibility, given other cookie recipes they discover. Provided with a visual organizer, students:

- make up the name of their cookie,
- list the main ingredients,
- illustrate what their cookie should look like when it is ready, and
- provide step-by-step directions, including what and how much to mix together, oven temperature, and cooking time.

We post the finished products, giving everyone a chance to admire the creativity of the group. (If we had the time, we might even dare to try out some of the recipes. As part of the fun, I have brought in cookies to share after this activity.)

Finally, we revisit our group chart and see if we can add to our responses to the opening question.

2. Extracting Important Words

Another challenge to my students involves reading a piece of information, taking notes, and then formulating their own paragraphs about the information. To practice that writing skill, we use an informational paragraph or two. After reading it together, we generate a generous list of significant words we found in it. I direct students to think about which words might belong together in a group and to determine what the heading might be for that group of related words. Each student develops one set of related words to display to the class. Then, classmates try to figure out what heading was intended for that group. After an exchange of justifications, we continue with another student's set of related words. Students are given back their display sets and directed to write a few original sentences about their topic with the help of the words they grouped together.

3. Drawing Upon One's Memory

Another approach for practicing the skill of casting given information into one's own words involves more listening than reading. I read a brief but engaging informational piece to the students. While I read, students draw simple picturesflno wordsflto help them remember the piece. After the reading/drawing, I direct students to talk to partners and try to remember as much as possible about the reading, using their drawings as memory helpers. Students organize what they remember into a main idea and supporting details. This organization works well on a group chart at first and then, as students become more familiar with the technique, independently. From this point, the step to students creating their own paragraphs follows comfortably. The organization of a report can be addressed within the context of an actual assignment depending on the requirements of the final project. It is refreshing to note the variety of schemes available for planning the paragraph-by-paragraph layout of a report from the structured outline form to the more flexible Web or creative metaphorical shapes, e.g., an umbrella, tree or turtle.

These activities work best if the informational content is directly related to the current curricular projects of the class. At the very least, they provide students a chance to better understand some of the ingredients in cooking up their own recipes for reporting.

The activities in the article were developed in conjunction with a professional development program presented by Hanson Silver Strong & Associates, Inc.

Ann van der Meulen is a Library Media Specialist at West Street Elementary School in Geneva, New York.

Notes

Teaching High School Students How To Use College Libraries Online

By Nancy Everhart

School librarians in Pennsylvania were looking for a way to introduce their students to resources on the state's online college catalogs. The librarian who wrote the workbook describes her effort here.

Many school library media specialists now provide high school students access to additional information sources by allowing them to log on to university online catalogs. This access is accomplished by direct connect, as part of a union catalog, on CD-ROM, or through the Internet. However, as more students go online, instructional materials specific to their needs becomes necessary. Such materials are critical to student understanding and efficient use of these catalogs, especially since many were designed before the days of the user-friendly interface.

The Pennsylvania School Librarians' Association recognized this dilemma by giving their Professional Development Award to this author to help investigate how high school students use Pennsylvania State University's online catalog (LIAS) from remote terminals. As a result of the project, a workbook was developed to aid high school students in using LIAS for completing research papers, whether working from the high school library media center or from home. The award was funded by Brodart Corporation, Williamsport, Pennsylvania.

Designing the workbook involved working with Penn State librarians and students. An ERIC online search identified key personnel on campus involved in using the LIAS. A meeting was set up to explain the project. Personnel offered valuable suggestions and

provided written materials, which were included in a preliminary draft, along with materials from the local campus librarian. A group of students evaluated the draft and also accompanied the author on a field test. The revised draft was presented to the Penn State librarians who edited it further. Finally, a 40-page workbook titled,
"Lion's PALS (Public Access LIAS for Students)" was printed.

The following critical needs necessary for students to work independently were identified and are presented in the workbook.

1. Technical information
Included are listings of equipment required, modem settings, local phone numbers, and log-on protocols.

2. Geographic information
Students were not familiar with the location of branch campus library sites throughout the state. A map noting these was produced.

When students decide on the library they want to search, they need to know how to restrict their search in the database. A chart listing codes for the specific libraries is provided. For example, if students want to search the collection of the Harrisburg library, they must type in *lib hbg* immediately on connection.

3. Scope of the database and levels of records

Knowing what is included in the database is important. Students need to know that records of other materials such as maps, government documents, audiovisual materials, and periodical titles, as well as books, are in the database. They need to examine LIAS records to differentiate among types of materials.

After students have typed in their search term, they are presented with a listing of closely related headings. They need to be encouraged to explore the database further, to move from headings, to citations, and finally to the full record of the materials.

4. Moving around screens

Specific terms are used in LIAS to move from screen to screen, retrace steps of a search and exit. These are not displayed on the screen, and students often became frustrated if guides were not available. An explanation of online help and the commands for available help is included in the workbook.

5. Locational skills

If students are interested in visiting the branch library to obtain materials, they need to know where to find the call number on the record. They need to be shown how a book appears on the

> Students need to be encouraged to explore the database further, to move from headings, to citations, and finally to the full record of the materials.

shelf with its Library of Congress call number on its spine compared to the online record. Because Library of Congress classification is unfamiliar to students, they need a brief explanation of how the books are arranged. College libraries are much larger than high school libraries. Therefore, students need to be told to look for maps or directories to help them locate their materials. Instructions are provided on how to check the availability of the material online before going to the library.

6. Title searching

Students often do not realize that several books with the same title may exist in a large database. They need experience searching for a title by the author's name. Because there may be many editions of the same work, they need help in narrowing the search to the exact book desired. Students also need suggestions for titles to search. They are reminded of bibliographies in books in their school library that they found useful, sources mentioned by their teacher or a subject expert they may have interviewed. Instruction is provided in searching for a periodical title online and how to interpret which issues of the periodical the library has.

7. Name searching

Aside from the recurring problem of not remembering to type in the author's last name first, students need to be able to distinguish between books by a person and books about a person. Authors in a university catalog tend to embrace more companies, government agencies and associations than are found in a typical high school library's catalog, and students need to be alerted to this.

8. Subject searching

Most student searches are by subject. Subject searching in LIAS utilizes Library of Congress subject headings, which are unfamiliar to students. Moreover, no *Library of Congress Subject Headings* books were available in the high school library. To overcome these deficiencies, two subject strategies were developed.

First, students are told to type in the title of a book they remember as a good source. If a match is found, they can use subject headings they find in the tracings of that record for their subject search. This may lead them to more subject heading possibilities. Second, they can follow a similar process using keyword, rather than subject searching, to lead them to appropriate subject headings.

9. Creating bibliographies

One of the most popular features of the workbook has been the page "Creating Bibliography References from LIAS Citations." A sample record for a book heads the page with correct term paper bibliographies for Turabian, APA, Chicago, and MLA styles. Even if it is decided not to produce an entire workbook, students will appreciate handouts on this process.

10. Advanced techniques

For students who wish to go beyond the basics, the last section of the workbook includes instruction in advanced features of LIAS. Boolean searching, truncation, and browsing the shelves electronically are some of the options for students with higher ability or previous experience.

Creating instructional materials for users of online catalogs is rewarding. In an era when jobs for library media specialists are being threatened, this idea could be further expanded as a public relations tool. Start by developing library worksheets for the colleges attended by students in your high school. Provide training for seniors in the spring soon after they have made their college choice and are highly motivated. Certainly, parents will appreciate this approach and so will university librarians! **TC**

Nancy Everhart, Ph.D., is Assistant Professor of School Library Media at St. John's University, Division of Library and Information Science, Jamaica, New York, and a former high school library media specialist. For a copy of her workbook, send $5.00 per copy to Dr. Nancy Everhart, Online Workbook, 221 Catawissa Street, Tamaqua, PA 18252.

CREATING BIBLIOGRAPHY REFERENCES FROM LIAS CITATIONS

There is enough information contained in a LIAS record so that you can write a bibliographic reference. What follows is a sample record and references written in the most popular styles that high school students use.

Strong, James H.
    Educating homeless children, issues and answers. / by James H. Stronge and Cheri Tenhouse.
Bloomington, Ind., Phi Delta Kappa Educational Foundation, c 1990.
    33 p. 18 cm. Series: Fastback, 313.
    Includes bibliographical references (p. 32-33).
    1. Homeless youth — Education. 2. Homeless children — Education.
Call#: HV4505.S77 1990
    Central Pattee Level 4 Blue

Turabian:
Stronge, James H., and Tenhouse, Cheri. Educating Homeless Children, Issues and Answers. Bloomington, IN: Phi Delta Kappa Educational Foundation, 1990.

APA:
Stronge, J.H. & Tenhouse, C. (1990). Educating Homeless Children, Issues and Answers. Bloomington, IN: Phi Delta Kappa Educational Foundation.

Chicago:
Stronge, J.H. & Tenhouse, C. Educating Homeless Children, Issues and Answers. Bloomington, IN: Phi Delta Kappa Educational Foundation, 1990.

MLA:
Stronge, James H., and Cheri Tenhouse. Educating Homeless Children, Issues and Answers. Bloomington, IN: Phi Delta Kappa Educational Foundation, 1990.

THE SENIOR EXIT PROJECT
A CHANCE FOR THE LIBRARY TO SHINE

By Patsy Troutman & Connie Pawlowski

FOR TWO WEEKS IN MAY the media center at Providence High School in Charlotte, North Carolina, puts on a new face. Gone are the student groups collaborating on class assignments, the reams of data belching from computer printers, and the shuffling and beeping of library inventory. There is, instead, the orderly procession of polished and scrubbed seniors taking their places confidently before panels of faculty and community judges to demonstrate their expertise on a topic of special interest. What better place for this culmination of eight months of concentrated research to take place than the library media center!

As part of the educational reforms across the country, demonstrations of competency have become a graduation requirement in many schools. Various models exist. Our school uses the Senior Exit Project, developed by Deana R. Chadwell at South Medford High School, Medford, Oregon. This project has three phases: a research-based paper, a product that applies the knowledge gained in the research, and an oral presentation to a panel of judges. All students, regardless of ability level, must show that they can retrieve and use information, work independently, organize their time, write correctly, think critically, and speak clearly.

Senior English teachers in cooperation with the media center initiated the project at Providence in 1993-94 on a small scale. For the following year, the planning team received training in the Oregon model and extended participation to all seniors. The school system added two other high schools to the pilot program. This past year, 1995-96, every senior in all 11 high schools had to complete a project, which counted for 20% of the final English grade; next year the Senior Exit Project will be required for high school graduation. Five other school systems in North Carolina piloted Senior Exit Projects this year, and a governor-appointed committee is recommending that all North Carolina high schools adopt the program.

Senior Projects give media professionals cause for celebration, for they give us a chance to serve and to shine. The library media program is an integral part of every phase of the project. With so many media programs in jeopardy today, the emphasis on authentic assessment could not have come at a better time. Having worked closely for two years in the pilot program, we can suggest some ways for library media professionals to get involved.

IMPLEMENTATION OF THE SCHOOL'S MISSION

Every school's mission is to graduate literate, productive young people. Media professionals can exercise leadership in the implementation of this mission by initiating a model in their schools. In Oregon it was English teachers who developed the Senior Exit Project; it could easily have been the school librarian.

If others introduce the project at your school, volunteer to be on the steering committee. At Providence the steering committee oversaw the project and coordinated the work of 14 subcommittees. The media specialists served as chairpersons of the video

Patsy Troutman and Connie Pawlowski are the Media Coordinators at Providence High School, Charlotte, North Carolina.

and Internet committees, a perfect fit. Since the project also served as an alternative evaluation system (replacing state-required class observations) for tenured teachers, faculty participation was highly structured.

REFERENCE AND READING GUIDANCE

All staff members serve as mentors, with a limit of six students per teacher. The students choose their mentors from the teachers they know or select from a list that identifies special interests and abilities of staff members. Mentors meet weekly with their charges to discuss plans, progress, problems, or needs. Although as media professionals we work with all seniors on the research paper, we also mentor students.

COLLECTION DEVELOPMENT

The Senior Exit Project greatly impacts collection development. Students select their topics, but the topic must be complex and comprehensive enough to challenge. It must be one that requires cumulative knowledge that the student can analyze, apply, and synthesize. Among the topics last year were: anterior cruciate ligament injuries, bass fishing, car racing, carpentry, chaos theory, mountaineering, neonatal intensive care, senile dementia, and virtual reality.

We quickly filled our consideration file to overflowing. Fortunately, we have access to the collections of public and academic libraries in our area. The school system's curriculum library was of tremendous help for education topics—even delivering the books to students by school courier. The high schools borrowed materials from each other, putting their belief in interlibrary loans to the test. Students, of course, printed out miles of articles.

To our dismay, school library access to the local freenet and the World Wide Web came after most research had been completed. Students had to use the Internet at home or in the school's vocational department. Their papers showed that they had connected to colleges, museums, libraries, organizations, and individuals. Next year, students will have full access to these resources in the library. E-mail will be available to students at school through their mentor's e-mail privileges.

INTEGRATION OF INFORMATION SKILLS

The research-based essay must include a works-cited page in Modern Language Association (MLA) format, showing that the student used a minimum of five sources with one being a primary source. Here was an opportunity for us to put on our teaching hats. We distributed a sample MLA bibliography and provided access to primary sources. During the weekly class visits, we provided one-on-one reference guidance.

At the same time, the media staff and the English teachers have begun preparing 10th-grade students for their senior project. We use the 10th-grade orientation as a launching pad; one teacher named it "Making Tracks to the Senior Exit." Students complete an interest inventory and narrow their focus to one topic of major interest. Using library resources, they print a preliminary bibliography, take notes, and use wordprocessing software to produce a one-paragraph document. (We paste the paragraphs on the outline of a shoe for a hallway display, which reminds all students of the upcoming senior project.)

CREATIVE USE OF INFORMATION

The media staff was especially involved when seniors began developing their products and getting ready for their presentation. The product must be an appropriate outgrowth or extension of the research. Students are required to spend at least 15 hours in independent work (40 hours or more are the norm). We prepared a list of available production equipment for each senior English class.

In addition to the library's desktop publishing and video resources, the seniors also had access to HyperStudio (Wagner), Microsoft PowerPoint, Video Toaster, and the Internet. As students began to schedule time in the media center, we quickly saw the need for more production equipment, the upgrading of some existing resources, and more inservice sessions in production for their mentors.

We allowed students to take some expensive production equipment — camcorders, cameras-35mm and digital, slide projectors, location lighting—home. Parents were required to sign for and pick up the equipment in person. We had no equipment losses and gained valuable media center PR.

All students, regardless of ability level, must show that they can retrieve and use information, work independently, organize their time, write correctly, think critically, and speak clearly.

Student procrastination was, as usual, a difficulty. In spite of some last-minute rushes, the products were impressive. One student wrote an original symphony; another learned sign language, taught a deaf student to swim, and documented it with a video. Students drew their own comic books, opened a small business, designed home pages, made furniture, completed community service projects, created computer animations, and demonstrated skydiving.

PUBLIC RELATIONS

In mid-May each senior presented to a panel of judges a six-to-ten minute speech about his paper and product and then defended his research in a question-and-answer session. The media center videotaped practice presentations both in classrooms and the TV studio; students critiqued themselves and each other.

Judges, both staff members and community volunteers, had to be trained. Working with a faculty committee, the media staff prepared a training video for the judges. It was shown and discussed at a school staff meeting and at scheduled public training sessions. The media staff maintained a small group viewing area in the library workroom for judges unable to attend formal training.

A staff committee scheduled the presentations and the equipment needed for each student. The media center was closed during class time for two weeks, but students could use the center before and after school and for extended hours two afternoons.

The staging of the presentations was a bonus for us. Community participants could see their tax dollars at work in the library. We observed many of them "checking out" our information technologies. Like other members of the school staff, we took our turns as judges. We also videotaped some presentations for documentation and future orientation to the project.

EVALUATION

The month of May is forever changed at Providence High. Even though the Senior Exit Project spells anxiety for some students, it is generally well-received by students, teachers, and parents. Teachers like the project because it makes instruction relevant, integrates the curriculum, and attacks "senioritis." Students complain but they also take pride in what they and their peers have accomplished. The community likes the Senior Exit Project because it showcases academic achievement. The media center staff applauds the way it integrates library skills and instills the concept of life-long learning.

Further Reading

Deana R. Chadwell, "Show What You Know." *The American School Board Journal*, April 1991, pp. 34-35.

———, "The Senior Project; South Medford High School, Medford, Oregon." *Exemplary Practices in Education*, April 1992, pp. 8-9.

THE COMPUTER LAB / LIBRARY CONNECTION

By Diane Pozar

Having the computer lab next door was only one reason for combining library and lab resources

WE'VE ALL READ ABOUT the importance of planning with teachers, integrating the curriculum and library skills, and making technology a part of the library. Last year I had success in all three areas and can attest that they do make a difference.

Two summers ago the middle school library was renovated and the computer lab was re-located next door with a connecting door. An enthusiastic computer lab manager helped ensure that collaboration became reality.

Shortly after the physical connection of the lab and library, two seventh-grade teachers were teaming and integrating English and social studies. Their first project was to have the students design travel brochures for one of the 13 American colonies. Based on their research of a colony, the students wrote advertising copy that would persuade people to move there. The students did their research in the library and laid out the brochures in the computer lab.

Along with books and other materials about the colonies, the library provided a list of ideas and questions to prompt the students' research: What kind of stores did the colonists have? What recreational activities were popular in that time period?

This project did not lend itself to copying text from other sources. I taught the students how to take notes. Students had to look critically at every piece of information, even their visual resources. For example, they couldn't include a picture of a room with electric lights when they laid out the brochures in the computer lab.

When these same seventh graders were assigned a science project, which also required a written and illustrated product, we followed the same procedure—brainstorming and note taking in the library, further research and production in the lab. By the third project these students were almost experts. This time they had to keep a journal as a colonial boy or girl. Familiar with the time period from their earlier project, they began to question facts they found. They were beginning to read and think critically. Note-taking skills improved. And the students saw me as a resource, asking my advice on their projects.

An eighth-grade teacher came to us to develop "something different" for a project on scientists. Our brainstorming lead to the idea of having the students "interview" and write a newspaper article about an imaginary visit by a scientist. The science teacher gave us a list of scientists and we checked library and computer lab resources for available materials. We created a master list for our use in directing students to the library or lab for specific items. It also helped us determine where we lacked up-to-date resources.

First we brainstormed questions the students could ask the scientist. Then they began their research. The resulting interviews were creative and obviously not copied. Some examples of headlines were: "Aristotle Philosophizes at Wallkill." "Niel Bohr Bombs at Wallkill."

To involve the whole school in the computer lab and library connection, we also sponsored a trivia contest. We asked teachers to submit three to five questions and answers from their subject area. We compiled these into separate trivia questions for the seventh grade and eighth grade. Some teachers agreed to give extra points to students who entered the contest. We solicited prizes from local stores, such as teddy bears, valentine candy, flowers and balloons and gift certificates from the local pizza shop. The prizes were displayed to motivate the students.

The students used the library and the computer lab to find the answers. They were helping each other and even arguing over answers. I know they were discussing the contest at home because parents commented on the questions.

Because of our efforts, teachers are coming to us offering to help us with projects and asking us to help with their assignments.

Diane Pozar is Librarian at Wallkill (New York) Middle School. The manager of the computer lab is Kim Kosteczko.

Notes

Notes

Reading and Literature Appreciation

As school library media specialists, we hope to nurture not only lifelong learners, but lifelong readers. Most first, second, third, and fourth graders *love* to read; they're just discovering that fabulous world of literature and they can't get enough of it. But something changes around the time students enter the upper elementary and middle grades. Perhaps it's because there are so many competing demands on their limited time; perhaps it's because reading is perceived as "uncool." Whatever the reason, formerly avid readers visit the library less and less frequently, and generally for research rather than pleasure. We need to reach out actively to this age group, to keep them reading through their high school and college years and into adulthood-especially in this age of *wonderful* young adult books, both fiction and nonfiction. Some of the suggestions offered in this chapter include reading aloud, booktalking by students as well as adults, and accessing author resources on the Internet.

When one of my K-5 school library media centers was closed for nearly a year for renovation, the collection in storage, I knew that I needed to remain a presence for these students in some way. I spent a day each week dragging a wheeled suitcase full of books from other libraries behind me through the halls, reading to every class in that school. The younger students were used to my reading aloud to them; I wasn't sure what the fourth and fifth graders would make of it. Fortunately, our state has a book award voted on by fourth, fifth, and sixth graders, and this school has a history of participation. I read these students two of the nominated titles before the library media center reopened. Whenever I looked up from my reading, I saw eyes glued on me. Even the teachers, who had been sitting at the back of the room grading papers, put down their work to listen. Reading to older students requires careful choice of material (since the initial reaction is generally that being read to is "baby stuff") and lots of expression and use of distinguishable "voices," but when it clicks it *clicks*! Years later, students from those classes wanted to read for themselves the novels I'd presented aloud.

I love to booktalk, something my students will attest to. But it's even more exciting when I'm busy helping one child, and from somewhere behind me I hear a young voice speaking to a classmate: "You've *got* to read this book. It's about . . . ." I know they've learned something from my booktalking technique when they conclude, "But I can't tell you the ending; you'll have to read it and find out yourself."

Middle and high school students are peer-oriented. Even when they trust my recommendations, they're more likely to believe the advice of a classmate.
Seek out those youngsters who are readers and leaders, and coach them on booktalking methods, formal and informal. Notebooks of booktalks or reviews written by students can also be helpful for reader's advisory when you're busy or unavailable.

All youngsters are fascinated by the fact that books are written by *real people*. Not every school can afford lots of author visits, but the Internet offers some great Web sites featuring ready-made mini-visits by favorite authors. At-risk readers might be attracted by items we point out on the Internet: an author's interesting biography, or a discussion of how he gets his ideas. Some might be excited by the opportunity to write to an author via either snail or e-mail. This latter activity ideally assumes some familiarity with the author's work, which means reading.

The Internet does not have to supercede books. It might even lead young readers to them.

☐ URL UPDATES

Children's Literature Resources on the Web:
HomeArts Web
www.homearts.com/depts/relat/
bookintr.htm

Dan Gutman
www.dangutman.com/

Electronic Resources for Youth Services
www.chebucto.ns.ca/~aa331/
childlit.html

Story Resources on the Web
www.enigmagraphics.com/
stories/index.htm

Tales of Wonder
http://darsie.ucdavis.edu/tales/

Reading Aloud in the Junior High Classroom

By Susan H. Williamson

Many educators are hesitant to read aloud to junior high students. But, despite the students' initial grumblings, I have found that oral reading can be a successful experience if teachers and librarians are enthusiastic and choose suitable novels.

Librarians who teach a scheduled library skills course may want to incorporate reading aloud in their classes. Those who do not teach a scheduled course can help encourage reading aloud to groups, recommending suitable novels to teachers.

Not all books are suitable for reading aloud to groups. The short bibliography at the end of this article contains titles that I have successfully read to junior high classes.

In order to capture the attention of junior high students, a novel must be exciting and within the framework of students' experience. Students who have avoided reading, regardless of their reading ability, tend to respond best to realistic fiction. While many quality novels, such as the Hinton books, have universal appeal, some novels tend to work only if the setting is similar to the students' community. While teaching in an urban area, I found *A Shadow Like a Leopard* a popular choice, but when I transferred to a rural community, I found books like *Where the Red Fern Grows* have greater appeal.

Historical fiction can be used successfully if students are prepared for it. *Shane,* a western, and *Sign of the Beaver,* set in colonial America, are both extremely popular with junior high students.

A successful literary experience, even though it is in a read-aloud situation, encourages students to read

Because male reluctant readers tend to be both more numerous and more recalcitrant, I have had greater success with books that have a strong male protagonist. Reading is often viewed as a "feminine" activity, and even boys who were readers in elementary school may forsake reading in junior high in order to strengthen their masculine image.

Because of their concern about their image, many boys will not let themselves empathize with a heroine, while girls at this age are usually capable of empathizing with any character regardless of sex.

The ability to empathize with a character is an important step in the process of becoming a reader. Poor readers often have difficulty

---

Susan H. Williamson is the librarian at Blairsville High School in Blairsville, Pennsylvania. She was formerly a reading teacher. Susan is a BOOK REPORT reviewer and her articles have appeared in other professional journals.

---

empathizing with characters and, thus, difficulty understanding literature. While reading aloud, one can guide students toward empathy and increase their understanding and enjoyment of a novel.

In order to make reading aloud palatable, you should choose books with these characteristics: fairly short chapters, a minimum of dialogue, and the use of action rather than description to illustrate characters' personalities.

I have read aloud *Sign of the Beaver* to 15 seventh and eighth grade classes with excellent results. The response to the novel was overwhelmingly positive; students looked forward to the few times a week I read from the novel. I usually read one chapter per session.

In this book, the chapters were of suitable length for the typical junior high attention span and often each chapter was a discrete adventure.

Students, especially less able readers, need to be prepared for the book they are about to encounter, even in a read-aloud situation. Because I teach in a rural area, all of my students were acquainted with hunting even if they were too young to hunt. Before beginning to read *Sign of the Beaver,* I discussed the idea of hunting for survival with my classes. (Research skills could be tied in at this point by having students research the background for the novel. Throughout the novel, research possibilities will occur and students can research material for their personal interests and to share with the class.) After we discussed hunting in the modern world, I asked students to pretend they were living in the wilderness of Maine during the late 18th century. They are all alone in a sturdy cabin with only a gun, a knife, and crops that will not be ready to harvest for several weeks. We discussed what it would be like to live under such conditions. They quickly realized that in the scenario described, hunting and fishing would be more than a sport; it would be their only chance for survival.

Now that my students were capable of empathizing with Matt, the main character of *Sign of the Beaver*, we were ready to begin reading.

We first meet Matt as he is saying goodbye to his father, who is leaving Matt on the newly completed homestead in the wilderness while he returns to Massachusetts to get the rest of the family. Matt's taciturn father gives him little advice, but he does leave the best gun with Matt. Except for the mysterious feeling that he is being watched, Matt adjusts to his new life.

This section and several others in the book are perfect for allowing students to respond to text and predict future events, a skill that many reluctant readers find difficult. The author relies heavily on foreshadowing, and because my students were not careful readers, they often did not notice the clues provided. Through my questions, I had students ferret out foreshadowing. We used this information to predict future outcomes. We discussed possible outcomes and voted on the most probable outcomes. Asking students to respond to text and predict future outcomes forces them to become more involved with the text. Listening becomes an active rather than a passive process. By voting on a possible outcome, students begin to feel as though they have a stake in what happens, and thus begin to pay closer attention.

A successful literary experience, even though it is in a read-aloud situation, encourages students to read. Because they feel more capable and have a basis for comparison, many students will be more willing to attempt to read a novel on their own. If they enjoyed the novel, they may be more willing to ask for help in locating other novels. Many poor readers have difficulty in locating suitable novels. A willingness to ask for help is often a first step toward becoming a reader.

Teachers may find that reading a novel aloud to their classes provides comparison for books students are asked to read silently. After reading *Shane* and discussing the various ways authors reveal character, my students matured in their ability to infer information about characters during independent reading. Even poor readers began to contribute to class discussion; they felt comfortable using *Shane* for comparison and as a reference point.

Both students and administrators may be skeptical the first time you read a novel aloud. Students may feel that being read to is an elementary school activity. If the discussion prior to the reading whets their appetites and if the first novel read aloud is a real attention-getter, students will soon enjoy the activity. I found that the same students who objected to my reading aloud initially were the ones who started asking that I read aloud more frequently. Principals in three different school districts, who were skeptical of reading aloud to this age group, have observed my classes. All have agreed after actually observing the activity that it was a great success.

If you find that students are not responding well to a particular novel, it is best to admit defeat and try another. Any of the novels on the following list have a great chance of succeeding, especially if you choose one that matches your students' interests.

Books for Reading To Junior High Students

S.E. Hinton, *The Outsiders*, 1967. Gang life is vividly portrayed in this first-person narrative.

S.E. Hinton, *Tex*, 1979. Tex's brother Mace is in charge while their father is off riding the rodeo circuit. Even the return of their father does not relieve the sibling rivalry; Mace will always be their father's favorite because Tex was conceived while their father was serving a jail sentence. Students enjoy Tex's antics.

Monica Hughes, *Hunter in the Dark*, 1984. Before he succumbs to leukemia, Mike is determined to hunt his first deer. He runs away to the Canadian wilderness and proves himself a man when he survives a storm and chooses to let his first deer live.

Myron Levoy, *A Shadow Like a Leopard*, 1981. When he blunders his attempt to rob Mr. Glasser, a once-famous but now impoverished artist, Ramon loses his chance to become a member of a street gang. As his friendship with Glasser blossoms, Ramon learns about the finer things in life.

Robert Newton Peck, *A Day No Pigs Would Die*, 1972. In order to provide for his family after his death, Robert's father must butcher Robert's pet pig. Pinky's death forces Robert to mature and he is ready to accept both his father's death and his new responsibilities.

Wilson Rawls, *Where the Red Fern Grows*, 1974. Students who live in hunting communities like this book despite its length. Billy works for two years in order to buy his hound and together they become the best hunting team in the Ozarks.

Jack Schaefer, *Shane*, 1949. Homesteaders are being forced to leave their land by greedy ranchers. When Shane, a mysterious gunman, joins the homesteaders they are ready to fight for what is theirs.

Elizabeth George Speare, *Sign of the Beaver*, 1983. Matt learns to survive in the wilderness Indian style after his gun is stolen.

Maureen Crane Wartski, *A Long Way from Home*, 1980. Kien finds that emigrating to America does not shield him from persecution. He must learn to fight prejudice if he is to make a new life for himself.

BOOKTALKS

Student Booktalks Can Motivate Readers

By Joni Bodart

While teachers and librarians can motivate students to read certain books by giving booktalks, we should not overlook the motivational power of student booktalkers. The identity of the talker can be as motivating as the booktalk itself.

In the classroom, booktalks by students can serve to integrate literature into all parts of the curriculum, to substitute for book reports, and to help students learn to analyze books. Having students critique each others' work teaches them not only how to critique but also how to accept criticism.

Booktalks can also be used more than once. Students can present their talks to other classes, grades, and schools. Talks can be videotaped and used in the school or the local public library. (Keeping track of circulation records can determine whose talks are most effective in persuading others to read.) The written "scripts" for talks can be collected in a notebook and kept in the school library for student and teacher use.

When teaching students to do booktalks, it is important to cover these points:

- Remind students that they've all done booktalks if they have ever told a friend about a book they particularly liked.
- Describe the various types of booktalks: first-person, plot summaries, mood-based or style-based talks, and so forth. Explain why each works with different types of books.
- Encourage students to choose a book that isn't widely known, one that not many of the audience will have already heard about because of its popularity.
- Stress the importance of reading the book and writing the talk before attempting the booktalk.
- Emphasize practicing and memorizing not the words of the talk but the sequence of thoughts or actions.
- If critiquing others' talks is part of the classroom booktalking, suggest that students make specific comments, not general ones such as "I liked it," or "You made the book sound good." They should also use the "sandwich" technique, giving positive feedback, then negative, then positive again. Be sure to mention that when people get too much negative criticism, they are not able to hear the positive feedback. Finally, students' comments should be constructive, focusing on how to make a booktalk better.

Every time I've taught kids how to booktalk, they've taken to it like ducks to water. Other librarians and teachers I've talked to concur. Kids not only love to hear booktalks, they also love to do them. In almost every class, I discover one or two students whose booktalks literally take my breath away.

Here are some talks on titles that were grabbers for me. I think kids will pick up on them just as fast. I selected them because of their covers (or in the case of the Zindel title, in spite of the cover, which stirred up my snake phobia), their titles or their authors. I hope you'll find something here to motivate reading in your school.

Dogwolf by Alden R. Carter. 1994, Scholastic, $13.95, 0-590-46741-7.

It was a strange summer, the summer I was 15, the summer I thought about all the fractions in my life and listened to the dogwolf howl. My name's Pete LaSavage. I'm part French and part Chippewa and part Swedish. It's never really bothered me before, being not all of something, but that summer I started thinking about it a lot.

My stepdad is a firefighter for the forest service, and that summer it seemed like there was just one fire after another. I spent a lot of time in the fire tower, looking for new fires. It gave me a lot of time to think, and a lot of time to listen to that dogwolf howl. Old man Wilson was off on a bender, so I went by his place every day or so to make sure there was food and water in the dogwolf's cage. I never saw him eat any of the food—he just sat and watched me fill up his water pan. When I left, he howled. I knew what he wanted, why he howled like that. I knew it sure as I knew my own name. He wanted me to set him free or put a bullet in his brain.

One afternoon after I'd baled hay all day, I heard the howling start again and I headed for Wilson's place with my deer rifle. I hadn't gone far when I realized that he'd stopped howling. I knew, even though it made no sense, that he was waiting for me.

I don't know why I didn't shoot him that day, why I just opened the gate of his cage, and waited for him to run. He was in my sights, but somehow I just couldn't pull the trigger. Just before he ran into the trees, he stopped short and turned to look at me. I lowered the rifle and for a long minute we looked at each other. Then he turned and loped into the trees.

There was no way for me to know then that what I'd done that day would change my life in ways I couldn't yet imagine.

Loch by Paul Zindel. 1994, $15, HarperCollins, 0-06-024542-5. [Reviewed in this issue.]

Remote Lake Alban in Vermont is very cold, very deep, and well-stocked with salmon, eel, and other bottom feeders necessary for the breeding of massive aquatic animals. Several of the locals have seen large shapes in the lake recently, and Cavenger believes that the salmon grid at the west end of the lake has trapped at least one huge creature inside.

No one really expects to find anything. After all, the men have been all over the world, looking for all kinds of strange animals that might or might not exist so Cavenger could publish the stories in his tabloid magazines. This time they aren't even using the expensive steel nets, but no net could have held the creature they will later call Rogue. It erupts from the water in front of the boat, a long scaly neck, huge jaws filled with dagger-size teeth, and glaring yellow eyes. The cam-

---

Joni Richards Bodart is a freelance consultant and booktalker, and the editor/publisher of Joni Bodart's Booktalker. *She lives in Denver, Colorado.*

eraman dies instantly, his body cut in half by the monster's first bite. Then it attacks the catamaran with Cavenger's daughter Sarah aboard before sinking back into the depths of the lake. It was unbelievably enormous and overwhelmingly angry and dangerous.

The crew's in shock, but Cavenger refuses to stop now that he has the story of the century within his grasp. He's determined to go after Rogue and capture, kill and stuff the creature if it's the last thing he does.

However, Cavenger doesn't know what's been happening behind his back. Loch and Zaidee, the son and daughter of a marine biologist on his crew, have befriended one of Rogue's offspring, a young plesiosaur about the size of a seal, and named him Wee Beastie. They are just as determined to save the plesiosaurs as Cavenger is to kill them.

Climb or Die by Edward Myers. 1994, Hyperion, $14.95, 0-7868-0026-7. [Reviewed in the January/February issue.]

Early October in the Colorado Rockies shouldn't have been that bitterly cold, and there shouldn't have been so much snow. The early blizzard surprised everyone. The father was positive that he could get his family to the cabin, even after he learned that the freeway had been closed. He knew about an old mining road, and soon they were all alone on a narrow path through the forest. With darkness closing in around them, it was no surprise the car ran off the road. Danielle and Jake, 13 and 14, weren't hurt, but their parents were seriously injured.

There were several feet of snow on the ground, and the family was more than 20 miles from the freeway. There was only one alternative—the weather station at the peak of Mount Remington. If the teenagers could reach the station, the staff could radio for help. Danielle had gone to mountain climbing school during the summer—now she'd have to use everything she'd learned to save herself and her family. Jake was the inventor in the family. It would be up to him to improvise the tools they'd need to get to the top of the mountain.

Will a few weeks of mountain climbing training and the ability to make something out of nothing be enough to save four lives?

The Gathering by Isobelle Carmody. 1994, Dial, $15.99, 0-8037-1716-4. [Reviewed in November/December 1994.]

Some people carry evil in them; some places seem to draw it to them, snaring both innocents and evil-doers. As soon as I saw Cheshunt, I felt its evil atmosphere reach out and touch me like a cold wind on the back of my neck. Looking at the place where I'd be going to school, it seemed like I was looking at something wrong and unnatural, something dead, contorted into grotesque shapes that defied definition, something bad that might get up and come after me. I hadn't wanted to move here, but Mother had insisted.

The townspeople didn't seem to welcome us. They acted as though they were afraid, always looking back to see if they were being followed. After two weeks, my only friend was the one we'd brought with us, my dog The Tod. He's part Chihuahua and looks like a tiny fox. He was with me the night all the strangeness started. I'd taken him for a walk, and we'd ended up at the school. The Tod vanished when I let him off the leash, and I was going after him when I saw two figures emerge from the storm drain near the science building. I recognized Bear Mahoney and Danny Odin. They weren't pleased to see me, and didn't believe my story about walking the dog, but they took me to meet the others—Nissa and Lallie. I'd noticed Nissa in the library a few days before. She was just as hostile as the other two had been, but Lallie said, "He chose to answer the Call. He is the fifth and last of the Chosen." With those words, it began, the strangest and most terrifying time in my life.

Evil was loose in Cheshunt, and the five of us had been chosen to bind the darkness and keep the evil chained. The evil forces that opposed us were very strong, and there was no way we could escape being damaged by them. Would we be able to withstand them and keep the chain strong?

Finishing Becca: A Story about Peggy Shippen and Benedict Arnold by Ann Rinaldi. 1994, Harcourt, $10.95, 0-15-200879-9.

A servant can learn a lot listening at doors, especially doors in a household with as many secrets as the Shippen household. I learned more than I ever thought I would, and that knowledge was the end of my life as a maid. Even now, I can hear Peggy Shippen's voice echoing in my head—"You've finished yourself now, Becca, haven't you?"

You see, that was the reason I went to that household in the first place. It was 1778, and we were at war with England. My stepfather was a bumbling dolt, and no farmer at all. There was hardly any money for food, and no way for me to get the proper kind of finishing education required of girls wanting to take their place in society. My mother arranged for me to be Peggy Shippen's personal maid, in exchange for lessons in French and needlework and painting. Mother said that pieces of me were missing, and that the lessons I would learn in that house would help me find them. She didn't know how right she was—the lessons I learned from that family did help me finish myself.

The first lesson I learned was to keep quiet about what I thought and what I heard, especially if Peggy was around or if Captain John Andre, the handsome British officer, was with her. Peggy was beautiful and determined to have her own way at any cost. She didn't care that her father was spending his fortune buying her clothes and entertaining the British officers. She didn't care that the colonial soldiers were dying of cold and starvation while she was demanding the most luxurious meals possible.

Peggy taught me that money can't buy everything, but it was my habit of listening at doors that caused me to leave Peggy Shippen and the man she married, Benedict Arnold. By that time, I knew much more about myself, my mistress, and the war our country was fighting than I had the day I came to work as her maid.

By that time, I was "finished," and, although Peggy didn't know it then, so was she.

Poison by Alane Ferguson. 1994, $16.95, Bradbury, 0-02-734528-9.

What would you do if you could eavesdrop on all kinds of conversations, and no one would ever know. You'd want to try it, wouldn't you? Just for fun? For me, it wasn't fun, not fun at all. In fact, it turned out to be pretty dangerous.

It all started when my dad decided I had to be his receptionist for the summer. That meant no lying around the pool with my friends, no time off, no nothing. But that wasn't the only reason my summer was ruined. Dad had divorced Diane, my stepmother. She was teaching me so much, about standing up for myself and not letting people walk all over me, about clothes and makeup and being proud of how I looked—and now she was gone. Dad wouldn't talk to me about it, and he wouldn't let me talk to her.

When Dad caught me talking to my best friend, Amber, while I was at work, he demoted me to the basement, to the communications room. Once I found out about the "goat," the gadget that would let me listen to any of the conversations in the building, I decided the demotion wouldn't be so bad. It might even be fun!

Nola, my father's secretary, says that the whole building is buzzing about what happened between my father and Diane. Maybe if I listened in, I could find out what really happened. Instead, Amber and I heard a conversation that wasn't just gossip. Two men were fighting over something that the younger man had left in Dover Cave. The older man was afraid that someone else would find it and spoil all their plans, plans that were worth millions of dollars. The phone rang before we could hear the rest of the conversation, and Amber unclipped the goat from the line before I could stop her. We didn't have any way of finding that line again.

The only clue we had was that something was hidden in Dover Cave. Amber didn't want to go, but I persuaded her that I needed a lookout while I went into the cave. When I found what they'd been talking about, I knew we were in big, big trouble. In the cave, in the very back, covered up with an old blanket, was Diane's body. My Dad had divorced her, but someone else had wanted her dead!

Notes

How can you get more of the highly recommended reading materials in your Media Center to circulate more? What about all those new books you purchased at last spring's reading convention? And those wonderful favorites of years past? This is a concern of every media specialist who harbors (surrogate) parenting pains when a special one sits on the shelf week after week—unappreciated, unused.

There are many ways to motivate our readers. This issue offers just such a sampling. The contests, the games, the booktalks and the author visits are but a few. This particular program can be adapted for any grade level and for any collection. It can be as multilayered as desired and definitely involves the classroom teacher. Additionally, it is a yearly event with a product outcome that remains in the media center for all students in the school to use.

TITLE OF PROGRAM: Raving Reviews!!!

DESCRIPTION:
Students become involved in reading, reviewing, illustrating, data entering and producing a yearly "book of books." It is an opportunity to direct the choices of the children by preparing a cart of the award-winning, highly recommended, old-time favorite novels that are often overlooked for the fluff and horror genre so popular with the students.

LEVEL: K-12

STUDENT WILL:
1. Read for comprehension.
2. Summarize story/novel in clear, concise language.
3. Critique story by evaluating it from a personal point of view.
4. Embellish appraisal of story by illustrating through drawings or creative writing.
5. Develop a sense of ownership and pride as Raving Reviews!!! is published and on display in School Media Center, local public library, community medical and dentist offices, etc.

Hands on Handout

By Susan J. Miller

ACHIEVED SKILLS:
Information Skills

- Recognize variety of literature genre.
- Select novel/story through evaluation of cart/books, preferred genre and on-site appraisal.
- List all bibliographic information of novel/story.
- Investigate professional reviews by scanning *School Library Journal, Book Report, Library Talk,* etc.

World Studies
- Create awareness of multicultures in diversified novel/story settings.

Technology
- Use computer word processing to input individual reviews.

Life & Personal Management
- Utilize time wisely to complete written reviews and input computerized review.

Language Arts
- Read for comprehension.
- Conceptualize story for analysis.
- Appraise and critique as needed.

Arts
- Incorporate sketching in review process.

PREPARATION:
1. Select titles for a designated circulation cart. Be varied, but stay away from the fluff and other "pop" reading fad.
2. Make attractive display of past Raving Reviews!!! professional review materials and several titles from previous years.
3. Arrange for display sites around the community — medical offices, public library, etc.

RESOURCES:
1. *Books We Love Best: A Unique Guide to Children's Books*, San Francisco Bay Area Kids & Foghorn Press: San Francisco, 1992.
2. Any issues of: *The Book Report, School Library Journal, LIBRARY TALK,* etc.
3. Computers, word processors.
4. Drawing supplies.
5. Spiral binding machine.

Susan J. Miller is Director of Media Services, Comstock Park Public Schools, Comstock Park, MI.

Editor's Note: In response to reader requests, we have initiated a new department called Hands on Handout. Each month we will feature a one-page reproducible item that is designed for you to share with your school community. It might be a lesson plan, a worksheet or game, or an executive summary of an important library-related issue for your administrators or colleagues. Each carries permission for you to reproduce the material within the building in which you work.

Reading Motivation: Using *All* Resources Available

CHILDREN'S LITERATURE RESOURCES ON THE WEB

By Joyce Kasman Valenza

IT'S BEEN CALLED THE ACADEMY AWARDS of children's literature. At 9:00 AM on January 12, the highest honors in children's media were announced at the ALA conference in New Orleans. After the final announcement of such prestigious awards as the Newbery, Caldecott, and Coretta Scott King, publishers, journalists, librarians and other book people ran to the nearest phones and modems to transmit the news to the many who care about children's literature.

But by 10:00 AM central time, the information was available on the Web. So many of the folks around the world interested in children's literature simply watched the American Library Association Web page for the announcements and examined the scanned book covers and information on the winners. There they could also get printable lists of all the winners since 1922.

The Web has made children's literature and children's book authors more accessible. Favorite children's authors, once remote and lofty, are now easy to visit through their home pages. Children can read interviews and can correspond by e-mail. And now, before selecting the Newbery book they are going to read, students can read descriptions and peek at covers. Language arts resource materials for teachers, such as stories, author information, poetry, Mother Goose rhymes, and literature guides, also are available on the Web. But here's the problem: dedicated book folks aren't always dedicated Web folks.

David K. Brown, began his Children's Literature Web Guide (**www.acs.ucalgary.ca/~dkbrown/**) in 1994 as a way to lure book people onto the Web. At that point, he says, "The personality of the Internet was basically that of a white male American graduate student, but it was becoming increasingly obvious that parents and teachers were discovering it, and I wanted them to be able to discover that useful resources were available." What has grown out of Brown's efforts is perhaps the most comprehensive of the children's literature sites and a great Web starting point. Brown, the Director of the Doucette Library of Teaching Resources at the University of Calgary, has attempted to gather and categorize the growing number of quality Internet resources related to books for children and young adults, but his contribution is not limited to print. "Because the film industry has embraced the Web in a big way, and because I love movies and movie reviews, I also collect information about movies based on children's books," he says. The site also includes awards, discussion groups, booksellers and publishers, thematic lists, teaching ideas, reviews, author sites, and resources for parents, teachers, and storytellers.

When asked to recommend the best resources in children's literature, Brown replies, "It's hard for me to pick best resources. I tend to get enthusiastic about things that I've just used or found recently." But he mentions Hearst Corporation's "Books Every Child Should Read" feature at the HomeArts Web site (**homearts.com/depts/ relat/bookintr.htm**). "It's a fine ongoing feature in which authors, ranging from Fay Weldon to Captain Kangaroo, recommend children's books, and discuss books that were important to them as children," he says. Brown also considers a site created by author Carol Hurst (**www.carolhurst.com**) to be "probably the best single source of ideas for teachers." Hurst's collection of resources includes reviews of great children's books, ideas for using them in the classroom, and collections of books and activities around particular themes, along with articles and sections from her own books.

Brown's personal favorite sites are those set up by writers and illustrators. One of the most notable, says Brown, was created by author/illustrator Jan Brett (www.janbrett.com). "The materials she distributes online are examples of things that couldn't be done before the Internet, such as printable pictures and projects and letters to support many of her picture books. When kindergarten teachers see the printable color masks she has created for her Web site, I know that their next Parent's Day presentation has just been planned."

Authors are indeed jumping on the Web as a way to promote their work, reach a broader audience, and communicate with their readers. Author Dan Gutman recently posted an impressive and unusual site, which offers a peek at his rejection letters and advice on how to plan an author visit. Gutman feels those rejection letters show children that people continue after disappointments and that even experts can make poor judgments. A couple of his best works were quite successful after being rejected by one publisher. Gutman, like many authors of children's books, earns a large part of his income from visiting schools. He wanted people around the country to find him easily. "When I was a kid," says Gutman, "authors were remote, not like real people. Now I visit about 50 schools a year. Once children meet me, they read my books with a different perspective." Gutman, who has been writing popular sports fiction for only about four years, believes his Web page levels the playing field, putting him on equal footing with other authors. "This is my way of promoting my work, and it is also fun. I hear from old friends and from people around the world. Children from the

Recommended sources for lovers of children's literature

Aesop's Fables Online Exhibit
www.pacificnet.net/~johnr/aesop/

American Library Association QALSC Home Page: Awards and Notables www.ala.org/alsc/awards.html

Amazon.com Children's and Young Adult
www.amazon.com/childrens

Carol Hurst's Children's Literature Site
www.carolhurst.com

Children's Book Council
www.cbcbooks.org/

Children's Doorway to Diversity
www.si.umich.edu/~miglesia/diversity/index.html

Children's Literature: Authors and Illustrators Fairrosa Cyber Library
www.users.interport.net/~fairrosa/cl.authors.html

Children's Literature Home Page
www.parentsplace.com/readroom/childnew/index.html

Children's Literature Web Guide
www.acs.ucalgary.ca/~dkbrown/index.html

CyberSeuss
www.afn.org/~afn15301/drseuss.html

Dream House: Mother Goose, Nursery Rhymes and Children's Songs
pubweb.acns.nwu.edu/~pfa/dreamhouse/nursery/rhymes.html

Electronic Resources for Youth Services
www.ccn.cs.dal.ca/~aa331/childlit.html

Harper Collins Big Busy House
www.harperchildrens.com/index.htm

Internet Public Library: Youth Division
www.ipl.org/youth/

Internet Public Library: Ask the Author
www.ipl.org/youth/AskAuthor/

Jan Brett's Home Page
www.janbrett.com

Kidlit (a magazine mostly for kids)
mgfx.com/kidlit/

Penguin Books Teacher's Guides

Puffin (Who's Who)

Readers' Theatre
www.aaronshep.com/rt/

Roald Dahl Index

SCORE Cyberguides
www.sdcoe.k12.ca.us/score/cyberguide.html

SimonSays (Simon and Schuster) Authors and Illustrators
www.simonsays.com/kidzone/auth/auth_index.html

Story Resources on the Web
www.swarthmore.edu/~sjohnson/stories/

Tales of Wonder
www.ece.ucdavis.edu/~darsie/tales.html

Top WWW Sites for Individual Children's Books, Authors, and Illustrators
www.underdown.org/topsites.htm

U.S. Department of Education Helping Your Child Learn to Read
www.ed.gov/pubs/parents/Reading/

Vandergrift's Children's Literature Page
www.scils.rutgers.edu/special/kay/childlit.html

Yahoo! Literature: Genres: Children's
www.yahoo.com/Arts/Humanities/Literature/Genres/Children_s/

YALSA: Young Adult Library Service Association—Booklists
www.ala.org/yalsa/booklists/index.html

Young Adult Links

schools I have visited submit book ideas because I promise that if a child offers a book idea that I use, I will dedicate the book to him," he explains. "It is great to get feedback from kids. How else are you going to know what kids like?" Gutman's favorite author pages are Virginia Hamilton's (**www.virginiahamilton.com/**), Bruce Balan's (**cyber.kdz.com/balan/cyberkdz.htm**), Eric Carle's (**www.eric-carle.com/**), and Jan Brett's (**www.janbrett.com**).

The Web also offers help for teachers interested in a more creative approach to introducing literature. One of the best examples is the San Diego County Office of Education's collection of SCORE Cyberguides, K-12 units of instruction based on core works of literature (**www.sdcoe.k12.ca.us/score/cyberguide.html**). These teacher-prepared literature guides for students supplement the study of good books with selected information from the Web. "Teachers will like the guides because they provide pre-selected sites for their students and specific tasks for them to complete," says Don Mayfield, one of the project's coordinators. Each cyberguide contains a student and teacher edition, statement of objectives, task and process by which to complete it, and rubrics and organizers to guide students and help them determine the quality of their products. Primary grade teachers might try the *Very Hungry Caterpillar* cyberGuide, based on the book by Eric Carle. The guide points to the Eric Carle Web site and asks students to find out about the author and create questions for Carle to answer. "Teachers who have used his Web site say that students consistently get responses within a week," says Mayfield. The cyberGuide for *The Crucible* by Arthur Miller asks students to take a virtual tour of Salem, visit the grave sites of the accused witches, read some of the testimony of the trial, and write a letter to the governor of the colony to explain why he should put a stop to the trials. In another activity, students research the McCarthy era and answer the question, "How did the political events of the 1950s influence the writing of *The Crucible*?"

David Brown admits there is a secret, subversive purpose to his own Web efforts. It's a purpose that I am sure many others involved in similar efforts would endorse. "If my cunning plan works, you will find yourself tempted away from the Internet, and back to the books themselves," says Brown. "Please remember that the Internet is not the most comprehensive source of information about children's books. Books and libraries cover the field far better than I can ever hope to. The Internet is a tremendous resource, but it will never compete with a children's librarian with a purposeful gleam in her eye."

Joyce Valenza is the Media Specialist at Wissahickon High School in Ambler, Pennsylvania, and is a winner of the 1997 Milken Family Foundation Educator Award.

Notes

Tips and Other Bright Ideas

MTV for Books

Students in our high school library class plan and put together booktalks on videotape to "sell" favorite books to their friends. The rules are simple: they cannot tell the story line, they cannot use the blurb on the book, and they must use good taste. Otherwise, they plan their talks, add music, and become the stars of their own videos filmed anywhere on the school grounds and using any props or other students they wish. The process of putting together an interesting "commercial" for the book usually inspires extra creativity and confidence, which makes the books more intriguing for their friends.—*Kathy McCurry, Fair Grove High School, Fair Grove, Missouri*

Training Students and Teachers

As school library media specialists, our responsibility is not just to our students. We also find ourselves offering inservice training to our fellow teachers, and sometimes even to the wider community. In addition, many of us, especially on the secondary level, not only enjoy the services of student volunteers but have turned their training into a for-credit course. As much as a refresher lesson on how to locate a Dewey Decimal number on the shelves or a presentation on Boolean searching in the electronic catalog, these activities constitute teaching information literacy skills.

Teachers can hardly be expected to incorporate technology, or even modern research methods, into their teaching repertoire if they are uncomfortable with the tools. And since library media specialists are generally the faculty members most familiar with the technology and programs, we are frequently called upon to design and teach workshops for our colleagues. Teaching teachers is not like teaching students. It's not even like teaching the general population of adults. These are people you may work with every day. You bring knowledge (and often opinions) about the content they teach, and their existing strategies; they bring preconceptions about you and about your machines, your software, and your new-fangled ideas about "collaboration" and "interdisciplinary units." There are faculty dynamics (as real as *family* dynamics) at work.

As in any class, most members are probably enthusiastic and curious. Others are indifferent-or openly hostile. Clear course descriptions and expectations, sensitivity to teachers' needs and starting points, practicality and relevance, and plenty of opportunity for hands-on practice go a long way toward ensuring a successful workshop. Even when time constraints and responsibilities preclude our taking on the actual teaching of the inservice course, we can be resource people, locating talented presenters and communicating to them the parameters of the workshop and the makeup of the class.

Many areas are fortunate enough to have a community college or other organization that arranges for adult education courses. Frequently, technology-related courses are held in local public or private schools that house large, well-equipped computer labs. The adults registering for the courses are often the parents of young people who attend those schools. Again, not every library media specialist can expend the time, planning, and effort required to teach these sessions. But when time and resources permit, such courses present wonderful opportunities for the library media specialist to practice public relations, familiarizing adults with the hardware and software their children come home talking about.

On the secondary level, I have often made use of student volunteers, who enthusiastically take charge of the circulation desk, shelve, keep collections in order, assist with displays, and even act as collection development liaison persons between me and their classmates. Through their training, these students gain a familiarity with the *reasons* for library procedures that their classmates generally never achieve.

In addition, my high school aides worked for me for a grade, determined by day-to-day observation and a final, comprehensive hands-on test.

One of my computer-teacher colleagues has a troop of students she can rely on to correctly shut down machines at the end of the day; they conscientiously leave notes regarding any problems they encounter and cannot fix themselves. And there are always a few youngsters at the middle school who declare themselves "on call" to figure out why a printer isn't printing, or to show a classmate (or, more commonly, a teacher) how to operate the scanner. (Barring a test, their teachers are usually quite amenable to letting these young people out of class. They've often been the recipients of help themselves, and know how important such services are.)

Students, especially on the secondary level, are often more willing to work with a peer than admit ignorance to a teacher. Well-trained student aides can be a useful extra set of hands when we find *our* hands full. When any or all of these activities can be organized, monitored, and developed into a progressive series of lessons, they can become a satisfying class for a motivated group of students.

Teaching information literacy skills is not confined to a curricular research project or limited to our school's classes and students. The opportunities are, literally, where we find them.

☐ URL UPDATES

Training Students as Technology Assistants:
  Daniel Elementary 2 home page
  http://www.kent.wednet.edu/KSD/DEtechnology/technology.html

TECHNOLOGY PLANS THAT WORK

feature

A Model for Teacher-Directed Technology Training

By Barbara Siegel

In September of 1992, the Hardy School (K-6) in Arlington, Massachusetts, armed with a three-year grant from the U.S. Department of Education, implemented a successful plan for integrating technology into the curriculum. This model, which can be readily adapted by other schools writing technology plans for staff development, includes three key components. Each year during a three-year period, one-third of the staff is trained on integrating technology into the curriculum. A new lead teacher is chosen annually to oversee this training, and each subsequent year, the trained teachers act as mentors for other teachers.

Teacher Selection
The teachers chosen for the first-year training should be those most interested in using technology who will commit to working with future trainees to share what they have learned. They should understand the hardware, software and training support they will receive as part of this pilot program.

Before instituting any plan, decide what resources will entice teachers to commit to the program. Schedule meetings on a regular basis for the entire staff where teachers in this pilot group will have an open forum to discuss

Before instituting any plan, decide what resources will entice teachers to commit to the program.

what's happening in their classrooms. When other teachers see the resources these teachers are acquiring, they will be stimulated to join the training program.

In the Hardy School model so many staff members became excited about the program that there were not enough openings to accept everyone who applied for formal training in the second year. This "bandwagon" effect allows the school to base selection of remaining teachers for the second and third years on desired grade distribution.

Lead Teacher Selection
A new lead teacher is chosen each year to oversee the training on using technology in the classroom. Since this individual is a member of the staff and does not evaluate the trainees, teachers feel comfortable working with one of their own colleagues and are more willing to accept help. Responsibilities of the lead teacher include selecting software and programs, modeling and co-teaching lessons, providing training and support, coordinating schedules for teacher planning, motivating the staff to use technology, and involving parents.

By having three different staff members assume a leadership role in this technology training and support, the school increases its own resources. After the "formal" period officially ends, the school has three strong leaders to spearhead future staff development.

Selecting Software and Programs
To have teachers integrate technology into their teaching, they must have access to and knowledge of appropriate programs. It is extremely important that the lead teacher work with the classroom teacher to assess curriculum needs in order to choose applicable programs. In this model, the lead teacher, after consultation with the classroom teacher, suggests programs at the suitable level that are

user friendly and meet the classroom teacher's curriculum goals. The lead teacher will assist the classroom teacher in integrating this software directly in the classroom. For example, one fifth-grade teacher at Hardy was instructing her class on the order of operations during a math lesson. The lead teacher suggested that she choose the software program *How the West Was One*, by Wings for Learning, as a resource for teaching this concept.

Modeling and Co-teaching Lessons

In this fifth-grade classroom, the lead teacher modeled *How the West Was One* with the entire class in a one-computer lesson. After connecting the computer to a large screen monitor, the lead teacher divided the students into small cooperative groups and assigned each individual in a group a role. Then she used the program with the whole class so the classroom teacher could see how effectively this program reinforced the concepts she was teaching. Later both teachers met and discussed the versatility of this software and how it could be set up in a classroom center.

In this process of training teachers to integrate technology into their teaching, the lead teacher generally begins by modeling lessons using the software. At the next stage, both the lead and classroom teachers plan units and co-teach them. Later the classroom teacher designs her own lessons with some consultation from the lead and other teachers. Eventually many classroom teachers are able to integrate much of the technology on their own and create their own lessons with minimal guidance from the lead teacher. Often trained teachers use this process as a mini-model for mentoring other staff.

Providing Training and Support

Teacher training can take place both on and off site. Throughout the school year, the lead teacher offers informal training sessions as well as scheduled workshops. Topics can range from learning how to use new programs in selected curriculum areas to explaining how word processing applications can be used for making revisions in process writing in a one-computer class lesson.

Teachers can go to workshops out of school and can observe teachers in other school systems using technology. The lead teacher takes responsibility for all arrangements and for providing substitute classroom coverage.

At the Hardy School, lead teachers were able to bring in outside trainers so the entire staff benefitted. Some of the subjects discussed were how to set up cooperative learning groups, how to use the one computer for the whole class, and how to effectively integrate simulation programs.

Coordinate Schedules for Teacher Planning

The Hardy School model realizes how important it is for teachers to spend time together to plan and communicate ideas. The lead teacher or her assistant teacher can cover classes for teachers so they can meet and discuss lessons encompassing technology. When much time is needed, substitutes can be hired to provide coverage. However, if budgets are limited, creative methods and flexible scheduling must be developed to allow teachers this planning time without hiring substitutes.

Motivating the Entire Staff

While officially only one-third of the staff is involved in technology training, the remaining staff cannot be isolated. The entire school community needs to take pride in what's happening in their school and to feel a part of it. At formal staff meetings all staff can brainstorm suggestions and work together. To make certain no one feels excluded, the lead teacher also goes into all classrooms and teaches mini-lessons using technology.

Involving Parents

Parents generally welcome the opportunity to help out in the classroom and are very supportive. Parents might work with small groups or individual students on programs. Some might type stories of pupils into a word processing program on the computer so that students will be able to revise them later. Others might free up a teacher so that she can work with other groups on technology. Of course, these parents must be trained by the lead teacher and a committee of other parent volunteers.

At Hardy, the school community was kept informed about the technology program. The principal sent home a bi-monthly newsletter which sometimes included articles

---

SOME ADVICE TO THE LEAD TEACHER

Find out each teacher's comfort level with technology.

Don't overwhelm anyone and respect entry levels. Praise goes a long way and gives people confidence to try new things.

Be flexible and willing to make changes.

Don't hesitate to change anything to improve upon it.

Encourage staff to collaborate.

Be a listener and a facilitator—let others share ideas.

Stay true to your role as a staff trainer in integrating technology.

Do not act as a fixer of equipment or a technician.

Use students as resources.

Communicate with the school community.

Make all aware of what's going on and be open about any problems.

A Model for Teacher-Directed Technology Training

from the lead teacher about how students were using technology in their classrooms. A local cable TV station filmed students describing and using technology.

Resources

Although the responsibilities of the lead teacher seem overwhelming, she has some powerful resources to help her meet her obligations. Her budget allows her to hire substitutes so that teachers can go to workshops, visit classrooms in other schools, and meet and plan with their fellow colleagues. The model also provides for an assistant teacher who can be used in numerous ways by the lead teacher.

Additionally, she also has some funds to purchase programs for individual teachers that fit into a special area of the curriculum. She should have discretionary use of these monies and carry the support of the administrator who appointed her.

At Hardy, the lead teachers were quite fortunate to have other powerful resources: the staff, the principal, and a technology consultant. Teachers were used to working

To have teachers integrate technology into their teaching, they must have access to and knowledge of appropriate programs. It is extremely important that the lead teacher work with the classroom teacher to assess curriculum needs in order to choose applicable programs.

with each other in a non-competitive environment and had developed a strong bond. The principal was also an ardent proponent of the staff development model and supported it in every way. The technology consultant (author of the grant) offered valuable guidance to everyone and brought vision to the project. Even if a school does not have all these resources, this model is an extremely effective one for staff training.

Mentoring Activities

Teachers who become first-year trainees make a commitment to work with other teachers. As their own self confidence grows, they begin to share more of their ideas with their fellow trainees as well as other staff. This first group begins to take on more leadership roles as the year progresses. Even before the end of the first year, many of these trained teachers are inviting others in to observe lessons they are doing. They begin to plan lessons with their grade-level colleagues. Eventually they work together on setting up units. For example, at the Hardy School, one teacher experienced in using technology planned a unit with her grade-level colleague on simple machines. In it they incorporated a CD-ROM program that explained how these machines worked.

The model also encourages teachers to use their students as resources in a variety of ways. They can work with one another within the class on technology. Students can participate in computer centers/stations and learn new programs to bring back to their own classrooms. Older students can mentor younger ones on computer activities which benefit both ages.

Finally, mentoring occurs among the three lead teachers who prepare each other for their new responsibilities. As the staff development evolves, so does the role of the lead teacher. She becomes more of a liaison for mentoring activities, and a coordinator of schedules so that teachers can communicate. By the end of the third year, training has become a collaborative responsibility shared by all.

Success Beyond

The Hardy School model has advantages beyond its official three-year training program. It establishes roots for an infrastructure of ongoing staff training through its mentoring activities. Since it is staff directed, it is more likely that the teachers will continue to take responsibility for their own professional development. **TC**

Barbara Siegel is a teacher at Hardy School, Arlington, Massachusetts. This grant was received under Barbara Fischer Long, principal of the Hardy School. It was written by Harvey Pressman, a technology consultant.

Notes

TECHNOTRAINING

From Entry Level to Proficient & Exemplary

A Design for Staff Technology Development

By Sara Dexter

National technology standards for teacher education are the framework for staff training in one school district.

At my school, the guidelines and goals for staff development we follow are the National Council for Accreditation of Teacher Education (NCATE) technology standards developed by the International Society for Technology in Education. NCATE recommends that every teacher be trained in technology, regardless of his or her content area or grade level.

Our district uses these NCATE standards as a framework to organize both our staff development classes and our discussions with teachers about integrating technology into their teaching methods and content areas. We have arranged the NCATE standards into a continuum reflecting our belief that learners must first connect what they are learning to what they already know and do.

Entry Level

Entry-level classes focus on learning the skills inherent in the software programs our district has adopted. Offered primarily in two-hour time blocks after school, these classes emphasize personal productivity rather than curricular applications. Held at a district office training lab and in the media centers of school buildings, they include Introduction to *Microsoft Word*, Additional Features of *Microsoft Word*, Introduction to *HyperStudio*, Digitizing and Using Video on AV Computers, Introduction to *PowerPoint,* and Introduction to *Excel*.

Progressive Level

Progressive-level classes focus on applying the capabilities of technology in the classroom. These two-hour classes are offered in three or four sessions through the district office training lab. They are usually held after school unless money for substitutes is available—in this case, a day-long class is offered. I team teach the classes with one of the district's curriculum area specialists. The progressive-level classes differ from the entry-level classes in that they provide ideas for and examples of projects using technology that directly correlate to the curriculum. Also, these classes provide materials for teaching students the software or hardware and include sample assignments and assessment tools.

Recent progressive-level classes include Supporting the Grade 4-6 Science Curriculum with Spreadsheets and Graphing, Student Presentations with the Standard Software, Technology Integrated into the District's Research Process, and Bilingual *HyperStudio* Projects for World Language Teachers.

Proficient Level

Proficient-level classes also focus on applying the capabilities of technology in the classroom but place more emphasis on higher-level thinking skills, grouping strategies and more complex applications. Working together to solve problems, manage information and make decisions is the goal of proficient-level classes. These classes are also offered through the district office training lab, either after school in series or in one session during the day. They are team taught and explore the philosophy of and theory behind classroom technology goals. Teachers might examine our district's thinking skills framework or alternate instructional strategies as part of these technology integration classes. These classes also provide materials to teachers for teaching students to use the software, as well as sample assignments and assessment tools.

> Our district uses these NCATE standards as a framework to organize both our staff development classes and our discussions with teachers about integrating technology into their teaching methods and content areas.

An example of a class offered at the proficient level is Databases in the Elementary Social Studies Curriculum, which illustrates how using a database can extend students' thinking about causal relationships and correlations. It also provides teachers a ready opportunity to directly teach students how to hypothesize, make inferences and develop other higher-level thinking skills.

DEXTER—

Exemplary Level

Exemplary-level staff development focuses on applying the capabilities of technology to transform the classroom through a research-and-development approach to integrating technology into teaching and learning. The goal is to push the instructional process toward "emerging views of the teacher and the learner" as described by NCATE, which each year funds some experimental projects that have these goals. Teachers at this level conduct investigations and, as technology trainer, I offer support for these investigations.

Recent teacher investigations include the following: piloting the use of a multimedia authoring program and overhead presentation panel to encourage more student research; providing Internet access for research and fostering Web publishing for high school social studies students; and investigating how laptop word processors can enhance the writing process for fifth- and seventh-grade students. **TC**

Sara Dexter is a Technology Trainer for Osseo Area Schools in Maple Grove, Minnesota.

Notes

NCATE STANDARDS DEVELOPED BY THE INTERNATIONAL SOCIETY FOR TECHNOLOGY IN EDUCATION

Entry-Level Skills
- Operate a computer system to use software successfully.
- Explore, evaluate, and use computer technology-based materials.
- Demonstrate knowledge of equity, ethical, legal, and human issues of computing and technology.
- Use computer-based technologies to access information to enhance personal and professional productivity. (For example: reference CD-ROMs, database, telecommunications.)
- Demonstrate skill in using productivity tools for professional and personal use. (For example: word processing, presentation software, multimedia authoring, spreadsheet, graphic utilities.)

Progressive-Level Skills
- Evaluate and use computers and related technologies to support the instructional process.
- Apply current instructional principles, research, and appropriate assessment practices to the use of computers and related technologies.
- Evaluate, select, and integrate computer technology-based instruction in the curriculum of one's subject area and grade level.

Proficient-Level Skills
- Demonstrate knowledge of uses of computers for problem solving, data collection, information management, communications, presentations, and decision making.
- Design and develop student learning activities that integrate computing and technology for a variety of student grouping strategies and for diverse student populations.
- Demonstrate knowledge of multimedia, hypermedia, and telecommunications activities to support instruction.

Exemplary-Level Skills
- Apply computer and related technologies to facilitate the emerging roles of the learner and the educator.
- Identify resources for staying current in applications of computing and related technologies in education.

TECHNOTRAINING

Singing the Praises of On-site Training

By Sandy Pope

Tailor-made training beats "one size fits all" every time.

During the past month, have you: Rescheduled a training session for the third time? Tried unsuccessfully to contact the vendor who installed your latest hardware or software? Searched for the elusive power switch on the network file server's UPS? Been asked by an administrator for a technology plan update?

If so, you must be the building or district media specialist/technology trainer/unofficial troubleshooter/tech coordinator! And chances are if you had to rank your most important task, training staff would be at the top of your list. In most schools, staff are at three different skill levels based on their personal computing experience, access to equipment, and acceptance of technology. Some are in the basic informational stage, others are ready to integrate technology and need practical help to do so, and still others are confident enough to try totally new methods.

Find Out What Teachers Want

Experience has taught me that the first step in designing or updating a relevant training program is to survey teachers about their current interests and needs. Also ask them to honestly evaluate the content and relevance of previous inservice offerings and the ongoing technical support they receive. We conduct an annual survey to find out what needs to be improved, what needs to be added, and what needs to be deleted from the training and support we offer teachers.

We've found that on-site training and support offer great advantages over "one-size-fits-all" seminars. It lends itself to the hands-on approach with demonstrations followed by guided practice. Another plus to keeping our teacher training in-house is that we *can* be flexible about rescheduling a session for the second, third, or even fourth time. We can also respond quickly to teachers' interest in learning to use new hardware and software. For example, if a PC-to-TV converter is purchased at the request of teachers having only one computer in their classrooms, they already understand the potential of that equipment. However, the actual connections and operation will remain a mystery until training (and color-coded dots) are provided. Plan the sessions to include examples of equipment and application use. Encourage practice during the sessions.

Provide Training That Meets a Variety of Needs

Teachers should be trained to use new equipment and software for their own personal or professional use as well as for instructional use in the classroom. Research shows that teachers want training in such applications as word processing, creating spreadsheets, and using grade book managers as well as in using computers to enrich, extend, or provide remedial help in their subject areas.

To make sure they've grasped the material, make sure your training sessions provide plenty of practice time. Those learning these applications skills in training workshops should complete a document using those skills. It's essential that teachers leave the final training session with a usable project. Similarly, they must find practical ways to integrate technology into their students' learning.

Offer Ongoing Support

You can support and extend what teachers learn in training by offering refresher courses or open lab time after school for them to work on their own individual applica-

> Teachers should be trained to use new equipment and software for their own personal or professional use as well as for instructional use in the classroom.

Notes

tions or on classroom projects. You may also want to offer follow-up by department or by grade level.

It's essential that teachers leave the final training session with a usable project.

Often, a teacher will request technology training or support for a specific classroom topic or thematic unit. News of a successful experience travels quickly, and other teachers will want to replicate their colleague's success. For this reason, one-on-one tutoring and lesson development is a good investment of your time. You would also be wise to schedule one-on-one sessions with building administrators who are often too busy to attend any or all sessions of training workshops.

Whether you are the official technology trainer or the unofficial "techie" at your school, you are undoubtedly aware of the advances other districts are making. If progress is slow at your site, it's easy to become impatient. Remember, unless there's a good reason to embrace it, most people avoid change. That's why one of your tasks—perhaps the most important one—is to continually show teachers the practical benefits of technology. **TC**

IS A WORKSHOP NECESSARY?

Have teachers asked for one?

Have you acquired new hardware or software?

Has your administrator requested one?

Have new teachers joined the staff?

Sandy Pope is the Coordinator of computer-assisted reading instruction at South Elementary School, Eldon, Missouri.

HANDS ON
Technology In-Service That Works

By Linda Skeele

Teacher surveys consistently rank additional training as a high priority. Yet the word "in-service" invariably brings pained expressions followed by tales of wasted time spent listening to someone lacking current classroom experience.

We kept these legitimate complaints about in-service in mind as we set out to train our entire faculty to fully utilize our new school's cornucopia of resources. In the span of two years, we changed from traditional classrooms and one computer, to non-graded primary classes with four to eight computers per room. Teachers who had previously shared one VCR now had access to distributed video, where a monitor and remote brought all forms of video and data into the classroom. Electronic encyclopedias and atlases, laser discs, CD-ROMs, modems, still video and CDI-TV are among the new technologies teachers had to learn in the nine days of in-service allocated to us last year.

Our faculty decided to take all our in-services together, as a school, so that every teacher and staff member had the same training. That way, we would all have a common base of instruction with which to help each other.

Prior to last June, all of my computer experience was on DOS-based machines, and I had to learn to use Macintosh machines in order to help our teachers. In one day, Mrs. Gano, the high school computer teacher, gave me a crash course on Mac basics. She also taught me how to use *ClarisWorks*, *SuperPrint*, *The Writing Center*, and *Bank Street Writer*. Afterwards, I took home all the manuals and an LCII; I spent the summer immersed in self-instruction. By late July, I was competent enough to assist the teacher at our first two-day in-service held in the high school Mac lab.

This first class covered Macintosh basics and three of the programs that we would have on our networked computers. Competency levels ranged from very low to quite high, although no one had worked extensively with the machines that would later be delivered to the new school.

For the in-services, Mrs. Gano condensed programs to the absolute minimums. Every thick manual became a few pages of basic information that went into looseleaf notebooks she provided to all staff members. Her condensed instructions are so clear that most of us never refer to the publishers' manuals. We keep Mrs. Gano's reference notebooks next to our teacher work stations and add information as needed.

This first in-service set the pattern for all our computer training: Mrs. Gano teaching, and each faculty and staff member (principal, secretaries, aides and cafeteria managers, as well

Notes

Notes

as classroom teachers) at a computer. Two or three of us whom Mrs. Gano had trained earlier moved about the room to help others. Participants were told to bring ideas and projects with them, and these became the basis for some of the practice sessions.

Our second in-service consisted of a full day spent learning about three different technologies. Southwestern Communications provided their professional trainer to teach our faculty the distributed video system. Again, our technology coordinator and I had been trained earlier, so we could help others. For an hour, teachers learned what the system is and how it functions. Then we divided them into four smaller groups and rotated them through the four different types of video on the system. Each group of five persons had 15 minutes with each type of media. During that time, they practiced starting, stopping and moving around each program. There was one experienced person at each station to help those who needed it.

After lunch, we split in half for two additional technologies. Lois Sanders, our Technology Coordinator, demonstrated loading and using the CD-ROM while I gave a ten-minute course in the Canon ZAP Shot Camera. Then we put the teachers on the equipment and had them practice for the rest of the time. The teachers carried the camera out into the building and took shots of their friends. During the last few minutes, we played back all their shots for the entire faculty. Some were good, some were awful and a lot were funny. The hands-on training was extremely effective. Within a week, the Chapter 1 Reading Teacher was doing a complicated project with the ZAP Shot, and requests to use the ZAP Shot cameras have continued to pour in.

Our first two in-services were excellent, but the third, held in late September, was outstanding. Every faculty member received a brand-new Macintosh Duo-Dock (a standard computer that has a portable PowerBook component) as a teacher work station. The first thing we did was show the teachers how to put a computer together and load software.

All twenty computers in their packing boxes were delivered into a large room. There, under Mrs. Gano's instruction, teachers opened boxes, attached keyboards, mice, power cords and PowerBooks, turned the computers on for the first time, filled out the warranty forms and began to load the four software programs that go on every machine in our school. At the end of the day, there were packing boxes all over the hall and only one lost cable. Yes, some of the software had to be re-installed, but teachers lost most of their fears about taking the computers apart. Now, nearly every teacher can take apart and reassemble his or her computer without resorting to manuals.

Still to come are sessions on how to use the modem on the computer network to access KETNET and INTERNET; advanced techniques for using the distributed video system; and a session on new CD-ROM and laser disc programs in science.

Like the previous sessions, they will follow our proven formula for a successful in-service:

1. Give the faculty a say in the type of in-service offered.

2. Reduce all instructions and manuals to a couple of pages of the most basic information.

3. Keep lectures and oral instruction to the absolute minimum.

4. Have a trained assistant as a resource for every eight to ten "students." These assistants can target teachers who need extra help and answer most questions. This way, overall instruction does not have to stop for every inquiry. Assistants do not have to be highly proficient.

5. Put participants on the equipment and let them learn as they go. Emphasize that no mistake is fatal to the equipment.

6. Make practice exercises useful. Teachers want to be able to walk into their classrooms the next day and implement what they learned.

7. Keep the pace fast enough so that the most able are not bored. Assistants can bring the less proficient along without holding up the rest.

8. Keep the atmosphere informal and relaxed. Most schools have to schedule in-services at the end of the school day when most teachers would prefer to be elsewhere. Our principal always provides drinks and a snack, which teachers greatly appreciate.

9. Provide a questionnaire for teachers to objectively evaluate each session.

10. Insert a little humor. Better yet, insert a lot of humor.

And remember, no amount of lecturing—no matter how well meaning and inspired—will ever convince teachers to use technology. They have to experience it for themselves. "Hands-on", practical in-services are the only way to go.TC

Linda Skeele is a Media Specialist at Western Elementary School in Georgetown, Kentucky.

Notes

TECHNOTRAINING

Tried and True Tips for Technology Training

by Mary Alice Anderson

Last summer our school district sponsored a three-day technology academy called "Celebrating Success with Technology." It focused on topics and technologies that teachers could immediately

> Highest registrations were for "Introduction to the Internet" and "Exploring Internet Curriculum Resources." Four *ClarisWorks* classes and two sections each of *KidPix* and *Storybook Weaver* were filled to capacity.

implement. Taught by teachers in our district, it consisted of a one-day overview of our district's technology plan, our community network, and our new technologies, followed by three-hour training sessions on consecutive days.

Since no central location was equipped with enough computer labs for our faculty, classes were taught at three different schools and at a lab at Winona State University. We provided snacks but not lunches and managed to keep the cost to $4,000, paid for by district staff development funds. Half the cost was for instructors' time; another expense was having our brochures professionally printed. This cost was somewhat offset by the free continental breakfast provided by our Apple Computer representative, who had agreed to do a show-and-tell software session. Another freebie was the software contributed by a local citizen that we used for door prizes.

The deadline for registration for this August event was June 8th, the last day of school. All classes filled immediately! About 120 individuals out of a teaching and support staff of 400 attended. Support staff, central office staff and substitutes from all levels were well represented.

Over the summer, we worked on final plans for the academy—our efforts paid off. The signs, banners and balloons we made or ordered contributed to the festive atmosphere of the event. Each of the 100 people who attended the overview session received a complimentary copy of TECHNOLOGY CONNECTION, an Apple pen, and a chance to register for door prizes of Apple gift items and gift certificates to a local computer store. Everyone who registered for a class received a mouse pad.

I was afraid the two-and-half hour opening session was too long, but teachers appeared genuinely interested in seeing software demonstrations and they asked good questions. Our afternoon sessions included a CD-ROM preview party and information about Luminet, Winona's community fiber optic network. They, too, were well attended.

The heart of the academy were the hands-on classes. Highest registrations were for "Introduction to the Internet" and "Exploring Internet Curriculum Resources." Four *ClarisWorks* classes and two sections each of *KidPix* and *Storybook Weaver* were filled to capacity. Another popular class was "Designing Lessons and Units that Integrate Technology." Other classes included "Finale" (music), "Grade Machine," "Working with

> **TIPS FOR A SMOOTH-RUNNING TECHNOLOGY ACADEMY**
> - Send preliminary confirmations to people as soon as they register and final confirmations a week before.
> - Use a computer at the on-site registration.
> - Provide an assistant for all instructors who work with more than 10 adult students.
> - Find instructors who have adult education experience.
> - Beforehand, query arts teachers and support staff to learn their special needs.
> - Offer some in-depth, day-long classes that allow people to apply what they've learned.
> - Offer classes that stress curriculum integration as well as classes that emphasize training in specific skills.

Final Budget *Celebrating Success with Technology* August 22-24, 1995		
Printing	$110.00	600 brochures
Gifts	$533.90	10 Apple mugs, 140 Apple pens, 2 Apple notepads
Mouse pads, Precision Line	$378.00	40 mouse pads, participant gifts
Snacks	$348.60	Warehouse Liq, pop; stk shp coffee/cookies (plus pd by Ed tech for cont breakfast)
Instructor salaries (estimate)	$2195.10	24 classes, 3 hours each + prep time & assistants
Secretarial time	$280.00	collect registration, mail confirmation letters
Balloons, banners	$18.80	
Postage & printing (estimate)	$74.00	done at bldgs or central office
Planning & setting up time (committee)	$160.00	
Disks	$155.20	
Supplies	$92.90	

Graphics," "Using Scanners," "Multimedia," "Coursebuilder," "Introduction to the Mac," *HyperStudio*, "Computerized IEPs" and "The Writing Center."

Our superintendent came to one of the Internet classes I taught to proudly deliver the URL for the district's new Web page and teach an Internet class. Several of the elementary principals attended multiple classes. Toward the end, I noticed that many people were understandably tired and overwhelmed. But all comments were positive and most people expressed interest in taking more classes. **IC**

Mary Alice Anderson is the Media Specialist at Winona (Minnesota) Middle School.

Notes

Byte-Sized Technology Sessions
Teachers Training Teachers

By Anita Booher and Michelle Taylor

Today's educators, administrators, and technology and curriculum specialists continually search for successful ways to train teachers in the new educational technologies. The lack of time and funding available poses a common problem in providing such training. In our high school and district the situation is no different.

When our school's staff returned to work in the fall of last year, the district network had been reconfigured, and there were new district-wide software applications. The district had moved from one "office suite" software package to another, to a different e-mail program, and to a new school management tool that incorporated a grading program and an electronic attendance system. In our building, we all struggled together to learn these applications. Those of us who took district-sponsored classes became unofficial mentors to other teachers. It was often necessary for us to answer our colleagues' questions a dozen times a day.

To curb the frequency and repetition of technical questions, we decided to offer two or three short after school training sessions to address the new school management system. We advertised that the sessions would focus on a very specific question or "how-to" point, and would last no more than 15-20 minutes. The training was conducted in the library so teachers could use computers and receive hands-on help. We provided each participant with a handout that reviewed the "how-to" topic step by step. Attendance was spotty, but teachers who did attend were glad to have the chance to have their questions answered and to share tips with colleagues. After receiving positive comments from the first group of attendees, we planned more sessions on additional topics. There was, after all, no lack of questions to be answered.

With the help of other technology committee members, we identified more than 12 frequently asked questions. The inquiries generally fell into four specific areas: basic computer use (e.g., mouse skills, keyboard commands, printer selection); the Internet (e.g., terminology, browser use, site recommendations); e-mail use (e.g., address books, enclosures, attachments); and word processing basics. After identifying these four areas, we approached the school's career ladder committee (which organizes a form of a merit pay plan) to request that training session attendance could count toward career ladder points. The committee agreed. We hoped the opportunity to earn career ladder points would provide incentive for more teachers to attend the sessions.

The series, announced as the "Byte-Sized Technology Sessions," included the after school mini-inservice training in the following four identified areas.

Basic computer skills:
Shortcuts-Keyboard Commands That Will Save You Time
Printing Choices-Using the Chooser
Find the Finder-What It Is and Does
Adam and Eve, or What You Should Know About the Bitten Apple (Apple menu)

Internet-related:
Playing with Favorites-How to Manage and Customize Your Bookmarks for Internet Sites
UR Terrific, But What's a URL?-Terminology and Some URLs to Explore for Fun
Helping Students Evaluate Web Sites
Fun Sites for Sending Electronic Greetings

E-mail-related:
Your Little Black Book-Setting Up Address Books for E-mail
All for One and One for All-How to E-Mail More Than One Person at a Time
Spread the News-How to E-mail Someone About a Terrific Web Site
How to Retrieve and Add Enclosures to Your E-Mail Messages

Word processing:
Jazz Up Your Handouts-Placing Graphics Into Your Word Processing Document
Slide Shows Without a Slide Projector—the Slide Show Feature
It's Tool Time-What It Can Do for You
The Stationery Feature-How to Use It and Save Time

Evaluations conducted after these sessions showed that the

Notes

majority of participants found the meetings helpful and would recommend them to colleagues. The attendees also requested that more sessions be offered. In response to these requests, we will soon embark on a new group of sessions. Training meetings will be held before school this time (6:45-7 a.m.), so teachers with extracurricular duties can attend. Because of restrictions within our career ladder plan, an alternative method was needed to compensate teachers for attending the morning sessions, which occur before contract hours. One of our administrators wrote and received a grant to provide money from staff development funds for this purpose.

The morning training will include repeats of all topics previously offered as well as new sessions that are geared toward information gathering via technology. Two new sessions will be "Surfing for Science" and "Hang-Ten for Health and P.E." Web sites related to these topics will be available. During the morning meetings, the use of specific online information sources also will be covered and a step-by-step process for approaching research will be presented. Our intent is to train the teachers so they can integrate these skills into their curriculums.

Our mini-training sessions have been successful because colleagues are teaching colleagues. These short doses of training on the school site are conveniently held within the workday, provide some compensatory incentive, and promote collegial camaraderie. Teachers say the sessions are beneficial because they give them the opportunity to have their specific questions and problems addressed. The educators also appreciate receiving practical and task-oriented information and handouts that assist them when practicing the skill at their convenience.

We already are considering conducting training sessions for new teachers when they arrive in the fall, and we are continuing to offer mini-sessions through next year to all staff members. These "byte-sized" training sessions have allowed our staff to move forward, beyond frustration, and to feel more confident and competent using the technology available to them. Furthermore, they have allowed the use of existing funding to be creatively applied to meeting teacher training needs. We realize that this training in no way replaces the need for systematic technology training at the district and school levels, but we have found the sessions to be a workable piece of the technology training puzzle.

Anita Booher is a Library Information Specialist, and Michelle Taylor is an Applied Technology Teacher at Park City (Utah) High School where they are co-chairs of the technology committee.

Notes

Stage a Well-Designed Saturday Session and They Will Come!

By Miguel Guhlin

Teachers may grumble about Saturday morning or after-school sessions, but they are so hungry for technology training they will come.

"What? Come on a Saturday? Are you out of your mind?" said one elementary teacher when I suggested that instructional technology-training sessions be held on Saturday mornings.

Several years ago that response would have discouraged me. But experience has taught me that although most teachers will claim that they will not attend technology training, the fact is, they will come on Saturdays and to after-school training sessions as well.

According to the United States Office of Technology Assessment, the role of the classroom teacher is critical to the full development and use of technology in schools. If teachers are not the focus of the technology training, then technology will fail. Happily, more teachers are recognizing the necessity of integrating technology into the curriculum.

Effective technology training begins with careful design of a staff development program. The following points must be considered in design and implementation.

1. Technology's potential is under-utilized. Over the years, various technologies have found their way into education. Most failed because administrators purchased them without involving teachers in the decision-making process or providing training in their use.

Although media specialists may write the proposal and technology plan, classroom teachers must be involved from the beginning because they will be the ones responsible for the actual integration. It is important to reassure them that extensive staff development will be provided.

2. Most teachers want to learn technology but lack time, access, and on-site support. In addressing this, it is wise to develop a campus technology plan that allows time for teachers to explore and learn to use a computer. Emphasize that while they may not become expert users, they will be able to use the computer and additional technology instructionally. Consider this staff development pattern:

a) Introduce ways to use technology for specific instructional tasks. Provide lots of hands-on time.

b) Provide individual follow-up modelling in the classroom.

c) Allow time for whole-class follow-up and sharing.

Training necessarily must take place before or after school, during the school day, and during the summer or on weekends. However, if a computer or the technology is not available in the classroom, teachers are seriously hobbled.

Research suggests that a classroom with one to four computers is a comfortable setting for teachers to begin using technology. Both students and teachers are more likely to use it when they need to, not when the computer lab is ready for them. Therefore, effective technology plans must allow teachers to earn hours towards obtaining computers for the classroom, and for weekend and summer use. This is a powerful incentive. Other incentives include providing copies of the software and manual that teachers are trained on, instituting educator computer purchase programs and providing summer and weekend loan programs.

On-site support is critical. Unfortunately, many technology coordinators are overburdened with classrooms and instructional technology duties. Site administrators must decide how to balance their load. Often, providing an extra planning period specifically for technology training works well. Coordinators can log their activities during that time and share them with the site administrator.

3. Lesson plans, related materials and curriculum guides must have clear and relevant objectives.

While hands-on training addresses a fundamental need to integrate technology, it has to be woven into the curriculum. In the beginning, teachers often take existing lesson plans and add technology. This approach works with some success, and it is a necessary developmental step for teachers. However, integrating technology will not be effective until it is used to do things that previously could not be accomplished without it.

Integrating technology involves redesigning lesson plans, a problem for the few teachers who use lesson plans from year to year without adjusting them to particular class needs. For the most part, however, teachers do change how they teach because they are genuinely concerned about their students' learning. The questions these teachers ask are: "How do we work technology into our already packed curriculum?" and "What do we do with the students once we start?"

The answer to the first question is not an easy one. Curriculum change is driven by what students need to know. In the past, math curriculums were driven by arithmetic and computation. Now, they are beginning to incorporate arithmetic and computation within the grander scope of creative problem-solving, decision-making strategies and cooperative learning. Technology is best suited to curriculum that involves discovery learning, developing higher-order thinking skills, and the comprehension and communication of ideas and information. If curriculum focuses only on lower-order thinking skills (basic skills) as a prerequisite to higher-order thinking skills (metacognition, problem solving and decision making), the computer will remain a drill-and-practice tutor.

The answer to the second question is much easier. After higher-order thinking skills are addressed, technology can become a tool for comprehending and communicating, serving both students and teachers. Nevertheless, writing lesson plans can be a difficult process. Developing databases that address these needs and assist in the development of lesson plans that incorporate technology is useful, but the job of integrating will fall on the classroom teacher and the curriculum writers.

As stated early in this article, the keys to integrating technology are the classroom teachers. Supporting them must be the first step in any technology training program. To quote the voice in the movie *Field of Dreams*, "Build it and they will come." Build a technology teacher training program addressing teachers' issues and they will come—after school, on weekends, during the summer, and in their free time.

REFERENCES

Finkel, L. (1990). Moving your district toward technology. The School Administrator Special Issue: Computer Technology Report, pp.35-38.

Office of Technology Assessment Report. Power On! New tools for teaching and learning. U.S. Government Printing Office, Washington, D.C. Stock #052-003-01125-5.

Snyder, T. (January, 1995). Technology is cool, teachers are cooler. Teaching with Technology NewsFlash; #33.

Solomon, G. (October, 1990). Share the Spirit: 15 Ways to generate excitement and support for classroom technology. Instructor.

Miguel Guhlin is District Instructional Technology Specialist for the Mt. Pleasant (Texas) Independent School District.

Boolean Burritos
How the faculty ate up keyword searching

Only have a few minutes for staff development?
This early-morning faculty meeting provided enough time for a memorable lesson.

By Sherry York

The online catalog had been up and running in the library for more than two years. The old, maple card catalog was gone. Most of the high school teachers had received orientation on using the new electronic catalog, and some teachers had even used it. However, very few teachers and students were using the online catalog to its full potential.

My goal was to introduce keyword searching to the teachers. My window of opportunity was the weekly, 30-minute, early-morning faculty meeting. I wanted to teach a lesson in a fun way, with audience participation rather than simply lecture while the teachers sat passively, looking attentive but mentally going over their plans for the day. As anyone who has ever presented to an audience of teachers knows, they are a tough crowd!

My limitations included lack of sufficient time to do an in-depth, hands-on program and the early morning time frame in which teachers groggily clutched gallon-sized cups of coffee as they trudged up the stairs to the library. On the plus side, I had a supportive principal who not only allowed but encouraged me to do short, library-related staff development programs. The group was fairly small but receptive and eager to learn.

Because I am a strong believer in the Big6™ process of problem solving, I applied it to this situation. I had already defined my task (Big6™, step 1). I spent some time leafing through my files of "really good stuff" culled from journals, printouts of ideas from the Internet, listservs and the like. At this point I had sought, located and accessed

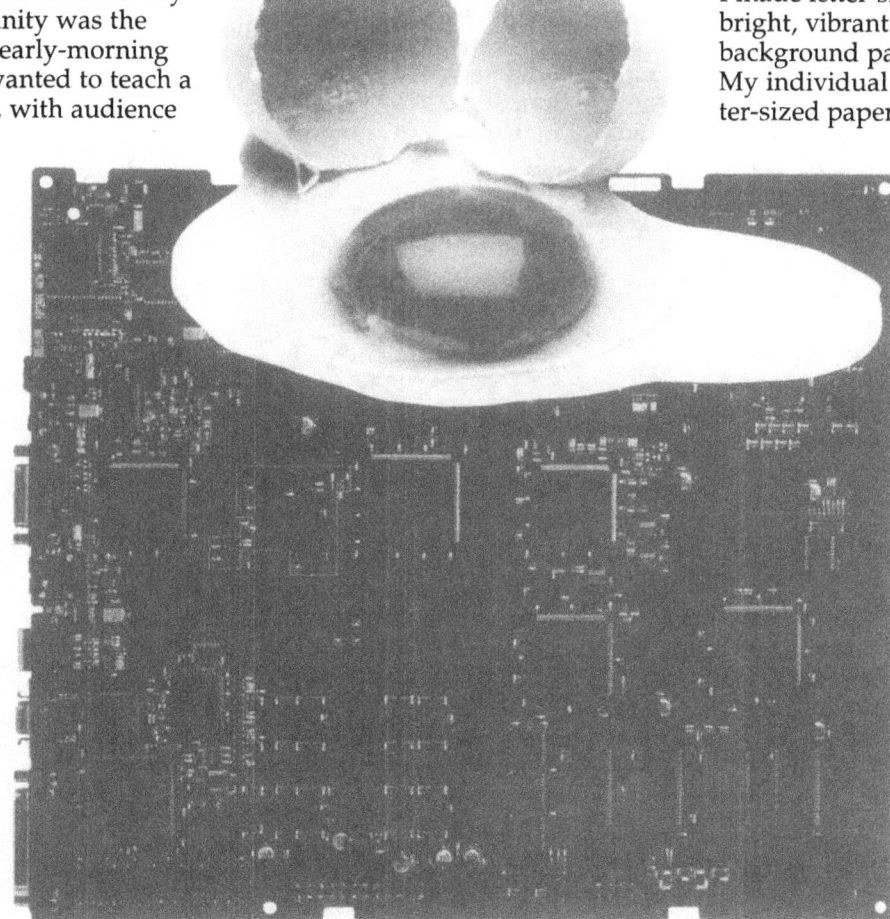

information (Big6™, steps 2 and 3).

I remembered, fortuitously, that some clever person either on the Big6™ listserv or in a Big6™ newsletter related an activity using ham and eggs to illustrate keyword searching. Food is something that gets my attention, but here in the Southwest burritos are more common than ham and eggs.

Boolean burritos, I thought. Yes! (For readers unlucky enough not to know the pleasure of authentic breakfast burritos, you have my sympathy.) Now I was ready to use my information to get this program together (Big6™, step 4).

Yes, Boolean burritos it would be. I began by making some props. I made letter-sized cards using very bright, vibrant colors for both the background paper and the letters. My individual ingredient cards (letter-sized paper) included one each for egg, ham, bacon, potato, beans, and salsa. Then I made two identical sets of operator cards. Each set of operator cards had the words "and, or, not" on a separate card. Now I was ready. I had synthesized information by organizing it 7to create a performance (Big6™, step 5).

At the meeting, I spoke briefly about the online catalog and its potential to help students (and teachers) locate precisely those books,

videos, posters, picture files, and vertical files that they needed for reports and projects. I talked about George Boole, the English mathematician who helped develop modern symbolic logic. I pointed out that Boole's logic was used in algebra, reasoning and computers.

Then I quickly distributed the six ingredient cards to teachers by handing one to each table of teachers and asking them select a "holder." I assured them that holders didn't have to speak or act. All they had to do was stand up, come forward and hold up the card at the proper time.

Next, I gave out the operator cards. Operators, I explained, had to be able to do more than simply hold a card. They had to be critical thinkers who could choose the appropriate Boolean operator when it was called for. After two "best" teachers were selected to handle the operator cards, we were ready to start ordering. We were ready to make Boolean burritos.

I called on teachers at random to make an order. When the ingredients were called for, the two ingredient card holders were to step forward. Then the operator would move between the two and display the appropriate operator. We had an order for one ham and egg burrito. That was easy. Then someone wanted bacon and egg. Easy. Ham sat down and bacon stood up. The same operator was still being used.

Then someone wanted bacon and egg with salsa. Now salsa stood up and joined bacon and egg. A second operator was required for this combination. Now we had five people standing.

Then the vegetarian librarian asked for a burrito with beans only. How many operators were needed for that? None. Beans stood alone.

Then we got into more complicated orders. How about one for an easy-to-please customer, egg and bacon or ham? Egg, bacon, ham, and two operators stood up. Did it make a difference where the operators were placed? Could a bacon and ham burrito be the result if the operator was misplaced?

What about a burrito for the greedy person who wants a deluxe: egg, bacon, potato, and salsa. How many ingredients? Four. How many operators? Three. While three operators and four ingredients might be fine for a burrito, our online catalog has spaces only for two operators and three ingredients (terms).

When would we use the operator "not"? The operator "not" didn't have much value in our orders, we decided. If we said, "Everyone will have bacon and egg and salsa unless they order otherwise," then individuals might order bacon and egg not salsa or egg and salsa not bacon.

> ny time you can make teachers laugh before eight in the morning, you've been successful.

How many different combinations could we make? Would they all be feasible? edible? useful? palatable? But our time was running out. We really had fun with the "ingredients" and "operators" moving back and forth. Everyone laughed a lot, and most important, they thought about keyword searching and Boolean logic. I would like to say that we stayed afterward and actually made burritos; instead, I thanked everyone for their participation, the bell rang and we headed toward our respective first period classes.

(During the next exam-schedule day, I did provide breakfast burritos (preassembled), orange juice and reinforcement in the teachers' lounge. The food was accompanied by a sign that read something like, "These Boolean Burritos are provided by the library with the compliments of the high school students who provided financial support by paying overdue fines during this term.")

Finally, what about evaluation, the last Big6™ step? The program turned out pretty darn well, if I do say so myself. Any time you can make teachers laugh before eight in the morning, you've been successful. If they learned keyword searching and Boolean logic at the same time, it must have been worthwhile.

Sherry York is Librarian at Ozona (Texas) High School.

TECHNOLOGICALLY SPEAKING

Don't Forget the Teachers: *Teaching Teachers to Search Electronically*

by Mary Alice Anderson

THE THEME OF THIS issue is "Teaching Research Skills Electronically." A first step in this process is teaching the students' teachers. Typically, teachers have not seen teaching electronic research skills as part of their job; they often assume that this is our role. Or, they assume the kids arrive in their classrooms already knowledgeable. The Internet and the exponential increase in the amount of information available are changing teachers' perceptions about what they want to know. As teachers realize what they need to learn, they realize their students are probably in the same situation.

So, how do we teach teachers? At Winona Middle School we rely on continuous staff development opportunities, which are a big focus of the media/technology program. We've offered a range of formal and informal staff development classes for over ten years. One of the most popular options has been an informal class called "exploration time" or "play time."

Teachers often say they'd like to have time "to just dig around and explore." This class begins with an overview of resources and searching strategies. Teachers are then free to work on their own. We hope they will find ways to integrate technology and resources into one of their curriculum units. It is interesting to observe how some teachers are just like the kids; they need time to poke around, are easily distracted, and often take some time before they settle down.

Another exploration class, simply titled "Exploring CD-ROMs," is a hands-on opportunity to see what's available in the media center. On some occasions only one or two people come to these classes. For example, the class may be held just for a few new teachers or for those teaching in a new curriculum area. Last fall both eighth-grade earth science teachers were teaching the curriculum for the first time; we arranged for time for them to explore electronic resources in the media center and I worked with them during summer curriculum writing sessions.

These informal classes give teachers opportunities to learn searching in a nonthreatening way with individualized instruction. Many good things have come of these classes; comfort levels increase, planning occurs, and teachers feel like they've accomplished something.

The earth science teachers each implement one resource-based teaching and learning unit each quarter and make excellent use of all of our electronic resources—from the online catalog to the Internet and topic CD-ROMs.

As the teachers move beyond entry-level technology skills, they are ready to move on to integration and application levels. Classes such as "Electronic Searching," which would not have drawn much interest two years ago, are popular. The Internet and networks are the hook. Teachers who were not interested before have had their interest piqued by the complexity of the Internet or because networks are making resources more accessible in their classrooms.

Added incentives for us in Minnesota are new graduation standards. These standards address accessing, evaluating and communicating information and working with core technological tools such as databases and word processing. Media specialists recognize this as nothing new, but teachers in our district and elsewhere are seeing the need to integrate these process outcomes in their curriculums and new partnerships are forming.

Other formal staff development offerings include classes on electronic searching, Internet search strategies and using various information tools. Some of our classes as described in a recent staff development brochure are:

Designing Lessons That Integrate Technology. How can you use technology in lessons you have already developed? What works, what doesn't? This will be a practical class with lots of tips and ideas suitable for K-12. People writing summer curriculum may find it especially useful. Plan to work on a project.

Internet Search Engines. Search engines can be very helpful in meeting your needs, but they differ from each other in many ways. Participants will practice using various engines, learning their search logic and strengths and weaknesses. Bring topics you're interested in searching to make this experience more beneficial.

Searching Electronically & Exploring Secondary Resources. Learn about search techniques and strategies common to electronic resources, such as *Computer Cat* and magazine indexes. Explore resources and learn how to use them in your curriculum.

Advanced Netscape. This class is designed for people who have been using the Internet and would like to learn more ways to search and really use the Internet to its fullest potential as an information tool. There will be opportunities to share ideas for successful curriculum integration and developing paperless projects.

"Designing Lessons..." is an exciting and important class. The class addresses practical considerations for providing a successful teaching and learning experience and aligning technology with curriculum outcomes. It's an opportunity to share successful projects and explain why they've worked. Hands-on time to actually work on a lesson is a major part of the class.

Notes

Some topics we teach in all classes are the differences and similarities among hypertext, keyword, subject and hierarchial searching and commonalities/differences between different resources. In all classes, we point out pitfalls and typical student successes and problems.

It's also important to teach the nitty-gritty aspects of using resources. Classes such as "Graphic Formats" and "Internet Plug-ins" might not seem relevant to searching, but they are developmental skills that enable students to fashion their own smooth search process.

Giving students an opportunity to work with the multimedia aspect of the Internet and other resources is motivational, especially for younger students. Some of our skill classes for teachers include:

Intermediate Netscape. Learn how to cut and paste out of *Netscape* into *ClarisWorks,* make bookmarks, and save to disk while surfing the Net.

Graphic Formats. Graphics come in GIF, JPEG, and PICT formats; they often need to be manipulated and changed to use them in various applications. Learn how—it's fun and not that hard.

Copy, Cut, Paste. Copy, cut, and paste are universal skills that you can use with most applications and between applications. Learn how to move information from one file or application to another. This is a *must* skill! The class can be taken as an introductory or refresher class.

Internet Plug-Ins & Helper-Apps. As the Internet becomes more advanced, tools are needed to use it to its full potential. You will learn which extras are becoming essential and how to download and install them to your machine.

As we teach teachers we learn how to provide meaningful staff development. Some ideas are:

■ Be understanding and patient. Teachers are busy. While we want them to have the knowledge to help their students, we must realize they are coming from a different viewpoint. Don't be too academic or theoretical, but don't be afraid to offer suggestions or say what needs to be said. Remain confident and positive that you have the knowledge to help others. As you work with your staff and get to know them, you will become more comfortable in offering suggestions.

■ Think about the curriculum of all content areas. Traditionally and too often, searching is taught only in English and social studies. With information technology pervasive throughout schools, it should be integrated in every curriculum. At Winona Middle School we are doing our higher-level instruction in science. An industrial technology teacher teaches searching skills to his students.

■ The Internet is a recognizable and understood resource. Don't teach Internet searching by comparing the Net to other online databases. Instead, use the Internet as a starting point and compare other databases to it.

■ Encourage teachers to have students design a search strategy and list keywords before they start work in the media center. Everyone learns during the process.

■ Develop "help sheets" for the electronic resources and give them to teachers and students. They are good for reference and nonthreatening. Ours are always visible on a stacking shelf in the media center; they are very popular and appreciated. Several of our help sheets are on the staff development section of our school's Web site (http://wms.luminet.net).

■ Involve teachers in staff development instruction. Teachers like to learn from other teachers.

■ Acquaint teachers with print resources such as *Internet for Schools,* 2nd edition, by Carol Simpson and Sharron L. McElmeel and *Searching Electronic Resources* by Marjorie Pappas, Gayle A. Geitgey, and Cathy A. Jefferson (Linworth). Both are useful for their overviews and transparency masters. Use them!

■ Use regular staff development and substitute teacher moneys to fund technology classes held during the school day. It's a wise use of money and garners a high rate of return.

■ Make staff development a top priority. Changes in our jobs may make it difficult to teach all the students, but it is possible to teach all of the teachers. It's time well spent; when teachers learn, everyone benefits.

Mary Alice Anderson is a Media Specialist at Winona Middle School in Winona, Minnesota, and an Editorial Consultant for TECHNOLOGY CONNECTION: The Magazine for School Media and Technology Specialists. *She can be reached by e-mail at maryalice@wms.luminet.net or on the Web at http://wms.luminet.net/teachers/manderso.html*

STAFF DEVELOPMENT

Fantasy and Fact in Computer Training

Lesley S.J. Farmer

We all know that students won't make the best use of computers unless they're required to use computer skills in the curriculum. And we know that teachers must be comfortable with computers in order to make assignments that take advantage of the technology. Furthermore, we know that sometimes neither scenario occurs. What's a computer literate librarian to do?

There are two options: a long-range, well-planned and implemented staff development model; or a "quick and dirty," train-on-demand model.

As a librarian, after years of working with teachers, I submit that the latter, though much less efficient and much more piecemeal, is the way to go. Sorry, folks. Even if the principal backs a thorough development plan, and there's a person to coordinate staff development, the most meaningful work is done one-on-one. Furthermore, it's driven by need and expertise.

What should the librarian do? Here are some ways to train teachers and students on-demand:

Teach through students; identify student aides who can teach both peers and teachers.

Teach for results; make sure that the resources presented fit the teacher's objectives for the upcoming lesson and facilitate the student's success (like poems on rats to complement Camus' *The Plague*).

Advertise library services that teachers and students can plug into, like video productions of class readings.

Create lots of "point-of-sale/use" flyers on how to use equipment. These may be augmented by library workbooks, audiocassette "tours" and brochures.

While the one-on-one approach may seem tedious, it can pay off because teachers hold a high stake in the process and outcome. Results are particularly exciting when teachers and students work as a team to understand and exploit the advantages of computer-based resources.

By training the adults in your setting, you can increase effective student use of the varied computer-based resources available. And the skills learned by teachers and students help them in their lifelong pursuits of knowledge.

What if *you* need the training? You can call on outside consultants or software packages, but the attitude you use to learn can help you whatever the format:

- taking notes on the concepts presented
- trying out the procedures enumerated in the software
- calling local or company experts for specific problems (and documenting the results)
- reading the documentation **TC**

Lesley S.J. Farmer is the Library Director of Redwood High School in Larkspur, California. She is the author of Creative Partnerships: Librarians and Teachers Working Together, *published by Linworth Publishing, Inc.*

Notes

HEAD FOR THE EDGE

Learned Helplessness

by Doug Johnson

Many teachers have fallen prey to the syndrome that Donald Norman in his book, *The Psychology of Everyday Things*, calls "learned helplessness." It's easy to acquire. People have learned to be helpless about many things—music, cooking, languages, carpentry, writing, swimming, to name a few. The same goes for computers. If we register negative experiences with an activity or skill, we rationalize our frustrations by saying "I was just never very good at _____."

For many years, school staff development for technology went something like this:

1) Teacher signs up for "Computer Basics" and completes the inservice session, leaving the training with a sense of mastery.

2) A week or two later, when Teacher gets a few minutes to use the building's computer, it's apparent that Teacher remembers little of what he or she thought was mastered. "I must need more training," is the response.

3) Next time technology training rolls around, Teacher signs up again for "Computer Basics" and completes the inservice session.

4) A week or two later, when Teacher gets a few minutes to use the building's computer, Teacher finds that he or she remembers little of what was taught. "Must need more training," Teacher thinks.

5) After one or two more repetitions of the effort, Teacher decides that he or she just isn't "good" with technology and begins to avoid computer inservice training at all cost.

It may be too late to save some teachers; the learned helplessness may be too deeply ingrained. But most teachers are salvageable, if the school's staff development program includes the following:

1) **Access, access, access**

   A computer in a teacher's room or office is probably the single best way to prevent "learned helplessness." Teachers need to be able to take computers home in the evenings, over the weekend, and especially during the summer. I have found that many teachers get tired of lugging computers back and forth, and, within a year of active computer use, buy a computer to use at home.

2) **Meaningful application**

   I am not sure technology advocates have done anyone a favor by suggesting that computers make one's life easier. They may save a little time here and there, but the real benefit of computing is that it makes one better at one's job! Our district staff development activities stress the use of the computer as a productivity tool *for the teacher*. We work hard to see that all teachers use word processing, e-mail, and a computerized record keeping system in the form of an electronic grade book, spreadsheet or database. I am convinced that teachers will not use productivity tools with kids until they have experienced the empowering effect of technology themselves. Oh, and teachers seem *not* to need instruction on how to use skill-and-drill applications.

3) **Time for practice**

   It's said that learning to use a computer requires about the same investment in time and energy as gaining rudimentary fluency in a second language. A savvy administrator, who knows that a teacher is earnestly trying to master computer skills, might provide more time by temporarily releasing that individual from some supervisory responsibilities, understand if they don't sign up for building committees, look for others to do special assignments, or find ways to reduce the number of preparations. Technology use should be accepted as a professional improvement goal. Inservice and workshop days for technology training are a must. Loaner laptops for teachers to check out can extend teachers' learning time.

4) **A technology environment**

   It's amazing what happens in a school when even a few teachers start using computers. It gives everyone else in the building courage. The internal dialog goes something like, "Geeze, if Johnson can learn to use a computer—and I know I am a heck of a lot smarter than Johnson—so can I."

5) **Support**

   We all need it, but some need it more than others. Support can be formalized by holding follow-up sessions to training a few weeks after the initial workshop. Just as important is having someone close at hand to call for help.

We advise new computer users to follow these steps when they hit a road block:

Essential Training Workshop Components

A brief nuts-and-bolts explanation of the topic.

Hands-on practice during every session.

Written or verbal feedback.

A talk-and-walk-through demonstration.

Adequate time for hands-on practice, note-taking and questions.

Creation of at least one document, chart, lesson, or teaching tool.

JOHNSON—
Continued from page 50

- Try again.
- Get a cup of coffee, stretch, and try again.
- Check the manual. (optional)
- Call another teacher who was in the training program.
- Ask your kids, neighbors' kids, or the local computer club.
- Call your media specialist. (Mine say they don't have a life anyway.)
- Call the computer coordinator.
- When all these avenues have been explored, call the district media supervisor. He can rarely help, but he's often very sympathetic.

6) A little fear mongering

Let's recognize that computer illiterate teachers are not good for kids. It's time administrators and fellow teachers stop accepting excuses for some teachers not having computer skills. But we may be too late. Kids and parents are already communicating that message very well. **TC**

Doug Johnson is the District Media Supervisor for the Mankato (Minnesota) Public Schools, and can be reached by e-mail at djohns1@west. isd77.k12.mn.us (or) palsdaj@vax1. mankato.msus.edu.

Notes

—A BOOK REPORT THEME SECTION—

Computers 101—Back By Popular Demand

By Ann Parker & Helen Adams

Teaching parents and others how to use the computers their children use proves to be a PR boost for the school.

WITH AN INITIAL $500 grant, the Rosholt Education Association began offering computer classes for adults in our small, rural Wisconsin district. We're now in our third year of coordinating this project, with plans for expanding our offerings. There have been a number of public relations benefits along the way.

The goals of the education association included postive personal contacts between parents and teachers and increased public support for the use of technology in the schools. The first four instructors were members of the association and were paid $25 for each evening class. Two lab assistants provided supervision and teaching assistance in the computer labs. They received $15 per session. The school board gave permission to keep the lab open for the evening classes.

The beginning computer classes consisted of four evening sessions plus two open lab sessions. The first three sessions dealt with such basics as how to format a disk, use a word processing program, and manage a database. In the fourth session, the library media specialists taught information retrieval using such resources as the online catalog, electronic encyclopedias, CD-ROM indexes, and the state library database. Adult students were also introduced to resources accessed by modem—state university library catalogs, online commerical services, and the Internet.

To publicize the first round of classes, we called the parents of the children enrolled in Chapter 1 classes and sent flyers home with each elementary school student. Posters were placed in stores. Articles appeared in the newspapers and in the district newsletter, which is distributed to all residents.

The available spaces quickly filled for the first two series of classes in February and March 1994. Retired

In evening classes, parents in the Rosholt, Wisconsin, schools are occupying the workstations filled by their children during the school day. Like the daytime students, they are learning how to use technology.

Notes

people, parents and community leaders signed up, and a third series was scheduled for April. Each class enrolled 15 people.

While evaluations by "students" and instructors gave high marks to the classes, there were some recommendations for improvement. For example, participants felt they did not have enough time to practice their new skills. Some enrollees were not able to use the computer lab because of the schedule. (We adjusted the instruction and lab scheduling to make the open labs more accessible.)

Another problem for adult students was the wide differences in the skills of the class members. People who used computers at work had difficulty being patient with the pace set to accommodate others who had never touched a computer before. We have tried to address this problem by being very specific about class content when we register participants.

Following the initial series of classes, we prepared a packet of information for the school board, including summaries of the evaluations, names of enrollees, and newspaper articles about the classes. At the time there was still a waiting list. The school board was receptive to our request for continued use of the lab for community classes.

Although we considered offering the classes in the 1994-95 school year for a fee, grant money was approved in the summer and we were able to offer classes again at no-cost to participants. The Rosholt Education Association agree to supplement the cost of the beginning classes if the amount exceeded grant funds. (The second beginning series was offered in October, January and March.)

In November and February, we also offered intermediate classes at a fee for those who had completed the beginning classes. The topics were review, database management and spreadsheets. The fee was $20 for four classes and two open labs. In addition, for $5 per session, community members could attend computer inservice session for the staff.

With nearly two years of experience as project coordinators we see a number of benefits from the classes. In a time of general dissatisfaction with teachers and the educational process, the quality and skills of our staff members have been demonstrated. Taxpayers have been able to see and use the computer labs purchased with public funds. There is an increased appreciation for technology in the schools.

We intend to continue offering classes related to technology. Among the topics under consideration are: how to select a home computer, telecommunications, selecting software for children, and using popular graphics and printing programs. We are also looking at the needs of adult students who have completed the intermediate classes but do not own a personal computer. They need open lab time to practice and maintain their skills.

As project coordinators, we found that helping adults continue their lifelong learning is a rewarding experience.

Ann Parker is a Language Arts Instructor and Gifted and Talented Coordinator at Rosholt High School. She is a former president of the Rosholt Education Association. Helen Adams is the High School Library Media Specialist and Co-Computer Coordinator for the Rosholt, Wisconsin, School District.

Setting Up A Community Computer Class

- Look for the need. Brainstorm, talk with parents and community members, or do a survey to determine if there is a need for classes.
- Be creative in finding sources of funding, or charge nominal fees.
- Look for personable, knowledgeable teachers who work well with adults and are enthusiastic about their topic. Good instructors are the key.
- Keep classes informal and non-threatening. Serve refreshments during breaks, be on a first-name basis with the adults, and combat evening fatigue with hands-on activities.
- Publicize classes. Keep the community informed with news releases after classes are in session. Send notices of future classes to former participants.
- Evaluate the project.
- Build on your success. Expand classes with intermediate and advanced levels as well as new topics.

Developing Library Courses For Credit in High Schools

By Sheila Berkelhammer and Betty Brandenburg

Two librarians describe how they planned and put into operation a credit course in library science for high school students.

A library and media course was introduced at our high school in 1974 for grades 9-12, and added to the middle school program in 1979 after the ninth grade was transferred to that building because of overcrowding at the high school. From our experiences, we offer these guidelines.

Objectives

The first step is to determine the needs and objectives to be met by a credit course in library media services. Once needs of the individual school have been identified, the credit course might speak to any or all of the objectives. Here are the objectives we try to meet at our school:
- To provide pre-vocational training for students interested in a library career, or in finding employment as media paraprofessionals or aides.
- To enable students to acquire extensive knowledge of the media center's resources for use in their own school work and in assisting others.
- To provide a service to the school.
- To teach students to work cooperatively as a part of the media center team and to understand the role an individual plays within a team.
- To instill pride and self-confidence in students, not only in their media center responsibilities, but throughout their school life.
- To foster an appreciation for books and libraries.
- To develop work habits and attitudes that will help the student in any career.

A list of objectives could include many other recognizable needs within a school and could be highly individual to that school.

Timetable

For a media course to get off to a successful start, at least one year's preparation is essential. The following schedule, based on our policies, might serve as a model.

September-November: Plan course objectives; begin outline of methods, procedures and policies; write course of study.

November: Submit course of study to the school board for adoption and approval, if this is necessary in the district.

December: Write course description for the guidance department for distribution to students and parents.

January-March: Students and parents select courses for the following year; guidance department begins scheduling; media specialist interviews student applicants.

April-August: Prepare evaluation tools, including initial screening test, and other course materials, especially a self-instruction manual (explained below); set up schedules of tasks; order materials; begin production of other instructional aids.

Sheila Berkelhammer is the librarian at Hillsborough Township High School in Belle Meade, New Jersey. Betty Brandenburg is the librarian at Hillsborough Middle School.

Content

An outline of course content, as well as a calendar (what will be taught when), should be established. For example, a course of study could be structured as follows in a school with four marking periods:

First Marking Period: Introduction to the media center, its materials, functions and policies. Included would be the card catalog, the responsibilities of the staff, circulation policies and procedures, classification systems, arrangement and location of materials.

Second . . .: Indexes and equipment. The use and function of such tools as the *Readers' Guide* and the operation of all audiovisual equipment in the center, including microfilm and fiche readers.

Third . . .: General reference and subject sources.

Fourth . . .: Literary and biographical sources.

Throughout the year students should be scheduled to learn how to shelve books, periodicals and audiovisual software, to process and repair materials, to check-in periodicals and new materials, to file catalog cards. They should also learn vertical file maintenance, library displays and publicity, materials selection and evaluation, equipment maintenance and operation, software production, photography, graphics, storytelling, library vocabulary, videotaping procedures, and so on.

Methods, Procedures and Materials

Schedules for some or all of the

expected to make use of the library's resources.

(packet)
Library Literacy: Some First Steps

Section 1. Introduction-Rationale

The library skills lessons in this series are only a beginning. They are a starting point. First, they provide a foundation for a systematic grounding in library skills. Second, they afford ad hoc tutoring in specific skills on a needs basis. Three, they offer enrichment opportunities to learning activities already in place. Together as a series or alone as polishing of specific skills, these lessons are a first step in our quest for library literacy among our students and staff.

Skills are arranged from simple to complex. Skill sets are repeated at different levels of difficulty in the series. Jerome Bruner's "spiral curriculum" is the guiding paradigm behind the lessons (see Bruner's *Process of Education*, Harvard Univ. Press, 1960).

Section 2. Orientation-Basic

In a grocery store, we often ask for the aisle location of a specific product. "Where's the cat food?" "In aisle 6," snorts the cashier.

The same logic applies to our library. First, we must be aware of the existence and location of materials before we can use them. This is the idea behind the library floor plan exercises. We need to know where we are before we can take advantage of what's available.

Hand-out: Floor plan of the library

Exercise:

Locate and label the following features of the library. Answer the questions.

1. Card catalog. What is it?
2. Periodicals. Where are the old ones?
3. *Readers' Guide*. What is it?
4. Daily and Sunday *New York Times*.
5. *New York Times Index*.
6. Vertical file. What is it?
7. *Horizon* collection. What is it?
8. The Masters School art collection of research material. What is it?
9. Books by graduates of the school. Cite an author and title of interest to you.
10. Books about college and career choice. Cite a title of interest to you.
11. Books about teaching. What in their call number designates them a special collection item?
12. Map case. Cite a title of an atlas.
13. Books 709-799. What is the subject?
14. Books 500-599. What is the subject?
15. Books 800-822. What is the subject?
16. Fiction books. How are they arranged?
17. Special foreign language book collections. What languages are represented?
18. *Harvard Classics*. What are they?
19. Reference books. What is a reference book?
20. New book display. Cite an author and title of interest to you.
21. Talking books. How do you borrow them?
22. Microfilm and microform readers. How many do we have?
23. Books on history. The call numbers range from __ to __.
24. Microfilm room. What is kept here?
25. Largest dictionary in the school. What's its name?
26. Circulation desk. How do you check out a book?
27. What part of the library do you expect to use most and why?
28. What part of this tour surprised you the most and why?
29. How much does the average book in our library cost?
30. What does the cost of the book tell you about returning library books?

Section 3. Skills-Basic

Lessons are provided for middle school and ESL students in classification and use of the card catalog, *Readers' Guide*, and reference books.

No students ought to use the library for class research until they are prepared in these four skills. (See *Basic Library Skills* by Nancy Polette, Milliken, 1971.)

Section 4. Orientation and Skills-Advanced

A blend of audiovisual and printed materials are used to build on fundamental concepts of library use. The key skills in this unit are: use of the card catalog, *Readers' Guide*, and reference books.

Because reference use is considered the traditional heart of academic library skills, five fundamental reference lessons are provided. They progress from general orientation to reference to detailed exercises in literature and social sciences.

Kits: *How to Survive in School* and *Using Library Resources and Reference Materials* (Center for the Humanities) and *Using Today's Library* (Eye-Gate).

Paul Rux is the Library Director at Masters School in Dobbs Ferry, New York. Paul's article on curriculum involvement appeared in the first issue of THE BOOK REPORT.

Section 5. Enrichment

The library staff is ready to develop special units with teachers in all subject areas. Lessons in this section are examples of what can be done with some cooperation and imagination. (See *Dear Faculty, A Discovery Method Guidebook to the High School Library* by JoAnne Nordling, Faxon, 1976.)

Section 6. Computer-Assisted Instruction

The library has interactive software programs for instruction in the use of almanacs, dictionaries, atlases and so forth. The disks can also be used as class activities.

Resources: *Right On!*, library instruction software series (Right On Programs, 755 New York Avenue, Huntington, NY 11743)

Section 7. Field Labs

The library staff believes we ought to get our students ready for the next level of library services: college and university libraries. We believe the curricular areas in the school ought to work with the library staff to develop interactive lab experiences—not tours—with collections in nearby university and college libraries. (This may include sophisticated public and community college libraries.) Such field labs would be the culmination of preliminary research begun in our library, and would prepare our students for effective use of library services at the next level of education.

Section 8. Database Searching

The library is committed to developing lessons for students in this area. From our computer we can access two major reference databases, *Dialog* and *Wilsonline*. After students become familiar with fundamental library resources, concepts and skills through print and audiovisual lessons, they should cap their library literacy efforts with database searching experiences.

TECHNOLOGY ORGANIZATION AND STAFFING

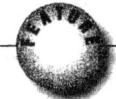

Training for Techies: A Schoolwise Commitment

By Lesley S.J. Farmer

Do you ever wish for a competent set of hands to help with technology in the library? Are you trying to figure a way to channel kid energy constructively? Do you want to provide technical service throughout the school without burning holes in your sneakers?

These three wishes may be granted with the establishment of a Technical Aide (TA) internship program in your library or school. Remember those days when junior high students wheeled around film projectors and replaced bulbs? Their latest incarnation is the junior techie. The job has become much broader in scope than in early media days, and students can possess a number of skills under the TA umbrella, including programming, keyboarding, instructing, graphics, organizing, and mechanics. (One side benefit is that girls are more likely to be involved in

---

TAMALPAIS UNION HIGH SCHOOL DISTRICT / Larkspur, California
Course of Study
In-School Work Experience
TAs in Technology

Background
This course is a specialty within the board-approved course of study for in-school work experience. As such, it conforms to existing credit limits, general objectives and course content, and placement procedures.

The main focus of this document is to detail the placement, content, delivery system, and assessment for the program.

I. Credit Limits
   a. Exploratory work experience may earn up to 20 units of credit.
   b. The total number of credits that may be earned is 40.

II. Objectives
   a. Explore school-related occupations
   b. Learn to use and care for equipment and application to workstation
   c. Further develop occupational skills related to job station
   d. Develop acceptable and desirable work habits

III. Placement Procedures
   a. The student plans the program with the counselor based on needs and interests.
   b. The student completes the In-School Work Experience form and TA application (including letter of recommendation from teacher or other adult who knows the student's skills and dependability) and submits them to the supervising teacher.
   c. The teacher interviews the applicant and consults with the counselor in terms of appropriate work assignments and periods.
   d. If the job is mutually acceptable, a program change slip is submitted, and the student begins work.

Tech Team (TA) Roles
Technology TAs (Tech Team) facilitate the use of technology within the school. They work under the direction of the educational computer specialist or other faculty member.

Tech TAs may work in several capacities:
1. lab assistant
2. trainer/coach for students and faculty (application use)
3. systems specialist (installation, troubleshooting, cleaning)
4. clerical help (software inventory, record keeping)
5. product developer (create instructional aids for teachers)

Each Tech TA should have the opportunity to carve out a niche in terms of teaching and learning, as long as it is aligned with the school's needs and resources.

Skills
There are two Tech Team levels—apprentice and journeyperson. First-year Tech Team members are apprentices, who start by shadowing a Tech team journeyperson or the computer specialist. Journey Tech Team members teach present skills to peers and learn additional skills. Apprentices should be at least sophomores; journeypersons should be at least juniors with one year of experience as an apprentice.

All Tech TA's must perform technical skills at or above a basic level. Those skills include those needed to pass computer literacy competence and ethical use and basic use of the Internet. Each type of work experience involves

the program.) As most schools encourage students to pursue voluntary service or career exploration opportunities, a TA program can provide needed personnel and service in the library as well as highlight library staff competence in technology.

The following program outlines one high school's successful foray into this kind of instruction and service. As author of this program, I pilot-tested the process. Here are a few tips to facilitate the program.

- The most critical factor in the program is student selection, with the best students self-selecting. Regardless of the technology, the best results come with a good match between student and teacher. If the students "buy into" technology service, then the main focus can be to find the right tasks for the students and help them grow on the job.

- Dependability and willingness win hands down over the high risk-taking hacker. Sometimes the student who is just a step or two beyond the rest of the class is the perfect coaching candidate because he remembers the stumbling blocks. Look for patient aides.

- The application process helps focus the student and teacher. An application form shows that the school is serious. An interview helps diagnose the student's interest and ability. References reveal the student's network of supporters. Monthly formal discussions about the internship provide follow-up assessments and facilitate needed modifications in the process.

- If a TA is shared with another teacher, clarify scheduling and supervision issues from the start. Check with the other teacher regularly to make sure a TA doesn't fall through the cracks.

- Make use of written or online instructional guides so students can self-pace their learning. Be sure to check with them about their progress before they leave

a unique set of skills beyond this basic set, which the student should exhibit or have a desire to learn.

1. lab assistant:
- word processing
- additional applications (may be subject-specific, such as science)
- lab procedures
- basic OS
- teaching or tutoring
- interpersonal skills, patience

2. trainer/coach for students and faculty (application use):
- advanced competence in applications (may be subject-specific)
- teaching or tutoring
- interpersonal skills, patience

3. systems specialist:
- software installation
- advanced OS (may specialize)
- troubleshooting
- equipment maintenance

4. clerical help (software inventory, record keeping):
- database/spreadsheet
- word processing
- attention to detail

5. product developer (create instructional aids for teachers):
- advanced competence in applications (may specialize)
- programming (optional)
- interface design
- design brief
- word processing

- graphics
- communications
- interpersonal skills

Assessment
Authentic assessment (how well the student performs) is the basis for grading. Specific criteria include degree and quality of competency, self-direction, cooperation, dependability, and responsibility.

Rubric for Grading:
A: Fully accomplishes the purpose of the task
- Student's work shows full grasp and use of technical concepts and processes
- Student works efficiently and accurately without supervision
- Student consistently arrives on time and stays on task
- Student consistently shows willingness to learn and help
- Student consistently works well with adults and students

B: Substantially accomplishes the purpose of the task
- Student's work shows essential grasp and use of technical concepts and processes
- Student generally works efficiently and accurately with little supervision
- Student generally arrives on time and stays on task
- Student generally shows willingness to learn and help
- Student generally works well with adults and students

C: Partially accomplishes the purpose of the task
- Student's work shows partial, but limited, grasp of technical concepts and processes
- Student works adequately but needs some supervision
- Student sometimes arrives late and is sometimes distracted
- Student occasionally shows unwillingness to learn and help
- Student works adequately with adults and students

D: Makes little or no progress in accomplishing the purpose of the task
- Student's work shows little or no grasp of technical concepts and processes
- Student works inefficiently and needs constant supervision
- Student has excessive absences or tardies
- Student does not stay on task
- Student is seldom willing to learn or help
- Student does not work well with adults and students

E: Makes no progress or undermines the purpose of the task
- Student's work shows no grasp of any concepts or processes
- Student does not work, even under constant supervision

each day, so accountability is highly visible and any necessary adjustments can be made quickly. Some students thrive with this approach; others become distracted or completely lost.

- Handle student pairing carefully. Shadowing works well if the more experienced student is dependable and reports back. Often one grade difference can make that relationship more professional. Over a semester, students working together often develop good friendships. Make sure these friendships benefit the work and don't detract from it. Sometimes friendly competition between TA teams (particularly if they work at different times) encourages students to do their best so they can be cited for their expertise and efficiency.

- Also have a fall-back task for TAs to do. In that way, if you're busy, the student doesn't have to stand around waiting for a directive. Have the students check the TA folder or schedule board when they arrive. You can write assignments for the day or include a list of activities for them to choose from. Train each student in one job, such as finding good Web sites or assisting students in the computer lab. Then you can say "the usual" as they check in with you for their assignment when you're too busy to teach them a new skill.

- Let TAs have a couple of free days per semester for those times when they have last-minute homework or need a cooling-off period. Students appreciate your sensitivity to their needs—and the sign of trust to control some of their time.

Lesley S.J. Farmer is the Library Director of Redwood High School in Larkspur, California. She is the author of Training Student Library Staff, *published by Linworth Publishing, Inc.*

- Student has excessive absences and tardies
- Student never stays on task
- Student is never willing to learn or help
- Student harms or harasses adults or students

Training Structure

Tech Team:
The computer specialist meets with the Tech Team for intensive orientation and training, ideally before school starts. Content includes part, if not all, of the following:
- ethical behavior and security measures
- lab use and troubleshooting
- Windows/DOS/Mac use and troubleshooting (one or more OS)
- generic installation procedures
- generic equipment maintenance
- basic training/teaching/tutoring techniques

Subsequently, the Tech Team meets weekly for training and updates. Training modules may include:
- operating systems: all platforms, advanced features of preferred platforms
- software applications: expanding variety of software and their crosswork, troubleshooting applications
- advanced Internet
- advanced troubleshooting: freezes, cables, cards, printers
- other hardware: camcorder, QuickCam, VCR, laser disc, scanner

- working with others: etiquette, conflict resolution
- teaching/tutoring skills: instructional strategies, teaching aids

Journey Tech Team may train other Tech Team members. The Tech Team may be scheduled in several ways:
- ongoing lab assistant (one per lab per period)
- teacher may sign up to use a Tech Team person as a one-time aide (e.g., set up multimedia machine) or tutor (e.g., train teacher on Internet skills)
- report to supervisor each time, and check tech need

Teacher-Specific Tech TA:
Each teacher has a plan for Tech TA work and learning experiences. The teacher and student should contract goals and objectives. On the whole, the student should spend one period a week in a learning experience, such as advancing their technical skill or honing work skill habits.

Training Framework

Training technical TAs differs from most classroom instruction in the number of students, grouping arrangement, length of time, instructional designate, and outcomes. While it is possible that the teacher would teach 20 students simultaneously for a full class period, presenting principles and providing practice time, that scenario is the exception rather than the rule. Particularly since the teacher often juggles staff training in the midst of classroom visits, training needs to be specific and quickly applied. Thus, single-concept task training is the norm. Additionally, guide sheets and reference pages are typical training devices, the concept being that after using these aids, the student can perform the needed task and will ask the teacher only specific, clarifying questions.

With these caveats noted, the following framework provides a full look at potential training sessions.
Function description: a one-sentence general description of the function
Objectives: a list of instructional learning objectives related to the function
Process: the main concepts and steps to consider when training students to perform the function
Demonstration ideas: tips to guide the trainer to facilitate student learning. Sample training aids may be provided.
Student activities: specific steps that students carry out independently or under initial supervision; sample guide sheets may be provided.
Follow-up: next steps in enriching or expanding the function or training
Evaluation: guidelines for assessing student performance and training experience; as much as possible, the criteria for evaluation should be given at the beginning of the activity. In the final analysis, if the student can competently perform the function independently, the training is successful.

TECHNOTRAINING

Training Students as Technology Assistants

by Esther Onishi and Erica Peto

Fifth and sixth graders teach younger students—and teachers too—how to use electronic resources.

Tech Team members at our school are fifth- and sixth-grade volunteers who attend weekly after-school training sessions that prepare them to help classmates and younger students in the technology lab. These students have also learned to install software, do minor repairs, clean equipment, and assist teachers. They help second-graders make *Kid-Pix Studio* (Broderbund) slide shows and assist third-graders who are using *ClarisWorks* to learn map skills. The work done by Tech Team members builds their confidence, develops their sense of responsibility, and polishes their self-esteem.

A media specialist, music specialist, and a fourth-grade teacher, all recent graduates of the City University Masters Program in educational technology, are Tech Team advisors. The Tech Team is part of a major restructuring of the way technology has been integrated at our school.

Now, instead of staying put in the computer lab, our technology specialist takes a mini-lab of computers with him and goes into classrooms for three weeks at a stretch. There, he supports the teacher in the classroom and infuses technology into the curriculum. The librarian does double duty in the computer lab, where she offers a one-hour "media block" that shows students how to

integrate technology with library skills to conduct teacher-assigned research and writing assignments.

Does the Tech Team sound like something you would like to have at your school? Read on for specifics on how to implement such a program.

Tech Team Components

After-School Program
Tech Team members attend training sessions one hour per week after school. They use this time for skill lessons and cleaning.

Technology Lab Assistants
Tech Team members help students and teachers during their media block period. They make up any class work they miss during this one-hour-per-week time.

Troubleshooting
Staff members request assistance by submitting a troubleshooting form to the Tech Team advisors. Work is then delegated to appropriate Tech Team members.

Cleaning
Tech Team members are responsible for cleaning and maintaining all hardware in the building.

Installation of Software/Hooking Up Hardware
Tech Team members install software school-wide at the request of the Tech Team advisors or as requested through the troubleshooting form for other staff.

Working with Others
This social skill, among others, is taught and reinforced throughout the year as tech team members work with staff members and other students. **Tc**

Esther Onishi is a Teacher and Erica Peto is a Media Specialist at Daniel Elementary School in Kent, Washington.

Download More Particulars from Their Home Page

You can download the following items from the Daniel Elementary World Wide Web home page (in *ClarisWorks* format for the Macintosh). From the Daniel Elementary 2 home page (http://www.kent.wednet.edu/KSD/DE/DE_home.html) choose TECHNOLOGY, then TECH TEAM: STUDENT TECHNOLOGY TRAINERS.

Tech Team Brochure
This explains the Tech Team program and student responsibilities as well as the selection process. One part is signed by the parent and prospective Tech Team member and is returned to the Tech Team advisors.

Troubleshooting Form
Printed on double-copy paper, these forms are filled out by staff members to relay a technology job to the Tech Team advisors. Tech Team students do the job

and fill out the bottom half of the form and return it to the initiating staff member.

Interview Questions

All prospective Tech Team members were interviewed prior to being accepted onto the Tech Team. They also had to receive approval from their classroom teacher.

Evaluation Form

This form is used each trimester by teachers Tech Team members have worked with.

Skills List

The following lesson plans are used for training students in the after-school training sessions; they are also handy to use with classes. Several of the lesson plans include computer templates, worksheets for students, and *ClarisWorks* slide show presentations.

1. Troubleshooting Form
2. Tech Lab Rules
3. Equipment Names
4. Working With Others
5. Save/Navigate/Retrieve
6. Working With Windows
7. Navigation Troubleshooting
8. Software Applications
9. *ClarisWorks* Editing
10. Cut/Copy/Paste
11. Integrating Graphics
12. *ClarisWorks* Slide Show
13. Hardware/Cleaning and Maintenance
14. Readying the Printers
15. Internet Navigation
16. *KidPix* Slide Show
17. *Grolier's* CD-ROM
18. VCR Use
19. Camcorder Use
20. Laser disc Use
21. Scanner Use
22. QuickCam Use

If you are unable to download these documents or have any comments or questions, please contact the authors at: eonishi@kent.wednet.edu or epeto@kent.wednet.edu.

Notes

A Quiz for Student Aides

By Mary Hauge

Mary Hauge is a librarian at Washington Middle School, Aurora, Illinois

The person who wrote the adage, "No job is so simple that it can't be messed up," must work with student library assistants. With tongue firmly planted in cheek, I dragged out my anecdotal records to develop an application for prospective student assistants.

STUDENT AIDE PROFICIENCY QUIZ

Name _____
    (First)   (Last)   (Alias)

Circle the correct response.

(1.) T F   It is permissible to do wheelies with the book truck once all the titles have been shelved.

(2.) T F   It is allowable to use the dater to stamp the hands and forearms of the borrowers to call attention to the correct return date.

(3.) T F   The correct form of address for the librarian is "Killer."

(4.) T F   The proper way to deliver library overdue notices is to fold them into paper airplanes and buzz the appropriate homeroom teachers.

(5.) T F   "Bring this book back or we shall have to hurt you" is an acceptable way to personalize the overdue notices you write.

(6.) T F   A video arcade is a good way to get extra money for the library. Collect a quarter each time you loan a disk to the computer users.

(7.) T F   Love notes found in returned books may be posted on the library bulletin board.

(8.) T F   Book cards are filed alphabetically by the sex of the borrower.

(9.) T F   One of the benefits of being an assistant is a private lounge complete with soda dispenser and private phone.

(10.) T F   In hanging up library displays, it is allowable to climb the book shelves instead of a ladder.

(11.) T F   The words "biography" and "bibliography" mean the same thing. *Readers' Guide* and *Reader's Digest* are the same, too.

(12.) T F   "Thou shalt not copy any part of thy anatomy" is the first rule of the photocopy machine.

(13.) T F   Student assistants shall pay the librarian the minimum wage for the privilege of working in this fine facility.

If you have answered "True" to all of the above questions, you are of the same caliber as student assistants in the past. Report to the library from the cafeteria as soon as you finish eating.

Notes

Tips and Other Bright Ideas

Model the Use of Technology

It's always a good practice to model the use of technology as you teach others to use it. One way to model a digital or paperless classroom concept is to put agendas, outcomes, and teaching materials for technology staff development workshops on the World Wide Web. This saves paper and demonstrates to teachers a way they can implement this in their instruction. This model works especially well for workshops about the Internet. Another good model uses classroom technology in an actual classroom. One of our teachers took a staff development group to her classroom for "show and tell" so that other teachers could see how she uses her scan converter, computer and monitor. -*Mary Alice Anderson, Winona (Minnesota) Middle School*

Use Students as Resources

Create a simple application form for 4th and 5th graders with blanks for name, address, phone, date, grade and space to tell why they want training on equipment and/or software. Group students by need and meet with each group for 45 minutes once a week for several weeks. If possible, put only three students on each computer and designate the center chair as the "training chair" to prevent arguments as to whose turn it is to use the equipment. Invite students to come in on their own time to practice what they have learned. After the final session, test them (formally or informally) on setting up and using the equipment. Issue those who are proficient a "resource person card" and encourage teachers to call on these students for help. This boosts student self-esteem and is of great assistance to teachers.-*Sandy Nelson, Lee County Schools, Fort Myers, Florida*

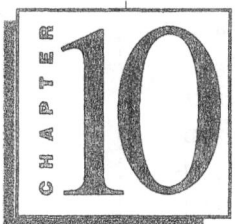

Assessing Information Literacy Skills

We've taught and reinforced print and electronic research skills with our students. We've planned cooperative lessons with subject area teachers; some projects have grown into multidisciplinary efforts. We've demonstrated a variety of presentation formats, from the traditional term paper to a hypermedia stack, a PowerPoint slide show, a Web page. We've shown students how to create their own presentations in all these formats and how to determine which would be most effective for a given assignment.

Now that the project is completed, how will it be evaluated? The product may be quite a different animal from what teachers are accustomed to grading. Once again, as the faculty members with the most experience in assessing multimedia projects, we can help develop rubrics that measure the quality of both the "contents" and the "container." The days of never seeing what students did with the information we helped them find may be over. We may even find ourselves part of an assessment team.

Listen to students discussing the "fairness" of various teachers' grading systems. (In the library media center, we're in an ideal location for such eavesdropping; students tend to forget we're there as they talk amongst themselves.) Students appreciate those teachers who are up-front with what is expected. They know from the outset of the course, or the project, the minimum they need to do for a specific grade- and the consequences for failing to meet that minimum as well as for exceeding it. The library media specialists and teachers whose work is reprinted here advocate this system for evaluating research projects. They also distinguish between *evaluation*, implying grading of a final project, and *assessment*, implying an ongoing function of guidance or coaching through intermediate steps to create the best final project possible. In real life, while sometimes our work is judged, accepted, or rejected as a "one-shot deal," more often we meet periodically with supervisors, co-workers, or clients to fine-tune a product as the work progresses and unanticipated needs, questions, or developments arise. Some of these articles address staff development and the assessment of the faculty's familiarity with various technologies. The assessment tools and rubrics described can easily be adapted for use with students in high school or middle school.

And this brings us full circle in the planning model. Having assessed a project, or a course, we know where students are in their grasp of information literacy. Our rubrics indicate where we'd like them to be. And to get there, we again meet with teachers to plan, design collaborative research activities, and continue to prepare our young people for the information challenges of tomorrow.

URL UPDATES

Technology Assessment and Curriculum: Teaching What is Tested
>   Jefferson County Public Schools
>   www.jefferson.k12.ky.us/contiuum/contiuum.html

MULTIMEDIA

Yes, They Put on Quite a Show,
BUT WHAT DID THEY LEARN?

Have you heard of the Kansas City Monarchs, the Pittsburgh Crawfords, the Indianapolis Clowns, or the Homestead Grays? These teams were part of the Negro baseball league formed in the 1860s. The link with racism is obvious to most students. However, the link with Adolph Hitler requires a slightly more astute youngster.

Students in history at Battle Ground Middle School are finding a number of links between their favorite topics that are not usually covered during the short school year. Josh is class expert on the Negro baseball league. Susan did her research on Ellis Island. Shannon has acquired in-depth knowledge about Adolph Hitler. Janet's project provides a look at the life of George Washington Carver.

These hypermedia projects span the school year and are presented to the entire class during the month of May. Motivation runs high because the students can choose the topic that interests them most, and they use IBM's *Linkway*, digitized images, and sound to develop their history projects. When all the projects are completed, they are put on the instructional network in the school and serve as reference tools. In this way, all the students can see the work of their fellow students.

Technology, in the guise of *Linkway*, has invaded the history class. Students, the teacher, and the library media specialist all function as a team during development of these technology projects. The research portion is facilitated by the library media specialist. The classroom teacher and the library media specialist provide some initial instruction in the use of *Linkway*. The students are given one day a week throughout most of the school year to work on the projects.

> *Students, the teacher, and the library media specialist all function as a team during development of these technology projects.*

While this sounds like a good use of technology, and it is, you may well ask, "How are these projects assessed? How do you know that students learned anything from them?" These questions were asked by the educators at Battle Ground Middle School and the other three schools using hypermedia for student projects.

For several years a team of educators in the Tippecanoe School Corporation has been working on incorporating the use of hypermedia at the secondary level. In the first two years the educators learned to use hypermedia themselves and discovered methods of successfully integrating hypermedia projects into social studies, history, geography, and science curricula. The third and subsequent years of the project found the group discussing, investigating, and developing assessment methods to use with hypermedia projects developed by students.

The discussion of assessment began with these questions: How do we know what the students are learning? How do we justify the amount of time spent on these hypermedia projects? The yearlong process of developing assessment tools began over lunch. The following questions were discussed:

What are the existing paradigms for assessing hypermedia projects?

What strongly held beliefs color our assessment?

What strongly held rules color our hypermedia use and assessment?

What assumptions do we have about assessment?

This discussion led to more questions. In order to continue the development of an assessment process, we held a daylong retreat facilitated by an outside expert on assessment. We also used some of the Grant Wiggins videotape series on assessment, "Standards Not Standardization." During the day, we developed two lists. The first list described the actions we wanted to assess as students developed hypermedia projects; the second list explained what these actions looked like and how we would recognize them. The list of desired goals included research, links in knowledge, decision making, self-reflection and assessment, creativity, design techniques, and technical computer skills. We ended the day with a tentative list of areas we wanted to assess, characteristics associated with these areas, and brief descriptions of how we would know it when we saw it.

> "How were these projects assessed?" and "How do you know the students learned anything from the time spent on them?"

From here began the detailed work of developing our scoring rubrics (see page 17). During a series of four after-school sessions, we developed scoring rubrics for presentation, cooperative learning skills, computer skills, and content knowledge. Discussion was lively, sometimes heated, as work continued. Changing from a traditional scoring method or from a method that relied heavily on evaluating computer skills alone was not easy. The topic of how to explain the assessment process to parents was discussed frequently. Finally, we had scoring rubrics we were ready to pilot test.

Pilot testing was done in several areas. First, one group had the students use the computer skills rubric as a peer assessment tool midway through the hypermedia project development. This session proved invaluable to the educators and the students. We found the scoring rubric worked well. However, we quickly discovered the need to hone students' skills in the area of peer assessment. Second, some of the group took the concept of our scoring rubrics and developed assessment tools for other classroom assignments. Student feedback was extremely positive as were the feelings of the educators involved. These kinds of comments from students were common: "Boy, Ms. K., now I really know what you want from our debate!" "Mrs. Trujillo, how can I not get an A on this project? You're telling me exactly what you are looking for."

One of the most rewarding and effective public relations tools was the pilot test involving parents. We had a parent assessment night during which the parents actually used the computer skills rubric to score a child's project. During the course of the evening, the scoring rubrics for knowledge, cooperative learning, and presentation were also discussed. The success of the event was gauged by the fact that parents were very reluctant to leave. They wanted to continue exploring the social studies references created by the students. In addition, the discussion among the parents about how concrete the evaluation was and how students could not claim they did not understand what was expected of them proved that our scoring rubrics and the assessment process accomplished what we educators had envisioned. Assessment of these projects had moved from a simple summative assessment of computer skills to a formative assessment of the complete project. The scoring rubrics also helped build, from the start of the project, student understanding of the expectations.

Final assessment of the projects was done by including the parent assessment, a peer assessment, the content area teacher assessment, the library media specialist assessment, and the assessment of another teacher, the principal, or a central office administrator. Student reaction to this comprehensive assessment was astounding. Often, the students would comment on the feeling of importance it gave them to have so many people examining their work. The students were very particular about the final product knowing that their audience would include more than the classroom teacher.

> *How do we know what the students are learning and how do we justify the amount of time spent on these hypermedia projects?*

As we educators completed the first year of using these assessment tools, we proclaimed the experience of developing them as one of the most powerful forms of staff development we had ever experienced. We felt our growth as educators was phenomenal. Finally, as we planned, the group has continued to share, with at least one educator, the new assessment strategies. The work of integrating technology into the curriculum, as well as changing assessment, has begun in the Tippecanoe School Corporation. Technology, assessment, and a team approach that included the library media specialist were the catalysts for the change. **TC**

© *Joanne Troutner, 1996.*

References:

Wiggins, Grant. et al. (1991) *Standards, Not Standardization Volume I: Rethinking Assessment.* Genesco, New York: Class.

Joanne Troutner is the Director of Technology and Media at Tippecanoe School Corporation, Lafayette, Indiana.

Rubric for Presentations Incorporating Technology

Criteria: Students' use of technology
1) Accurately reflects the ideas presented.
2) Communicates clearly.
3) Contributes meaningful content to topic presented.
4) Is technically/mechanically competent.
5) Reflects higher-order thinking skills.
6) Is appropriate to the audience.
7) Is well-developed and organized.

Scale
A: Fully accomplishes the purpose of the task; is well done; exceeds requirements
B: Substantially accomplishes the purpose of the task; is adequate; meets requirements
C: Partially accomplishes the purpose of the task; needs revisions; meets limited requirements
D: Makes little or no progress in accomplishing the purpose of the task; should restart; meets little or none of the requirements

Assessment of Presentation

Oral	• Good eye contact • People at back of room can hear • Demonstrated ease with topic • Smiles, shows enthusiasm in voice	1 Unsure/poor eye contact 2 Limited eye contact/some questions 3 Poised/answered questions
Mechanics	• Punctuation • Spelling • Grammar—Basic verb tenses • No slang • Graphic further explains or clarifies text • Supported facts	1 Poor grammar/spelling 2 Some problems 3 Complex sentences/correct grammar
Matching Information to Presentation	• Graphics help explain text • Graphs/charts best form to convey information • Graphics serve a purpose	1 Graphics distracting 2 Graphics superfluous 3 Graphics reinforce information

Assessment of Cooperative Learning Skills

Shared Labor	• Contributes orally in class • Contributes with written material to the group project • Contributes ideas to group • Willingness to contribute	1 Little contribution 2 Adequate contribution 3 Equitable contribution
Dependability	• Attends class • Meets deadlines • Brings supplies	1 Sometimes 2 Usually 3 Always
Integration of Work/Collaboration of Effort	• No bickering or whining • Ability to compromise • Willingness to adapt work as needed • Revise work as needed to fit group project • Accepts constructive comments • Ability to tactfully provide constructive comments • Gives positive feedback to group	1 Sometimes 2 Usually 3 Always

Assessment of Computer Skills

Screen Design	• Button placement consistent • Type contrast pleasing • Type style appropriate • Icons appropriate • Arrows point correctly/sized • Picture size appropriate • Graphics understandable/appropriate	1 Can't read it/inconsistent 2 Okay/usable but confusing/can navigate folder 3 Clear/appealing/navigate easily
Program Operation	• Contains Menu or Quit button on every page • Buttons work as stated • Pop ups, if used, are clearly marked • Sound, if used, is clear	1 Doesn't work/has lots of bugs 2 Works but has some bugs 3 Pretty bug free
Program Design	• Has title page with credits • Appropriate use of branching • Pop ups appropriate • Branching opportunities • Returns to a recognizable point, i.e. menu • Uses intuitive icons as much as possible	1 Many deadends/doesn't flow 2 Works but could be better 3 Pretty well designed/logical flow
Use of Linkway Resources	• Uses pictures/graphics appropriately & often • Uses sound appropriately • Uses paint feature appropriately • Uses types of buttons appropriately	1 No graphics/sound/links 2 Acceptable use/missed opportunity/few links 3 Optimal use

Assessment of Knowledge

Research	• Uses varied sources—books, magazines, vertical file, databases • Has notes with source documented • Has bibliography • Cites sources • Avoids plagiarism	1 Has less than required number of resources 2 Has required number of resources 3 Has more than required number of resources
Subject Knowledge	• Mentions factors leading up to or resulting from topic • Relates topic to time period • Historically accurate	1 Little or no understanding of where topic fits in history 2 Some understanding 3 Clear understanding
Organization of Information	• Logical progression of information • Thesis is clear • Introduction clearly states purpose • Conclusion clear • Graphic further explains or clarifies text • Supported facts	1 Strange connections between information 2 Limited connections between information 3 Logical connections between information
Content and Accuracy	• Facts are up-to-date • Pictures accurately tie to text • Sound ties to text • Demonstrates depth of knowledge	1 Inaccurate/lack of ties 2 Accurate but partial requirements 3 Accurate and fits requirements

Head for the Edge

Getting What You Ask For

By Doug Johnson

I've discovered a great technique for getting what I want for Christmas. I describe the hoped-for gift—precisely. I've learned that if I simply ask for a tie, heaven only knows what I'll receive. If I ask for a red-and-gray tie, my chances improve. But if I lead my daughter by the hand to the Jerry Garcias at the local department store and ooh and ah over one or two, I am pretty sure to get something to my taste.

As educators begin to work with students on performance skills that cannot be evaluated by standard paper and pencil tests, their ability to write an assessment instrument that clearly articulates a desired quality level becomes critical. Whether in the form of a rubric, a checklist, or a benchmark, creating tools that describe what is expected of learners can help educators dramatically improve instruction.

Library media specialists have a leadership role in implementing these new forms of assessment. Having experienced project-based learning, we can use our experiences to teach teachers effective means of evaluating performances and projects, both through inservice workshops and by modeling the assessments of joint library/classroom projects. Our media specialists and teachers are becoming increasingly proficient at writing good assessment instruments. Here are some of their secrets:

1. **Describe what you want in observable terms.** Remember the tie analogy? The more specific you can be with the indicators of quality, the easier it will be for students to determine quality for themselves. A hypermedia stack about a historical period might include checklist items such as:

- location and years
- proper clothing
- correct transportation
- tools and weapons
- people doing their daily work
- key events—what happened that was so important we're still studying it?
- main geographical features
- symbols (religious, job-related, or holiday) that were important to people in your region
- important or famous people, sayings, or documents.

2. **Use two strands of assessment: content and container.** Remember getting back English papers that had one grade for content and one for mechanics? Projects that use technology to help communicate the content really need two separate sets of assessment criteria—one for the content and one for the electronic container of that content. Whether it is videotape, hypermedia stack, electronic slideshow, word processed document, desktop published brochure, spreadsheet, or database, you need to develop an assessment tool that describes the effective use of the container. Quality container criteria for the hypermedia stack above might include:

- a minimum of eight cards, each with a uniform background and layout style
- easily seen and understood navigation buttons
- a logical organization and structure
- readable text
- graphics, sounds, and movies to add to the understanding of the topic.

3. **Use examples of past high-quality work.** Students need to see or read actual examples of high-quality work. The "critical elements," as Mankato media specialist Kathy Wortel describes them, need to be listed. One of the dangers of using examples is that students may be tempted to copy them too closely. To prevent their doing so, change the assignment enough to make that impossible. If a research assignment looks at the attributes of effective leaders, one year ask students to choose scientists as subjects, the next year social activists. If geographic regions are the topic, questions one year can be about environmental issues, the next year about the effect of geography has on living conditions.

4. **Give criteria to the learner at the time you make the assignment.** Assessment tools need to be shared with students at the time the assignment is given, not after it is complete. That way students have a roadmap to follow as they work on the project. The goal should be *no surprises*. Here is the task. Here are the quality indicators. Go to it.

5. **Use the assessment tool to help guide revisions.** Jean Donham at the University of Iowa reminds us that the term assessment has its roots in a Latin word that means "to sit down beside." One of the great philosophical differences between doing an assessment and an evaluation is, an assessment is a tool that encourages continued growth rather than simply judging a completed task. The assessment tool should help students see where they are strong and where they can improve. And by using these tools while the project is in the works, rather than simply when it is completed, you can actively encourage such growth and improvement.

6. **Use multiple assessors.** The best checklists I've seen have places for input from multiple sources. The teacher, of course, should comment on whether a quality indicator has been met, as should the stu-

Head for the Edge

dent. The media specialist can add his or her unique perspective. Parents should be given the opportunity to review with their children the progress of the work. And in special cases, experts in either the subject of the research or the use of the media can provide insights unavailable elsewhere.

7. **Revise your tools each time you use them.** No assessment instrument is perfect the first time it is used. Criteria might be unclear. Too many indicators might restrict creativity or originality. We have found and eliminated nearly all uses of superlatives (good, better, best) in creating rubrics. The terms are empty without precise descriptors of what actually makes something "better" than something only "good." Keep your assessment tools in digital format, a word processing document, or database, for easy updating and reuse.

Writing good assessments takes time, practice, and thought. And that goes not just for instruments that measure student performance, but also for tools that measure the quality of programs and professional performance. The more experience we as educators have in articulating what we hope to get, the better chance we have of getting it. Remember Johnson's Law of Assessment: You'll only get what you want if you can describe what you want. And that applies to both Christmas ties and student performance.

Doug Johnson is the District Media Supervisor for the Mankato (Minnesota) Public Schools and can be reached by e-mail at djohns1@west.isd77.k12.mn.us (or palsdaj@vax1.mankato.msus.edu.) Doug's new book, The Indispensible Teacher's Guide to Computer Skills, *has just been released by Linworth Publishing.*

Notes

Authentic Assessment of Information Literacy Through Electronic Products

Electronic resources make it easier for students and teachers to demonstrate to a skeptical public the depth and diversity of schooling.

By Lesley S. J. Farmer

THE DEMAND FOR tougher standards for high school graduation, by both local and national constituents, signals the need for school accountability. Parents and the community demand that a diploma mean more than a certificate of completion of a certain number of hours.

How can learning become authentic? One possible solution is outcomes-based education that uses authentic assessment. This article explores this concept and its implications for information literacy.

What is Outcomes-Based Education

Essentially, outcomes-based education embraces the concept of measurable goals-setting. When developed and stated clearly, outcomes specify what schools want students to accomplish. Outcomes describe standards that graduates will meet or exceed. Outcomes are set within a framework of performance, which is measured against an objective standard rather than in relationship to the abilities of other students.

Additionally, outcomes use an assessment tool to determine whether or not a student achieves the standard. Outcomes tend to be stated in global terms. Typically one to ten outcomes would describe a course. On the other hand, the performance indicators more resemble instructional objectives; they are detailed and specific.

The Education Task Force (ETF), a consortium of K-14 public schools in Marin County, California, has been developing a series of outcomes to drive education and provide seamless articulation between school levels. One of the outcomes generated by ETF is:

Authentic assessment is not a one-time event. Just as in the work world, assessment in schools is an ongoing activity.

Using technology as a tool to access information, analyze and solve problems, and communicate ideas.

To put the outcome in concrete terms, each element is given a descriptor:

The student demonstrates competence in the use of authoring tools, graphic applications, and telecommunications. Uses technology in many disciplines to solve problems. Selects and employs a variety of electronic technology resources for research and communication. Creates products using technologies. Uses technology responsibly, legally, and ethically.

Another step specifies the performance indicators demonstrating that the student has achieved that outcome. For high school graduates, technology indicators include:

Within a curricular context the student will produce a solo project which exhibits mastery of the following technologies, authoring tools, graphics, telecommunications plus items from at least two different technology categories. Students may propose projects that encompass such processes as design, construction, and modeling. Or, the student will develop a portfolio that incorporates the use of three or more technologies with sample works from at least four subject areas.

Two other indicators fill out the list. Additionally, benchmark indicators are identified for second, fifth and eighth graders. For instance, the fifth-grade benchmark includes "cross-curricular project presented by a small group, utilizing at least two authoring tools plus two other technologies."

Standards

While it is not the intent of this article to focus on standards, certainly standards play a role in authentic assessment. Schools and educational groups are already busy creating standards, from the classroom to the national level. Such standards describe the level of acceptable or desired competence but vary widely in their perspective. Standards can be analogous to "setting the bar": an athlete is expected to high jump (outcome) a five-foot bar (standard).

The Mid-continent Regional Educational Laboratory (McREL) distinguishes between content and performance standards. The critical difference is that a performance standard describes a task that a student is supposed to accomplish in order to demonstrate his or her knowledge or skill. In terms of fractions, a content standard might be "the ability to use fractions to solve problems"; a performance standard might be "a student should be able to accurately calculate how to share two pies among seven people equally." Content standards most closely resemble outcomes. Performance standards correlate to outcome indicators. Subcomponent standards refer to benchmarks, just as with outcomes-based educational terms.

Authentic Assessment

Assessment, in general, refers to gathering and analyzing information about students in order to determine their abilities. Assessment is a basic part of education because it enables one to determine whether students "get it," whether they meet the standard. Not surprisingly, outcomes are directly associated with authentic assessment. The underlying theory is that outcomes need to be authentic: that is, true to life and reflecting lifelong learning skills. Outcomes should also answer essential questions and use high-order thinking skills. Thus to measure outcomes, authentic assessment is usually called for, referring to a complex set of performances. It's the difference between describing how to ride a bike and actually putting the foot to the pedal and pumping down the street. Thus a scantron "bubble" test would be an unlikely authentic assessment tool; a student-directed play would more closely correlate to real life, and a Junior Achievement business venture would constitute a still more authentic assessment, especially as students count their profits.

Authentic assessments can assume many forms. In his book *Assessing Learning in the Classroom*, McTighe categorizes assessment items as

Product: lab report, story, poem, art exhibit, model, videotape, spreadsheet.

Performance: dance, demonstration, athletic competition, debate, recital.

Process: conference, interview, journal.

The assessment task itself should have these characteristics:

- multidimensional and complex in nature
- incorporated modalities of learning
- demonstrated progress over time
- learned with practice rather than based on native talent
- built on practice and feedback
- aligned with school outcomes and goals.

This approach to accountability not only helps students see the relevance of their learning but also reflects society's demands for education that prepares students for the world of work. Authentic assessment helps bridge the two worlds. By designing substantial projects, students demonstrate their ability to work with peers and accomplish specific tasks. They show that they can apply theoretical concepts to solving lifelike problems. As a result, education doesn't seem to operate in a vacuum; it truly prepares students for the rest of their lives. Real learning for real results.

Authentic assessment is not a one-time event. Just as in the work world, assessment in schools is an ongoing activity. As a person creates a draft or

> **With the surge in educational technology, information literacy skills can be assessed in new and creative ways.**

a model, that effort is analyzed and feedback is given so the product will be the best possible. So, too, in education; as students make a first attempt in a project, teachers should provide meaningful feedback. Students should assess their own work and their peers' to insure the best final results.

Rubrics

The next question that arises is, how does one assess projects objectively? Outcomes-based education typically includes rubrics that describe the performance at different levels of competencies. These rubrics are developed at the same time as the outcomes so that everyone involved in the outcome has a clear understanding of what is being measured and the degree of competency required at each level. A sample rubric for the ETF outcome quoted above appears in the box (page 13).

As the sample shows, the difference between levels of competence often lies in degree or thoroughness, such as "wide variety" versus "diverse" or "some" versus "many." These key words act as critical features to distinguish one level of competency from another. As teachers and students develop rubrics, they identify what is "good" by identifying these critical differences. Concurrently, rubrics are "anchored" in actual products or performances, so everyone knows what a "4" looks like in comparison to a "3" or "2" or "1." How different is this approach from the practice where a teacher gives an abstract goal or assignment and doesn't show any examples of the desired product at the beginning!

Electronic Projects

Key to achievement in outcomes-based education are the benchmarks that demonstrate authentic learning. The design and development of a product or presentation becomes the contextual vehicle for learning concepts and skills. Typically, a project spans several lesson units and crosses subject disciplines. Because of the amount of research and synthesis involved, products may demand an extended period of time. Products are often developed by a group of students, and the teacher acts as a facilitator. Thus, the product to be assessed also needs to be open-ended enough to allow each student to bring to it his individual gifts and to maximize individual learning.

Implications for Information Literacy

With the surge in educational technology, information literacy skills can be assessed in new and creative ways. The following examples highlight the potential for authentic assessment of information literacy skills using electronic products.

Newspaper or magazine simulation. Students recreate another time period or historical events by producing a newspaper or other publication of the day. For instance, a simulated paper on the day that Julius Caesar died might include scanned pictures of ancient Rome. Students would need to research Marc Antony, the Roman Senate, Roman mythology, and maybe Roman cuisine. They might find out about Roman entertainments, such as the Coliseum attractions, and incorporate advertisements for them. They would need to organize their findings in the form of newspaper layout and report writing. Students would probably use a Roman typeface, including the use of "V" for every "U"

Technology and Product Rubric

OUTSTANDING 4	HIGHLY COMPETENT 3	COMPETENT 2	NOT YET PROFICIENT 1
complexity in defining problems and stating thesis	clearly defines problem/states thesis	defines problems/states thesis	does not define problem/state thesis
accesses relevant information from a wide variety of sources	accesses relevant information from diverse sources	accesses relevant information	does not access relevant information
shows thorough understanding of the problem, concepts and processes	shows good understanding of the problem, concepts and processes	shows general understanding of the problem, concepts and processes	shows little or no understanding of the problem, concepts and processes
provides an exceptionally clear, coherent, complete, and organized explanation	provides a clear, coherent, complete, and organized explanation	provides a reasonably clear, coherent, complete, and organized explanation	provides an unclear or incomplete explanation
rarely contains technical errors	contains few technical errors	contains some technical errors	contains many technical errors
contains relevant information	contains relevant information	contains relevant information	contains very little information
uses correct language mechanics and usage	uses correct language mechanics and usage	uses correct language mechanics and usage	contains many errors in language mechanics and usage
production and composition are excellent	production and composition are good	production and composition are fair	production and composition are poor
integrates diverse technology effectively	integrates technology effectively	integrates technology	does not integrate technology

(since "u"s hadn't been invented yet).

Videotape production. Students can tape interviews with local experts about regional environment issues, and compare/contrast the talks with videos of affected nature. The video essay can demonstrate student ability to locate primary sources, identify main ideas, distinguish between fact and opinion, synthesize and sequence their research, and visually communicate what they learned.

Computer-Aided Design (CAD). Students can develop a model neighborhood, which could demonstrate their knowledge of community services and interrelationships. The project can be strengthened by introducing a crisis, such as a fire or major layoff. Students could also complement their CAD project through the use of spreadsheets to quantify the neighborhood economic "ecology." This added project shows how students have located and applied statistical information.

Multimedia presentation. Students can design a political advertising campaign on *HyperStudio* (Wagner) or other software program. Cards showing the candidate's background and political stance would concretely demonstrate student research results. Pictures portraying issues would show the student's ability to locate and select visual sources. Multimedia presentations can result in particularly useful assessments, for students would be learning globally or rationally rather than sequentially.

Web page publication. Students can create "WebQuests" about a topic, providing an electronic equivalent to a bibliographic essay. Selecting and describing significant Web links demonstrate the student's ability to locate and evaluate Internet sources. Web pages can also show how students organize their information for easy access.

Ways to Get Started

Here are some ways you can begin to introduce authentic assessment in your school.

■ Collect examples of authentic assessments of electronic products.

■ Build on existing strategies that incorporate electronic products. An easy method is to videotape a simulation; for example, students re-enacting a U.S. Senate proceeding instead of writing a paper about a Senate bill.

■ Collaborate with another teacher to design an interdisciplinary unit that weaves in authentic assessment and electronic products.

■ Brainstorm with students to identify electronic products that would demonstrate deep learning and also apply to daily life.

■ Use phrases such as "What does it look like?" "What do you feel when. . ." "How do you know?" as you think about and discuss assessment.

■ Start with a clear-cut presentation, such as a lab procedure or a step-by-step demonstration, and develop two rubrics, one that describes competence of the content and another that describes the presentation itself.

■ Have students develop electronic portfolios of their work in which they have to choose items that show progress over time and represent their best efforts. Then have students write reflective letters explaining their choices and assessing their own progress.

Lesley S.J. Farmer is the Library Media Teacher at Redwood High School in Larkspur, California. She is also the consulting editor for the Professional Growth Series published by Linworth and an editorial consultant to the magazine TECHNOLOGY CONNECTION. *She is the author of a number of books, including* Workshops for Teachers: Becoming Partners for Information Literacy *(Linworth).*

CONNECT YOUR STUDENTS ELECTRONICALLY TO LEARNING

Technology Assessment and Curriculum:
Teaching What Is Tested

By Mary Jo Milburn and Carolyn Rude-Parkins

Although some schools and some teachers were enthusiastic computer users more than 10 years ago, as many as half of the elementary teachers in a 1994 study had never used computers. The implications for their students in terms of lost opportunities in a country where 47% of workers used computers on the job in 1993 are staggering.

When technology use for instruction is optional, educators have the luxury to adopt it or not. However, when it becomes part of the district's curriculum and assessment process, the district officially places a value on technology integration that may provide the needed incentive.

Jefferson County (Kentucky) Public Schools (the 20th largest in the country, with 93,000 students and over 10,000 computers) defined the need to document student competence with technology. Although computers initially were installed more than 10 years ago, there was no curriculum or organized approach for evaluating their impact. Although many students have more advanced skills in additional technology areas, the district needed first to get baseline data on basic computer skills.

The district's initiative included curriculum development, which focused on creation of a Computer Application Skills Continuum and correlated classroom activities, and assessments, which were developed to test each item on the Skills Continuum.

CURRICULUM DEVELOPMENT

The District Instructional Technology Committee, composed of teachers, principals, counselors and librarians, was identified as a think tank of ideas for the assessment. Elementary, middle and high school teachers, along with staff members of the Computer Education Support Unit, developed and tested the Skills Continuum, assessments and activities. They were proponents for training and use of the products with district teachers and administrators.

Computer Application Skills Continuum

The Computer Application Skills Continuum identifies performance indicators in the areas of keyboarding, word processing, database, and spreadsheet for kindergarten through grade 12. The various indicators were developed with the understanding that the level and types of skills reflect the changing technology applications required of students in different grades. The skills are cumulative and by grade 12 students should have experience with the major functions typically used in software application packages of each type. They should have also experienced numerous ways to use each type of application.

Teacher reactions to the Skills Continuum included the comment, "following the curriculum has proven to me that students don't have to play games to be excited about computer class." Figure 1 gives some examples of entries on the Skills Continuum. (For a copy of the full Continuum, access the Jefferson County Public Schools home page on the World Wide Web at http://www.Jefferson.K12.US/continuum/continuum.html.)

Computer Curriculum Materials and Training

Inservice training on the Skills Continuum was conducted for teachers and school technology coordinators (STCs). Because of the variety of computers and applications programs in the schools, training on 15 different combinations of platform and software packages was conducted. Over 50 inservice sessions were held in a three-month period, with emphasis on the integration of

	Grade 5	Grade 10

D A T A B A S E	• Enter data on a formatted template
	• Browse records by scrolling
	• Search for specific information
	• Answer questions using database
	• Create simple database
	• Search for one attribute
	• Find specific record
	• Use search and tab functions
	• Sort data
		• Create database:
		   arrange data
		   sort data
		   find data
		   match data
		• Enter new record
		• Alter fields in existing record
		• Generate report
		• Print report with headers
		• Interpret data
		• Find data using Boolean Logic
		• Insert information from a database into a word processing document

Figure 1. Sample: Computer Application Skills Continuum

these computer skills into the regular curriculum.

STCs and participating teachers received Skills Continuum posters, and curriculum materials developed by teachers were disseminated via training sessions. The first set of materials, *Instructional Technology: Combining Interdisciplinary Units and Technology to Create a New Environment*, was produced in versions for elementary and middle/high school. These booklets were compilations of units developed by STCs as part of their training to implement the Kentucky Educational Technology System (KETS), one goal of the Kentucky Education Reform Act (KERA). The second set of materials, *Computer Cookbook*, was developed in versions for elementary, middle and high school. The *Cookbook* uses a catchy format to demonstrate activities for each skill on the Skills Continuum. (Figure 2 gives an example of a *Computer Cookbook* activity.)

ASSESSMENT

The assessment is an instructional tool to help the district and schools identify strengths and weaknesses. The District Instructional Technology Committee determined that grades 3, 5, 7, and 10 would be assessed.

Using the Skills Continuum, assessment items were developed for each entry and test protocols were pilot tested during the year. (Figure 3 shows example assess-

ment items.) A major consideration in writing the final assessment protocols was the different platforms and software packages involved. Over 5,000 disks were formatted and duplicated for use in 150 schools to test a random sample of more than 4,000 students.

Information pertaining to the Continuum and assessment was presented to STCs, principals, and central office administrators in meetings during the fall. A videotape presenting details of the assessment was also produced and downloaded to schools for presen-

---

DATABASE RECIPES

DISH: Movies and Microchips

GOALS: • To create and enter data in a database
• To search a database for specific information

TECHNOLOGY SKILL LEVEL: Intermediate

SUBJECT AREAS: Social Studies, Language Arts

INGREDIENTS: Software: word processing, database, spreadsheet, movie and music guides

BAKE: Two weeks

DIRECTIONS:
• Ask students what movies they have seen in the last month and list them on the chalkboard.
• Ask students what information would be most important if they were telling their friends about the movie. Examples: Title, male star, female star, director, Academy Award, type/classification, price, length, theme song.
• Have students create a database using the field names listed by the class.
• Find the male and female stars and movie theme songs that have won an Academy Award by sorting through the data.
• Have the students find the information that they submitted for the database.
• Have the students use the "find" function to list all movies by famous directors such as Steven Spielberg, Ron Howard, Penny Marshall, or Spike Lee.

PARENT/EXTENSION ACTIVITIES
• Create a database at home of the movies that your family has seen. Add to it as you attend or rent new movies. (This may be done on index cards if a computer is not available.)
• Become movie critics like Siskel and Ebert and add comments to your database. What do you like or dislike about the movie? Would you recommend it to a friend?
• Develop your own rating system (1-10, 1-5 stars) and add to your database. Neighbors and friends can read your entries and get opinions before renting or attending.

Figure 2. Sample: Computer Cookbook Activity

Grade 5 - Southeastern States Database
SOUTHEASTERN STATES DATABASE QUESTIONS
1. What is the capital of South Carolina? _____
2. Which of the southeastern states has the largest population? _____

Grade 5 - Fast Food Spreadsheet
FAST FOOD SPREADSHEET QUESTIONS
1. How many calories are in Burger King's Whopper, fries, and shake? _____
2. What is the amount of cholesterol in Domino's pepperoni pizza? _____
3. Which food has 1,125 calories? _____
4. Which meal had the least number of fat grams? _____
5. Which meal had the most calories? _____
6. What is entered in cell D9? _____

Figure 3. Sample: Assessment Items

tation during faculty meetings. A brochure was developed and sent to all parents of students in Grades 3, 5, 7, and 10. The assessment was implemented in late spring.

BASELINE ASSESSMENT RESULTS

The results of the first-year assessment reveal patterns of student competence across the grades and across competencies. (See graphs of the results in Figure 4.) In keyboarding skills, student competence rose at a steady rate from grade 3 to grade 10. In word processing skills, results were highest at fifth grade, then declined at middle and high school. In database management skills, the highest average score was in grade 5, with a drop at middle and a rise in high school. In spreadsheet skills, again the highest score was in grade 5, with subsequent drops in middle and high school.

Except for keyboarding, the greatest competency was shown at grade 5. Clearly, elementary schools focus time and attention on providing experiences for their students on these skills. Middle schools and high schools appear to offer less opportunity in these areas. These differences may be explained by higher student-to-computer ratios at the higher grade levels, lack of specialized computer teachers, and lack of technology integration activities in the content areas. Overall, middle and high school students simply have less opportunity to learn technology skills.

FUTURE DIRECTIONS

The results suggest several actions should be taken immediately. The student-to-computer ratio should be lowered, particularly in middle school, by adding up-to-date hardware and software. More exposure to hands-on activities that integrate technology with content area tasks should be provided for middle and high school students. Older students must understand the relevance of keyboarding, word processing, database and spreadsheet skills to job opportunities and further education, in order to make it worth their time to seek out these skills.

Although this assessment is performance-based, it does not include the examination of authentic student work, products more in line with the philosophy of KERA. Teachers commented that they would prefer to assess application of skills via performance-based activities created throughout the year in a variety of curriculum-related activities.

In the coming years, the assessment will be expanded to additional students by request in some schools. Other areas will be assessed, such as multimedia, electronic information retrieval, ethics and legal issues. The expanded Computer Application Skills Continuum and curriculum materials are already under development. **TC**

Mary Jo Milburn is a Curriculum Specialist in the Computer Education Support Unit of Jefferson County Public Schools in Louisville, Kentucky. Carolyn Rude-Parkins is Associate Professor and Director of the Education Resource and Technology Center at the University of Louisville (Kentucky).

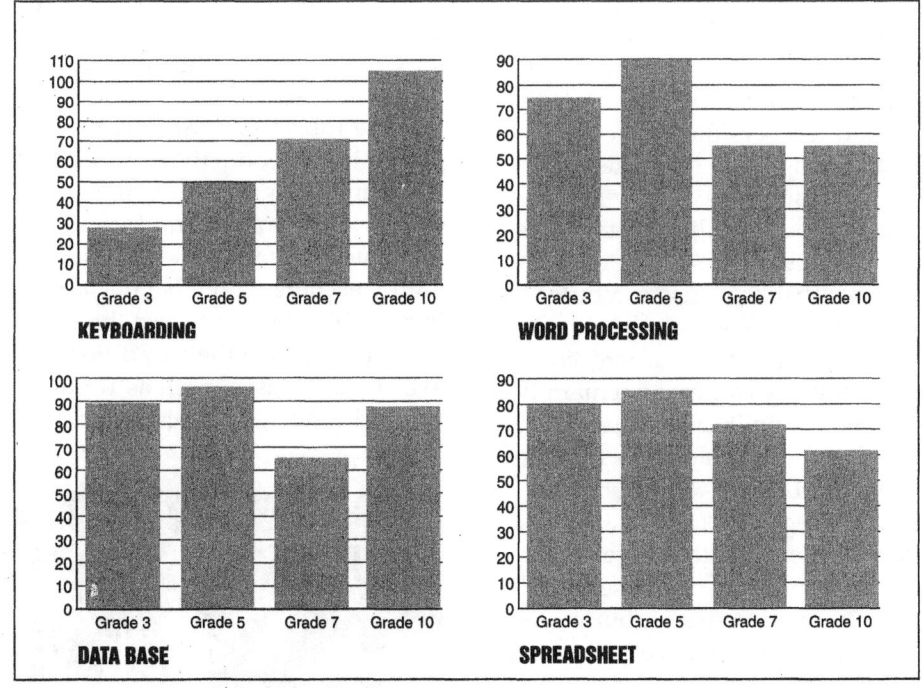

Figure 4. Baseline Assessment Results

ASSESSMENT — THEN AND NOW

What Does It Look Like?

Part 1
The CODE 77 Rubrics

By Doug Johnson

Parents and administrators want computer-literate teachers. Students seek out teachers who meaningfully use technology, and teachers themselves acknowledge that computer skills are increasingly necessary and important in fulfilling their professional duties. The specific computer skills that comprise computer literacy, however, are rarely articulated. As it applies to teachers, computer literacy can easily remain ill-defined—a politically correct buzz word without meaning or purpose.

When Mankato Area Public Schools began its formal staff development program five years ago to train teachers to use technology, I wrote a series of rubrics, or graduated performance indicators, to describe what the district expected a computer-using teacher to be able to do after 30 hours of formal computer instruction and six to nine months of practice. The name of our program, CODE 77, stands for Computers On Desks Everywhere in District 77.

These rubrics primarily address professional productivity and are the foundation on which more complex technology and technology-related professional skills are built. Teachers who have mastered these skills are able to use the computer to improve their traditional instructional tasks, such as writing, record keeping, designing student materials, and presenting lessons. These skills also build the confidence teachers need to use technology to restructure the educational process. (For rubrics describing the Advanced Teacher Computer Use skills, see this month's *Head for the Edge* column.)

Each of the ten rubrics has four levels:

Level 1 Pre-awareness
Level 2 Awareness
Level 3 Mastery
Level 4 Advanced

We initially designed our training efforts with the assumption that most teachers would be at Level 1 or 2. By the end of the training, we anticipated that teachers would be at Level 3 or 4 in most skill areas and would have advanced at least one level in all areas.

These rubrics have served two

purposes in our district. We have been able to judge the effectiveness of our staff development efforts by asking teachers to complete an anonymous self-assessment before and after training using the rubrics. Then simple graphs showing the percentage of training participants at each level before and after training are constructed to share the results with the staff development committees and the administration. The rubrics also provide a "road map" for teachers to improve their computer skills. By examining the specific skills described, teachers know in what areas they need to take classes or to continue practice.

Below are both the instructions to teachers for completing a self-assessment and the rubrics themselves. Feel free to use and modify the rubrics for your district's needs and as technology changes. These rubrics can also be modified to benchmark student performance. See Jamieson McKenzie's adaptation of these rubrics for that purpose at http://www.bham.wednet.edu/assess2.htm.) TC

Doug Johnson is the District Media Supervisor for the Mankato (Minnesota) Public Schools, and can be reached by e-mail at djohns1@west.isd77.k12.mn.us (or) palsdaj@vax1.mankato.msus.edu.

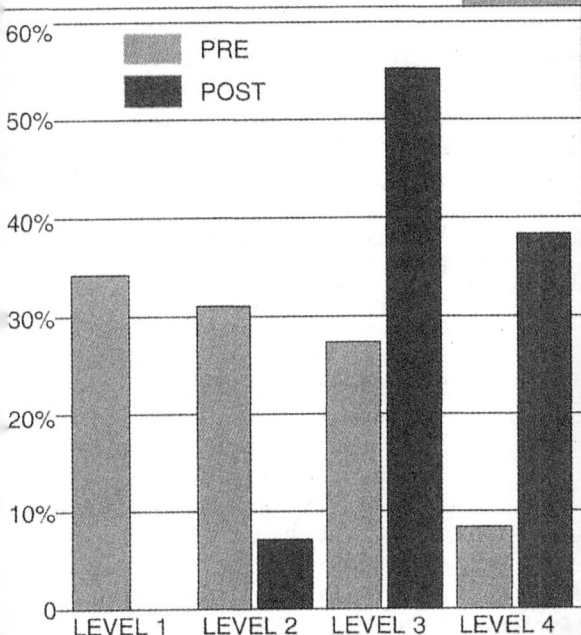

CODE 77 Self-Evaluation

Please judge your level of achievement in each of the following competencies. Circle the number that best reflects your current level of skill attainment. At the end of the training program, you will complete the same set of rubrics to reflect your level of skill attainment at that time. (Level 3 is considered mastery.) This tool is to help measure the effectiveness of our training program, and to help you do a self-analysis to determine the areas in which you should continue to learn and practice. Keep a copy of these rubrics to refer to during the training.

I. Basic computer operation

Level 1—I do not use a computer.
Level 2—I can use the computer to run a few specific, preloaded programs. It has little effect on either my work or home life. I am somewhat anxious I might damage the machine or its programs.
Level 3—I can set up my computer and peripheral devices, load software, print, and use most of the operating system tools like the scrapbook, clock, note pad, find command, and trash can (recycling bin). I can format a data disk.
Level 4—I can run two programs simultaneously and can have several windows open at the same time. I can customize the look and sounds of my computer. I use techniques like shift-clicking to work with multiple files. I look for programs and techniques to maximize my operating system. I feel confident enough to teach others some basic operations.

II. File management

Level 1—I do not save any documents I create using the computer.
Level 2—I save documents I've created, but I cannot choose where they are saved. I do not back up my files.
Level 3—I have a filing system for organizing my files and can locate files quickly and reliably. I backup my files to floppy disk or other storage device on a regular basis.
Level 4—I regularly run a disk optimizer on my hard drive and use a backup program to make copies of my files on a weekly basis. I have a system for archiving files that I do not need on a regular basis to conserve my computer's hard drive space.

III. Word processing

Level 1—I do not use a word processor, and I cannot identify any uses or features it might have that would benefit the way I work.
Level 2—I occasionally use the word processor for simple documents that I know I will modify and use again. I generally find it easier to handwrite or type most of my written work.
Level 3—I use the word processor for nearly all my written professional work: memos, tests, worksheets, and home communications. I can edit, spell check, and change the format of a document. I can paginate, preview, and print my work. I feel my work looks professional.
Level 4—I use the word processor not only for my work but also with students to help them improve their own communication skills.

IV. Spreadsheet use

Level 1—I do not use a spreadsheet, and I cannot identify any uses or features it might have that would benefit the way I work.
Level 2—I understand the use of a spreadsheet and can navigate within one. I can create a simple spreadsheet to add a column of numbers.
Level 3—I use a spreadsheet for several applications. These spreadsheets use labels, formulas, and cell references. I can change the format of the spreadsheets by changing column widths and text

Rubrics for Basic Teacher Computer Use

style. I can use the spreadsheet to make a simple graph or chart.
Level 4—I use the spreadsheet not only for my work but also with students to help them improve their own data keeping and analysis skills.

V. Database use
Level 1—I do not use a database, and I cannot identify any uses or features it might have that would benefit the way I work.
Level 2—I understand the use of a database and can locate information within one that has been pre-made. I can add or delete data in a database.
Level 3—I use databases for personal applications. I can create an original database by defining fields and creating layouts. I can find, sort, and print information in layouts that are clear and useful to me.
Level 4—I can use formulas with my database to create summaries of numerical data. I can use database information to mail merge in a word processing document. I use the database not only for my work but also with students to help them improve their own data keeping and analysis skills.

VI. Graphics use
Level 1—I do not use graphics in my word processing or presentations, and I cannot identify any uses or features they might have that would benefit the way I work.
Level 2—I can open and create simple pictures with the painting and drawing programs. I can use programs like *PrintShop* or *SuperPrint*.
Level 3—I use both pre-made clip art and simple original graphics in my word processed documents and presentation. I can edit clip art, change its size, and place it on a page. I can purposefully use most of the drawing tools, and can group and un-group objects. I can use the clipboard to take graphics from one application to another. The use of graphics in my work helps clarify or amplify my message.
Level 4—I use graphics not only for my work but also with students to help them improve their own communications. I can use graphics and the word processor to create a professional-looking newsletter.

VII. Hypermedia use
Level 1—I do not use hypermedia (*HyperStudio*), and I cannot identify any uses or features it might have that would benefit the way I work.
Level 2—I can navigate through a pre-made hypermedia program.
Level 3—I can create my own hypermedia stacks for information presentation. These stacks use navigation buttons, sounds, dissolves, graphics, and text fields. I can use an LCD projection device to display the presentation to a class.
Level 4—I use hypermedia with students who are making their own stacks for information keeping and presentation.

VIII. Network use
Level 1—I do not use the online resources available in my building, and I cannot identify any uses or features they might have that would benefit the way I work.
Level 2—I understand that there is a large amount of information available to me as a teacher that can be accessed through networks, including the Internet. With the help of the media specialist, I can use the resources on the network in our building.
Level 3—I use the networks to access professional and personal information from a variety of sources, including networked CD-ROM reference materials, online library catalogs, the ERIC database, and the World Wide Web. I have an e-mail account that I use on a regular basis.
Level 4—Using telecommunications, I am an active participant in online discussions, and I can download files and programs from remote computers. I use telecommunications with my students.

IX. Student assessment
Level 1—I do not use the computer for student assessment.
Level 2—I understand that there are ways I can keep track of student progress using the computer. I keep some student-produced materials on the computer, and I write evaluations of student work and notes to parents with the word processor.
Level 3—I effectively use an electronic grade book to keep track of student data, and I keep portfolios of student-produced materials on the computer. I use the electronic data during parent/teacher conferences.
Level 4—I rely on the computer to keep track of outcomes and objectives students have mastered. I use that information in determining assignments, teaching strategies, and groupings.

X. Ethical use understanding
Level 1—I am not aware of any ethical issues surrounding computer use.
Level 2—I know that some copyright restrictions apply to computer software.
Level 3—I clearly understand the difference between freeware, shareware, and commercial software and the fees involved in the use of each. I know the programs for which the district or my building holds a site license. I understand the school board policy on the use of copyrighted materials. I demonstrate ethical usage of all software and let my students know my personal stand on legal and moral issues involving technology. I know and enforce the school's technology policies and guidelines, including its Internet acceptable use policy. I have a personal philosophy I can articulate regarding the use of technology in education.
Level 4—I am aware of other controversial aspects of technology use, including data privacy, equitable access, and free speech issues. I can speak about a variety of technology issues at my professional association meetings, to parent groups, and to the general community.

Rubrics for Restructuring (Continuation of The CODE 77 Rubrics) Part II

By Doug Johnson

Is technology being used in your school to accomplish anything that otherwise would be impossible? Other professions have used technology to make possible:

- banking services from home
- medical CAT scans custom-fitted
- blue jeans at a mass-production cost
- full-text searching for information in national databases
- the globalization of industries
- astronomical amounts of data from unimaginable distances
- customized news and information services
- distance training and customer support services.

Yet education is primarily using technology only to reinforce traditional educational practices.

Most teacher training classes are designed to give teachers a familiarity with the computer skills that help them improve their professional productivity: basic computer operation, word processing, telecommunication, and record keeping. (See *The CODE 77 Rubrics* in last month's issue.) But if technology is to realize its powerful potential for improving education, it must be used for more than just automating the traditional methods and practices of teaching.

The rubrics below are designed to help teachers move to the next level of professional computer use. Rather than the computer simply being a tool that allows a common task to be done more efficiently, these skills fundamentally change how instruction is delivered, how student performance is measured, and how teachers view themselves as professionals. The technology is used to restructure the educational process to allow it to do things it has never been able to do before. These include using technology to ensure that:

- all students master the basic skills of reading, writing, and computation
- all students practice authentic information literacy and research skills and the higher-order thinking skills inherent in them
- all students have access to top-quality resources, including human resources, regardless of location
- all teachers provide students and parents with
    - individual education plans

- continuous feedback on how well students are meeting their learning goals
- opportunities for virtual student performance assessments
- all teachers have the tools and ability to:
  - locate the research findings that will guide their use of technology
  - collect the data that measures the effectiveness of their practices.

These advanced rubrics are designed for the same purposes as the beginning CODE 77 rubrics—to help schools measure the effectiveness of their teacher training efforts and to guide teachers on their own learning path.

CODE 77 Self-Evaluation Rubrics for Advanced Teacher Computer Use

I. Instructional software use

Level 1

I do not use instructional software as a part of my instructional program, nor am I aware of any titles that might help my students meet their learning goals.

Level 2

I use a few computer programs as an instructional supplement, as a reward, or with special needs students.

Level 3

I use several programs (drill and practice, simulations, and tutorials) chosen by my department or grade level to help all my students meet specific learning objectives. The software allows me to teach or reinforce concepts more effectively than traditional methods. When it is available, I use the software's management system to help assess individual student performance. I use technological resources to meet the needs of students who do not respond to traditional methods of instruction.

Level 4

I seek new programs for evaluation and adoption. I know sources of software reviews and stay current on new developments in computer technologies through professional reading and conference attendance. I share my findings with other professionals.

II. Information literacy skills

Level 1

I am not familiar with the term information literacy, nor do I know why such skills are important.

Level 2

As a part of my curriculum, I have library research projects, and I support the library skills taught by the media specialist. I am aware that there are electronic resources available to my students.

> *If technology is to realize its powerful potential for improving education, it must be used for more than just automating the traditional methods and practices of teaching.*

Level 3

My curriculum includes multiple projects that have an information literacy component. These are team-taught with the media specialist. I understand the Big Six or a similar information literacy process and design student projects so they require higher-level thinking skills, use electronic information sources, require the use of computer productivity software, and are authentically assessed. I guide my students in accessing, evaluating, and using information and experts from worldwide sources through the Internet and videoconferencing.

Level 4

I am actively involved in curriculum-planning teams and advocate for multidisciplinary units and activities that require information-literacy skills. I share successful units with others through print and electronic publishing and through conference presentations and workshops.

III. Modification of instructional delivery

Level 1

I have one or two effective methods of delivering content or teaching skills to my students. I do not use technology that requires me to change my instructional methodology.

Level 2

I have tried units or projects that are student-directed, use small groups, or are highly individualized, but I primarily use teacher-directed, whole-group instruction.

Level 3

I use a variety of instructional delivery methods and student grouping strategies routinely throughout the year. I can design activities and approaches that best fit the learning objectives and the technology available to me. I can use small groups working cooperatively or in rotation to take advantage of student-to-equipment ratios of greater than one-to-one. I modify instructional methods to take advantage of the learning styles of individual students.

Level 4

I continually try new approaches suggested by research or observation to discover the most effective means of using technology to engage my students and meet curricular goals. I work with a team of teachers to create, modify, and improve my practices in this area.

IV. Assessment of student performance

Level 1

I evaluate my students using objective tests only.

Level 2

I evaluate some student performances or projects using subjective criteria. I save some student work for cumulative folders and parent conferences and print some electronically-produced student work.

I use a wide range of assessments to evaluate student projects and performances. I can create assessment tools like checklists, rubrics, and benchmarks, which help students assess their own performance and allow me to objectively determine the quality of student work. I ask students to keep a physical and an electronic portfolio of their work. Students and their parents have the means to continually access the recorded progress students are making toward their learning goals through networked grade books and portfolios. Students are given the opportunity to demonstrate skills through performance to a wide audience via data and video networks. I have a means of aggregating performance data for my class, which I use to modify my teaching activities and strategies.

I continually try new approaches suggested by research or observation to discover the most effective means of using technology to assess student learning. I work with a team of teachers to create, modify, and improve my work in this area.

V. Individualization of the educational program

I modify my curriculum or instructional methods only for students with identified special needs.

I occasionally give students the choice of assignments in my class, but all class members (unless they are in special education) must meet the same learning objectives within the same time frame. Skill remediation is done during summer school or informally during or after school.

Level 3

With the assistance of the student, parents, and appropriate specialists, I create an individualized learning plan for each of my students. I track the accomplishment of learning goals in the plan using a computerized tool. I use this tool during parent conferences and for school or state reporting. Students and their parents have networked access to this tool for continual monitoring of progress and plan modification.

Level 4

I provide suggestions about the content and design of the individualized computerized planning and report tools.

VI. Professional growth and communication

Level 1

I do not use electronic resources for professional growth or communication.

Level 2

I can find lesson plans and some research in online databases. I use e-mail to correspond with parents and other teachers.

Level 3

I use the Internet and other online resources to obtain research findings, teaching materials, and information related to the content of my classes. I read electronic newsletters and journals to stay current on educational practices. I participate in electronic discussion groups and chat rooms that are related to my area of education, and I contribute to and use the best practices discussed there. I use a computerized presentation program when giving workshops or speaking at conferences. I use technology to take part in distance learning opportunities for my own professional development.

Level 4

I organize professional growth opportunities for other teachers and feel comfortable teaching other staff members about the use of technology.

VII. Research and evaluation of technology use

Level 1

I have not attempted to determine whether the use of instructional technology has made a difference in my students' learning or classroom climate.

Level 2

I gather, use, and share anecdotal information and observations about student use of technology in my classroom.

Level 3

I use action research and aggregated data to accurately determine whether the technology and methodology I am using has an impact on how well my students learn and on school climate.

Level 4

I participate in formal studies conducted by professional groups and academics on the impact of technology on student learning. I have designed such studies as part of my own professional education. I report to other professionals electronically and in print the findings of my research.

To help teachers master these complex skills will be a greater, more time-consuming task than the simple hands-on classes in which word processing, e-mail, and file management were taught. And it can't be done by the technology department alone. Staff development in technology will require a collaborative effort with experts in the content areas, child development, curriculum, assessment, research, and evaluation.

These challenging skills will take time, effort, and courage to master, but schools with teachers who do so will be in a superior position to meet future educational demands. **TC**

Doug Johnson is the District Media Supervisor for the Mankato (Minnesota) Public Schools and can be reached by e-mail at djohns1@west.isd77.k12.mn.us (or) palsdaj@vax1.mankato.msus.edu.

Notes

Ethical Issues

The wealth of information available to students today creates a dilemma. Young people have access to an incredible variety of resources. They can create the sort of reports only graduate students and professional presenters would consider a few years ago. On the other hand, the prospect of locating and working with all this information can be so daunting that some students will opt for the simplest route to a grade. They'll cut and paste bits from a handful of CD-ROM encyclopedias and nicely illustrated Web sites. Sometimes they may even print out a ready-made paper, courtesy of the Internet. Most teachers were able to catch term papers plagiarized from *World Book* through vocabulary and sentence structure. But with student-written pieces rife in cyberspace, it is not as easy as it used to be to spot the appropriation of another's work without permission.

Now more than ever, it is not enough simply to turn young people loose in the fields of research. We need to provide guidelines, as well as constant reminders that information (especially direct quotes) needs to be cited, both in one's notes and in the final product. We unfortunately need to make students aware that not everyone posting information on the World Wide Web is as conscientious and ethical as we are encouraging *them* to be. Just as, in past years, we taught youngsters to look carefully at the copyright dates of books and the political biases of certain periodicals, today we also have them pay attention to sources as well as dates of Web sites to determine reliability.

The potential for teaching information literacy skills in this new environment is exciting. For years educators have talked about promoting critical thinking among students. The confusing wealth of sources available today makes this more a necessity than an option. And as multimedia resources augment traditional tools for both research and presentation, so do innovative report formats join the old-fashioned term paper in the repertoire of class requirements among progressive teachers, reducing the temptation to "cut and paste" and plagiarize. With our existing backgrounds and comfort with developing technologies, we school library media specialists can be in the vanguard, introducing both teachers and students to modern information literacy skills with which to manage both classroom and real-life problems and questions.

URL UPDATES

Using Technology to Cultivate Thinking Dispositions:

www.hern.hawaii.edu/hern95/hern95.html

How To Help Students Deal With 'Too Much Information'

By Edna M. Boardman

I GAVE A STUDENT A TRIP THROUGH the sources she might use for her somewhat offbeat research topic. Here, I told her, were the books she might use, pointing out several sections in the collection where they were shelved. One book has a useful bibliography because many of the titles are available in this library. I suggested subject headings, CD-ROM disks to explore, other libraries in town to consult, and persons to interview.

She turned away. "I think I'll do it on capital punishment," she said. "There's just too much information."

I kicked myself down the hall, because this was by no means the first time this had happened. I had dumped so many possibilities on the student that I had spooked her into taking refuge in a topic treated by dozens of students each year. There was little new for her to learn. She already knew the parameters of the issue of capital punishment from listening to many discussions of the subject.

The quantity of information available to our students explodes. The answer to "what do you have on..." is no longer a book and two or three periodical articles, as it was a few years ago. Now our students can tap into databases that flash the bibliographical information and location of hundreds of books on the computer screen. They can find thousands of articles on full-text CD-ROMs and can quickly scan CD-ROM encyclopedias and other reference sources. And, through still other indexes, a wide array of periodical articles, accessible through interlibrary loan, are available on any conceivable topic.

My concern focuses on the student I tried to serve. What was going on in her mind when, instead of glorying in the mass of new-to-her information, she took refuge instead in a more manageable topic? Since the information glut is not going to go away, how can we help students like her select what they need without triggering panic?

I think I know how other students are coping. Some will do a paper on, say, seat belts and air bags in grade seven, then basically repeat the same material in every paper, discussion group, or speech through grade 12. Since they move from teacher to teacher and building to building, it is difficult for an individual teacher to identify this pattern. The product is pretty good because the student, after a while, knows the subject very well.

Sometimes I feel as if I could meet 80% of the demand for research materials in my library if I collected materials on about a dozen topics: abortion, drunken driving, capital punishment, seat belts, censorship.... You can easily complete the list.

Sometimes I feel as if I could meet 80% of the demand for research materials in my library if I collected materials on about a dozen topics: abortion, drunken driving, capital punishment, seat belts, censorship.... You can easily complete the list. It is troubling to think that, as our information base explodes, with more available in more interesting formats on more topics, too many students show an inclination to retrench—to force us to create, for their daily assignment use, a collection too heavy on a limited number of topics.

It is important to collect excellent materials on the "popular" topics.

Edna M. Boardman is a Library Media Specialist at the Magic City Campus of Minot High School in Minot, North Dakota.

When teachers give research assignments, they have two important goals: teaching content and teaching process. It would hardly serve our students well to get so uptight about their narrow topic preference that we cut back on the possibilities for process—selecting a topic of interest, narrowing, choosing a point of view, and arriving at a conclusion.

The first step in dealing with this problem, I think, is to become aware of its existence. What a teacher took for granted when materials were more limited—that most students would do well to find a dozen pieces of material treating their topic—is no longer true, and this requires a rethinking of assignments.

Teachers and library media specialists need to—

• Gang up on students to keep them from reverting to their comfort zones, even in assignments where the choice of topic is open. One of the marks of giftedness is the ability to stick with and grow with an area across developmental stages. Most students who report on capital punishment and seat belts class after class are not in a growth mode.

• Pay more attention to how students select their topics. In communications courses, research and technical skills, the ability to organize and reason and present are what the teacher is looking for; the actual topics of the piece is a secondary consideration, but perhaps should not be. As I look back on my teaching in the high school English classroom, I think the most serious mistake I made was to make the choice of topic almost entirely my students' problem. Helping them explore possibilities and find interesting things to write about is surely a teacher's obligation.

• Explore more consciously the process of choosing from the mass of material available. This is not done too well, I think, because I still see students who quickly grab whatever they first see relating to their chosen topic and run with it. Part of the solution may be as simple as showing students examples of how long 1,000 words is. Let students look at a 10-page paper. I spot panic when students begin their projects with little awareness of how much reading or writing they have to do to produce the end product. When I suggest greater selectivity, students still say, "I can't narrow my topic. I've got 12 pages to fill!"

• Spend some class time helping the students to evaluate sources. One author is better or less well qualified than another. One has researched the material more carefully than another. One periodical publishes the results of scientific research, the other is into "infotainment." One magazine has a political bias or some other agenda to promote, but another searches for the truth and lets the chips fall where they may.

• Give students more help in narrowing the topic and emphasizing that limited aspect without narrowing it so much that nothing can be found about it. Teachers who force students to declare a topic before research has begun and then stick with it, no matter what, create great frustration. The occasional student switches topics at the slightest hint of difficulty, and that one needs some attention too. It helps if students recognize up front that there will be large quantities of information. The challenge to students is not to find something "about" their chosen topic but to determine what will fit their needs.

• Struggle with the students as they explore the indexes. This is a teaching job of the library media specialist as well as of the teacher. If a student has typed "Rain Forest" into the online catalog, look with the student at what pops up. The dozen or more books on the printout are not of a piece, though I think students are often only vaguely aware of this. One book deals with the practical products of the rain forest. The book by William Beebe is a historical piece. Two books are about one of the few temperate zone rain forests—in Washington state. There is a book about endangered animals and another about the problems of the contemporary peoples of the rain forest. Yet another focuses on what might happen to the climate of the earth if current rates of rain forest destruction continue. Is this "too much information" again? Probably. But there is no way that we can or will go back to a time when a student had access to only a book or two about the rain forest and had to make do with the limitations no matter what.

It may even help to ask students to stand back and look at the media themselves—the means through which we get information. I think this is difficult for them to do because the mass media fill their lives so completely that it is like taking notice of the air they breathe.

The direction is definitely to continue to expand and multiply the sources arrayed before the researching high school student. Now we need to tackle the job of helping them deal with the quantity itself.

Notes

Easy To Find *But* Not Necessarily True

By Steve Baule

Finding information has long been one of the "cornerstone" skills of librarians. "Asking the librarian" was a common step in the student's research process ten years ago. However, many of us have found that technology has changed this. No longer do we regularly face a line of students needing assistance to find books on wolves, genetic engineering, drug abuse or whatever is the topic of the week. The teachers haven't stopped making these assignments; the kids are gone because they are surfing through cyberspace.

Besides the solid information on wolves they found at the Natural History Museum site, they have also found "true" stories of werewolves, a new punk band named Black Wolf, and statistics on Wolf, South Dakota. To the eighth grader, the werewolf information may be the most interesting. And since it is on the Internet, it must be true.

We now face a greater challenge in helping students evaluate the information they find. This becomes particularly difficult when students are sifting through hundreds or even thousands of items that might be found with a simple keyword search on the World Wide Web.

Our first task is to teach young people to look at four aspects of evaluating information found on the Web:
1. The purpose of the article or other information
2. The author's credibility
3. Publication date and the date of the last updating
4. Wording of site titles.

The Purpose of the Article
You should help students learn to determine the purpose of information they find on the Internet. Teach them to ask questions such as, Is the site trying to sell a product? Who sponsors the site? Is the sponsor a library, a museum, or other organization that provides solid information? What is the purpose of the site? Does it specialize in information on the research topic or is this information part of a program on other topics?

The Author's Credibility
When teaching about the credibility of a source, use the bizarre. Ask the students where they would go for information about UFO sightings in Arizona and give them a sample listing of articles to choose from. Use a range of sources, such as *Time* or *Newsweek* and tabloid newspapers. After a few minutes of discussion, you may be amazed how well students understand the reliability of popular news sources.

Some further questions for teaching young researchers to evaluate sources are: Was the information developed by a student or teacher of the topic? Did the author identify himself or herself? What does the author's willingness to identify his or her credentials say about credibility?

Publication Date and Date of Updates
When was the information published or posted on the Web? Is the information current? Was the information posted before or after the event you are researching occurred? If we could reach every student with these questioning techniques, the nation would probably have fewer conspiracy theories.

Wording of Site Titles
Students get better search results if they look for their research topic or keyword in the title of Web pages. This eliminates many irrelevant treatments of their topics. In addition, teaching students and teachers how to narrow searches and make the best use of search engines is a good use of time. Make sure they know where to find the "help" feature for each of the search engines.

Going Back to Print
Going to the Internet for every information need may be trendy, but it isn't always a good use of time. Searching for the name of the capitol of India on the Internet is not as efficient as using an almanac from the bookshelf. One assignment that recently came through our library required the student to find a picture of the first atom bomb. When the librarian started for the shelves, the student told her that the teacher said the picture had to come from the Internet.

Promoting good print materials and non-Internet electronic sources for each assignment to both students and teachers is essential. One method is to develop "pathfinders" or research-helper handouts that list the appropriate sources for assignments. Among the resources, list books, electronic resources, and World Wide Web sites. Work with teachers to ensure that students include at least one or two references from each type of source listed in the handout.

Asking teachers to avoid Internet-only assignments is another method to encourage students to use the best source. Make sure the teachers understand the need to allow students to use the best source for their assignments. Explaining to teachers that, in the past, they seldom required students to use only one resource in a research assignment may drive home the point that requiring an Internet search may not be the best directions.

When explaining the new dimensions of finding information, remember to end your instructions to students and teachers with "and if you need assistance, ask a librarian."

Steve Baule is Director of Information Technologies, New Trier High School in Winnetka, Illinois. He is an editorial consultant for TECHNOLOGY CONNECTION. His book Technology Planning *is available from Linworth.*

CONNECT YOUR STUDENTS ELECTRONICALLY TO LEARNING

feature

Using Technology to Cultivate Thinking Dispositions

By Violet H. Harada and Joan Yoshina

Creating a Critical Thinking Culture

Mililani Mauka Elementary in Honolulu, Hawaii, sought to address the issue of integrating critical thinking skills and technology in instruction by providing staff development opportunities for its faculty. The school, which opened in 1993, serves 650 students (K-grade 6). All classrooms, the library, and offices are networked for voice, video, and data communication. A computer lab with 32 stations offers direct connection to the Internet. For the past three years, the staff has explored ways to create a critical thinking environment in the school. With consultants from Harvard University-based Project Zero, teachers and support staff discussed ways to encourage higher order thinking. Using a model of effective thinking developed at Harvard by David Perkins, Eileen Jay, and Shari Tishman, the faculty studied seven dispositions critical to the thinking process: being broad and adventurous, sustaining intellectual curiosity, clarifying and seeking understanding, planning strategically, being intellectually careful, seeking and evaluating reasons, and being metacognitive.

In his book, *Smart Schools: From Training Memories to Educating Minds* (Macmillan, 1992), Perkins emphasizes the need for teachers to encourage these dispositions by "naming them, modeling them, creating time for them, helping students see how to pursue them, and rewarding them." The staff studied ways to translate these dispositions into practice.

Incorporating Technology

An additional challenge was to determine how available technology might be incorporated into the learning environment. Last summer, a teacher-librarian team from the school participated in a federally-funded training initiative as part of the Hawaii Education and Research Network (HERN). The team worked with educational experts in such areas as Internet resource development, interactive curriculum design, and collaborative learning strategies, to design multidisciplinary units of study.

Following the summer training, the team shared its work with teachers in grades 4 through 6. In the fall, the teachers implemented units in social studies and science that emphasized a resource-based approach to learning and incorporated the use of the Internet and multimedia/CD-ROM resources.

Teachers worked closely with the librarian and computer lab coordinator to provide students with access to various sources of information. Organized in teams, students created their own Web pages which were posted on the school's home page (http://kalama.doe.hawaii.edu//hern95/pt006/). The crucial point was that faculty consciously used technology to support a critical thinking environment.

Technology Supporting a Thinking Environment

The teachers and librarian wanted students to build knowledge and meaning by connecting their prior understandings with new information. To encourage students to *be broad and adventurous*, teachers allowed them to select their own topics within a larger theme. For example, the sixth graders could select any international conflict to study as part of a semester-long unit on conflict and compromise. In making their selections, students visited Web sites that dealt with current conflicts around the world. Hypertext links on the Web provided students with multiple branching opportunities that motivated them to search. Browsing and exploring also extended to electronic resources in the library and television newscasts at home with their parents.

Teachers and the librarian stimulated *sustained curiosity* in students by challenging them to generate thoughtful questions about what they were discovering. A girl, who found information on the Internet about Haitian emigration, wondered, "Why are people leaving?" Another student, browsing through an article on China in an electronic encyclopedia asked, "Why are female babies mistreated?" Questions like these became the springboards for students to select topics and issues of personal interest.

The team also used strategies, including cooperative teams and conferencing, to help students *clarify and seek understanding* as they gathered information. For several weeks, students moved back and forth between classroom, library, and computer lab finding pieces of information and taking notes. Working with computers, in particular, nurtured collaborative learning. It was common to observe one team member taking notes using a CD-ROM atlas while another member checked sources on the Internet. The partners would then compare information and develop a common set of notes. In the process, students often helped each other in reading and comprehending passages.

Because students knew they were going to create illustrated Web pages with their information, they also were required to *strategically plan* their steps toward this goal. Students brainstormed the steps in their action plans, shared them with the class, and reworked their plans based on the feedback.

Use of sources on the Internet provided the librarian with an opportunity to alert students to inaccuracies and errors they might encounter. They were reminded that as authors on the Web, they needed to *be intellectually careful* and to practice responsible reporting. Students also discovered that a valuable part of the learning experience was *seeking and evaluating reasons*. For example, as sixth graders searched for the causes and effects of the international conflicts they were studying, they reported finding "lots of information on the Web and in books but we had to read between the lines to find the reasons for things happening." Again, peer collaboration and adult conferencing helped students over these hurdles.

Finally, strategies to build students' *metacognitive awareness* were built into the information-searching process. Students wrote in research journals at least twice a week to reflect on their own thinking and learning. By thinking about what they were doing, why they were doing it, and what their next steps might be, students gained valuable insights into their own actions. One fourth grader could hardly contain her enthusiasm when she wrote, "I feel great about [the] Internet. When we saw what Hillside School did [student products posted on Web66], we got really excited. I never in my whole life thought one of my projects would be on a nationwide thing!"

Students also collaborated with the librarian and teachers to create an evaluation for their Web pages. Because they helped select the criteria and devise a rating scale for each criterion, students were eager to test out the evaluation by using it on their peers' drafts as well as on their own work.

If there was any question about the powerful appeal of the Internet as an authoring vehicle, it was dispelled when students saw their finished works posted. A sixth-grade teacher said, "We turned off the lights in the computer lab and watched the computer screens. When the kids saw their first Web page, they broke out in spontaneous applause."

Conclusion

Students and faculty at Mililani Mauka Elementary are discovering that technology used appropriately can fulfill its tremendous educational potential. To accomplish this, teachers must examine why, when, and how students should use this technology. It requires educators with a clear sense of destination so

> *By thinking about what they were doing, why they were doing it, and what their next steps might be, students gained valuable insights into their own actions.*

Using Technology
Continued from page 11

students don't get lost on the information superhighway.

Author's Note:
The HERN Project is a three-year, $2.1 million research project funded by the National Science Foundation's National Infrastructure for Education initiative. The project is currently in its second year. Educators at all levels in Hawaii are invited to apply for participation in a 12-month program that focuses on the impact of statewide Internet services and on the restructuring of learning opportunities in Hawaii. A portion of the HERN grant funds is used for faculty/staff development and support services in connection with the HERN research agenda. **TC**

Joan Yoshina is the Library Media Specialist at Mililani Mauka Elementary School in Honolulu, Hawaii. Violet H. Harada is an Associate Professor at the School of Library and Information Studies, University of Hawaii. She also serves as a consultant to the school.

Notes

Head for the Edge

Teaching Ethical Technology Behaviors

By Doug Johnson

By Doug Johnson

Much to my children's embarrassment, I've never been shy about letting people know when I find their behavior impolite. My kids burrow a little deeper in their movie theater seats when I tell the talkers in front of us to pipe down. My son tries to look as unrelated to me as possible when I tell a group that their bad language is offensive. I've been known to explain to dog owners why they should pick up after their dogs, to students why they should say please and thank you to cafeteria helpers, and to smokers why they should believe signs that say, "No Smoking." My children don't understand why I am not popped in the nose on a regular basis. I don't really enjoy these little fits of Miss Mannerism, but I am firmly convinced that if everyone rationally admonished others of their bad behavior when they saw it, we would soon be living in a far more civilized world. As educators, this job of teaching polite, and more important, ethical behaviors, is not an option but our duty.

In direct and indirect ways, children begin to learn ethical values from birth. While the family and church are assigned the primary responsibility for a child's ethical education, schools have traditionally had the societal charge to teach and reinforce some moral values, especially those directly related to citizenship and school behaviors. And since most of the ethical issues that surround technology deal with societal and school behaviors, they are an appropriate and necessary part of the school curriculum.

Business Ethics magazine suggests that businesses take a proactive approach to ethical issues. That advice is also good for schools and classrooms: Media specialists and teachers must:

- Articulate ethical values related to technology.
- Clearly display lists and create handouts of conduct codes and acceptable technology use. The "Ten Commandments of Computer Ethics" by the Computer Ethics Institute at *www.cpsr.org/program/ethics/cei.html* is a good list to use as a model.
- Reinforce ethical behaviors and react to non-ethical behaviors. Technology use behaviors should be treated no differently than other behaviors — good or bad — and the consequences of student behaviors should be the same. It is important not to overreact to incidences of technological misuse.
- Model ethical behaviors. Students learn more from what we do than from what we say. All rules of ethical conduct we expect from our students, we ourselves must model. Verbalization of how we personally make moral decisions is a very powerful teaching tool as well.
- Create technology environments that help students avoid temptations. Computer screens that are easily monitored (no pun intended), passwords not written down or left easily found, and the habit of logging out of secure network systems all help remove the opportunities for technology misuse in the media center or classroom.
- Encourage discussion of ethical issues. "Cases," whether from news sources or from actual school events, can provide superb discussion starters and should be used when students are actually learning computer skills. Students need practice in creating meaningful analogies between the virtual world and the physical world. How is reading another person's e-mail without permission like and unlike reading that person's physical mail?
- Stress the consideration of principles rather than relying on a detailed set of rules. Although sometimes more difficult to enforce in a consistent manner, a set of a few guidelines rather than lengthy set of specific rules is more beneficial to students in the long run.

By applying guidelines rather than following rules, students engage in higher level thinking processes and learn behaviors that will continue into their next classroom, their homes, and their adult lives.

Additionally, students' understandings of ethic concepts need to be assessed. Technology use privileges should not be given to students until they have demonstrated that they know and can apply ethical standards and school policies. Testing of appropriate use needs to be done especially prior to student gaining online privileges such as e-mail accounts or Internet access. The school should keep evidence of testing on file in case there is a question of whether there has been adequate instruction about appropriate use.

Schools also have an obligation to educate parents about ethical technology use. Through school newsletters, talks at parent organization meetings, and through school orientation programs, the school staff needs to inform and enlist the aid of parents in teaching and enforcing good technology practices.

As information professionals, we are in a unique position to remind other educators that it is not enough to teacher our students how to use technology, but we must also teach them how to use it well. But don't do it around your children. It's embarrassing!

Doug Johnson is the District Media Supervisor for the Mankato (Minnesota) Public Schools and can be reached by e-mail at djohns1@west.isd77.k12.mn.us (or, palsdaj@vax1.mankato.msus.edu.) Doug's new book, The Indispensible Teacher's Guide to Computer Skills, *will be published this month.*

Johnson's 3 P's of Technology Ethics:

1. Privacy – I will protect my privacy and respect the privacy of others.

2. Property – I will protect my property and respect the property of others.

3. a(P)propriate Use – I will use technology in constructive ways and in ways that do not break the rules of my family, church, school, or government.

HEAD FOR THE EDGE

Copy, Paste, Plagiarize

CD-ROM encyclopedias, full-text magazine indexes, and other digital information sources have developed a bad reputation among certain teachers and media specialists. It's not that the information contained in these electronic tools is inferior to that found in their print brethren. It's that students—many of whom are more computer literate than their teachers—can easily copy big chunks of text from these resources and paste them directly into their word-processed reports. Some, of course, submit the work to the teacher as original—bringing the old educational specter of plagiarism into the digital age at the speed of light.

In the good, old, purely-pencil-and-paper days, the teacher or media specialist frequently had the luxury of monitoring students as they took notes by hand from books and magazines. Note-taking was often a required part of the research assignment. Nowadays, it's rather heartless to ask the student researcher to sit at a computer and convert those data dancing on the screen to pencil and paper, and then laboriously keystroke them back into the word processor. I certainly can't imagine any professional researcher using such a cumbersome method of gathering and processing data. In fact, anyone who deals with lots of information and has a computer knows that once text or graphics or sound or video is in its wonderfully malleable digital form, you'll do just about anything to keep it that way. (That's why I hate the fax machine, but love e-mail attachments.)

So how can we discourage electronic plagiarism?

Carol Tilley <ctilley.dahs@incolsa.palni.edu> from Danville, Indiana, asked that question on LM_NET last year. She categorized the solutions suggested by media specialists this way:

1) Instruct teachers and students on ethics in information.
2) Require students to hand in copies of printouts used in research assignments.
3) Change the nature of the research assignment to require a higher level of thinking skills.

Instruction on copyright and intellectual ethics needs to be ongoing for both students and teachers. Unfortunately, knowing what is right is too often not enough. Requiring students to turn in printouts, as Carol suggests, is a temporary fix, and, she says, "encourages students' perceptions that they are not to be trusted."

The most effective means of preventing plagiarism requires that teachers assign research assignments that focus on original reasoning by the student. Research that is simply "about" a topic leads to copying. But activities and tasks that ask for conclusions, ask for answers to interesting questions, ask for comparisons, ask for solutions to problems, ask for points of view—all these lead to original writing. These kinds of assignments help a student narrow a topic, focus effort, and exercise higher level thinking skills. They might, heaven help us, even be interesting and meaningful to the student!

If a teacher asks a student to just write "about" bats—he's likely to copy that report right out of *Grolier's*, electronic or print. (If my fourth-grade son were given such an assignment, I'd encourage him to take the encyclopedia page that is "about" a topic back to the teacher, and innocently suggest that someone else has already done the assignment.)

But if, instead, that teacher asks a student to:

- find out if people could use the same techniques bats use to fly at night;
- show how bats are like or unlike other mammals;
- build a bat house and explain its design;
- create an appeal to prevent people from killing bats;
- write a story from a bat's point of view; or
- speculate about why people are afraid of bats

she'd see work from the student which almost has to be original!

Don't blame students for using plagiarism to keep from having to reinvent a boring wheel. If you want originality and creativity, you gotta ask for it! **TC**

by Doug Johnson

Doug Johnson is the District Media Supervisor for the Mankato (Minnesota) Public Schools and can be reached by e-mail at djohns1@west.isd77.k12.mn.us (or) palsdaj@vax1.mankato.msus.edu.

The Process-Based Approach

If your district has not already done so, it should be looking at adopting a "process-based" approach to information literacy which would replace that tired library skills/research curriculum. Plagiarism prevention is only one happy side effect of such a switch. Some great places to find out more about process-based literacy instruction include:

Colorado Department of Education (1994) *Model Information Literacy Guidelines.* Denver, Colorado.

Eisenberg and Berkowitz (1990) *Information Problem-Solving: The Big Six Approach to Library and Information Skills Instruction.* Norwood, NJ: Ablex Publishing.

Michigan State Board of Education (1994) *Information Processing Skills: Scope and Sequence Planning and Integration Matrix.* Lansing, Michigan.

Wisconsin Educational Media Association (1993) *Information Literacy: A Position Paper on Information Problem-Solving.* Appleton, Wisconsin.

Technology to the Rescue of Senioritis Victims

Voila! Instant term paper!

By Susan J. Miller

This past summer, a colleague shared a tale of horror during one of our technology training sessions. It was about last spring's graduating class and electronic resources! It began with her daughter's best friend, Dottie.

During a senior class trip to the Bahamas, Dottie roamed the beaches with her friends and allowed one of the locals to braid her hair. At a dollar a braid, it was amazing how the native was able to twist 50-plus braids from her short hair. But, what the heck??? It was nearly the end of 12 years of schooling and there were only 11 days of class left. So, why not look extremely cool? She splurged! The braids would last at least a week or longer and that meant she could be a bit lazy in the mornings before school.

In fact, she had planned on being a bit lazy about everything until the last day of school. Senioritis, she admitted. Perhaps that is why, the day they got back to school, her class was in total shock when Mr. Carr assigned a research paper.

Right! Like they wanted to go down to the library and research inventions and inventors during the last few days of school! Sure!!! Maybe, that's why my fellow librarian wasn't surprised to see the kids "invent" ways to complete this assignment. Technology came to the rescue!

With the wealth of information available at our finger tips, the students of today can easily download any amount of text to fulfill their assignments. How many times has a group come into your media center determined to complete their task by spending as little time as possible searching and as much time as possible socializing. The kids explain how they can go online at home without waiting "in line," go to the downtown library after school, or use the CD-ROMs they have.

Electronic resources are second nature to many of the young people in our high schools. That's the dilemma...the kids are technologically literate from the manipulative aspect and technologically illiterate from the process point of view. They can get to it, print it, highlight it, clip it, and regurgitate it. But have they owned it? Have they learned it? Have they embraced it? Do they really know the process of searching for it? It being information.

My friend shuddered when she overheard Dottie declaring the seniors' cleverness in how they gathered the information for the research paper. On the printouts, several of the kids covered *Encarta* with white-out or clipped off *Grolier's* at the top of the page. Others used the old familiar, low-tech ruses—recycling their older siblings' papers or adding an appropriate word to the title of papers done years ago.

We media specialists, spending our summer learning more about technology, debated this "crime." Are we educators so ignorant as to not outstep these sly kids? Is it too easy for students to access information and then pass it as their own production? To be honest, we blamed the teacher who accepted these papers as original work, but we also concluded that the responsibility was partly ours.

As the building media specialists, we must work more closely with the students to design, implement, and revise electronic research skills. The classroom teachers cannot keep up with all the new modes of information access—the simple and advanced search strategies, the best sources (URLs), the wasted efforts (cruising aimlessly), or the disallowed sites (pornography). We must be obvious to all the students as they occupy our space.

Go to the kids (even the one without hair but with tattoos) and quiz their efforts. Ask to see what they have found so far. Suggest other sources, better search techniques, different keywords. Introduce the newest CD-ROM. Build rapport so the students can comfortably ask questions or respond to your inquiries without feeling intruded on.

Invite the child who is obviously struggling with the electronic resource to come back during lunch or after school. If you are sure this kid won't respond to that, arrange with the teacher to send the student on a pass, alone or with a cohort, to work one-on-one at the terminal.

There is so much we can do to assure our students are using electronic resources as part of a processed, complete product. We are ever-evolving in our profession. And, one of the most evolving components is the total commitment and physical involvement we must establish with our students. This cannot be replaced by whole-class instruction in research skills. The most important part of our job is the kids. The most fun part of our job is the kids. We need to work with those cunning "seniors" prior to the last research assignment.

When the kids light up because they have conducted a successful search and have many sources from which to draw, they are well on the way to an assignment done well. With the results of this research, the kids can now apply the process of disseminating information; they can dissect it, churn it, and produce their own original work.

If Dottie and her senior pals had known how quickly they could have "processed" the ever-ready electronic information and actually learned from it, this horror story could have been averted. It is a story we can attempt to dissuade chapter by chapter (class-by-class).

Susan J. Miller is the Director of Media Services in the Comstock Park, Michigan, Public Schools.

Tips and Other Bright Ideas

Bibliographic Posters

For students and teachers' questions about bibliographic citations for reference materials, we have produced posters, which are hung on the wall above the computer stations. We typed two examples of citations for books, encyclopedia articles, newspapers and periodicals, and electronic resources on separate sheets of paper. At a photocopy store, we enlarged the sheets on colored paper—a different color for each type of reference source. Teachers and students use these posters, saving time for themselves and the library staff.—*Marghe Tabar, St. Paul Academy and Summit School, St. Paul, Minnesota*

Notes

Bibliography

BOOKS

Berry, Margaret A., and Patricia S. Morris. *Stepping into Research: A Complete Research Skills Activities Program for Grades 5-12.* West Nyack, NY: Center for Applied Research in Education, 1990.

Bolner, Myrtle S., and Gayle A. Poirier. *The Research Process: Books and Beyond.* Dubuque, IA: Kendall/Hunt, 1997.

Breivik, Patricia Senn, and J. A. Senn. *Information Literacy: Educating Children for the 21st Century.* New York: Scholastic, 1994.

California Media and Library Educators Association (CMLEA). *From Library Skills to Information Literacy: A Handbook for the 21st Century.* Castle Rock, CO: Hi Willow, 1997.

Craver, Kathleen W. Teaching Electronic Literacy: *A Concepts-Based Approach for School Library Media Specialists.* Westport, CT: Greenwood, 1997.

Eisenberg, Michael B., and Robert E. Berkowitz.. *Information Problem-Solving: The Big Six Skills Approach to Library & Information Skills Instruction.* Norwood, NJ: Ablex, 1990.

Farmer, Lesley S. J. *Workshops for Teachers: Becoming Partners for Information Literacy.* Worthington, OH: Linworth, 1995.

Garrett, Linda J., and JoAnne Moore. *Teaching Library Skills in Middle and High School: A How-to-Do-It Manual.* New York: Neal-Schuman, 1993.

Handler, Marianne G., and Ann S. Dana. *Hypermedia as a Student Tool: A Guide for Teachers.* 2nd ed. *Englewood, CO:* Libraries Unlimited, 1998.

Heller, Norma. *Projects for New Technologies in Education, Grades 6-9.* Englewood, CO: Libraries Unlimited, 1994.

Information Power: Building Partnerships for Learning. Chicago: American Library Association, 1998.

Library Research Skills Workbook, Grades 7-12. Worthington, OH: Linworth, 1990.

McElmeel, Sharron L. *Research Strategies for Moving beyond Reporting.* Worthington, OH: Linworth, 1997.

Mendrinos, Roxanne. *Building Information Literacy Using High Technology: A Guide for Schools and Libraries.* Englewood, CO: Libraries Unlimited, 1994.

Pappas, Marjorie L., and Gayle A. Geitgey, and Cathy A. Jefferson. *Searching Electronic Resources.* 2nd ed. Worthington, OH: Linworth, 1999.

Rankin, Virginia. *The Thoughtful Researcher: Teaching the Research Process to Middle School Students.* Englewood, CO: Libraries Unlimited, 1999.

Skills for Life: Library Information Literacy for Grades 6-8. Ed. by Marsha Kibbey. Worthington, OH: Linworth, 1993.

Skills for Life: Library Information Literacy for Grades 9-12. Ed. by Paul Rux. Worthington, OH: Linworth, 1993.

Stripling, Barbara K., and Judy M. Pitts. *Brainstorms and Blueprints: Teaching Library Research as a Thinking Process.* Englewood, CO: Libraries Unlimited, 1988.

Stuurmans, Harry. *Nine Steps to a Quality Research Paper.* Worthington, OH: Linworth, 1994.

Sykes, Judith A. Library Centers: *Teaching Information Literacy, Skills, and Process, K-6.* Englewood, CO: Libraries Unlimited, 1997.

Teaching Information Literacy Using Electronic Resources for Grades 6-12. Ed. by Mary Alice Anderson. Worthington, OH: Linworth, 1996.

Volkman, John D. *Cruising through Research: Library Skills for Young Adults.* Englewood, CO: Libraries Unlimited, 1998.

Wolf, Carolyn E., & Richard Wolf. *Basic Library Skills.* Jefferson, NC: McFarland, 1993.

Yucht, Alice H. *Flip It! An Information Skills Strategy for Student Researchers.* Worthington, OH: Linworth, 1997.

WEB SITES

Big Six Skills
    www.big6.com

Global School House
    www.gsn.org

Information Literacy: Essential Skills for the Information Age
    http://ericir.syr.edu/ithome/pubs.htm

Information Literacy Standards
    www.ala.org/aasl/ip_nine.html

Information Power
    www.ala.org/aasl/ip_implementation.html

Internet Training
    wms.luminet.net/training